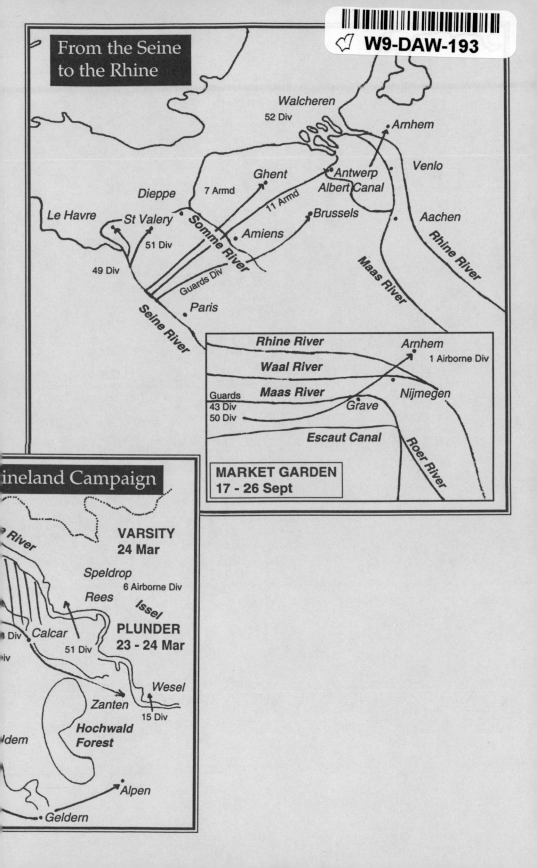

From the Seine to the Rhine

Walcheren
52 Div

Arnhem

Venlo

Ghent

Antwerp
Albert Canal

7 Armd

11 Armd

Dieppe

Brussels

Aachen

Le Havre

St Valery

Amiens

Somme River

Rhine River

51 Div

Maas River

49 Div

Guards Div

Seine River

Paris

MARKET GARDEN 17 - 26 Sept

Rhine River

Arnhem

1 Airborne Div

Waal River

Maas River

Nijmegen

Guards
43 Div
50 Div

Grave

Escaut Canal

Roer River

ineland Campaign

River

VARSITY
24 Mar

Speldrop

6 Airborne Div

Rees

Issel

Calcar

PLUNDER
23 - 24 Mar

51 Div

Div

iv

Wesel

Zanten

15 Div

Hochwald
Forest

dem

Alpen

Geldern

Code Word
CANLOAN

The story of a group of Canadian Army officers who
volunteered to serve in the British Army in Europe between
D-Day, 1944, and VE-Day, 1945, in a scheme called ...

Code Word
CANLOAN

WILFRED I. SMITH

Dundurn Press
Toronto & Oxford
1992

Editing: Freya Godard
Design and Production: GSN
Printing and Binding: Gagné Printing Ltd., Louiseville, Quebec, Canada

The writing of this manuscript and the publication of this book were made possible by support from several sources. The publisher wishes to acknowledge the generous assistance and ongoing support of **The Canada Council, The Book Publishing Industry Development Program** of the **Department of Communications, The Ontario Arts Council,** and **The Ontario Publishing Centre of the Ministry of Culture and Communications.**

Care has been taken to trace the ownership of copyright material used in the text (including the illustrations). Credit for each quotation is given at the end of the selection. The author and publisher welcome any information enabling them to rectify any reference or credit in subsequent editions.

J. Kirk Howard, Publisher

Canadian Cataloguing in Publication Data

Smith Wilfred I. –
        Code word CANLOAN

Includes index
ISBN 1-55002-167-2

1. Canada, Canadian Army – History – World War, 1939–1945. 2. World War, 1939–1945 – Canada. 3. World War, 1939–1945 – Great Britain. I. Title.

D768.15.S55 1992   940.54'21   C92-095303-4

Dundurn Press Limited
2181 Queen Street East
Suite 301
Toronto, Canada
M4E 1E5

Dundurn Distribution Limited
73 Lime Walk
Headington, Oxford
England
OX3 7AD

Contents

Transiens in Britanniam

In Memory of Our Fallen Comrades

Aitken, John A.
Anaka, Harry J.
Andrews, Ellis G.
Arnett, Francis L.J.
Arthurs, Ralph B.
Baker, Charles T.
Baldwin, Ivor B.
Beaton, Gordon E.
Belanger, Henry E.
Bennett, William A.
Blackham, John P.
Bourget, Joseph A.R.
Bowman, John E.
Box, Vernon E.
Brais, Joseph C.Y.
Brown, Gordon M.
Brown, Norman A.
Brownlee-Lamont,
   Wilfred W.N.
Bushell, Andrew F.
Carstairs, Kenneth W.
Caseley, Willard S.
Cawsey, Aubrey C.
Coates, Kenneth
Cochrane, James
Cockburn, Ernest E.
Cohen, Lawrence
Coll, William J.
Comolli, Benoit D.J.
Cooper, Charles W.
Cope, Alfred R.
Cowan, Duncan R.H.
Cowan, William M.
Cox, Hubert C.
Crabb, Allen P.
Crehan, Maurice J.
Crighton, Arthur D.
Day, James P.
Duclos, Pierre
Duncan, Donald A.
Dynes, Frederick J.
Edwards, David E.
Ells, Frederick A.

Gilmour, James H.
Glass, Edward D.
Goddard, Ronald M.
Harcourt, Earl H.
Harding, Albert R.
Harris, Alfred J.
Harrison, John R.
Hartman, William G.
Hastings, Donald K.
Heald, Clarence F.
Hemelryk, Joseph
Hilborn, David G.
Hingston, Basil, W.H.
Hopkinson, George G.
Hughes, Harry F.
Hunt, William G.
James, William A.
Jeffries, Peter
Jones, Hubert M.
Karls, Justin T.
Keast, Robert J.
Kelly, Bernard J.
Kipping, Albert E.
Kotchapaw, William J.
Kuhl, Allen W.
Lalonde, William J.
Laurie, John A.
Lee, Donald K.
Levine, John O.
Luffman, George H.
Lynn, Brian F.
MacDonald, Alistair K.
Main, Harold W.
Mann, Eldon B.
Marsh, Robert G.
Matthew, John B.
McAllister, Howard C.
McDermott, George A.
McGregor, James
McKenna, James L.
McKibbon, Hugh D.
McLeod, Hugh D.
Merchant, Evatt F. A.

Nelles, Larry D.
Nicholas, William E.
Niznick, Harry
Noiseux, Joseph A.C.A.
Paff, Lorne H.
Pape, John C.
Pearce, Wilfred A.
Phelps, Thomas A.
Purchase, John R.
Reid, Stirling A.
Richardson, Leonard J.
Robertson, Robert K.
Robinson, William B.
Rodger, Anderson
Roper, Harry C.
Rose, Malcolm R.
Rosenthal, Hyman
Rush, Mathew C.P.
Schwark, Harold L.
Scott, Frederick
Sheely, Henry G.
Smith, Donald J.
Smith, Lawson M.
Smith, Thomas A.M.
Stevenson, Howard M.
Stewart, Jackson
Stewart, Fernie B.
Stewart, Richard N.
Suttie, James M.
Thomson, Raymond W.
Thoresen, Raymond F.
Trudeau, Maurice A.
Ward, Allan
Wayte, Albert E.F.
Wellbelove, John A.
West, Philip G.
Wilson, Edward A.
Wilson, Richard N..
Wood, Dudley H.
Young, Everett E.
Young, Leland A.
Young, Peter B.
Young, Richard O.

Foreword

THIS BOOK, compiled with great dedication, perseverance, and skill by Wilfred Smith with the assistance of his military comrades and with the support of their Canloan Army Officers Association, brings a valuable and living memory of the past and the priceless voluntary contribution made by the 673 young Canadian officers who came to Britain in the spring of 1944 to serve with many British regiments and the Royal Army Ordnance Corps.

It was an immensely proud moment for me when I was asked to write the foreword to a book which, I hope, will take a place in the homes of all CANLOAN officers and their families and of all of those who, in British regiments, had the privilege of serving with them. I also hope it will be read by a good many others who will wish to know of the respect, admiration, and regard in which these officers were held by the British and Canadian public alike for their courage, sense of joyous comradeship, discipline, and devotion to duty.

The request to write this foreword included an instruction that the content was to be entirely in my own hands, but with a reminder that Winston Churchill once said that if he had had more time his writing would have been shorter rather than longer. I also believe in short forewords but wondered why I had been chosen and what qualifications I had for the unique and unbounded privilege of writing this one.

I hoped some justification could be made of my Canadian citizenship, of which I am justly proud, and perhaps this had some bearing on my selection. I hope that the pleasure of my time as child and schoolboy spent in the grandeur of British Columbia may have persuaded those CANLOAN officers who served with me that they were unfortunate not to have come from that wonderful province. They were occasionally reminded of the advantages.

I had the good fortune to have three CANLOAN officers in my battalion, each of whom served with great courage, distinction, and loyalty, being completely integrated and staunch members of the 9 DLI team. They became perhaps even more "Geordie than the Geordies" and were immensely proud to wear the DLI cap badge, as others were to wear the cap badge of the regiments or RAOC to which they were posted. In my experience, this feeling exemplified the way the CANLOAN officers quickly adapted themselves in order to merge and identify themselves with their British regiments. It was not an easy task to suddenly penetrate the firm friendships and loyalties of British battalions that had been together for a long time, and it showed the strength of character of the CANLOAN officers and their desire to make the scheme work. It also reflected great credit on the Canadian Army and their training establishments, such as Camp Sussex, where a "spirit" was developed which gave their officers professional confidence in battle and the determination to enhance the high reputation of Canada and its fighting services.

During my unforgettable visit to the CANLOAN reunion in Ottawa in 1974 as guest of honour, this spirit and pride and close adherence to their British comrades were abundantly evident. At dinners and receptions it was arranged that groups of CANLOAN officers were assembled under large banners or standards depicting the British divisional or regimental sign with which they had served.

A deep debt of gratitude is due to those who have produced this human record from the conception of the scheme and who have collated the stories and experiences of those who took part in the victorious and liberating march from the Normandy beaches to Berlin, a march Sir Winston Churchill described as "unsurpassed through all the story of war." *Code Word CANLOAN* has the great advantage of describing events in a simple, easy-to-read style of personal occurrences, unlike so many histories of campaigns dealing only in strategy, plans, and battles as seen from the eyes of the higher commanders.

The "feel of the battle" is emphasized throughout as experienced by the infantry soldier, particularly the junior infantry officer, and in doing so, the book brings out the human aspect and the personal perception.

I hope that all who read this book will be inspired by the example and proud achievement of those whom it portrays.

General Sir John Mogg, GCB, CBE, DSO, DL
Oxon., England
September 1989

Preface and
Acknowledgments

FEW PEOPLE, except the surviving participants, have ever heard of CANLOAN, the code word for an arrangement during the Second World War by which a number of Canadian Army officers participated in the fighting in northwest Europe between D-Day 1944, and VE-Day 1945, by voluntarily serving in regiments of the British Army. The ferocity of the fighting in which these officers were engaged is indicated by the extent of their casualties (75 percent) and the number of awards for gallantry – nearly 100, more than 40 of them Military Crosses. At the special request of the War Office, a number of RCOC officers also volunteered to serve under the same conditions as the more numerous infantry officers

It is not surprising that the activities of these officers are not well known, for the numbers involved (623 infantry and 50 ordnance officers) were relatively small, and the duration of the scheme (between one and two years) relatively short. More-over, since the participants, though Canadian Army officers, served in the British Army, they were not included in the histories of Canadian regiments or other Canadian wartime activities. And since the participants were few in number and scattered thinly throughout the British Second Army, they were referred to only occasionally in British regimental and divisional histories.

Despite the obscurity of the CANLOAN scheme, its significance has been recognized by Canadian official military historians. The Historical Section of the Canadian Army prepared several reports on the scheme at the end of the Second World War, and CANLOAN officers are pleased to quote a reference from Col. C.P. Stacey, *The Canadian Army, 1939–1945: An Official Historical Summary* (Ottawa, 1948), 296: "The Canloan scheme may be accounted decidedly successful; the gallant young officers lent to the British forces under its terms did the country credit and made a distinguished and significant contribution to the military effort of the Commonwealth and the winning of the war."

A more extensive account was included in Colonel Stacey's *The Victory Campaign: The Operations in North West Europe, 1944–1945* (Ottawa, 1960), 633–35. Until now these references and a brief introduction in the several editions of the *CANLOAN Roster* have been the only published accounts of the CANLOAN scheme. This has been a matter of concern to the surviving CANLOAN officers, who are keenly aware that they, who are the most interested in a history of the scheme, are disappearing at an alarming rate. When the national Canloan Army Officers Association was formed in 1954, a history of CANLOAN was prominent among its goals, but the project was delayed for various reasons. Finally, at the 11th national reunion in Ottawa in 1986, I agreed to prepare a history of the CANLOAN scheme. Although I had begun a career as an historian 40 years earlier, I had joined the staff of the Public Archives of Canada in 1950, and my duties there had made extensive research and writing impossible until my retirement from the position of Dominion Archivist in 1984. A history of CANLOAN seemed to have greater urgency than the other historical projects to which I had intended to devote my time in retirement.

While the interest of participants in a history of their activities is obvious, the CANLOAN scheme also provides a context for studying more general subjects relating to human behaviour, such as the motivation for volunteering for armed combat, adaptation to cultural differences, the relationship between young Canadian officers and the British officers with whom they served and the British troops whom they commanded, the role of infantry commanders in battle, quality of leadership, the relationship between wartime experiences and civilian careers, and aspects of group loyalty in Canadian and British military associations.

The primary documentary sources for a history of the CANLOAN scheme are records of Canadian Military Headquarters in London (CMHQ), records of National Defence Headquarters in Ottawa (NDHQ), and British War Office records, particularly the regimental war diaries at the Public Records Office in London, as well as other public records and private papers in Canada and the United Kingdom. Other valuable sources are regimental and divisional histories and the *Canloan Review* from 1949 to the present.

Because the CANLOAN officers were scattered throughout the British Army, their story, to a considerable degree, is 673 individual stories, much of the information concerning which can be obtained only from the surviving officers or those with whom they served. This history is a co-operative project that owes a great deal to the officers and next of kin who have completed questionnaires and provided unpublished memoirs, as well as to the many British comrades who have written narratives and comments concerning the CANLOAN scheme and individual CANLOAN officers. All of this material has been gratefully received. Several CANLOAN officers, including Jack McBride and Rex Fendick, have written book-length memoirs, which have been deposited in the National Archives of Canada.

Other CANLOAN officers have contributed many hours to the preparation of the history as members of the History Committee of the Canloan Army Officers Association and as editors: Tom Anstey, Rex Fendick, Doug Gage, Gordon Chatterton, Bob Inman, Phil Labelle, and the late "Tommy" Tomlinson, RCOC. Tom Anstey, as well as serving as principal editor, has used his computer to good effect in producing appendices, an index, and various versions of the text. Erik Spicer, the parliamentary librarian and a military history buff, has kindly reviewed the text. The military staff of the British High Commission have given valuable assistance, and Tom Parker has provided excellent liaison with the publishers. I am grateful to all those at Dundurn Press who were involved with the book, for their competent treatment of the text and consideration for the author. Special thanks are due to George Beck, "Mr. CANLOAN," who has missed no opportunity to urge fellow CANLOAN officers to contribute to the history as a national project in honour of the comrades who did not return. It is hoped that this history will do justice to their sacrifice and contribute to the recognition and appreciation that are their due, and that it will provide an adequate record of the experiences of a group of young Canadians who voluntarily placed their lives in jeopardy and whose behaviour in combat while commanding British troops reflected credit on their country.

W.I.S.
Ottawa, 1992

1

The CANLOAN Scheme

IN 1944, on the eve of the Allied invasion of Normandy, the British Army was desperately short of junior infantry officers, whereas Canada had a temporary surplus of such officers. In the hope of solving both problems at the same time, the military authorities of the two countries agreed that a substantial number of junior Canadian infantry officers would be lent, on a voluntary basis, to Britain.

The appeal for volunteers was answered by several hundred Canadian officers who were eager to get into action and who seized the opportunity to go overseas. Though not an elite group in the usual sense of the word, they were nevertheless chosen to reflect credit on Canada and the Canadian Army.

The volunteers, 623 infantry and 50 ordnance officers, became a distinct entity with distinctive CDN numbers, separate administrative arrangements, and an operational code word, CANLOAN.

The officers who were accepted assembled at a camp near Sussex, New Brunswick, for briefing and refresher training under the direction of Brig. Milton Gregg before being sent, in several drafts, to the United Kingdom. They were given their choice of British regiment, and eventually one or more of them served in almost every battalion in the British Second Army.

Though the Canadian officers were widely dispersed, their individual exploits contributed to a highly respected CANLOAN reputation and a sense of unity and esprit de corps remains strong after nearly half a century.

There has always been an element of mystery about the origin of the CANLOAN scheme. A wartime cabinet minister recalled that it was arranged by his colleague Col. the Hon. J.L. Ralston during a trip to England in 1943.[1] Other sources connected the scheme with the Adjutant-General (AG) of the British Army, Gen. Sir Ronald Adam. It was said that he had been grounded by fog in Gibraltar at the same time as Colonel Ralston and that they agreed on the loan of Canadian junior infantry officers to the British Army.[2]

Another version of the story has the Canadian AG, Maj.-Gen. H.F.G. Letson, meeting his British counterpart in Gibraltar. (Official documentary sources, however, rule out Gibraltar.)[3] A report on the CANLOAN scheme prepared in July 1945 in the Historical Section of the Canadian Army is quite precise about its origin: it was arranged in London on 9 October 1943 while the two AGs were having lunch together.[4] This has been confirmed by 93-year-old General Letson. But the late Sir Ronald Adam, in his unpublished memoirs, authenticates the Gibraltar story. He says that he was there on 9 December 1943, that he met the Minister of National Defence for Canada, Colonel Ralston, and persuaded him to lend the British Army several hundred Canadian infantry officers.[5] Other claims of paternity for the scheme have been made on behalf of Brig. R.E.G. Roome of National Defence Headquarters in Ottawa and Maj.-Gen. P.J. Montague of Canadian Military Headquarters (CMHQ) in London. Two conclusions are evident. First, the CANLOAN scheme was not devised by any one person on any single day. Second, some such arrangement was almost inevitable in view of the desperate shortage of junior infantry officers in the British Army in the fall of 1943 and the embarrassing surplus of such officers in the Canadian Army in Canada.

The shortage of British infantry officers in 1943 was perhaps the most critical aspect of a chronic manpower crisis in the British Army. When war broke out in September 1939, the strength of the British Army had been brought up to 428,000 from a peacetime strength of only 112,000. After Dunkirk 275,000 men were called up, and no fewer than 120 infantry battalions were formed, creating an almost impossible task of finding officers and men for them. By 1941 it was clear that British manpower resources were becoming gravely strained. Ninety-four out of every 100 males between 14 and 64 had been mobilized into the armed forces or war industry. From March 1941 manpower allocation was rigidly controlled by the War Cabinet, and a limit was placed on the manpower for each service. The allocation for the Army was 2,100,000, a limit that remained for the rest of the war. Since manpower resources were fixed, any increases in requirements could be met only by moving personnel within or between services or by breaking up units. This process became continuous.

At the beginning of the war 50 percent of the British Army consisted of infantry units. This proportion rose to 60 percent after Dunkirk. By 1942, however, the proportion of infantry had dropped, incredibly, to only 20 percent, and the Royal Artillery, including anti-aircraft (AA) and coastal defence, had become the largest arm, with 22 percent; 25 percent were tradesmen.[6]

In the summer of 1943 the requirements for the invasion of northwest Europe in 1944 were being drawn up. The man charged with the responsibility for finding the necessary reinforcements was the AG, Gen. Sir Ronald Adam. The War Office predicted that at least two infantry divisions and several independent brigades might have to be broken up by the end of 1944. One solution that Sir Ronald Adam endorsed was to transfer 35,000 men from other arms to infantry for re-training. The demand for officers was particularly urgent. The British Army had widespread military responsibilities in India, East and West Africa, Egypt, and the Balkans in addition to the large-scale operations in North Africa and later Italy. Sir Ronald Adam reported, "In the first six months of 1943 we had to send 30,000 officers and potential officers overseas."[7]

In the search for infantry officers no stone was left unturned: even non-combatant organizations such as the Pay Corps were combed for officer material. Many recruits were obtained from the Republic of Ireland, smaller numbers came from the United States, usually American citizens living in the United Kingdom, and still others came from English populations in countries such as Argentina. Given the extent of the need and the urgency of the search for junior infantry officers, the response of General Adam to the opportunity to obtain several hundred trained infantry officers from Canada was predictable.

One result of the massive expansion of the Canadian Army during the war was the necessity of finding a very large number of new officers. This problem was not apparent immediately. The mobilization instructions in 1939 provided that each unit being mobilized should find its own officers. They could be found from their own active list or reserve list of officers, by transfer from other units, from members of the Canadian Officers' Training Corps (COTC) with certificates of qualification, or by promotion from the ranks. There was no shortage of officers from these sources. In the first year of the war the Canadian Active Service Force (CASF) had a full slate of officers who already had commissions in 1939. The officer supply became urgent, however, when the Army began to expand in earnest in the summer of 1940, after "the deliverance of Dunkirk," with the formation of the 3rd, 4th, and 5th, and later three home defence divisions.[8]

Before the production of reinforcement officers on a large scale could begin, the apparatus for a scientific system of selection and training had to be developed. Already several policies had been established. First, the granting of commissions and promotions was to be on the basis of merit alone. This was announced by the then Minister of National Defence, Norman Rogers, as early as 3 October 1940. He emphasized that there was to be "no political or personal bias of any kind." Secondly, for the future "every candidate for a commission in the Canadian Army must first pass through the ranks."[9] A decision to this effect was made in August 1940 and was announced in Parliament by Colonel Ralston, who was then Minister of National Defence. A related principle was that there should be a clear path to a commission for every recruit. Provision was made for recruits, on enlistment, to be given a series of tests. An important one was the "M" test, which indicated intelligence. If, during training, the motivation, leadership, and physical condition of a candidate with a high "M" score were satisfactory, the candidate was streamed into the officer-training system. The minimum time in the ranks for officer candidates was four months for active units and one year for reserve units.

In the United Kingdom a selection committee of senior Canadian officers was appointed in the autumn of 1940 to interview candidates recommended by unit commanders and to select those to attend the Officer Candidate Training Unit (OCTU) near Aldershot, Hants, England. In the spring of 1941 two officers' training centres (OTCs) were opened in Canada, one at Brockville, Ontario, for eastern Canada, the other at Gordon Head, British Columbia, for western Canada. At these OTCs the training syllabus provided for officer cadets to have four weeks of "common to all arms" training, followed by six weeks of special-to-arm training and, in the case of infantry, two weeks of platoon tactics. At the end of the course the successful candidates were commissioned as second lieutenants and sent to a Canadian infantry training centre (CITC) as "one-pip wonders" for a month of advanced infantry training combined with experience as instructors, usually resulting in promotion to full lieutenants. The system then called for more experience as instructors at basic training centres or advanced training centres, leading to postings overseas as reinforcement officers or to units in Canada.

Early in 1942 the OCTU in the United Kingdom was closed, and candidates from Canadian units in Britain were henceforth sent back to Canada to obtain their commissions at either Brockville or Gordon Head. At this time an increased demand for reinforcement officers was generated for the Canadian Army. The formation of three home defence divisions and the anticipated casualties overseas led to a reorganization and expansion of the whole program of selection and training of Army officers. At NDHQ an Officers' Selection, Promotion, Reclassification and Disposal Board was established with Brig. Howard Kennedy as chairman. Two Officers' Selection and Appraisal Centres (OSACs) were established, one at Three Rivers, Quebec, for eastern Canada and one at Chilliwack, British Columbia, for western Canada. Both were functioning in the spring and summer of 1943. At each OSAC, Officers' Selection and Appraisal Boards were established. They comprised senior officers of all corps together with psychiatrists, psychologists, and educational officers, presided over by brigadiers. At these OSACs each officer candidate underwent a series of tests to assess his fitness for a commission, and an interview by the board. The successful candidates were sent on to the Officers' Training Centre at Brockville or Gordon Head. Both OTCs were expanded in 1943, and a third one established at Three Rivers.[10]

The expanded system for the production of officers was no sooner in full operation than it was found to be too efficient. In August 1943 the Adjutant-General estimated that there would be a surplus of 2,000 officers by April 1944.[11] There were several reasons for a sharp reduction in officer requirements. It had been decided to disband the three home defence divisions (6th, 7th, and 8th) and to reduce the coastal and anti-aircraft defences. This would release several hundred officers of various ranks. In addition, the casualty rate after the invasion of Sicily had been much lower than expected.

Although it was not feasible to interrupt classes in mid-stream, everything possible was done to slow down the production of officers. In September the OSAC at Chilliwack was closed and the Three Rivers OSAC was moved to the Brockville OTC. As well, the OTC at Gordon Head was closed and thus, after September 1943, all officer training was conducted at the Brockville OTC.

Though the home defence divisions, especially the 7th and 8th, never reached full strength, they did have a large complement of officers, many of whom by reason of senior rank, age, and perhaps physical condition did not fit into the normal reinforcement stream with its emphasis on young junior officers. It occurred to Colonel Carey, the Director of Personal Services at NDHQ, that the British Army, with its larger and more widespread establishments, might have need for the services of officers not needed by Canada.

On 22 September 1943, NDHQ in Ottawa requested CMHQ in London to find out whether the British Army could absorb any of the surplus officers, especially ranks above captain, who were above reinforcement age.[12]

By 30 September the idea of lending Canadian officers to the British Army had been discussed with the Army Commander, General McNaughton, and with the Deputy Adjutant-General (DAG) at the War Office. Though it appeared that the British did not need the senior officers, there was keen interest in the concept of a loan of officers and recognition that the British Army was generally short of officers. The DAG felt that the proposal of a loan was basically sound: "The possibilities should be thoroughly canvassed as the resultant deal would be in the nature of an outstanding example of international cooperation, the ultimate benefits of which might be far-reaching."[13]

General McNaughton insisted that no officers should be transferred if the Canadian Army needed them and that any officers who were transferred should be checked carefully, since he did not want, as he said, "to dump poor stuff on the British."[14] The conclusion was that the idea of a loan should be explored further. It is quite possible that the eventual loan of junior officers might have resulted from subsequent discussions, but meanwhile there was a more direct approach.

On 9 October 1943 Major-General Letson, the Canadian Adjutant-General, who was in London on one of his periodic visits to CMHQ, asked his counterpart, Sir Ronald Adam, whether there was anything more the Canadian Army could do to help Britain. Adam replied that in the circumstances the greatest contribution Canada could make would be to lend a large number of trained junior infantry officers in view of the desperate shortage in the British Army and the anticipated casualties in the impending invasion of the Continent. General Letson said that he was confident something could be done; he would find out the numbers that could be made available and would discuss the matter with the War Office.[15]

On 1 November General Letson and Brigadier de Lalanne, DAG, went to the War Office for a discussion with Maj.-Gen. F. Hare, Director of Organization, and Brig. C.B. Robertson, his deputy director, on the possibility of supplying Canadian officers to the British Army. General Hare endorsed Sir Ronald Adam's appeal for young, trained infantry officers. Officers in the Royal Artillery (RA) and the Royal Armoured Corps (RAC) were being reallocated to infantry as quickly as possible, and the cadets in those corps were being diverted to infantry during their officer training, but there were neither sufficient numbers nor sufficient time. He said that the British Army also needed officers for the Royal Army Service Corps (RASC). General Letson made several suggestions as a guide to an arrangement:

- Junior Infantry and Royal Canadian Army Service Corps (RCASC) officers should be placed on loan with the British Army with the understanding that they could be recalled if needed by the Canadian Army.
- The loan should be entirely voluntary.
- Canada should be responsible for their pay.
- The age limits should be the same as for the Canadian Army overseas.

Though numbers were not discussed, General Hare said that several hundred could be taken immediately. He also suggested that if Canada wished "to keep a string on these officers" they should agree to limit service to Europe.[16]

It was apparent that the matter had considerable urgency. Brigadier de Lalanne, DAG (A), immediately informed Brigadier Roome, DAG (O), at NDHQ of the meeting at the War Office and asked him to prepare a proposal for the Chief of the General Staff (CGS) and the Minister of National Defence. Both had already been informed of the proposed loan, and both approved in principle. Since the meeting at the War Office, several points had been discussed. On the question of rank it was agreed that only subalterns were needed, although a few captains might be accepted. De Lalanne suggested a ratio of one captain to eight lieutenants. It was decided that the Canadian Army would select the volunteers and that the British Army would accept them without question, but if they were later found to be unsuitable they would be returned to the Canadian Army.[17] The matter of numbers had not been resolved, but the statistics available suggested that there were at least 1,500 surplus officers (1,200 infantry and 300 RCASC) and that that figure was to be used tentatively in preparing the submission for the Minister. It was taken for granted that the officers would be volunteers and that "by reason of their experience, training and general bearing [they] should reflect credit on the Canadian Army."[18]

By 29 November 1943 a memorandum to the Minister incorporating the eight main points of the tentative agreement had been prepared by the Directorate of Personnel for signature by the AG and dispatched to Colonel Ralston through the CGS, General Stuart. Since Stuart was in London at the time, the formal proposal of the CANLOAN scheme was made in a secret telegram from Letson to Stuart on 4 December 1943 (AG 90). It repeated the eight points: volunteer infantry and RCASC officers to be lent to the British Army; withdrawal if required by the Canadian Army; pay by the Canadian Army; promotion while on loan approved by Canadian authorities; service restricted to Europe; one captain to eight lieutenants; British to accept Canadian selection; and return to Canadian Army if unsuitable. When the approval of these general conditions by the CGS and the Minister had been obtained, CMHQ would negotiate a detailed agreement with the War Office. Letson concluded the telegram with: "Have no idea how many would volunteer but do NOT repeat NOT deem it advisable to canvass situation here until such time as approval has been obtained."[19]

It was at this time that Colonel Ralston met Sir Ronald Adam in Gibraltar while both were returning from visits to their respective troops in Italy. This is Sir Ronald's account of the meeting:

> I was lucky enough to be marooned in Gibraltar at the same time as Col Ralston, the Canadian Minister of National Defence. We were both delayed on the Rock on our way back from tours overseas, as it was impossible to get back to England when head winds were blowing. After a day's walking round the Rock, I managed to persuade him to let me have 200 young Canadian officers to provide first reinforcements for the 21st Army Group. We made special arrangements for their welcome and introduction to units. They were such excellent material that units took them with them on D-Day, leaving others to wait as reinforcements.[20]

Adam, Colonel Ralston, and General Stuart were all staying at Government House, where Sir Ronald gave a lecture to a group of officers in the garrison on 9 December. The Canadians attended the lecture, in which Adam discussed the manpower crisis of the British Army as the 21st Army Group prepared for the invasion of northwest Europe. Both before and after the lecture Adam and Ralston discussed the reinforcement officer crisis, and the two men, both of whom had been commanders of infantry battalions in the First World War, had no difficulty in agreeing on the importance of junior infantry officers. When writing his memoirs, however, General Adam's memory failed him on two points. First, it had not been necessary to persuade Colonel Ralston to let the British Army have young Canadian officers as reinforcements. Even though the official request for Ralston's approval (the telegram of 4 December) was waiting for him and General Stuart in London, they had both approved the loan scheme in principle before leaving Ottawa. Secondly, the figure of 200 was wrong because the numbers that were being discussed unofficially between CMHQ and the War Office were between 1,500 and 2,000. Indeed, just three weeks after the meeting in Gibraltar, General Adam told General Stuart during lunch in London that the British Army could take 2,000 infantry and 500 service corps officers.

The discussions that both General Adam and Colonel Ralston had found so fruitful resumed in London on 21 December. Certainly, Ralston was prepared to give his support to the CANLOAN scheme, and when he returned to Ottawa the submission requesting Cabinet approval was being prepared at NDHQ. This submission was sent in the form of a memorandum from the AG, General Letson, to the Minister on 28 December. It began with an account of the surplus of officers in Canada and suggested that steps be taken "to enable such trained officers to usefully serve in the field." It then referred to the shortage of infantry and service corps officers in the British Army and to General Adam's opinion that a loan would be "a most important contribution to the united war effort." It recommended that up to 1,500 Canadian officers who might volunteer be lent to the British Army under the eight conditions that had been enumerated.[21]

This draft was followed, on 4 January 1944, by a supplementary memorandum from General Letson. First, he informed the Minister of General Stuart's meeting with General Adam when the latter had said that the British would like to have as many as 2,000 infantry and 500 RCASC but would be pleased with a first instalment of 1,000 infantry and 300 RCASC. Next, he gave a report on the supply of officers as of the end of November. Estimates showed that after allowing for requirements of the Canadian Army, including a year's supply of reinforcements overseas and full establishment for one division and instructional staffs in Canada, there would still be a surplus of 1,503 infantry officers and 231 RCASC officers. Finally, General Letson outlined the advantages to Canada and the Canadian Army of the proposed loan. It would release for service in the field officers who were not needed immediately but who would gain battle experience that would be invaluable later to the Canadian Army. It would also permit the continued commissioning of selected noncommissioned officers (NCOs), which was considered good for morale. The memorandum concluded with a strong recommendation for approval of the submission to Cabinet.[22]

On 5 January 1944 the proposed loan was dealt with by the War Committee of the Cabinet. There was little discussion. The Prime Minister, W.L. Mackenzie King, insisted that the officers should be subject to immediate recall whenever the Canadian Army needed them and that they should be eligible for all the advantages of the demobilization arrangements for the Canadian Army. Subject to these conditions and the approval of the Minister of Finance for the payment of pay, allowances, and pensions, the loan was approved.[23]

Although General Stuart had requested General Letson to "get on with the selection" as soon as Cabinet approval had been obtained, it was decided at NDHQ that it would not be advisable to issue a call for volunteers until the main conditions of the loan could be explained to them. After meetings with General Stuart and General Montague on 30 December and 23 January, Sir Ronald Adam agreed to call a conference of officers from the War Office and CMHQ to work out the details of an agreement. The conference, held on 4 February, was attended by 24 officers, all but two of them from the War Office. The Canadian representatives were Brig. C.S. Booth and Brig. E.G. Weeks, both on the staff of CMHQ. Maj. A.B. MacLaren, later CANLOAN liaison officer, was present as an observer. The chairman, Brig. J.H.A.J. O'Donnell, DAG (Co-ord.), asked if it was true that the request for 2,000 infantry officers could be met; Brigadier Booth assured him that no difficulty was expected in obtaining that many volunteers. The Canadians were assured that that number could easily be absorbed, and, in view of the urgency, it was hoped that the first 650 could be available in the United Kingdom during the first week of March. The Canadian officers must have been surprised to be told that there was no current British need for RCASC officers.

The chairman noted that several points had been agreed upon already. They included:

- There would be a number of French-speaking Canadian officers, provided that they were completely bilingual and "temperamentally suited" for service with British troops.
- All officers would be volunteers who were acquainted with the conditions of service.
- Volunteers would be junior infantry officers in a proportion of one captain to eight lieutenants.
- Service would be limited to the European and Mediterranean theatres to facilitate the return to the Canadian Army if required.

In a cordial spirit and businesslike manner the conference proceeded to deal with more than 20 elements of the agreement. The participants agreed that the volunteers would be of the standard of efficiency for reinforcements to the Canadian Army overseas; that officers would be paid at Canadian rates; that British practices regarding promotion would be followed; and that officers would be dispatched from Canada in drafts of approximately 250. The first 600 would be posted directly to field units of the 21st Army Group, and efforts would be made to post officers to British regiments affiliated with their parent Canadian unit. In regard to discipline, no sentence of cashiering or dismissal would be confirmed by a British commander below the rank of lieutenant-general; and CMHQ would appoint an officer to liaise with the War Office on all matters relating to the Canadian officers, including honours and awards, documentation, and casualty reports.

There were slight differences of opinion on several matters. The War Office representatives had assumed that the British age limits for junior officers would be observed, that is, 30 for subalterns and 35 for captains, but the Canadians insisted that the Canadian regulations should apply, namely, 33 and 37 respectively. The intention was that the British could return officers who were found to be unsatisfactory but that they should first have three months to prove themselves. Applications for return from Canadian officers were to be permitted only in exceptional circumstances. General Letson had already insisted that the Canadian Army must be entirely responsible for selecting the officers, that "mass returns" by the British would be intolerable, and that the three months' grace should be accepted, as it was without argument by the British. The British agreed that the volunteer officers could wear their own service dress, badges, and buttons but insisted that they would normally wear battle dress with the badges of the unit to which they were posted. This was later amended to provide that they would wear "Canada" flashes on their battle dress.

There were two final matters. The War Office requested that 50 junior officers from the Royal Canadian Ordnance Corps (RCOC) be lent to the Royal Army Ordnance Corps (RAOC) under the same conditions as the infantry officers. Finally, it was agreed that for ease of reference a code word for the scheme was desirable.[24] The Director of Organization at the War Office agreed to look after this matter.

A letter from the War Office to CMHQ dated 21 February 1944 confirmed all the above and proposed that the code word for the scheme, suggested by Maj. L. Ridgeway of the War Office, be "CANLOAN."[25] In the meantime, on the basis of notes by Brigadiers Booth and Weeks, there had been exchanges between CMHQ and NDHQ on several points. Finally, on 10 March an official response from General Montague at CMHQ to the Under Secretary of State at the War Office confirmed all the points in the agreement, including "CANLOAN" as the code word.[26]

On 16 February the scheme was announced by the Minister of National Defence in the House of Commons. Colonel Ralston gave an outline of the loan, which did not yet have a name, and of which, in the interest of security, he would not give numbers. Meanwhile the machinery for obtaining the volunteers was already in place. The CANLOAN scheme was approved and was being implemented.[27]

2

The Volunteers

A PLAN TO IMPLEMENT the loan agreement was submitted to the Canadian Adjutant-General on 10 February 1944 by Col. R.S. Carey, Director of Personal Services at NDHQ. The British Army was to be lent a maximum of 1,450 infantry and 50 ordnance officers. This was to be done by instalments of about 250 at two-week intervals between 15 March and 14 May 1944. All eligible officers in the Canadian Army were to be given an opportunity to volunteer. For the first draft, quotas were suggested for each military district (MD), ranging from 50 for MD 4 (Montreal) to five for MD 12 (Regina) and totalling 300, of whom 250 were expected to survive the final selection. Officers selected in each military district were to be given embarkation leave and then sent to a concentration centre for refresher training from the date of arrival to the date of dispatch overseas.[1]

A memo, dated 11 February 1944, from Colonel Carey to the Adjutant-General, noted:

> It is considered that selected rft [reinforcement] officers should be of such standard as to training and physical fitness which will reflect credit on the Canadian Army. In this connection it is pointed out that rft officers trained in Canada cannot be considered suitable for the field as any trg [training] received can only be considered theoretical since it is generally impossible to give them the necessary practical man management and leadership trg in units in this country.

The memo repeated the words of the War Office in pointing out the urgency of the loan: "On the assumption that they are completely trained, the first 600 would go directly to field units of 21 Army Group."[2] This seemed to suggest that the first 600 volunteers should receive intensive training in Canada before going overseas and that the rest should receive training overseas before being posted to field units.

Colonel Carey's plan was adopted at once, and on the day after its receipt, the official call for volunteers was issued in a directive from General Letson to the General Officers Commanding (GOCs) in Pacific and Atlantic Commands, all Commanders of Military Districts, and the Commander, Camp Borden. He summed up with the words, "The matter is urgent and should be given first priority."[3]

Enclosed with the directive was information to be made available to volunteers. The General considered it "essential that the attitude of officers volunteering toward commanding Imperial troops and being under Imperial officers [be] such as to render them suitable for employment with the British Army."[4]

The initial response to the appeal for volunteers (see Appendix A) seemed to meet the high expectations of the authors of the CANLOAN scheme. The opportunity to serve in the British Army was welcomed (see Appendix B) by hundreds of young army officers from coast to coast in Canada as a release from the frustration of uninteresting duties, but chiefly as a ticket to the invasion of northwest Europe. Many officers had been mobilized with, or subsequently posted to, regiments that, for various reasons, had not been sent overseas. Others had been overseas, had risen through the ranks, usually from private to sergeant, had been returned to Canada for officer training, and wished to get back overseas. A few, who had had difficulty in getting overseas as reinforcement officers because they were at or near the age limit or had minor physical defects, hoped the new scheme would provide some latitude. Others were favourably disposed towards service in the British Army because they had been born and educated in the United Kingdom or Ireland or their fathers had served in British regiments. Others were simply keen to see action and had already volunteered for everything that seemed to offer the opportunity to get overseas quickly. These included under-age youths who had lied about their ages to get into the Army, a number of Americans who sought action in the Canadian Army, others who had already volunteered, without success, for Royal Canadian Air Force (RCAF) air crew, paratroops, and various alternatives. As CANLOAN officer Doug Gage said, "We have volunteered for everything else to get overseas; why not this?"[5]

Many officers in other corps, particularly artillery officers in coastal defence, were so anxious to get overseas that they were willing to take additional training to qualify as infantry officers. The greatest number of CANLOAN volunteers, however, came from the staffs of basic or advanced training centres. One, Jack McBride, has described the reaction to the CANLOAN scheme by the officers at the Canadian Infantry (Basic) Training Centre (CI(B)TC), St- Jean, Quebec:

For me CANLOAN happened in the middle of a very wintry March afternoon in the middle of a course on Fieldcraft and Camouflage in Sherbrooke, Québec. It was in 1944 and the war was in its fifth year. My home base was the Infantry Training Centre in the old Dragoons' Barracks at St Jean, Québec. It was, as was every training centre, glutted with junior officers waiting and hoping to get on an overseas draft. Their time was spent alternately in the training of recruits and attending specialized courses. And at this particular time I was on the above mentioned course ... But our mood was such that it all seemed so pointless and I found myself reflecting on the bad luck that caused me to miss a draft ... And then one day we were all ordered to report to the drill hall. The purpose was to tell us that the British Army wanted volunteers from Canada for service with British Regiments, to fill a serious shortage of junior officers required for the opening of the second front. If any of us wished to volunteer we were free to do so. It was an appealing idea. The British Army had an acute shortage of platoon commanders, whereas the Canadian Army had an embarrassing surplus. What a happy solution all round!

That same afternoon those of us from St Jean who had volunteered boarded a train to return to our home base and we spent the time speculating on how many others at the Barracks would be going too. We arrived during dinner and as we entered the mess the din gave us our answer. The whole damned lot had volunteered, although it was inevitable that in the final screening some would be left behind. But nobody thought too much about that right now. With dinner over, there was a natural migration to the bar. That session was a long, noisy, and very happy one. Finally the CANLOANs, as we were now called, went off on leave to await further orders.

Within a few days we were called. Each volunteer was personally interviewed by a British Army selection committee. It accepted most of the St Jean group and when we finally reported back from leave the CO [Commanding Officer] laid on a fitting farewell. Wearing service dress, we did a march past led by the pipes and drums and an honour guard. We then marched out of the barracks for the last time and through that famed old military town of St Jean which had seen so many men march through it in so many wars.[6]

Norman Orr, another of the volunteers from St-Jean, confirms the enthusiastic response to the CANLOAN scheme. Though there were differences – the ceremonial send-off was unusual – similar experiences occurred at many other training centres from coast to coast, from Aldershot in Nova Scotia, Utopia in New Brunswick, Farnham in Quebec, Ipperwash, Borden, and Petawawa in Ontario, to Portage la Prairie and Shilo in Manitoba, Regina in Saskatchewan, Currie Barracks (Calgary) and Red Deer in Alberta, and Vernon in British Columbia. Harry Hihn recalls that 17 volunteered at once from Camp Ipperwash, and Alex Cunningham said there were enough volunteers from Camp Borden to warrant a special coach to take them to Toronto on leave and later to Montreal on the way to Sussex.

Jack McBride notes that the officers in training centres alternated between training recruits and taking specialized courses. The premier course was the rugged battle drill course at the Canadian Infantry School (CIS) at Vernon, British Columbia, but there were many other courses that were supposed to give successful candidates an edge in getting on a draft. Lieut. Jack Matthews, serving with the Prince Edward Island Highlanders in Port Alberni, British Columbia, heard about the CANLOAN scheme before the official announcement and immediately wrote to his CO, applying for service overseas with the British Army. He listed the courses he had taken, which included platoon weapons, woodcraft, mountain warfare, and forest, bush, and jungle warfare.[7] Don Diplock was one of several officers in training centres who had been selected to go to the Royal Military College (RMC) at Kingston, Ontario, for training as battalion intelligence officers. This had seemed a reasonable assignment for Diplock and his pal, Donald Good, both graduates of McGill University. But they didn't hesitate to leave RMC in response to the call of CANLOAN. Early in 1944 there was a rumour that there was a demand for paratroop officers and that after training in Montana one was sure to get posted overseas. Wilf

Smith was among those who applied, and he also put in a bid for Boobytraps and Demolitions. Such efforts often backfired, however, since the applicants were "frozen in present location" while waiting for a response that never came.

The case of the Pictou Highlanders Regiment (the Pictous) illustrates the frustration that produced so many instant volunteers for the CANLOAN scheme, in units that had not gone overseas. Several future CANLOAN officers had joined the local county regiment long before the war, John Druhan in 1930 and Stewart Cameron in 1933, for example. Both were sergeants when the Pictous were mobilized on 25 August 1939. All ranks were keen to get overseas and into action, but for the next three years the regiment was engaged in coastal duties "bravely defending Mulgrave, Dartmouth, Halifax and surrounding areas." The Pictous became a reinforcement unit with a constant drainage of men for other units, but some officers requested permission to resign their commissions and revert to privates in order to get on an overseas draft. These requests were refused, as were requests to transfer to other units. As Stewart Cameron recalls; "It became increasingly more embarrassing to come home for a week-end and be greeted with, 'Are you still here?'"

Finally in August 1942, a striker force of five officers and 152 other ranks was provided by the Pictou Highlanders to land on Madagascar, then held by Vichy France. The force was commanded by Capt. John Druhan and included three other future CANLOAN officers – Stewart Cameron, Lawson Smith, and Warren Thompson. At the last moment the project was cancelled, and the force was posted to Bermuda for garrison duties. Returning a year later to Halifax, the officers were desperate for an overseas posting. Cameron, Smith, and Thompson haunted the adjutant daily and finally one day he greeted them with: "Do you bastards still want to go overseas? If you do, sign this."

It was, of course, the CANLOAN scheme, which provided the desired release. A total of 17 officers from the Pictou Highlanders, who were stationed in Saint John, New Brunswick, volunteered. Ten of them were original Pictou officers; the rest had been posted to the regiment from training centres. In fact there were 18, but one, Lieut. Jack MacKenna, was accepted but had to drop out because of an injury received at a farewell mess party. Apparently the CO, Lieut.-Col. J.A. Adamson, MC, ED, on receiving so many applications, decided to let the selection be made at MD headquarters. All 17 were chosen, much to the Commanding Officer's horror, since he lost half his officer strength, including his second in command, Maj. Charles A. Manning.[8]

Many of the volunteers from other home defence regiments had similar experiences. Eric Hall, who had joined the Victoria Rifles of Canada (the Vics) with a commission in 1940, was seconded as a training officer at Huntington, Quebec, while the regiment was in Newfoundland. He rejoined the Vics as they travelled to the west coast to make up, with the Royal Winnipeg Rifles and the Royal Rifles of Canada from Quebec, a rifle brigade for the defence of Hong Kong. Prevented from sailing (fortunately, as it turned out) by a shipping mishap, the regiment went successively to Halifax for coastal defence duties, to Moncton, New Brunswick, and finally to Niagara Falls, Ontario, to defend the power dam and canal at Queenston. CANLOAN was a welcome release.

Tom King, who had been commissioned in September 1939 and later promoted to captain, travelled with the Kent Regiment from coast to coast, from Halifax, Nova Scotia, to Port Hardy, British Columbia, during the next four years. He reverted to lieutenant to be accepted as a CANLOAN volunteer.

Glen Harrison, an officer in the Winnipeg Light Infantry, had gone with them to Vernon, Victoria, Comox, Nanaimo, and Prince George, all in British Columbia. He had taken courses in battle drill, mountain warfare, and weapons. He knew that his "unit would not go overseas – ever." He welcomed CANLOAN. So did Martin Kaufman and seven other officers in the Prince of Wales Rangers in Terrace, British Columbia, and Reginald (Rex) Fendick and five fellow officers in the Saint John Fusiliers (MG) in Prince George, British Columbia. And so did many other officers who wished to escape from home defence duties. A special irritant was the changing nature of regimental personnel. The National Resources Mobilization Act (NRMA) of June 1940 had in effect introduced conscription for service in Canada, but one had to volunteer for service overseas. As the need for reinforcements overseas increased as a result of casualties, first at Dieppe and later in Italy, they were drawn from units in Canada. The overseas volunteers were replaced by "NRMA" men, conscripts who would not opt for overseas service, usually called "zombies." This effectively killed any chance of going overseas as a battalion.[9] Many of the CANLOAN survivors have referred to the fact that it was increasingly unpleasant to serve in units composed almost completely of zombies, with only the officers and a few NCOs willing to serve overseas.

Arnold Willick is a good example of the officers who were unhappy in the home defence regiments. He had enlisted in Niagara Falls, Ontario, and worked his way through the ranks to a commission and was eager to get overseas. It is difficult to improve on his own account:

> I had volunteered for everything I felt I was qualified for or believed I could contribute to ... but because I had been tagged as an instructor I was held back. When transferred to the Edmonton Fusiliers as a training officer I believed that we were training the unit to go overseas. On completion of a gruelling three-month period of training, the Battalion was sent, with a few trucks, rifles and Bren guns, to guard the hydro canal which supplied water for the powerhouse at Queenston, Ontario. This was the ultimate letdown, since this was my home. Then Captain Don Saul came in one night and asked me if I would volunteer for the British Army. The official request had just reached his desk. My response: "give me thirty minutes to run home, kiss my wife and baby daughter goodbye and pick up some laundry and I will be ready." Needless to say, the Army doesn't move that rapidly, but I was among the very first group into Sussex, and I was one of the first 52 officers to get to the British Army.[10]

Several of the CANLOAN volunteers had special connections with the United Kingdom. Arnold Allen volunteered because his father, who had died in 1935, had been born in England and would have liked his son to serve in the British Army. John Anderson had been born in Scotland and his father had served in the Argyll and Sutherland Highland Regiment (A. & S.H.) in the First World War. Kenneth Brown's father had served with the Coldstream Guards Regiment. Philip West's grandfather, father, and several uncles had served in the Imperial Army, and Arthur

Connor's father and older brother had a combined service of more than 30 years in the British Army. John Aitken, Bill Mitchell, and Howard McAllister were among those who had been born in England, and Frederick Dynes and Bernard Kelly had been born in Ireland. Eric Hall had grown up and attended school in England. In fact, he had qualified for a commission in Cranleigh OTC. Joseph Hemelryk had spent five years at a public school in England, and Donald Oland from Halifax had attended Beaumont College in Windsor.

One CANLOAN volunteer had an unusual connection with Britain. Wilfred Brownlee Vanderlip had been born in Portland, Oregon. He had attended university in California, obtained a bachelor's degree and continued for a year of postgraduate work before obtaining a position as a researcher with the Imperial Economic Commission in London, England. In October 1940 he enlisted as a private in the Canadian Army at CMHQ in London and was posted to the 48th Highlanders of Canada. At this time he changed his name to Wilfred Wallace Nigel Brownlee-Lamont. He was promoted to corporal in 1941 and sergeant in 1942. Recommended for a commission, he was sent to Canada for officer training. He obtained a commission in the RCASC at Gordon Head in February 1943 and his second pip at Camp Borden. After volunteering for the CANLOAN scheme, he attended the two-month special course at Brockville to qualify for infantry. Overseas he joined the 2nd Battalion, the Gordon Highlanders (Gordons), was wounded in Normandy, rejoined his unit on release from hospital, and was killed two weeks later.

More than one-quarter of the CANLOAN volunteers had a special incentive to participate in a scheme that promised an early overseas draft. They were the men who had already served overseas in the Canadian Army, who had, in most cases, worked their way through the ranks from private to sergeant or warrant officer, had been recommended for a commission and sent to Canada for officer training at Brockville, Ontario, or Gordon Head, British Columbia. Sometimes these cadets were given special duties on board ship when returning to Canada, as is described by Del Struck:

> We were given a short course in handling POWs (prisoners of war) at a large camp in Oldham, and proceeded to board the *Louis Pasteur* with about 4500 to 5500 Afrika Corps prisoners. Some 80 cadets and a few Marines and the normal crew were the entire guard detachment. When we arrived at New York, we thought the entire American Army had been sent to greet us: tanks, artillery, infantry, you name it. We really did not have a senior officer in charge, so when the senior American officer, I think a Lieutenant-General, came aboard to accept the prisoners, they were probably handed over by a cadet. The Afrika Corps – what excellent soldiers. They walked off the ship with their uniforms pressed, medals shining and in perfect order, more the look of victory than the defeat they had endured.[11]

Many of the cadets on the *Louis Pasteur*, and others who had returned to Canada for commissions, on graduation from Brockville or Gordon Head were pounced on for service as instructors and posted to the staff of the OTCs or the battle drill course at the CIS, Vernon, which was commanded by Brig. Milton Gregg, VC, CBE, MC, ED, who had a good eye for talent. Most of the staff were overseas men who, considered indispensable, might well have spent the rest of the war in Vernon if CANLOAN had not come along. Even so, when the instructional staff volunteered as a body, many of them were persuaded by Brigadier Gregg to instruct at Camp Sussex before being fitted into a draft.

The enthusiasm of the overseas men was contagious. Most future CANLOAN officers had encountered them as fellow cadets at OTC or as instructors and had heard tales of the delights of life in the UK – the friendly girls, the Palais de Dance, Piccadilly Circus, Trafalgar Square, even Hammersmith and Putney, plays in London, leaves in Scotland, and that grand institution, the pub. Appetites were whetted, undoubtedly contributing to the warm reception given to the CANLOAN scheme.

A few future CANLOAN officers had gone overseas with commissions. Frederick Chesham, for example, had had a commission as early as 1935 and had served in several militia units before joining the permanent force as an officer in the Royal Canadian Regiment (RCR) in August 1939. He served overseas with the RCR until 1942, when he returned to Canada as a captain in the newly mobilized Canadian Fusiliers (City of London Regiment). He was aide-de-camp (ADC) to Maj.-Gen. Arthur Potts, General Officer Commanding (GOC), 6th Division, and was an instructor at Vernon, British Columbia, before participating in the expedition to Kiska that ended in January 1944.

Another who had gone overseas as an officer was J. Stuart Townshend, who had a commission in the Calgary Highlanders as early as 1932. At the outbreak of war he transferred to the Princess Patricia's Canadian Light Infantry (PPCLI) and went to England in December 1939 with the 1st Division. In the spring of 1940 he returned with 100 German POWs for internment in Alberta. For the next four years, however, he was firmly stuck at the training centre at Portage la Prairie, Manitoba. He was able to spring free by joining CANLOAN.

At least one future CANLOAN officer had given up a commission in order to go overseas. Ralph Arthurs, who was born in Ottawa, served in a militia unit, the Algonquin Rifles, from 1933 to 1940, the last four years as a lieutenant. In 1940 he enlisted in the Royal Canadian Engineers (RCE) as a sapper and was posted to No. 2 Tunnelling Company in Gibraltar. He spent 18 months on "the Rock" as sergeant in charge of tunnelling before being returned to Canada for officer training in 1943. A member of the first CANLOAN flight, he was posted to the 5th Battalion Duke of Cornwall's Light Infantry (DCLI) and was killed in action on 11 July 1944.

A few future CANLOAN officers had gone overseas as senior NCOs. Arthur Connor had joined the 48th Highlanders in 1929 and in 1936 was a sergeant. He transferred to active service (retaining his rank), went overseas with the 1st Division, and in 1940 participated in the exciting dash to France as the Germans were closing in. He was an instructor at the Canadian OCTU in England under the command of Brigadier Gregg until it was closed in 1942. Connor, by then a warrant officer class II, was posted to the western Canada OTC at Gordon Head, British Columbia, first as an instructor and then as a cadet. After obtaining his commission, he was posted to the basic training centre at Brantford, Ontario. He was rescued by CANLOAN.

Several of the future CANLOAN officers with overseas experience had a special incentive to return to the UK. James Taylor had gone overseas with the Calgary

Highlanders in the 2nd Division in 1940. By the spring of 1943 he had risen to the rank of sergeant-major and had married an Englishwoman. After returning to Canada for a commission, he became an instructor at CIS, Vernon. CANLOAN was an opportunity to rejoin his wife, and when his draft reached London he was allowed to run down the street to where she was serving on a barrage balloon site. Peter Pearce had married while serving with the Canadian Forestry Corps in Inverness, Scotland. After obtaining a commission at Gordon Head, he joined those who were instructors at Currie Barracks, in Calgary, until CANLOAN came along. After the war he remained in Scotland.

A special group of volunteers with overseas experience were those who had participated in the Dieppe raid in August 1942, particularly seven of them who had been decorated for gallantry: "Adam Brygider, Distinguished Conduct Medal (DCM); John Buchanan, Military Medal (MM); Fred Knight, MM; John MacDonald, MM; George McDermott, MM; John Marsh, MM; and Ernest Thirgood, MM." When they volunteered for CANLOAN they were well aware of what was involved.

At the opposite end of the scale in terms of military experience from the CANLOAN volunteers from overseas were the products of the university Canadian Officers' Training Corps. The COTC syllabus included the subjects required for basic and advanced training as well as some distinct officer training; during the war participation was compulsory for all university students who were otherwise eligible for military service. Whereas training during the university term, which was in addition to regular university courses, was held chiefly in classroom or drill hall, the annual summer camp provided opportunities for concentrated field training. Since the COTC contingents usually consisted of several platoons, some students held ranks as high as lieutenant. In this respect it would be difficult to beat the record of Harold (Moody) Richards of the University of New Brunswick COTC contingent. Between May 1940 and June 1942 Richards held successive ranks of corporal, sergeant, company sergeant-major, regimental sergeant-major, 2nd lieutenant, and temporary lieutenant. He was adjutant when he was struck off strength (SOS) on enlisting in the active force. The number of CANLOAN volunteers who enrolled with commissions or went to OTC immediately after enlisting was about the same as those who had returned from overseas for commissions after years of experience as NCOs. There was no comparison in the amount of their military experience, but since most of the COTC graduates had been out of university only a year or less when CANLOAN was announced, many of them were still enthusiastic about the Army. They had not yet become thoroughly "browned off" with the monotony of training troops in infantry training centres (ITC). Following is an extract from a letter from the Aldershot ITC on the eve of CANLOAN:

> Jack is just as happy and enthusiastic about the Army as I am. I've been very busy as my four NCO instructors are home on New Year's leave, leaving the sergeant and me to carry on. I've enjoyed it, though, and we have got the men off to a good start in advanced training. We have the obstacle course every day. Friday we had a ten-mile cross-country march through deep snow, up steep hills, through woods, over streams, etc. and all the platoon finished, as they are rapidly getting into top condition, and so am I after my brief administrative position as acting company commander.[12]

A number of officers welcomed the CANLOAN scheme because it seemed to provide an opportunity to serve overseas in spite of their age or minor physical defects. Fred Burnaby, for example, had been told when he graduated from Brockville OTC that he was too old at 34 to be sent overseas as a reinforcement officer; he was posted to No. 2 District Depot and later Camp Borden as an instructor. Two years later he was accepted for the CANLOAN scheme and was, in fact, under the regular age limit for captains to go overseas. Another volunteer who had been prevented from going overseas because of his age was Robert Barr. Born in 1907, he had graduated from the University of Saskatchewan and McGill Law School and was a practising lawyer. He enlisted as a private in the Regina Rifles in 1940, was promoted to sergeant almost immediately, and was later sent to Gordon Head, British Columbia, for a commission. Later at Camp Shilo, Manitoba, he became assistant adjutant and was promoted to captain and then major. When CANLOAN came along he used his considerable influence and persuasiveness to have himself accepted as a captain despite his age and questionable physical condition.

Perhaps the most prominent example of a volunteer who had been considered overage was Donald Findlay. He had been practising law in Toronto since 1931 and had served in the Queen's York Rangers since 1926; when his unit was mobilized in 1939 he was a major. When the Rangers were disbanded in 1943 he was posted to the General Staff in Ottawa, considered to be too old for overseas service. Alerted to the CANLOAN scheme at an early stage, he was an instant volunteer, reverting to captain to qualify; he received the first CANLOAN number, CDN/1.

There were many other officers for whom CANLOAN was a welcome opportunity. Though their circumstances differed, they all shared an unusual keenness to get into action. There were, for example, the dozen or so Americans who had come to Canada with the hope of seeing action in the Canadian Army, but had encountered obstacles in the reinforcement stream. Tim O'Keefe, later known as "the wild American Irishman in a Scottish kilt" when he was in the 7th Battalion, the Black Watch, was a lawyer trapped in Montreal on permanent court-martial duty when CANLOAN offered him an escape hatch.

Then there were the boy soldiers. Earl Cloutier had lied about his age when he was 14 to enlist as a signaller in the 1st Canadian Field Battery, the Royal Canadian Artillery (RCA), and at the age of 17 he had enlisted as a boy soldier in the RCR. His efforts to get overseas in the Canadian Army and in the Canada/United States Special Service Force had been frustrated when he was assigned as an instructor at Brockville and elsewhere before and after obtaining a commission. John Harrison had lied about his age to enlist in the Calgary Highlanders and had been discovered, although he got overseas eventually. Alex Cunningham was aided by a kindly medical officer who had recommended that a year be added to his age so that he could get a commission at 19. Arthur Stone had joined the local militia unit, the Lanark and Renfrew Scottish Regiment (affiliated with the Black Watch), as a piper at the age of 12. In 1941 in Toronto he was still underage but enlisted in the active force as a member of the pipe band. A chum in the orderly room (a drummer) had added his name to a draft for advanced training, and there he was recommended for a commission. Two years later he was posted to the Pictou Highlanders in Saint John and was among those in that regiment to welcome CANLOAN.

Several volunteers felt that the CANLOAN scheme enabled them to carry on their family tradition. Ross LeMesurier's father had been wounded in the infantry in the First World War, and his two brothers had been killed in action. Two cousins had also served, one of whom was killed after earning a Military Cross (MC) and bar. His mother's two brothers had served overseas, both earning MCs and one a DSO and Mentioned in Dispatches (MID) as well. His brother, a lieutenant in the 48th Highlanders, had been wounded. It was unthinkable that Ross would not fight in the war, and CANLOAN gave him the opportunity.

Others who volunteered for CANLOAN had tried many other avenues to a more active role in the war, such as the RCAF as air crew and paratroops. And finally there were some free spirits who had had trouble with the military system. The outstanding example is Leo Heaps; it would be difficult to improve on his own account:

> I had come only because the Canadian Army was so anxious to see the last of me. Successive commanders had branded me "not of officer calibre," "no initiative," "not aggressive enough" and I tended to agree. The Canadian Army decided to discharge me and recall me as a private. Even when a kindly brigadier took pity on me and gave me one more chance to qualify in the infantry I failed. No one had ever failed before to qualify for the infantry. I should definitely not be here.[13]

Heaps was at Aldershot, Nova Scotia, when the CANLOAN scheme was announced. He was accepted and in England was posted first to the 1st Battalion, the Dorset Regiment (Dorset), which landed in Normandy on D-Day. Wounded and returned to hospital in England, Heaps showed great persistence and enterprise in getting into the 1st Battalion, the Parachute Regiment (Para.) in the 1st Airborne Division. At Arnhem, where his exploits won him an MC, and subsequently when his initiative, courage, and enterprise were demonstrated in organizing the return of many Arnhem escapees, Heaps's performance demonstrated that CANLOAN was flexible enough to profit from the talents of a free spirit who, as he said, "yearned to break away from routine and regulations."

Finally there were the officers who were willing to convert to infantry from other corps in order to get overseas. There were several volunteers from the RCASC, half of them from MD 13 (Calgary). One of these, Tom Anstey, recalls, "Junior officers in the RASC were too many by about a factor of 10, hence there was little hope of any of us seeing active service."[14] Gordon Booth, another RCASC officer, had got bogged down at Camp Borden as an instructor: "It did not look like I would ever get overseas as an RCASC officer. I was sent to Debert on two drafts but each time they were cancelled and I was returned to Camp Borden."[15]

Many of the officers who were willing to take a special eight-week course to qualify as infantry officers in order to be accepted in the CANLOAN scheme had obtained commissions in the RCA and were serving in the Atlantic provinces in coast artillery or anti-aircraft (AA) batteries. Several of these officers have explained their reasons for volunteering.

Fred Burd was with the light anti-aircraft battery in Goose Bay, Labrador, before being posted to a heavy anti-aircraft battery in Dartmouth, Nova Scotia. He describes his duties there:

Much of military service is cloud-cuckoo-land but the next 6 weeks was in the running for first prize: I was posted to No. 1 GOR [gun operations room] hidden in one of the old magazines on Citadel Hill [Halifax], and theoretically the nerve centre of the anti-aircraft defences of Halifax-Dartmouth. In practice, I think there would have been few places in the world where it would have been equally safe for a German aircraft to fly over. My main job, and that of my fellow duty officers, was to spend our duty hours sitting in comfortable leather chairs surveying CWACs [Canadian Women's Army Corps] pushing arrows over map tables as they received plots from the RCAF.[16]

Harold Richards reports:

The 14 or so months I spent in 1 Halifax Coastal Artillery (compared to three to four years spent by some other future CANLOANs such as Peverley, McInerney, Lamb and Merchant, among others) left us all rather frustrated. Fort life was uninteresting by and large, although necessary to the defence of Canada. Most of our troops were "Zombies." Remember that Canada was still, at this time, not sending conscripts overseas, but only volunteers – so the officers were "Active" and the troops, including most of the NCOs, were conscripts. There existed the real danger that the war would end, and most of us had never fired or seen a shot fired in anger.

It started for the Gunners in mid-March, 1944. I was then at Devil's Bty [battery], it was a Saturday afternoon. The Bty CO was on week-end pass, and George McInerney was acting CO. He had a call from the RHQ [Regimental Headquarters] that any gunner officer who met the medical requirements could volunteer to transfer to infantry and join the CANLOAN scheme for appointment to the British Army. By Sunday morning nine officers from 1st Coast had submitted their willingness to sign on. Altogether, out of a complement of about 22 officers in the 1st Coast, 14 either went CANLOAN or volunteered in the first instance. This gives some indication of the frustration of being in a static coast defence operation.[17]

The second notice to GOCs concerning volunteers for the first draft of 300 was dated 23 February 1944. It identified the concentration point as A-34 Special Officers Training Centre (SOTC), Sussex Military Camp, New Brunswick. Officers selected were to report there 7–8 March. The notice also stressed the importance of selecting officers "well-oriented towards service with the British Army and well-motivated toward future action."[18]

Within the first week several MDs had filled their quotas: MD 2 (Toronto) had already exceeded its quota of 10 and expected more volunteers; MD 3 (Kingston), with a quota of 10, had received 26 volunteers; and Camp Borden had exceeded its quota of 40. MD 4 (Montreal), with the largest quota (50), expected to fill it. On the other hand, MD 1 (London) had only half its quota of 35; MD 5 (Quebec City) had only 3 volunteers and did not expect many more. MD 6 (Halifax) and MD 10 (Winnipeg) had about half their quotas.

To be accepted for service in the British Army, a volunteer had to obtain two certificates: one from his DOC or camp commandant attesting that his military qualifications were at least equal to the standard for overseas reinforcements for the Canadian Army; and another from an OSAC board assessing motivation, attitude, aptitude, adaptability, personal characteristics, and general suitability for meeting British Army standards and the requirements of the loan scheme. These certificates did not, however, guarantee dispatch overseas, since the commandant of A-34 SOTC had the authority to reject any officer who, in his opinion, was not suitable for service in the British Army.

The first reaction from the OSAC boards appeared favourable. Brig. C.B. Topp, Chairman of OSAC Board No. 2, wrote to the Secretary of the Department of National Defence on 15 February 1944:

> The Board has today interviewed 15 officers selected within MD 13 for service in the British Army. All have been found suitable for this special duty except one who needed proof of age (later accepted). It was a stimulating experience for the Board to see these fine young officers. They include a number who have returned to Canada from England for training as officers after long service in the field as NCOs. It is our hope that their service will not be entirely lost to the Canadian Army. Selection of these candidates reflects great credit upon the District authorities concerned. It is obvious that the officers have been carefully chosen and that they will represent the Canadian Army with British units very well indeed.[19]

A later report from Brigadier Topp from Camp Shilo was, however, less enthusiastic. He wrote on 1 March 1944 that his board had interviewed 19 volunteers, all of whom had been recommended, some with minor reservations. Several others were unsuitable and had withdrawn.

> With some outstanding exceptions the standard of officers here was lower than that of those seen elsewhere. The first group of officers interviewed appeared to radiate energy and enthusiasm to a marked degree. They were brisk and snappy in their movements and left an impression of aggressiveness and drive. The group here were more stolid and did not display the more superficial ear-marks of the trained soldier to the same extent. They have the required qualities, however, and we feel that the polish they will get at the Special OTC at Sussex will quickly overcome any slackness that may exist. The MD 10 quota also includes a number of officers who returned from overseas for their commissions after long service as NCOs. These, generally speaking, were the best of the group seen. It is clear that they have set the example. The Board finds it difficult to understand why so few officers have volunteered for this service from the quite large number here. The Commandant of A-15 CITC [Canadian Infantry Training Centre] states they have all been fully informed as to the conditions of this duty but that many of them seem to lack confidence with respect to being able to handle British personnel.[20]

Reports from the other military districts were less descriptive, tending only to give the names of the volunteers who were interviewed and approved. On 28 February 1944, 22 volunteers were interviewed at Camp Borden and 10 at Brockville; all the volunteers from MD 12 (Regina) went directly to Sussex to be interviewed there. On 29 February, 15 volunteers were interviewed at CI(B)TC at St-Jean and 11 more there on 1 March. The volunteers who were interviewed in Winnipeg on 3 March restored the enthusiasm of Brigadier Topp. He reported:

Seven officers from MD 13 who had volunteered and were absent on embarkation leave when the Board was in Calgary were interviewed in Winnipeg. The officers seen today were fully up to the standard of those interviewed in Calgary and are a particularly fine lot of young men. Six of the seven had been serving overseas for a long period as NCOs and had returned for training as officers or had been selected here after returning as instructors.[21]

Visits to several centres after the departure of the first draft suggested that it might prove difficult to obtain the number of volunteers expected. In MD 4, Montreal, it was confirmed that "French-speaking reinforcement officers [were] not anxious to volunteer because of lack of confidence in their knowledge of the English language and a fear that the difference in background between a French speaking officer and his English troops would create difficulties."[22]

The first quota was filled on 22 February 1944, and on 2 March the request went out for the second quota of 300 volunteers, who were to report to A-34 SOTC, Sussex, on 21 and 22 March. Already, however, doubts were being expressed at NDHQ about the possibility of obtaining the number of volunteers that had been promised. Consequently new classes of volunteers were admitted, and a public relations campaign was undertaken.

On 3 March 1944 the Adjutant-General announced that volunteers for the CANLOAN scheme would be accepted from officers at NDHQ who possessed the necessary qualifications. On 9 March he announced that it had been decided to offer CANLOAN service to RCASC officers, to officers in coastal defence and anti-aircraft units, and to other artillery officers not qualified in mobile artillery. Volunteers would be sent to OTC Brockville for a two-month qualifying course beginning 7 April, which would be recognized as qualification for infantry reinforcement. On completion they would go to Sussex. Any captains would be required to revert to lieutenant. It had been reported earlier that there were 64 captains and 230 lieutenants in coastal defence units eligible for CANLOAN. This seemed to be a means of boosting considerably the flagging numbers.[23]

A Capt. W.E. Estey reported from MD 4 on 28 February 1944 after the departure of the first quota that, although there were still 30 to 35 English-speaking officers and a great many French-speaking officers in his district, he estimated that only 10 to 15 volunteers could be expected in future quotas. He considered that for the success of the scheme it would be necessary to request volunteers from every source and to undertake a range of public relations measures. This reinforced an earlier suggestion from NDHQ that various methods be adopted "to present to Canadian officers the factual and inspirational advantages of volunteering for service with the British Army." One suggestion was a pamphlet, which was eventually produced. Entitled *Opportunity for Early Overseas Service with the British Army* (sec Appendix A), it outlined the reason for the loan and contained 36 questions and answers concerning the details of its conditions.

By 10 March it was clear at NDHQ that the number of volunteers was falling short of the commitment to the British, and it was decided to mount a major publicity campaign. In a memorandum on the subject Brigadier Roome outlined several suggestions:

• articles in K*haki* and *Canadian Affairs* magazines;
• articles in weekly newspapers written from Sussex on such subjects as "Lt-Cols reverting to go British," "Splendid training at A-34 under Brig Gregg, VC";
• radio programmes which included broadcasts from Sussex with interviews with volunteers, the Coca Cola broadcast from Sussex and items in the regular Armed Forces radio programmes; and finally
• speakers with experience with the British Army using titles such as *A DSO winner relates his experience with the British* and *Here is that opportunity. This is so good it is rational!*

A sample article contained some "inspirational" passages:

> The loan solves in an exciting manner the problem of many junior officers who, under ordinary circumstances, might not see combat service for a long time. It is the opportunity of a lifetime. Stop grousing about not getting a crack at overseas service. Get your buddies together and volunteer as a group. This is a challenge for adventure that occurs only once in a lifetime. A decision now is the key that will open to you a field of personal action that will assure participation in the forging of the security of the British Empire and the United Nations.[24]

Before launching the proposed publicity campaign, the Director of Army Recruiting on 14 March 1944 appealed to the Chief Recruiting Officer in each military district, addressing each by his first name or nickname:

> This letter will have a decidedly personal touch because I think you deserve some explanation regarding the series of teletypes that you will have received. It came about in this way: I was called in to a meeting where I learned that the usual dry directive issued from NDHQ in connection with the demand for loan officers to the British Army had not met with the proper response. Ways and means were discussed as to how the required number of officers could be produced. Without much ado I stated that the District Recruiting Officers could do this job in less time without fanfare and with dignity becoming the Canadian Army. The other methods suggested had to do with publicity, advertising, radio and speech-making – which, incidentally, will be used in the event that you fall down on the job ... So you see that I have put you on the spot and it is up to us to acquit ourselves of this task in such a manner as to raise the prestige of recruiting personnel to the elevation that it rightfully belongs ... All of you must realize that these men are wanted for the PBI [Poor Bloody Infantry]. All we old soldiers have known for a long time that this war is going to be won by the Infantry – Queen of Battles.

He enclosed a speech which, he said, might be used if the recruiting officers couldn't think of anything better:

> Today, gentlemen, I come here to ask for volunteers to serve with the British Army – as fine an Army as can be found anywhere in the world. Behind its regiments are centuries of pride and the most glorious traditions. These are the men you have wanted to fight beside; these are the men you may lead. Napoleon said, in substance, "Give me French

officers and British soldiers and I will lick the world." Now you have an opportunity to imprint new words in the minds of posterity and to pioneer the pride that will live when it is proven that it is the Canadian officers and the British soldiers who can lick the world ... The Mother Country needs you – and needs you because you are what you are – a well-trained Canadian officer. I want those of you who wish to volunteer to come up to this table in an orderly fashion. I say orderly because I don't want to be killed in the rush.[25]

It is fair to say that such rhetoric resulted in few volunteers. The MDs reported at the end of March that the recruiting drive was falling well short of its objective. The District Recruiting Officer from MD 3 (Kingston) sent several acknowledgment forms (see Appendix B) but spoke of difficulties, for example: "Artillery officers feel that having held commissions in the RCA since 1940 and 1941 and priority in training it would be a waste of time and effort to transfer to the British infantry." He concluded, "It is felt that some other method of obtaining the required number of infantry officers for the British Army should be introduced as it would appear that the present system is not satisfactory."[26] Similar gloomy reports came in telegrams from the other districts:

- MD 13: A shameful response from the RCASC. It would seem that "they are quite content to remain here knowing there is no call for reinforcements in their branch."
- MD 12: "Situation has been carefully checked and no applications can be expected."
- MD 1: "All sources exhausted."
- MD 4: "Every potential source exhausted. Future possibility nil."
- MD 6: "Enclosing 48 acknowledgments but future possibilities remote as RCASC not interested."
- MD 7: "Nil return."
- MD 10: "Enclosing 17 acknowledgment forms but every potential source exhausted."

The recruiting officer in MD 10 (Winnipeg) listed all the officers he had interviewed: 23 infantry, 119 artillery, and 7 RCASC and those who had volunteered: 4 infantry, 13 artillery, and no RCASC. He reported that of 66 eligible infantry officers 43 had volunteered and had gone to Sussex; the remaining 19 had definitely refused.

None the less, some recruiting efforts were successful. Gordon Chatterton recalls that Lieut.-Col. Jock McGregor, VC, who was employed in British Columbia to publicize the CANLOAN scheme, had a good deal of influence on his decision to join.

Almost daily reports showed that all potential sources were being canvassed, including instructors at all training schools, officers who were away on courses, those with temporary low PULHEMS[27] because of injuries, even those with insufficient experience in man-management who might develop in the near future. The only bright note was a report from MD 6, Halifax, on 6 April listing the volunteers from coastal defence artillery units who were leaving for Brockville to take the special course.

On 10 April the recruiting efforts were abandoned. In a letter to commands and military districts, General Letson wrote,

> After dispatch of the third quota of infantry officers who have volunteered for service in the British Army on loan from the Canadian Army, no further quotas will be allocated to Commands or Districts for the present. Volunteers from other arms who are to proceed to undergo Special to Infantry training at OTC Brockville commencing 7 Apr will be dispatched [to Sussex] on the conclusion of this course two months hence. This movement will mark the end of the present arrangements for the loan of infantry officers.[28]

An obvious question is why the number of infantry volunteers for the CANLOAN scheme fell so far short of the 2,000 that the British Army hoped to have and the 1,450 that had been authorized by the Canadian Cabinet. When he was interviewed in August 1945, Major MacLaren, the CANLOAN liaison officer at CMHQ, said he believed that 2,000 volunteers could have been obtained "if it had been thought desirable to use up all the Home Defence officers who wished to get overseas and into action."[29] Since he was in England he was apparently not aware of the extent of the efforts in Canada to obtain volunteers. Certainly officers in home defence units were not only permitted but actively encouraged to volunteer. Though some COs and camp commandants were at first reluctant to lose their best officers, they were not able to withstand the pressure that was eventually exerted and the high priority that NDHQ gave to the CANLOAN scheme. (Nevertheless, some COs did actively discourage potential volunteers.) However, there were no more volunteers because there were no more eligible officers who wanted to volunteer. The authorities at NDHQ had simply miscalculated the number.

There is no doubt that the junior infantry officers who did want to go overseas and into action and who were frustrated by being frozen in training centres and home defence units had made their dissatisfaction known to authorities at all levels. They may have given the impression that all eligible reinforcement officers wanted to go overseas and would welcome any opportunity to do so. Statistics on available officers indicated a potential of up to 2,000 infantry officers, not counting possible conversions from other arms. It is possible that insufficient allowance was made for officers who, though quite capable of carrying out military duties in Canada, would not pass the medical requirements for reinforcement officers. Some infantry officers were reluctant to serve in the British Army, perhaps, as Brigadier Topp suggested, because they lacked confidence about commanding British troops. Most officers in other arms, particularly field artillery and RCASC, were never convinced that they could not get overseas with their own corps. And then, of course, it would not be surprising if some officers were reluctant to volunteer because of the certainty that CANLOAN officers would be in the invasion of northwest Europe, where the casualties were sure to be heavy. Lastly, there is no doubt that a good many officers simply did not want to leave the "good thing" they had going in Canada.

Rather than ask why officers did not volunteer, as the district recruiting officers were told to do, one should ask why so many did volunteer. We have seen that there were a number of officers – more than 500 in infantry and nearly 100 in other arms, RCA and RCASC – who were anxious to get overseas and into action in the forthcoming invasion of the Continent. For them CANLOAN was a godsend; the fact that so many officers were willing to revert to lower ranks is indicative of the spirit that animated the CANLOAN volunteers. Those who gathered at Sussex were a small but enthusiastic and highly motivated group whose members were bound to reflect credit on the Canadian Army and the CANLOAN scheme.

The effort to obtain 50 Royal Canadian Ordnance Corps volunteers differed in several respects from the recruiting of infantry officers. First, it was in response to a special request from the War Office, whereas the initiative in the loan of infantry officers came from Canada. Second, the recruiting of RCOC officers began two months later, about the time that the recruiting of infantry officers ceased. Third, since it was a limited objective there was never any danger that it would not be attained. Finally, since there was no surplus of RCOC officers, there was a problem in finding replacements for all the volunteers.

On 14 April 1944 General Letson informed GOCs and DOCs that arrangements had been completed for the loan of 50 RCOC officers to the British Army for employment with the Royal Army Ordnance Corps; that the conditions of the loan were similar to those described in the instruction of 11 February for infantry officers; and that officers of higher rank than captain should be given the opportunity to revert to either captain or lieutenant, keeping in mind the ratio of one captain to eight lieutenants, that is, the chances of being accepted were eight times better for a lieutenant than for a captain. The same arrangements concerning interviews by a selection board and the sending of nominal rolls to NDHQ applied, but for the RCOC volunteers the final selection would be made at National Defence Headquarters. General Letson concluded with these words:

> It is realized that difficulties may be encountered in regard to this loan, but because of the urgency, it is essential that every officer who is eligible be given the opportunity to volunteer. As there is no surplus of Ordnance officers no assurance can be given that replacements will be forthcoming, or, that when available, they will be as able as those officers who will be released. It is appreciated that the lack of immediate replacements will throw an additional burden on the remaining officers and commanding officers will try to carry on as efficiently as possible with the personnel at their disposal.[30]

Arrangements were made to give an opportunity of volunteering to RCOC officers attached to the Department of National Defence. Some were outside Ottawa, in Montreal, for example. Applications were to be sent through NDHQ to the Director of Ordnance Services, but the final selection was to be made at NDHQ, where it would be decided whether volunteers could be spared without replacement or, if a replacement was considered essential, action could be taken to find a suitable substitute.

By the beginning of May the first 30 RCOC volunteers had been selected. They sailed on 10 June, making up the seventh CANLOAN flight. Colonel Saunders, Director of Ordnance Services at NDHQ, insisted he could not make a final selection of the remaining 20 until he had a list of all volunteers from each military district and had read the reports of the selection boards on the candidates. The list, when compiled, included 94 volunteers from training centres and home defence units.

They seem to have been fully occupied in work that was usually interesting, but, given the opportunity, they would like to be more closely involved in the war that was being waged overseas.

Reg Shelford had been on the staff of the *Winnipeg Free Press* since he graduated from university in 1936. He enlisted in the local militia field battery, RCA, in 1940 and qualified as a lieutenant in the RCA in 1941. When he decided to "go active," he received a message that he was to take the next qualifying course at Brockville for ordnance officers. The message came from his boss, Victor Sifton, owner of the *Winnipeg Free Press*, who, as a dollar-a-year man in Ottawa, was Master-General of Ordnance. After an interesting assignment as supply officer for ordnance stores in MD 13, where he was involved with 10,000 Afrika Corps prisoners of war, he took an advanced ordnance course at Barriefield, Ontario. He was Inspecting Ordnance Officer for MDs 10 and 12 and dealt with delicate problems concerning ammunition, when CANLOAN offered him the chance to seek new challenges overseas.

Roger Smith was also from Winnipeg. After serving in the University of Manitoba COTC he was enrolled in the RCOC with a commission on graduation, and during the next four years he served on several ordnance bases in different parts of Canada. When the CANLOAN scheme was announced he was among those who applied. Since seniority was a factor in selection he was accepted and retained his rank as captain.

Arnold Allen of Ottawa had enlisted as a private in the RCOC in December 1941. Posted to the depot at Amherst, Nova Scotia, he had been recommended for a commission. After graduation from Brockville OTC and corps training at Barriefield, he was posted to the Directorate of Mechanization, Master-General of Ordnance at NDHQ. When he saw the notice about CANLOAN he felt that his late father, a clergyman who had emigrated to Canada, would have approved of his son's serving in the British Army.

Alex Ord had enlisted as a private in the RCOC on the outbreak of war. Commissioned in 1942, he served in several ordnance posts in British Columbia before the announcement of CANLOAN. He asks, "Who wouldn't volunteer for some excitement after four and a half years around home?"[31] On the whole, though, the RCOC officers, while volunteering in considerable numbers, did not show the same urgency for release from posts in Canada as the infantry officers.

3

From Sussex to the Second Army

IF THE PURPOSE of a concentration point was to assemble the CANLOAN volunteers and dispatch them from Halifax, the well-known "Eastern Canadian port," then the obvious place was No. 1 Transit Camp, Windsor, Nova Scotia, for that was its purpose throughout the war. When the CANLOAN scheme was approved by Cabinet and selection and dispatch overseas were being discussed at NDHQ, it was assumed that Windsor would be the assembly point. Even the detailed plan for implementing the scheme that was presented to the AG on 10 February 1944 included instructions to send the volunteers who were selected to No. 1 Transit Camp. This part of the plan was deleted at the last moment for two reasons: first, Maj.-Gen. Howard Kennedy, the Quartermaster-General, reported that there was no shipping available for CANLOAN drafts from Halifax, since the demand for space far exceeded the capacity; so the only hope would be to negotiate for space on ships sailing from New York and, since Windsor didn't seem to be suitable for that destination, other options should be considered. Second, when the War Office indicated its intention to send the first 600 volunteers directly to field units of 21st Army Group, it was realized that they would require intensive refresher training before leaving Canada. The concentration point, then, instead of being merely an assembly point, should have first-class training facilities and staff.

A quick survey of military districts revealed that there was little spare accommodation in the main training centres. Four other possible camps were considered, and their favourable and unfavourable features were listed and compared: No 1. Transit Camp, Windsor; A-34 CITC, Maple Creek, Saskatchewan; Niagara Camp, Ontario; and Camp Sussex, New Brunswick. Windsor and Maple Creek had poor training areas, no range facilities, and not enough instructional staff; Niagara had good training facilities but no accommodation or staff; and Sussex had good accommodation and training areas but no administrative or instructional staff. It was decided to combine the best elements from several sources, namely to establish at Camp Sussex a temporary school to train up to 800 reinforcement officers at one time; to move A-34 CITC, including all administrative staff and equipment, from Maple Creek to Sussex; and to select additional administrative staff from No. 1 Transit Camp and instructional staff from OTC Brockville, the CIS, Vernon, British Columbia, and the Training Brigade Group, Debert, Nova Scotia. Already two essential appointments had been decided: that of Brig. Milton Gregg, VC, as commandant of the school and of Lieut.-Col. H.M. Jones as chief instructor. The Deputy Chief of the General Staff was to call a meeting of all the interested directorates at NDHQ to ensure that the establishment of the special training centre had the highest priority and that there would be no delays in obtaining necessary equipment, facilities, and personnel.

At the meeting, which was held in Ottawa on 18 February 1944, it was decided that the designation of the new school would be A-34 SOTC (Special Officers Training Centre). It was to be established on a temporary basis of not more than three and a half months from 1 March. Assignments were given to no fewer than 20 directorates, ranging from care of the vacated buildings at Maple Creek to repairs to buildings at Camp Sussex, accommodation for CWAC personnel, changes in the establishments of MDs 12 and 7, medical and recreational services, and even wood for the stoves in the huts.[1] Special attention was given to officers' mess furniture. The Chief of the General Staff wrote to the Master-General of Ordnance on 19 February, "An essential and important factor in the training at Sussex of Canadian officers who are to be loaned to the British is mess etiquette and conduct generally in the officers' mess and it is therefore considered most essential that suitable and adequate mess facilities be provided for the 600 reinforcement officers who will be concentrated there commencing 7 March."[2]

There was only one week between the meeting in Ottawa and the transfer of A-34 from Maple Creek to Sussex (on 24 February) and the arrival the next day of Brigadier Gregg and Colonel Jones. It was another two weeks before the arrival of the first group of volunteers. During those two weeks, with the co-operation of the staff of MD 7 Headquarters in Saint John, which Brigadier Gregg said was "of the highest order," the hundreds of things that had to be done to get the camp ready for its new function were carried out speedily and efficiently.

Probably the most important action, and one that was to have an impact greater than could have been foreseen, was the appointment of Brigadier Gregg as commandant of A-34 SOTC. Every aspect of his long and distinguished military career combined to make him the ideal person for this unusual assignment.

Milton Fowler Gregg was born in New Brunswick in 1892. He taught school for several years before entering the University of New Brunswick in 1913. After his first year he enlisted in the Army in 1914 and throughout the First World War served with the Royal Canadian Regiment with distinction and great gallantry. He won the Military Cross at Lens in 1917, a bar to his MC at Arras in 1918, and the Victoria Cross for most conspicuous bravery and initiative during operations near Cambrai in September 1918, when he personally accounted for 11 enemy and captured 25 prisoners and 12 machine guns. He was wounded in action several times.

Between the wars Gregg served as Sergeant-at-Arms in the House of Commons and was an officer in the Governor-General's Foot Guards. At the outbreak of war he volunteered for active service immediately and went overseas with the 1st Division. After he had commanded the West Nova Scotia Regiment, his outstanding leadership and training ability led him to the establishment of the OCTU in England. When it was closed early in 1942, Gregg took the pick of his training staff with him to Canada. Now with the rank of brigadier and as commandant of OTCs and OSACs at Brockville, Gordon Head, Three Rivers, and the CIS at Vernon, he was involved in the training of a large proportion of the officers who eventually came to Sussex as CANLOAN volunteers. He knew and understood them, he liked their spirit, and he regarded them with affection and pride. He was to them a source of inspiration and a symbol of what became the CANLOAN spirit.

Brigadier Gregg was ably assisted by Lieut.-Col. Hubert Jones, who had been born in Marmora, Ontario, in 1899 and had enlisted in the First World War at the age of 16. After service in Bermuda he went overseas to England and to the front in France. He was at Ypres and was wounded on the Somme in 1916. During his convalescence in England, his age was discovered and he was transferred to the Boys' Battalion. After the war he obtained an accounting degree in Belleville and joined the militia, where he was commissioned and promoted to major. In 1940 he went active as a captain and was Assistant Adjutant at A-32 CITC (Peterborough) before joining the staff of the OTC at Brockville in 1941, where he was promoted to major in July and lieutenant-colonel in September. He was General Staff Officer and Chief Instructor when Brigadier Gregg was Commandant. Their partnership was renewed at Camp Sussex. Colonel Jones would have given anything to have joined his son, Hubert, as a CANLOAN officer.

The leaders were joined by instructors chosen from the staffs of various training centres. From Brockville OTC came Captain Robichaud and Lieutenants McIntyre, Mailhot, Glass, and McBratney; from S-17, Captain Brayley and Lieutenants Downey and Meek; from other training centres, Lieutenants Wickenham, Rumble, Owen, Robertson, Andrews, Lynn, Hunter, Huggan, and Rose; and from units, Lieutenant Wyckes from the Victoria Rifles of Canada and Lieutenant Bissonette from le Régiment de Québec.

In addition to these officers and others who were added later to the instructional staff, a number of the volunteers in each CANLOAN draft were selected to be instructors during their stay at Sussex. In most cases they proceeded overseas with their group and their places were taken by officers from the succeeding "intake." The average term of duty for these officers was only four weeks.

During the short existence of A-34 SOTC it produced a newspaper entitled *The SOS* (Silhouettes of Sussex), whose CANLOAN editor, Lieut. Philip A. Labelle, had been a reporter with the *Ottawa Journal* and whose art editor, Lieut. James M. Buchanan, was a commercial artist who later designed the crest of the Canloan Army Officers Association. An article in the *SOS* described the arrival of the CANLOAN volunteers at Camp Sussex in a humorous vein that captured elements of reality:

Feet dragged slowly along a new platform. Bodies moved languidly towards an unseen voice. The newly-arrived, huddled together seeking for friendly faces, were sardined into a truck. That was the beginning. Emptiness in the pits of nervous stomachs soon was dispelled as the routine of admission to camp was carried on. Jocose Zombies roared loud "Suckers" ... Documentation, allotment of huts, beds and messes and drawing of equipment followed. Loud yells of "Why you old ..., what are you doing here?" rang through the newly-opened huts. Happy beaming faces glowed with pride as screaming instructors pronounced their rifles filthy, their postures hunch-backed, their eyes bleeding. Delightedly they gambolled over dusty roads, lovingly they hugged heavy ropes, pulling themselves nowhere above the ground ... Their days were filled with open mouths lying comfortably in dentists' chairs eagerly awaiting the ecstasy of drills boring deep into decayed enamel. Long lines of tingling arms, bared to the shoulder, thrilled to the touch of a thousand needles. Queues of contented men stood waiting for pictures to be taken, documents to be signed, pay to be handed out. Throngs rushed to paper-tearing evening lectures and to deliciously prepared mess dinners. Cheers of joy welcomed the announcements of these momentous occasions, eyes dimmed if they weren't forthcoming – and so the days went on. Oh yes. I forgot. There was training (?) too.[3]

Training, of course, was the raison d'être of A-34 SOTC, whose mandate was announced in NDHQ Training Instruction No. 1, 8 March 1944: "The object of this school is to ensure that the candidates are fitted to command sub-units in British field regiments immediately ... and that they are of sufficiently high standard of training and physical fitness to reflect credit on the Canadian Army."[4] The syllabus, which was designed to train officers to the same standard as those leaving for Canadian reinforcement units in the United Kingdom, stressed physical fitness, weapon training, night training, field works, including mines and booby traps, infantry tactics, mess conduct, and principles of leadership and man-management.

Brigadier Gregg told the instructors that they would be called upon to exercise their utmost skill and ingenuity, for while the training program was simple and elementary in the method in which it was presented, it must be made effective, vivid, and exciting. He urged them to study each candidate and report any lack of spirit or of the right attitude. He emphasized that every candidate must give evidence of cheerful vitality or he would be no good in anybody's army. He insisted that all must be in top physical condition when they left and that all organized training moves be on the double. He urged the instructors to set an example of skill, enthusiasm, and efficient work, to put their hearts and souls into the task.[5]

As part of the reception procedure, each officer was interviewed privately by the Commandant and the Chief Instructor, who had the reports of the selection boards. A general assessment was made of the candidates, and it was at this time that some in each group were selected as instructors. At the end of the course the performance of each officer was assessed and decisions made concerning his future. If considered efficient but not suitable for service in the British Army, officers would be posted to the Training Brigade Group to proceed overseas as normal reinforcement officers. If considered inefficient they would be returned to their district depots. If considered not quite ready they could be kept at Sussex for an additional period. Shortly before the completion of the training of the first intake of 279 volunteers, Brigadier Gregg estimated that 18 would be returned to their depots, 5 would be dispatched to the training brigade, and 16 would repeat all or part of the course. That would leave 240 to be sent to the British Army. In fact, of the first intake, 250 went overseas in four "flights"[6] during the two weeks between the end of March and the middle of April 1944.

To what extent was the team of Brigadier Gregg, Colonel Jones, and their instructing staff successful, in the short time at their disposal, in preparing the CANLOAN volunteers to command British infantry platoons in action? What Brigadier Gregg at the time called "a simple and elementary program" and years later called "this weird short course" was a considerable challenge to instructors. We have noted the variety in the backgrounds of the CANLOAN officers, who probably ranged from the most to the least experienced officers in the Canadian Army. For a refresher course intended to ensure that all officers had attained a minimum standard of training, it was necessary to aim at the lowest common denominator. This meant that nearly all of those taking the course would be familiar with its contents – infantry weapons, battle drill, and platoon tactics. Many of them had been instructing these subjects, sometimes for several years. This seemed to guarantee a measure of boredom. As Rex Fendick has observed, "A group of bored officers without responsibility can be very difficult and awkward."[7] In addition, the CANLOAN officers as a group were not disposed to be tolerant of "the powers that be." It has been noted that "among the characteristics of the CANLOAN officer was a lurking spirit of intellectual rebellion against authority."[8] Much of the course was identical to that undergone recently by many CANLOAN officers as cadets at OTCs in Brockville, Gordon Head, and Three Rivers, and with some of the same instructors. Now, however, the candidates were wearing officers' pips instead of cadets' white flashes;[9] they were equal in rank to the instructors, not threatened by an RTU (return to unit), and so not disposed to be submissive. Several were even known to taunt instructors they knew and dare them to join the CANLOAN ranks. In fact, the course tended to evoke memories of OTC and recall the motto associated with their officer training: BBB (Bullshit Baffles Brains). One CANLOAN officer was observed sitting in the camp orderly room with his feet on the desk making rows of paper dolls. His explanation: "If they are going to treat us like children we may as well behave like children." When the first flight of the CANLOAN scheme reached England, two of the officers visited CMHQ and were asked about the course at Sussex. They were most critical, insisting that it was chiefly basic training and an example of the "Brockville complex," treating officers like recruits.

A prominent feature of the stay at Sussex, the one that CANLOAN officers recall most vividly, was the emphasis on physical fitness: battle drill in the hills several miles from camp, the obstacle course, doubling everywhere, even to the canteen. Doug Gage remembers the route of a familiar run:

> Through camp, out the main gate, through town, up the hill, back through the fields to where there was normally a foot bridge across the stream that formed the camp's western boundary but which was removed during the winter so the ice wouldn't take it out, out on the ice, into the water, wading across waist deep, clambering up on the ice on the other side and running into camp and straight into the showers.[10]

Another officer recalls activities outside camp: "All will remember panting their hearts out over the beautiful but rugged countryside."[11] Alex Cunningham remembers forced marches while carrying a heavy PIAT (projector, infantry, anti-tank), when he weighed 135 pounds soaking wet. Then there was physical training at 0600 hours.

Fitted in between the repetitive training and the strenuous exercise were administrative arrangements that involved interminable waiting and much discomfort: interviews, photographs, physical examinations, inoculations, and dental work. It was considered important, in view of the alleged scarcity or inefficiency of British Army dentists, that all dental work be done before departure.

There was a legitimate criticism that those most important elements in the syllabus, leadership and man-management, were difficult to develop without troops to lead or men to manage. In addition to lectures and "tactical exercise without troops," candidates were assigned duties in rotation as section, platoon, and company commanders and were expected to carry out the duties of those positions. It was probably the best that could be done under the circumstances.

Altogether, it is not surprising that there was some grumbling and occasional flashes of rebellion. More remarkable is that there were so few complaints, and most CANLOAN officers recall the stay at Camp Sussex with pleasure because of the generally helpful attitude of the staff, which was evident from the time of arrival. Incidentally, it is not quite clear who the first CANLOAN arrivals were. Members of the first intake were to report by 7 and 8 March, but several came as early as 3 March. The first recorded arrivals were two Pictou Highlander officers from B Force (Bermuda), Lieuts. Stewart Cameron and Warren Thompson, but a group from A-14 Aldershot, Nova Scotia, also arrived on the 3rd. Four volunteers, Capt. Joseph Hemelryk and Lieuts. Leonard B. Robertson, C. Clifton Cassady, and Burton E. Harper, who were attached to the Dufferin and Haldimand Rifles stationed in Camp Sussex, simply moved their kit from one hut to another. They claim they reported to CANLOAN within the first hour of its operation.

As far as possible groups that arrived together were kept together. For example, the author arrived on 7 March with a group of eight from A-14, Aldershot. All were assigned to the same platoon and to adjoining beds in the same hut and were trained together throughout the course. Everywhere, incoming officers met old friends from OTC, specialized courses, overseas, training centres, and regiments. Many new friends were made from all over Canada. The experience created a friendly atmosphere. Roger Smith recalls, "At Sussex we had an assembly of old friends and lived, trained and partied together. It was a good, happy time."[12]

There was tolerance in regard to accommodation and leave that also created a favourable impression among the volunteers. Three couples, Don Diplock, Donald Good, Maurice Trudeau, and their wives, were allowed to rent quarters in a house outside camp. So were a number of others, including George McRae, James Duncan, Gordon Chatterton, Tom King, and their wives. Weekend leaves were not hard to get. Most of the New Brunswickers went home every weekend, and others spent occasional weekends with their wives or girl friends in Saint John or Sussex. Others went home, often considerable distances. Two, for example, who lived in Trenton and Dartmouth, Nova Scotia, respectively, one weekend went by train to Moncton and flew to Halifax by Trans-Canada Airlines. The town of Sussex offered little in the way of entertainment except for restaurant meals and shopping, though some officers recall good meals at the Fox Hill Farm. The presence of nurses from No. 19 Canadian General Hospital added immeasurably to the pleasure of off-duty hours. There were dances in addition to convivial sessions at the bar in the mess and even a respectable offering of movies in camp. Then there were poker and crap games, occasionally lasting all night. As a last resort on a Saturday evening one could listen to "Hockey Night in Canada" and "The Hit Parade" on the radio.

The criticism that the training program was repetitive was countered by the efforts of the instructors to make their subjects interesting. We have seen that Brigadier Gregg urged them to make a simple and elementary program "effective, vivid and exciting." This was a tall order, but they usually succeeded, and the CANLOAN officers appreciated their efforts. Much admired was Jack Brayley, who was known as "Jack the Ripper" from his habit of tearing off the sheets of brown paper that bore the outlines of his lectures. Gerry Robichaud was another experienced instructor from OTC and a member of the Gregg team. The addition of many CANLOAN officers as instructors for their draft helped to defuse any antagonism towards the instructional staff, especially since their qualifications and experience were so impressive.

On the whole there was a cheerful acceptance of the course as a reasonable refresher. Some officers like Tom King thought it stimulating after years of home defence duties. Others, like Ernest Thirgood, with a Military Medal from Dieppe and years of instructing, considered it a holiday. Another volunteer thought it "tough but fun." Certainly the conditioning would stand all in good stead later on. Some found the up-dating on weapons useful, particularly the new anti-tank weapon, the PIAT, as well as the lectures on mines and booby traps.

Then there was information about the British Army. A British major gave information, instruction, and advice about commanding British troops, regimental customs, even mess etiquette. Tom Anstey says, "My main recollection of Sussex was the daily route march which was designed to make us hungry enough to eat the evening regimental dinner. Is it true that we had these dinners each evening so that the Brig could teach us to eat with the fork in the left hand and the knife in the right?"[13] The extent of information and instruction about the British Army was limited, perhaps because of the realization that many customs were unique to particular regiments. Much space in the *SOS* was filled with historical sketches of British regiments.

An important factor in reducing criticism and creating a cohesive influence in each of the CANLOAN drafts was the great respect and affection for Brigadier Gregg, "the Brig." Fred Burd, who was at Sussex for only a few days, recalls that even in that short time the Brig. made his charismatic presence felt. Fred Burnaby thought him an inspiring person, as did many others. After Brigadier Gregg had interviewed each candidate at the beginning of the course, he henceforth called each by name when he saw them. Short, dark, and wiry with bright eyes, quick movements, and a total lack of reserve, he was always at ease with candidates, engaging them in conversation at any time, picking them up in his jeep, ready to see them and help them in all sorts of individual problems and difficulties, of which there were many.

Finally, there was an ever-present spirit of anticipation, heightened morale, and esprit de corps. Martin Kaufman recalls it as the most exciting thing about Sussex.

Brigadier Gregg reminded his instructors that the fact that the CANLOAN officers were "on the edge of an interesting experience" would affect their attitude during the course. The sense of anticipation, even exhilaration, was expressed in several ways. One was the tendency to break into song on every occasion: on the march, in the backs of vehicles, and when waiting in queues. They sang the old favourites from the First World War, "It's a Long Way to Tipperary" and "Mademoiselle from Armentieres," and the current wartime songs like "Roll Out the Barrel" and "The White Cliffs of Dover." They sang the Canadian Army favourites such as "The Quartermaster's Store," and above all "Ralston's Army":

Why don't you join up?
Why don't you join up?
Why don't you join old Ralston's Army?
Two bucks a week,
F— all to eat,
Great big boots and blisters on your feet.
If it wasn't for the war
I'd have buggered off before.
Ralston you're balmy!

Another sign of the spirit that pervaded the camp was the antics, which ranged from simple pranks to serious hell-raising. Doug Gage recalls falling in on a parade after lunch and watching the chimney of his hut blowing smoke rings. Jack Matthew, in his platoon, always had a supply of blank rounds and often threw a few into the pot-bellied stove before leaving the hut. More noisy and disruptive were thunderflashes. Some pranks that caused damage to property or threatened injury resulted in disciplinary action. Among all the 673 who passed through the camp, the Pictou Highlanders stand out as the champion hell-raisers. One of them, later a distinguished senior public servant and commanding officer of a fine old regiment, was returned to his depot. He was cleared later and completed the course at Sussex. Another was saved from a similar fate by the personal intervention of Brigadier Gregg, and several were got to sea in time to avoid possible disciplinary action.

From this anticipation, high spirits, and affection for Brigadier Gregg there evolved a feeling of kinship, which in retrospect can be seen as the cementing of a CANLOAN bond. Hank Richard has expressed it well: "The spirit of Sussex continued aboard ship as we sailed to adventure." All who shared in this great adventure were brothers and were recognized as such whenever two or more of them met at the front, on leave, in hospitals or reinforcement holding units, and they will be for as long as they live.

Throughout the short existence of A-34 SOTC there were constant negotiations about the availability of ships, the dates of sailing, and the number of free spaces, which would determine the size of each "flight." (See Appendix C for the list of flights.) Even when all this was known there were frequent, even last-minute, changes. At least once the call for a flight to leave found several members in dentists' chairs. They left with hastily inserted temporary fillings.

Shortly before the first flight left, Brigadier Gregg mentioned to his friend,

Brigadier R.E.G. Roome, DAAG(O) at NDHQ, the remarkable calibre of some of the CANLOAN volunteers. Brigadier Roome suggested that he send a list of those who, by virtue of ability and experience, could be considered exceptional officers. Brigadier Gregg complied, noting in a covering letter that they were "specially good lads in the first flight from here. I can vouch for all of them to do a good job and feel that it would be an excellent thing if you could arrange for special consideration in their case on the other side."[14] The first list consisted of the names of ten officers, five of whom had been overseas, and notes concerning their service. They were Capts. Eric W. Hall and Donald S. Meagher and Lieuts. Ralph B. Arthurs, René J.A. Blanchard, Earl C. Cloutier, Robert L. Hunter, Raymond Ludford, Alastair K. MacDonald, Henry G. Sheely, and Arnold J. Willick.

Two days later Brigadier Gregg sent a list of "specially good chaps" in the second flight. All except one of them had been overseas. They were Lieuts. Hubert C. Campbell, Lionel H. McAulay, Clarence J. Rodgers, Dominique Lambert, Edward P. Manning, Francis L.J. Arnett, Havelock H.R. Nicholson, Cyril D. Whittington, Maurice C. Carter, John W.M. Marsh, Glen S. Harrison, and John R. Harrison. All had been instructors, most at Brockville.

A final special list of sixteen officers was sent by Brigadier Gregg on 29 April. In a personal note to Brigadier Roome he wrote,

Dear Reg: These are drawn from the 250 flight. In this as well as the lists from former flights, we have what appeared to us the most outstanding all-round officers. This does not always mean that they are the ones with the most varied and interesting backgrounds.[15]

Those on the list, nine of whom had been overseas, were Capts. James B. Hamilton, Donald E. Holmes, Orlando de Luca, Hugh D. McLeod, Henry J. Morley, Gerry J.G. Robichaud, and Gordon B. Taylor; and Lieuts. Andrew Connor, Robert C. Fee, Harry F. Hughes, Lawrence P. Kane, William J. Kotchepaw, Hugh W. Macdonald, Cameron E. Morrison, James W. Taylor, and John A. Wellbelove.

These lists were forwarded by bomber mail to CMHQ with the request that they be passed on to the War Office in order to give the Imperial Army some particulars regarding these outstanding officers in order that they might be fitted to the best advantage into the British Forces. It is not clear what action was expected, but there is no evidence that any attention was ever paid to the special lists.

One final duty remained for Brigadier Gregg: to honour his promise to members of his instructional staff that they would be given a place on an overseas draft. In a letter to Brigadier Roome on 4 April he gave a list of fifteen instructors to be added to the third, and final, "intake." In a personal note he told of the problems they had had in getting overseas because of being taken out of the reinforcement stream and given assignments as instructors. He had given a solemn promise to get them over with CANLOAN and begged Brigadier Roome not to let him down. The list included Captains Brayley and Robichaud as well as Colonel Jones's son, Hubert. A few days later he asked to have five more names added to the list, but he had to make a trip to Ottawa to ensure that all those to whom he had given promises were on the small sixth flight. Then he received a desperate letter from a Capt. Beverley Howard, an artillery officer who had taken the battle course at Vernon and qualified as an infantry company commander. When he returned to his unit in Halifax he found that thirteen officers had gone to Brockville to take the infantry course for CANLOAN. He felt that he didn't need it and applied to go directly to Sussex. When he found that his application had not been forwarded and that the last draft had been called, he appealed directly to Brigadier Gregg, reminding him of their chats at Vernon. The Brig responded and Howard was squeezed into the last intake and sixth flight. That left only the 88 officers who had taken the special course at Brockville and spent only a few days at Sussex, and finally the 50 RCOC officers who were not required to undergo training at Sussex.

At this point, when the third flight was leaving, the War Office had to be informed about the shortfall of volunteers. On 7 April 1944, General Letson sent a secret cable to CMHQ asking that Sir Ronald Adam be informed that, although strenuous efforts had been made to secure infantry volunteers, the total of 623 were all who had been accepted after the medical checks and surveys of attitudes and motivation. Brigadier Booth at CMHQ wrote on the dispatch, "This is pretty much of a let down from 1500"[16] and requested discussions at a senior level before notifying Sir Ronald Adam. Sir Ronald was told eventually and, of course, took the news with good grace, being grateful for the number of officers who had volunteered and been accepted.

In spite of the earlier reports that no shipping space from Halifax was available, the eventual arrangements were most satisfactory and in many cases ideal. Several of the drafts, including the first two flights of 52 and 57, the fifth flight (which included the entire second intake of 250), the eighth flight (which consisted of the 88 graduates of the special course at Brockville), and the last, 20 RCOC officers, sailed on standard wartime troopships. The other four CANLOAN flights, however, were fitted into peacetime passenger accommodation in small ships, usually with a similar number of women, where they enjoyed five excellent meals a day and open bars.

Instructions concerning CANLOAN in the Army Council Instruction (ACI) No. 504 (see Appendix E), stated "each officer, on being posted to a British unit, will be allotted a personal number by the War Office. This number will have the prefix CDN. It is important that the prefix always be used."[17]

Officers in the wartime Canadian Army did not have personal (regimental) numbers but were identified for all purposes by rank and name. Other rank (OR) regimental numbers were not used after an officer was commissioned. British officers, on the other hand, each had a personal number. Thus the British assigned CDN (CANLOAN) numbers to fit their own system. At the same time the unique CDN number ensured instant recognition so that pertinent data could be extracted and forwarded to the Canadian Records Section promptly. Though CDN numbers were allotted in the UK, they were based on the nominal rolls for each flight as it left Sussex. The first flight, for example, listed officers who were struck off strength from A-34 on 29 March 1944. It started with 8 captains, who were listed in no particular order, followed by 44 lieutenants in alphabetical order. CDN numbers were assigned in the UK from the first name, Capt. Donald M. Findlay, who became CDN/1, to the 52nd, Lieut. Allister M. Young, who became CDN/52. The second flight had CDN numbers 53 to 109, and so on for subsequent flights, except that for the large fifth flight, the CDN numbers did not correspond directly to the order of names on the nominal roll.

The first flight left Camp Sussex on 29 March, travelled by train to Halifax, and went directly on board their ship, the SS *Andes*. The conducting officer of the draft was CDN/1, Capt. Donald M. Findlay, who has been mentioned in a previous chapter as one of the officers who reverted in rank from major in order to become a CANLOAN. The flight was accompanied by a British officer, Capt. F.H. Rowland. The *Andes* was a new ship, built for southern cruises but taken over as a troop ship before her first cruise. Like most wartime troop ships, she was dry (without a bar) and was crowded, with at least 10 officers in each cabin. Since there were only two meals a day, served in four sittings, there were queues throughout the day. With a speed of up to 30 knots the *Andes* had no need for convoys or escort. Despite the northern route and the cool spring breeze, the sun was warm and many in the group acquired respectable tans. Otherwise the time was spent playing cards and English games such as "Housie." On the fifth day land was sighted, and at noon on 6 April the *Andes* docked at the Princess Landing Stage in Liverpool, where she was welcomed by the RCAF band playing "The Maple Leaf Forever." CDN/29, Lieut. John (Jack) McBride, who has given the most complete account of the voyage, insists that it was at this time, not earlier, that the famous 52 Club, perhaps better known as the Deck of Cards Club, was formed. A deck of cards was "borrowed" from the ship's lounge, and each of the 52 members of the flight drew a card. McBride recalls, "There was a great bit of business of everybody signing everybody else's card and all agreed that subsequent failure to produce the card when called upon to do so would cost that member a round of drinks."[18]

To this day the surviving members of the club insist that they still carry the original cards and have never had to buy a round of drinks. On 7 April, Good Friday, a group of officers came on board for an official welcome. According to CDN/47, Capt. Arnold Willick, there were at least 20 senior officers from colonel and up, "more Army brass than the average subaltern would see in a lifetime."[19]

The party was headed by Lieutenant-General Watson, Commander, Western Command, who welcomed the group on behalf of the AG, Gen. Sir Ronald Adam and the British Army. Then came the selection of regiments. Being the first to arrive, they had a clear field of choice. Although they were confined to the ship for the rest of the day, probably half of them managed to get ashore, setting off a search by the security people. Most got back on board undetected, but a few were escorted by military police. At 0500 hours the next day the members of the flight left the *Andes* and were quietly placed on a train and sent to London for dispersal to their new units.

The second flight left Sussex on 3 April. It was another small group, 57 in number – the Heinz Flight. At Halifax they boarded the *Louis Pasteur*, the ship on which Del Struck and 15 other future CANLOAN officers had escorted Afrika Corps POWs in 1943. They docked at Liverpool a week later and were welcomed by Brig. T.J.B. Boswell and his party from the War Office.

The third flight left Sussex on the evening of 5 April and sailed from Halifax on the 7th, while the first flight was being welcomed in Liverpool. For the 93 members of this flight, the 17 days of the voyage from Halifax to Edinburgh are considered to be among the most pleasant interludes during the war, resembling a holiday cruise more than a troop movement. The highlights of the voyage have been listed by CDN/127, Lieut. John (Jack) Bedford:

The *Cavina* was a good ship. In peacetime she carried her cargo of bananas from Central American countries back to England and the continent. She weighed about 7,000 tons. She performed gallantly in heavy seas and left her passengers memories like these:

... a wonderful group of Canadian Red Cross girls heading for overseas duty;
... a couple of stewards who miraculously produced "extra rations" for a nominal fee. Their names were (honest to God) Pat and Mike;
... a capable CO Troops by the name of Sandy Millar (Major Alexander M, CDN/117), late of the RCMP, Vancouver (what a job he had!);
... Lieutenant Jack Irwin (the Reverend John T, CDN/164) taking the Easter Sunday service aboard ship;
... good meals, liquor at tax-free prices and a nameless CANLOAN officer who pulled a gun and threatened to start his own private war;
... some mighty fine young men like Len Bushell (Lieutenant Andrew F, CDN/134), Johnny Bowman (Lieut John E, CDN/130), Gordie Beaton (Lieut Gordon E, CDN/126), Pat Blackham (Lieutenant John P, CDN/129) and many more who paid the supreme sacrifice (21 members of the group);
... "douse that light!" yelled more than once at careless smokers by the Officer of the Watch;
... the seasickness that many landlubbers found they had to endure;
... the endless hours spent on deck watching other ships in the convoy and praying they'd all make it safely;
... the thrill of seeing land two weeks and two days after sailing;
... landing at Leith, Scotland on a Sunday (no bars open);
... the coming aboard of UK officials who assigned us to our units – some Scottish, some Welch, some Durhams, a little bit of everything;
... the hospitality of the Mountain Division who entertained us that Sunday in their mess;
... the concert we attended in Usher Hall, Edinburgh, before taking the overnight train to London; and
... postings from the London Depot.

Within hours we were spread out the length and breadth of the British Isles.[20]

The fourth flight, consisting of 48 CANLOAN officers, later to be known as the Bayano Boys, was similar to the third in the type and size of their ship, the length of the voyage, and the fact that the vessel was shared by about the same number of women. An account of the voyage was written by CDN/332, Capt. Frederick (Fred) H. Burnaby:

It was in the spring of '44, April 14 to be exact. Fifty fighting men began to take the war seriously. We were on our way overseas at last. Snow was still on the ground and the

Atlantic air was raw. The train from Sussex to Halifax stopped for a few minutes at Moncton. Wives who had been with us at Sussex were waiting on the platform in the hope of a last farewell embrace ... Just before dark our special car was placed alongside the freight shed at the Halifax docks. As we detrained we looked for the troop ship which was to carry us overseas. All we could see were the tops of two small masts projecting above the roof of the freight shed. Could this be it? Led by Russ Waters [Capt. J. Russ, CDN/365, conducting officer] we walked through the freight shed and up the gangplank into the saloon of the *Bayano*, a 5,000-ton part-cargo, part-passenger ship which had not been converted to conform to wartime utility. As we looked around the saloon at the comfortable furnishings and beautiful women, we sensed there must have been a mistake. We were soon assigned to staterooms and resigned ourselves to the luxury and comfort. The war was better than could be expected.

A recce [reconnaissance] of the ship revealed that she was a former banana boat running between England and the West Indies. Now, in wartime, she was carrying a cargo of pork and 100 passengers of whom 50 were women and children and we were the other 50. There was a complete dining saloon with white table cloths and menus and waiters. Most important of all there was a bar although it was closed until the ship left harbour. The women were mostly wives who were returning after being guests in Canada during the Battle of Britain.

At noon the following day the *Bayano* pulled away from the dock and anchored in the harbour along with dozens of other freighters and tank-landing craft. When we wakened the next day we were at sea, out of sight of land and surrounded by at least 100 other ships. As we got farther out into the Atlantic the wind grew stronger and waves became mountains of water. At times when our ship was in a trough no other ships could be seen. Then we would rise to a crest and look down on the rolling, tossing, twisting, turning tank-landing craft and feel sorry for the crews who handled them. One afternoon I was standing at the stern of the *Bayano* looking westward with my mind full of thoughts of home. I could see a black speck on the horizon, which was a member of our convoy with engine trouble. As I watched there was suddenly a cloud of smoke where the dark speck had been. She had been torpedoed by an enemy submarine.

As we approached the British Isles the wind subsided and it was pleasant to bask in the sunshine of the upper deck. Soon we had our first sight of the British Isles. It was the Mull of Kintyre in the southwest of Scotland. Next we saw on our right the lush emerald-green shores of Ireland. In the early hours of the following morning, May 1, we slowly moved through the fog up the Mersey River to Liverpool. The ship anchored in the river and we were taken ashore in a lighter. We sat around in an empty freight shed for an hour or so waiting to be welcomed to England by a Colonel Blimp. Within an hour we entrained for London where we were assigned to British Regiments.[21]

A supplementary account of this voyage, entitled "Mutiny on the Bayano," was published in the *Canloan Review*. It referred to

the dark and stormy night when one long-legged CANLOAN tried to climb up the ship's mast to the crow's nest ... and had to be subdued. And the time poor old Waters (Captain J. Russ) had to parade five of the lads before the ship's captain. Seems they had played crap all night and refused to get up the next day. They glared at Waters for days.[22]

The fifth flight, known as the 250 Flight or the Big Flight, comprised the entire second intake at Sussex, equal to the total of the first four flights. It left Sussex on 3 May and arrived at Liverpool on 11 May. The highlights of the voyage have been recounted by CDN/378, Lieut. George H. Beck:

Early on May 1, 250 CANLOANs boarded a troop train for Halifax. There had been a frenzied last minute round of documentation, needles by the dozen, tooth extractions, kit parades. I remember we drove like gentlemen to our train, passing on our way the sweet sisters of No 19 Cdn Gen Hospital slogging down the road in full marching order with tin hats and respirators at the ready. We covered them with dust as we sped by. They were somewhat provoked. It was a strange reversal of the usual lot of the PBI [Poor Bloody Infantry].

At Halifax the huge gray shape of the 30,000 ton *Empress of Scotland* (formerly the *Empress of Japan*, renamed for obvious reasons) towered by the dock-side. Brigadier Gregg was at the gangplank to bid each one of us Godspeed. No. 19 Gen Hospital boarded with us. They got staterooms midships while the whole 250 of us were squeezed into what had been a rather small Tourist Smoker. The pipe berths were three deep and one had to move sideways to thread one's way to the single doorway. Latrine facilities were sketchy. There were only three basins, wash-up, troops for the use of, which were served by a couple of feeble cold-water taps – but this is the usual lot of the Infantry.

Other things were just as grim – no bar, only two meals a day, no place to sit or play cards, but the bare deck. Also there were duties to be done such as troop-deck supervision. The ship was under command of the RAF being stuffed with "pigeons" returning from closed-down RAF training stations in Canada. A warrant officer with an annoyingly cheerful Cockney voice nattered all day long on the blower. Every 0600 hours it was "Wakey! Wakey! Rise and Shine!"

The only lounge was so far away from our boat-station that we could never reach it after morning boat drill in time to get in. It was always chock-a-block with RAF. So one morning our Adjutant called a meeting for all CANLOAN in the lounge which was to be out of bounds to all others after boat drill. For one day we hogged the lounge, using nursing sisters to hold our places when we went to dinner. However this scheme backfired for on each of the ensuing days the other groups pulled the same stunt.

The *Empress of Scotland* sailed on her own using her speed as her submarine defence. Planes passed over the mastheads each day signalling with their lamps. The crossing was very pleasant – calm seas and sunshine.

On the morning of the fifth day we saw our first landfall on entering the Irish Sea. The first misty view of a strange coast is always a thrilling moment charged with a sense of adventure and unreality. This first sight of Britain was no exception for me, being surpassed only by my first look at the smoking shores of Normandy a month later. The Irish Sea was crowded with warships of every description having their last work-outs for the bloodbath of June. The estuary of the Mersey was a strange sight with the fairway dotted by weird ack-ack towers and protruding bows or masts of ships which had been sunk by bombers or mines. These were our first signs of battle. Liverpool had had a pasting.

We docked at the Princess Landing Stage and filled in the time waiting for our turn to disembark by watching the anti-aircraft gunfire and the huge nets full of our trunks swinging over the side and crashing down on the dock. An Air Force band played for us from the dockside while a huge Colonel Blimp came aboard to welcome us to Britain in what seemed like incomprehensible Hindustani. By nightfall we were speeding south for London in a special train with an issue of American K rations for supper.[23]

The sixth flight was a small one of 34 which comprised the rest of the first two intakes, several of the instructors, and those delayed by illness. It was the only flight that did not sail from Halifax. The *Beaverhill*, a CPR ship of 10,000 tons, left Sydney, Nova Scotia on 19 May and arrived in the UK on 2 June.

Flight seven was a second voyage of the *Cavina* and, like the third flight, evoked expressions of pleasure from its passengers. They consisted of the first 30 RCOC CANLOANs, a similar number of Canadian women, chiefly nurses, and 25 military government officers. Typical comments were "A beautiful little ship," "unbelievable," "good food, pleasant parties, good fun."

The eighth flight was on a second voyage of the *Empress of Scotland*. It comprised The 600 Group (all CDN numbers in the 600s), the former RCA and RCASC officers who had taken the special infantry course at Brockville. Like the earlier trip with The 250 Flight, it went quickly, sailing on 16 June and arriving on 23 June. During the voyage one CANLOAN officer, CDN/600, Lieut. John Anderson, was surprised to run into his brother, who was in the RCAF and happened to be posted to England at the same time.

The ninth and last flight, in another short voyage from 24 July to 29 July, consisted of the remaining 20 RCOC officers and one infantry officer. He was CDN/630, Lieut. N.W. (Wally) Ingraham, who, as an artillery officer in coastal defence, had volunteered for CANLOAN, and had completed the course at Brockville. Taken ill during the few days at Sussex before his draft was to sail, he was in danger of missing the last boat. Wally was particularly anxious to get overseas because, while he was serving in Canada, his older brother, Wilbur, who had been attending Acadia University, had gone overseas as a platoon commander in the Cape Breton Highlanders and had just been killed in Italy. Ingraham conveyed his sense of urgency to the nursing staff at Sussex, who took it as a challenge to get him on the last flight. That was why he was the only infantry officer in the ninth flight. He served with the 3rd Battalion, the Monmouthshire Regiment, survived the war, and married Lillian, his Sussex nurse.

The voyages across the Atlantic, especially the 17-day voyages of the *Cavina* and the *Bayano*, gave the CANLOAN officers the opportunity to contemplate their decision to volunteer for service in the British Army, about which most of them knew very little. The few lectures at Sussex and capsule histories in the *SOS* were a slim basis for serious consideration, so nearly all were content to wait and see. In any case, the British Army was for most a means of getting into action, a subject that was never far from their thoughts. There were no illusions about the prospects. Different sources and statistics were cited, but there was general agreement that the active life of an infantry platoon commander in battle could be measured in days, if not hours. Nevertheless, most of the young men who had deliberately sought a guaranteed participation in the coming battles believed that despite the odds they would be among the survivors and refused to worry. There were occasional comments about future casualties. For example, the author recalls a brief consideration of the question: "If given a choice, which would you rather lose, eyesight or testicles?" But such conversations were rare. The chief effect of the approach to battle was a mixture of anticipation, excitement, a heightened awareness of the richness of life because it might be brief, satisfaction, even pride in being part of a struggle that would determine the future of mankind – the feeling that if a man managed to survive, he need not be ashamed to tell his children what he had done, and if he didn't survive, he had not died in vain.

The more immediate matter of becoming an integral part of a British regiment evoked interest, curiosity, and perhaps some apprehension. Reality began with the reception by the British Army as each flight arrived in the United Kingdom.

4

Getting Acquainted

THE RECEPTION OF THE CANLOAN officers in the United Kingdom was the responsibility of the British Army, because, to all intents and purposes, they ceased to be in the Canadian Army when they left Sussex. For example, the members of the fifth, or 250, flight had their service documents stamped "SOS CA [Canada] 3 May 44" when they left A-34 SOTC, and "TOS CANLOAN 4 May 44" when they embarked in Halifax.

There were differences in the arrangements for the reception of the various flights, but several elements were common to all: a welcoming speech on behalf of the British Army by a regional commander or a senior officer from the War Office; the distribution of a leaflet that explained the purpose and nature of the CANLOAN scheme; the assignment of officers to battalions in the British Second Army; and the allocation of the CDN number as already described.

The most elaborate reception, which has been mentioned in Chapter 2, was the one on 23 April 1944 in Edinburgh for the third flight, consisting of 93 CANLOAN officers and 10 Canadian Red Cross nurses, who were included in the reception. After the early-morning arrival of the SS *Cavina* in the harbour of Leith, a tender brought Colonel Sibbald of the War Office from shore with three other officers to look after the assignment to units. An hour later another tender brought Maj.-Gen. N.M.S Irwin, CB, DSO, MC, Commander of the East Scotland District, to welcome the Canadians on behalf of the Commander, Scottish Command. He was accompanied on the tender by the brass band of the Royal Scots (RS), which circled the *Cavina* and continued to play throughout the General's visit aboard. The tenders then took everybody to the dock, where they were piped ashore by the pipes and drums of the King's Own Scottish Borderers (KOSB) and met by representatives of the six Army messes in Edinburgh, each of which had been assigned a number of officers to entertain for the day. Transported to the officers' messes for lunch and a social visit, the officers were then taken on tours of Edinburgh sights, including the Castle, Holyrood, Palace and St. Giles' Cathedral. They returned to the host messes for dinner, then attended a variety show at Usher Hall. At 2100 hours they boarded buses to the railway station, where they were piped aboard the *Flying Scot* to be whisked off to London during the night.

It was a grand reception from the moment when the *Cavina* dropped anchor in Leith Harbour to the last fading notes of the pipes as the train pulled out of Waverley Station. The hospitality of the British Army hosts, the visits to buildings that bore witness to centuries of history, the lively entertainment at the theatre, all created a most favourable first impression of Britain and the British Army. All went off without a snag, even the handling of the baggage. CDN/146, Lieut. Elmer Fitzpatrick, who was rather apprehensive when put in charge of the baggage detail, was able to report that every trunk and kit bag reached London safely.[1] Though not always so elaborate, the receptions which were accorded the other eight CANLOAN flights were equally cordial.

When the CANLOAN flights arrived, each officer was handed a copy of a leaflet "with the compliments of Gen. Sir Ronald Adam, Adjutant General to the Forces" (see Appendix D). In it he extended a welcome on behalf of the Army Council, explained the reasons for the CANLOAN agreement, and outlined its chief features – those dealing with pay, promotion, dress, documentation (with emphasis on use of the CDN numbers), medical procedure, and return to Canada.

On 13 April 1944 Maj. Angus B. MacLaren was appointed Deputy Assistant Adjutant General (Liaison) (DAA (L)) at CMHQ with the duty of maintaining contact with the War Office on matters relating to CANLOAN officers as well as being the person directly responsible for CANLOAN affairs at CMHQ. A few days after his appointment Major MacLaren reported on the favourable impression given by the British leaflet ("Damned decent to go to this trouble, etc."). He suggested that a Canadian leaflet be prepared to show that the Canadian officers were not being neglected by the Canadian Army, to assure them that the Canadian Army would continue to be concerned about their welfare, and to inform them that a liaison officer had been appointed to look after their interests.[2] This suggestion was forwarded through several levels at CMHQ and on to General Letson in Ottawa, but it got no support and no more was heard of it. In retrospect, it seems that it might have been a good idea to ensure that CANLOAN officers knew about the identity and function of the liaison officer. He was kept informed about all matters relating to CANLOAN officers, including postings, promotions, decorations, and casualties, and he reported constant activity on their behalf. However, the officers' general impression of him was not favourable, and he came to be the focal point for complaints.

For several flights the allocation to units (see Appendix F for a list of British regiments) took place on board ship before landing, but for the majority, including the large fifth flight, the interviews leading to postings were held at the Officers' Transit Depot in the Grand Central Hotel opposite Marylebone Station in London. CDN/453, Lieut. Reginald (Rex) F. Fendick, recalls,

The processing was a fine example of the very best staff work. We were assembled in a large lobby of the hotel with small tables set up around the edges of the room, each manned by one or two British staff officers and clerks and each table with a sign erected over it naming a British regiment. We were invited to go to the table of our choice, where we were told which battalions had vacancies and where we were given the chance to choose our unit.[3]

When Gen. H. Letson had first discussed with Sir Ronald Adam the possibility of a loan of officers to the British Army, he had been particularly enthusiastic about the idea of Canadian infantry officers having the opportunity to serve with British regiments that were affiliated with their Canadian regiments. He recalled the fraternal contacts that he had had in the First World War with the British Rifle Brigade, which was affiliated with his own Vancouver regiment, the Duke of Connaughts Own Rifles. To facilitate this type of posting, it was intended to send a nominal roll indicating Canadian regimental attachments. Unfortunately the roll for the first flight was sent in error by sea mail instead of bomber mail and arrived after the first flight had landed and been dispersed.

In any case, it turned out that most of the CANLOAN officers had no attachments to Canadian regiments and were designated CIC (Canadian Infantry Corps). For example, the nominal roll of the third flight of 93 officers showed only eight belonging to Canadian regiments: two to the Pictou Highlanders, four to the Edmonton Fusiliers, and one each to the Royal Irish Fusiliers of Canada and the Victoria Rifles of Canada.

Most successful in being posted to an affiliated regiment were the officers from the Black Watch (Royal Highland Regiment) of Canada (RHR). In the first flight alone, of 52 officers, 10 were assigned to battalions of the Black Watch (BW), 6 to the 1st Battalion, and 2 each to the 5th and 7th Battalions, all in the 51st Highland Division. Eight of these officers came from the RHRs. Altogether, of the 27 CANLOAN officers who served in BW battalions, 16 came from the Canadian Black Watch.

Several Canadian regiments were affiliated with the British Seaforth Highlanders. No fewer than five CANLOAN officers who had served with the Seaforth Highlanders of Canada were able to join the 7th Battalion, the Seaforth Highlanders, in the 15th Scottish Division. The Pictou Highlanders were also affiliated with the Seaforth Highlanders, but since there were 17 Pictou Highlanders the Seaforths were not able to absorb all of them. Three, CDN/255, Capt. John W. Druhan, CDN/196, Lieut. Lawson M. Smith, and CDN/542, Lieut. Earl W. Cameron, were accepted by the 7 Seaforth, and two more, CDN/153, Capt. Charles A. Manning and CDN/56, Capt. Roderick F. Mackay were posted to the 2nd Battalion in the 51st Highland Division. Many of the remaining Pictou Highlanders joined the 2nd Battalion, the Glasgow Highlanders and others the 9th Battalion, the Cameronians – the other battalions in the same brigade as the 7 Seaforths.

Four of the six officers who had served with the Saint John Fusiliers and had volunteered together for the CANLOAN scheme were able to join their affiliated British regiment, the 6th Battalion in the King's Own Scottish Borderers (KOSB).

CDN/499, Lieut. Edward D. Glass, who had been overseas with the 48th Highlanders in the 1st Canadian Division, was able to report to his regiment in Toronto that he had been welcomed by the affiliated British regiment, the Gordons, and that "the CO has insisted that I wear our regimental flash (the 48th Highlanders) alongside their own.[4]

More often than not, however, there were no vacancies in affiliated regiments or their battalions were in other theatres of operations, such as in Italy with the 8th Army. Although several CANLOAN officers had served in the RCR, whose affiliated regiment was the Gloucestershire Regiment (Glosters.), there were no vacancies at the time. Of the five Canadian officers who served eventually with the 2 Glosters., none had served in the RCR. Several officers were posted to regiments that were their second or even third choice. There were some mistakes, though remarkably few. Capt. Eric Hall, on finding that there were no vacancies in a regiment affiliated with the Victoria Rifles of Canada, mentioned that he was born in Essex, just outside London. Told that he would be posted to the Essex Regiment (Essex), he picked up his travel documents and at the end of a train journey found himself a reinforcement officer, not to the 2 Essex, but to the 1/5th Battalion, the Queen's Royal Regiment (Queens)!

In the event, the provision for assignment to affiliated regiments applied only to a relatively small proportion of CANLOAN officers. Many more of the officers took advantage of a second provision in the agreement concerning posting: the choice of being posted with a friend to a battalion within a designated division. Sometimes there was prior agreement on the choice of either an English or a Scottish regiment, but the essential condition was that two, and sometimes more, friends wished to serve together in the same unit. In some cases these partnerships had lasted for several years; in others they were as recent as the sharing of a cabin in the voyage to the United Kingdom or even as the holding of consecutive numbers in a nominal roll.

Lieuts. CDN/241, D. Donald Diplock, CDN/242, Donald M. Good, and CDN/251, Maurice A. Trudeau had served together at A-12 CITC, Farnham, Quebec. As has been mentioned, they and their wives had shared a temporary home outside the camp while at Sussex. When their flight was being assigned to regiments they decided to stick together and were posted to the 1/5th Battalion, the Welch Regiment. When Donald Good was sent to a reinforcement holding unit shortly before the 53rd Division left for Normandy, the three friends regarded it as a breach of faith by the British Army. Many CANLOAN partners were separated in this way.

CDN/514, Capt. James C. Duncan, and Lieuts. CDN/469, George D. McRae and CDN/457, Glen S. Harrison, who all came from Winnipeg, were together at Sussex and went together to the 7 Cameronians in the 52nd Division. CDN/192, Lieut. Leonard B. Robertson and CDN/190, Lieut. Stirling A. Reid had been together at the OSAC at Three Rivers and OTC at Brockville. Reunited at A-34 SOTC, they decided to stick together and were posted to the 2nd Battalion, the East Yorkshire Regiment (E. Yorks.). For them and for others, it was more important to be posted to the same battalion than to a particular regiment. In some cases two friends were together throughout their military careers. This was true, for example, of CDN/520, Lieut. Robert J. Jackson and CDN/515, Lieut. Delmar H. Struck, who served together overseas in the Highland Light Infantry of Canada, returned to Canada together for commissions, were instructors together, and served together throughout their service on CANLOAN. Similarly, CDN/453, Lieut. Reginald (Rex) F. Fendick and CDN/464, Lieut. Francis A. McConaghy served together throughout the war in the Saint John Fusiliers, 6 KOSB, and the same company of the 2nd Battalion, the Middlesex

Regiment (MX). After the war Conc McConaghy was Rex's best man at the Fendick wedding in New Brunswick.

Many CANLOAN officers were willing to accept the suggestions of the British staff officers regarding the selection of a unit. In the first draft, for example, more than a dozen were nudged in the direction of the infantry brigade of the 7th Armoured Division – the 1/5, 1/6, and 1/7 Queens, which eventually received more than 30 CANLOAN officers.

At one point there was a pressing invitation to join the Airborne Divisions, and nearly 100 CANLOAN officers eventually served in battalions in the 1st and 6th Airborne Divisions (AB). CDN/478, Lieut. Tom H. Anstey, has described his assignment:

> "Who wishes to join the 2nd Battalion, The Oxfordshire & Buckinghamshire Light Infantry (Oxf & Bucks), 6th Airborne Division?" sang out a British officer. My hand was up, not because of any reaction on my part, but because Jim Cochrane (Lieutenant James, CDN/409), had my wrist firmly in his hand and his hand was up. We were quickly on the train to Bulford!"[5]

The greatest number of CANLOAN officers who served in a single battalion were the 23 who were posted to 7 (Galloway) KOSB. No fewer than eight officers in the small third flight were posted to this battalion. Several CANLOAN officers who asked for a Scottish regiment were posted to 7 KOSB without being aware that it was an airborne unit. Other popular battalions were 6 KOSB and the 10th Battalion, the Highland Light Infantry (HLI), with 16 each, 2 Glasgows with 15, and 7 Seaforths with 14. Several had 13, including the 2nd Battalion, the South Staffordshire Regiment (S. Staffords.), which was also in the 1st Airborne Division, the 3rd Battalion, the Monmouthshire Regiment (Mons.), and 1/6 Queens (both in armoured divisions), the 6th Battalion, the Royal Scots Fusiliers (RSF), and 4 Dorset. On the other hand, several battalions had only one CANLOAN officer: the 2nd Battalion, the Royal Ulster Rifles (RUR), the 2nd Battalion, the Royal Lincolnshire Regiment (R. Lincs.), the 7/9th Battalion, the Royal Scots (RS), and several battalions of the Parachute Regiment (Para.).

It was assumed that the loan arrangement did not apply to the regiments of the Brigade of Guards. In fact, when Winston Churchill had suggested that Guards units be brought up to strength by reinforcements from line regiments, General Montgomery had protested: "You cannot take line reinforcements and draft them into Guards units just like that; the two types of discipline are quite different and it does not work."[6]

Nevertheless, in mid-July 1944 the War Office received a request from the CO of the 1st Battalion, the Grenadier Guards (Gren. Gds.), that five Canadian officers, who were listed by name and CANLOAN number, be posted to his battalion.[7] CDN/606, Lieut. Frederick W. Burd has explained what lay behind the request:

> People have often asked me, "How in the world did you end up in an elite unit like the Grenadier Guards?", and my truthful reply has had to be, "Because my name began with B." All hundred-plus of us were lined up in alphabetical order and divided into fifths. The top fifth was posted to No 40 RHU which happened to be the holding unit through which

all Guards personnel passed and which was commanded by a Colonel in the Coldstreams. He was an avid bridge player, as was Bill Burnett (Lieutenant William J, CDN/607), and after several evenings of bridge together he said to Bill, "I think that the Guards should have some of you chaps." Accordingly he took the next morning's train to London and visited the five Guards Regimental Headquarters in turn. The Grenadiers, with their characteristic efficiency, were the first to act and indented for five CANLOAN. The War Office gave rather a frosty reply to the effect that it had not been intended that CANLOAN officers should go to the Guards, but that as a special exception five would be allowed to do so, but that there would be no more such postings.

Now the question arose, which CANLOAN should go? Enter the alphabet once again, starting with the As and going down the list. John Aitkin (Lieutenant, CDN/599) wanted to go to the Gordons (he was killed in August 1944); John Anderson (Lieutenant, CDN/600) had his heart set on going to a Highland regiment (he went to the 5/7 Gordons); Francis Andrew (Captain CDN/601) and Holland Bate (Lieutenant, CDN/602) also elected to go elsewhere, so the choice reverted to Tom Birchall (Lieutenant Thomas H, CDN/603) who became the first of our Grenadier group. Cam Brown (Lieutenant F Cameron, CDN/604) and Wilf Brownlee-Lamont (Lieutenant Wilfred W N, CDN/605) both wanted Highland regiments so I (CDN/606) became the second Grenadier, followed by Bill Burnett. Clarence Campbell (Lieutenant, CDN/608), Erk Carter (Lieutenant Erskine E R E, CDN/609) and Will Caseley (Lieutenant Willard S, CDN/611) all went to the KOSBs while Jimmy Carson (Captain Jim F J, CDN/610) went to the HLI, so the fourth Grenadier was Dick Chard (Lieutenant Richard N, CDN 612). Larry Fazackerley (Lieutenant Lawrence, CDN/669) jumped the alphabetical queue as he had earlier served in the Canadian Grenadier Guards.[8]

Most of the eighth flight (the RCA and RCASC retreads) went to the School of Infantry at Barnard Castle for a special course which, while of only 17 days' duration, was considered far superior to the two-month course at Brockville. After that the officers who had been selected for the Grenadier Guards were given another course to indoctrinate them into the ways of the regiment.

The stay in London was brief for the first 600 CANLOAN officers, who were to go direct to field units. In addition to the allocation to units for those who had not done so before disembarkation, there was just time for a visit to a Canadian bank where pay for each officer was to be deposited, a telegram home to report safe arrival, and a quick tour of London. Then all dispersed singly or, more often, in pairs and sometimes in groups of up to half a dozen, to divisions, most of which were located near the south coast ready for the invasion of northwest Europe. In retrospect the allocation to units was most notable for the excellent staff work. In most cases the various battalions had been notified about the postings of CANLOAN officers by name and number. Thus they were expected and accordingly welcomed on their arrival.

Several of the CANLOAN officers were introduced to their divisional commanders. CDN/258, Lieut. C. Russell Parke was one of a group in the fifth flight posted to units in the 15th Scottish Division, which had its headquarters at Horsham Castle. He reports: "While we were being briefed at the Castle, through a window stepped the kilted six-foot four-inch figure of the Divisional Commander, General MacMillan."[9] The Canadians, unaccustomed to meeting generals, were impressed by this informality. Those in the first flight who were assigned to 154 Brigade in the

51st Highland Division were sent to brigade headquarters to meet the Brigade Commander and then to divisional headquarters to be presented to the Divisional Commander, Major-General Bullen-Smith. He told them, "There is an Army way to do things and a Highland Division way and you will do things the Highland Division way."[10]

Those in the first draft who were assigned to the 43rd Wessex Division met the Divisional Commander, Major-General Thomas, when he returned from church on Easter Sunday, resplendent in glistening boots and breeches. Most CANLOAN officers went directly to the battalions to which they were posted for a welcome by the commanding officer. Most received a cordial welcome. As early as 14 April 1944, when only two flights with a total of 109 officers had arrived in the United Kingdom, Lieutenant-Colonel Sibbald at the War Office reported that British divisional commanders were "high in the praises" of CANLOAN officers. They had told Colonel Sibbald that their battalion commanders were "crying for more Canadian officers."[11] This reaction was confirmed recently by a former CO of the 4th Battalion, the King's Shropshire Light Infantry (KSLI), which absorbed 11 CANLOAN officers: "At the time we received CANLOAN officers we were desperately short of platoon commanders and had reluctantly accepted that many of our platoons would be commanded in action by sergeants. The CANLOAN officers joined us as a breath of fresh air."[12]

And a former company commander of the 7th Battalion, the Somerset Light Infantry (Som. LI), recalls, "When the CANLOAN scheme was told to us by our CO I remember every company commander cried spontaneously, 'Please, can I have some?', or words to that effect."[13]

There were, however, some natural reservations concerning the Canadian officers who arrived in battalions shortly before D-Day. Colonel Thornycroft of 2 KSLI recalls,

> As a battalion, before D-Day, we had trained together for a long time and had tremendous friendships and loyalties among ourselves which stood one in great stead. To be suddenly bundled into a team of this sort in the middle of action without the time or opportunity to get to know those around you was very demanding and required great strength of character.[14]

There were also bound to be questions about the ability of the Canadian officers to fit into the regimental team. There is a story about several CANLOAN officers who were welcomed by a regular Army commanding officer with the caution, "Now I know all about you Can-i-deans – so don't pull any of your colonial monkeyshines!"[15] And the first CANLOAN officers to be presented to the CO of 2 E. Yorks., Colonel Hutchinson, were surprised when he looked at his watch and said, "I didn't ask for any colonials but did say that if they arrived before 1700 hours today I would accept them – welcome aboard."[16]

On the other hand, the six CANLOAN officers who were paraded to meet the Commanding Officer, 7 E. Yorks., were surprised when he introduced himself as "a fellow colonial," Lieut.-Col. "Digger" Goss, an Australian. The use of the word "colonial" was an irritation to many CANLOAN officers until they got used to it.

CDN/302, Capt. Thomas B. King and CDN/152, Lieut. Harold F. (Hank) Henry were among those who corrected superior officers who referred to them as colonials. This term, and the attitude of which it was a symptom, tended to be used by a few officers, particularly those with Indian Army experience. CDN/47, Capt. Arnold Willick recalls, "We rapidly formed a bond of friendship with the younger territorial officers, who described the Indian Army types as the Poona boys."[17]

Another CANLOAN officer who speaks for many of his colleagues notes, "There was none of the colonial bit by officers in the 15th Scottish Division. The young Scottish officers were much like ourselves in temperament and treated the Canadian officers like brothers from the beginning."[18]

On the whole, personal difficulties or even reserve between Canadian and British officers were unusual. What British officers remember most about the arrival of the CANLOAN officers is how easily and completely they fitted into their new units. Typical remarks are, "They integrated completely with us; they were one of us as far as we died-in-the-wool British officers were concerned,"[19] and "We treated them exactly as one of us. It was never 'them' and 'us.'"[20]

The last is not quite true, for many CANLOAN officers remember best the special treatment they received from the British officers and the extent to which they went out of their way to make them feel at home. Many of the commanding officers set an example in this respect. One of the most prominent was the CO, 2 E. Yorks. Colonel Hutchinson wrote to the next of kin of the CANLOAN officers posted to his battalion to say that they had arrived safely and had joined 2 E. Yorks., which was well trained, and that there was no need to worry. To help the Canadian officers become acclimatized to the British environment, Colonel Hutchinson accompanied them to places of interest, including the famous old HMS *Victory* as well as the Navy yard and naval messes in Portsmouth and Winchester Cathedral. Since his four CANLOAN officers had not had experience with assault landing craft, as had the rest of the battalion, and since 2 E. Yorks. was to lead the D-Day assault on Sword Beach, the CO arranged for the troops, accompanied by him, to go on board a naval vessel to practise landings.

Other battalions made special arrangements for their CANLOAN officers. Those posted to 4 KSLI were sent on a four-day exercise with their platoons to give them an opportunity to get to know the men they would lead in battle. There were many other examples of special treatment which helped to ease the transition to what was at first a strange environment, but which quickly became home.

A typical reaction to the reception by the British Army is in a letter from one CANLOAN officer to another at the time:

What do you think of the British army? I think it is great stuff myself. As you say, the "limies" have turned out to be some grand people. They treat us so well that at times I'm almost ashamed of the things I used to think about them. Tea five times a day "laid on" with cakes after "Cheerio, old boy," "five quid and tuppence ha'penny." It's one grand experience.[21]

When CANLOAN officers fitted well into their British units it was a tribute to their adaptability, for their new environment differed in nearly every respect from that to which they were accustomed. One factor to overcome was differences in language. Reports of the arrival of CANLOAN flights in the United Kingdom frequently mention being greeted by a "Colonel Blimp" speaking "unintelligible Hindustani." This was an immediate reminder of fundamental differences between Canadian and British accents and expressions. In fact, however, communication between officers was not to be a serious problem, although for many months either British or Canadian officers were puzzled or amused by differences in vocabulary (one young British officer was fascinated by the Canadian expression "That should go over big").

Often this could not be said about communication with other ranks, who, in many cases, seemed to be speaking a foreign language. The 30 or so CANLOAN officers who were posted to the five battalions of DLI found it difficult at first to understand the "Geordies." Similar difficulties were experienced with Welch and Scottish troops and with the many regional English accents, such as Cornish and even Cockney. Capt. Tom King, as a platoon commander in the 6th Battalion, the Bedfordshire and Hertfordshire Regiment (Bedfs. Herts.), attended his first company office at which his Cockney platoon sergeant gave testimony. Asked if he would confirm his sergeant's statement, King confessed that he had not understood a word the sergeant had said. In some cases, though, platoon sergeants were very useful as interpreters for their Canadian officers.

Some concern was expressed at the 2nd Army level about the standard of training and efficiency, as junior infantry commanders, of the CANLOAN officers who were assigned to field units. Certainly the officers themselves shared that concern. One report noted that the CANLOAN officers "had a high degree of individual training but apparently had had little opportunity of serving with platoons and consequently there was room for improvement in regard to man management." This was true in many cases, but ultimately it would be performance under battle conditions that would reveal the quality of leadership; later reports indicated that it was more than satisfactory. Meanwhile the CANLOAN officers found no serious difficulty in adapting to British military procedures since they were familiar with the weapons, drill, infantry tactics, and other subjects. In some cases, as has been mentioned, officers spent brief periods at divisional battle schools, were given practice in assault landing or short courses in specialized subjects, such as WASP flame throwers. Usually, though, officers who were assigned to rifle companies were expected to carry on at once as platoon commanders, and they usually did. Of most immediate concern was the relationship with the human elements in their battalions – the officers, NCOs, and men. One first impression was that there was excessively strict discipline in the British Army. A newly arrived CANLOAN officer reported, "A corporal comes to attention when speaking to a sergeant and calls him 'sir', and, when any of them speak to an officer, well —! Everybody salutes an officer as far as they can see him, even if his back is turned."[22]

It came as a surprise, however, to discover the informality that existed among the officers in a battalion. Differences of rank were emphasized on parade, but off parade it was as if differences did not exist. With the exception of the commanding officer, who was always called "Sir," all other officers without exception – majors (including the second in command), captains, and lieutenants – called each other by their first names or, preferably, their nicknames. Some of these were predictable –

"Lofty" for short men, "Tiny" for large ones, "Dusty" Rhodes and "Chalky" White – but some nicknames were quite remarkable and hardly conducive to formality. Since most battalions were decentralized, occupying a variety of civilian buildings or even tents, there was rarely the normal battalion officers' mess to which the lectures at Sussex had referred. More often there were separate messes for the five officers in each rifle company, and in them fellow officers lived on terms of the greatest informality.

The difference between officers and NCOs was great, and an elaborate code of conduct was observed in relationships between the two. CANLOAN officers were impressed at once by the remarkably high calibre of the British NCOs and warrant officers. They were, indeed, the backbone of the regiment, the repository of its traditions and the executors of its commands. They were so efficient, resourceful, and reliable that, even though they were invariably respectful, officers could be forgiven for feeling at times that NCOs could get along very well without them. Generally speaking, Canadian officers felt that they must earn respect from NCOs and men by being able to perform better than the troops they led in every respect from firing on the range, to stripping a Bren gun, performing on the obstacle course, and demonstrating knowledge and leadership qualities. In the British Army, however, it seemed that officers received respect almost automatically because of their rank.

The relationship between officers and other ranks that CANLOAN officers encountered was the product of many years of experience in the British Army, familiar to, understood, and accepted by all concerned. The Divisional Commander of the 51st Highland Division spoke to his CANLOAN officers about the Army way and the Highland Division way of doing things. Later the Brigadier continued where the General had left off:

> I'm aware that there is a certain degree of fraternizing tolerated between officers and other ranks in the Canadian Army. At least that's what I've been led to believe. I shouldn't think it would be too advisable to pursue this practice in units of the British Army, and, on that point, the Highland Division and Army are in complete agreement.[23]

Although this information was not always given explicitly in briefings to CANLOAN officers, the message was conveyed to all of them at an early stage. The Brigadier explained that this was not class distinction but an effective arrangement that worked both ways: "The soldier resents any attempt by an officer to intrude on his sphere. 'Whit's he makin' wi' us for?' he asks. There is also a tendency to regard such an officer as lacking confidence in himself, and above all, the British soldier must have absolute confidence in his officers."[24]

Though this situation was well understood, many if not most CANLOAN officers were nevertheless at some time guilty of overstepping the traditional boundary by becoming too familiar with other ranks. They encountered criticism, ranging from raised eyebrows, to friendly hints and formal rebukes for incidents such as buying a round of drinks in a pub for their sergeants and working with troops in unorthodox ways. On the whole this does not seem to have been held against them by the troops. A typical remark was made by an NCO in the 5th Battalion, the East Lancashire Regiment (E. Lan. R.), who recalled that CDN/345, Lieut. Justin Karls was "well-liked for his easy going way as you found with all Canadians."[25] The batman of Lieut. Andrew Bushell in the 7th Battalion, the Royal Norfolk Regiment (R. Norfolk), writes, "He treated me like a friend, not just officer and private."[26]

Others appreciated having an officer sit on their bunks and talk to them about their families. That there were no adverse consequences from such fraternization does not mean that the British system was wrong, but simply that Canadians were expected to be different from British officers and that their ways were generally well received.

Not only other ranks but officers, too, considered that Canadians were different. They were expected to be "a miraculous composite of Red Indian, Mountie and bushman who played and drank hard, had no regard for authority but who were good guys."[27]

Though few could live up to this image, it was remarkably widespread. It tended to make CANLOAN officers aware of the high standards that were expected of them and to recall the speeches that insisted that the reputation of Canada rested on their shoulders. And it is difficult to believe there was no connection between the Red Indian image of Canadians and the number of patrols by CANLOAN officers in northwest Europe.

When the CANLOAN scheme was first proposed it was intended primarily to provide "first reinforcements" for the 21st Army Group in the invasion of northwest Europe following the expected heavy casualties among junior infantry officers. In his account of the origin of the scheme, Gen. Sir Ronald Adam, the British Adjutant-General, added, "They were such excellent material that some units took them with them on D-Day, leaving others (non-CANLOANs) to wait as reinforcements."[28]

This was true to a limited extent. For example, the first four CANLOAN officers who were posted to 2 E. Yorks. were assigned to platoons that they commanded in the assault landing on D-Day, while an equal number of British officers in the battalion went to a reinforcement holding Unit (RHU). This was true also of the 2nd Battalion, the South Wales Borderers (SWB), and several other battalions. Usually, though, the first CANLOAN officers to arrive were assigned to any existing officer war establishment (WE) vacancies and later arrivals were sent to the appropriate RHU. For example, 4 KSLI, which was short of platoon commanders, was able to absorb four CANLOAN officers into their order of battle in April and May 1944. Similarly the 1/6 Queens assigned six CANLOAN officers to platoons. During the same period the 4th Battalion, the Wiltshire Regiment (Wilts.), was able to assign only two CANLOAN officers to WE positions while sending six others to an RHU. Several battalions, including 2 Essex and the 2nd Battalion, the Royal Hampshire Regiments (R. Hamps.), had no CANLOAN officers when they went to Normandy, although they received nearly 20 as reinforcements. Altogether, at least half of the CANLOAN officers who arrived in the United Kingdom before D-Day were assigned to WE positions in battalions, and the rest were posted to RHUs.

Success in retaining strings on first reinforcements varied. In the case of 4 Wilts., for example, which retained two CANLOAN officers and posted six to an RHU, none of the latter ever rejoined the battalion. The RHU landed in Normandy before the 43 Division, and the Wiltshire reinforcements went to 2 Essex, the 1/7 Queens, and the 2nd Battalion, the Devonshire Regiment (Devon). On the other hand, 2 Glas. H.

was able to keep control of their reinforcements, chiefly ex-Pictou Highlanders. They had vacancies for only two CANLOAN officers while in the UK, so others were attached to companies in the battalion, then sent to RHUs until reinforcements were required in Normandy, when a dozen CANLOANs filled battalion vacancies.

Shortly after the first 500 or so CANLOAN officers had reported to their new battalions, some of them were informed that they were entitled to disembarkation leave. At one stage in the negotiations between the War Office and CMHQ, it had been agreed that CANLOAN officers would be allowed two weeks' leave on their arrival in the United Kingdom. This information, however, was not widely circulated. It was not included in the pamphlet given to each CANLOAN volunteer, nor was it in the War Office Army Council Instruction 504, which governed the administration of the CANLOAN scheme. All CANLOAN officers had had embarkation leave before reporting to A-34 Sussex. They arrived in the United Kingdom about the time, or shortly after, all leave for units in the 21st Army Group had been cut off, and in view of the short time available to get acquainted with their new regiment, new duties, and new troops before the invasion, a period of leave at that time was considered by some to be inappropriate. In fact, several CANLOAN officers elected to pass up the leave and spend the time getting to know the men in their platoons. There was no uniformity in the granting of leave in the different battalions. It appears that only a few officers were given the two weeks' leave. More were given one week, several only 48 hours, and many were not given leave at all, which was a cause for concern when it came to the attention of the authorities at CMHQ.

For those Canadians who were given leave it was a wonderful opportunity to become acquainted with Britain and the British outside the boundaries of their military activities. For most, the first view of British countryside was from the windows of their railway coaches as they sped from the ports of debarkation to London. Their impressions were similar to those of CDN/362, Lieut. Arthur N. Stone, who refers to

> the time spent in gazing at the fairy-like land in never diminishing wonder. The fields were a delicate green and any one of them would have made a creditable lawn in Canada. Everything was in miniature: tiny fields, houses, roads, even the trees looked smaller. The horizon was closer and trees were set in picturesque little groves of neat, broad and bushy boughs.[29]

And another officer, writing to his family in Canada, reported:

> The country we are in is simply lovely with crops growing, miles of well-trimmed hedges, the roads shaded with splendid trees, little picturesque cottages with roses or honeysuckle covering the bricks and each with blooming flower gardens. There are ivy covered churches, vicarages and more imposing mansions surrounded by walls. And then there are the pubs. The weather has been perfect and altogether we are in love with the whole country.[30]

With appetites whetted by the brief visit to London on the way to their regiments, many CANLOAN officers returned for longer visits on their leave. Many of them found a home there at the Junior Officers' Club in Kensington. It was staffed by Red Cross officers, several of whom had shared the voyage to the UK with CANLOAN officers, who were thus assured of a warm welcome. One group of enterprising CANLOANs even rented a four-bedroom apartment near Piccadilly. One of them recalls, "Naturally our haven became popular with CANLOANers and after Benny [CDN/84, Lieut. Benjamin Laxer] had relieved them of their hard-earned cash (in poker games) they were allowed to sleep on the living room floor."[31]

Several CANLOAN officers took advantage of the opportunity to visit the native county of their new regiments so they could report on their return that they had actually been in Yorkshire, Essex, Dorset, Monmouthshire, or wherever.

CANLOAN officers were pleased to discover that their "Canada" flashes ensured them a warm reception by British civilians nearly everywhere, and they often had difficulty in buying a drink in a pub. At the beginning of the war, Canadian troops in Britain had a reputation for heavy drinking and rowdiness that persisted for a long time, but during the long occupation of Sussex and Kent by the 2nd and 3rd Canadian Divisions a network of friendships had developed and the popularity of Canadians was widespread. In Scotland, of course, Canadians were always made to feel at home in both the First and Second World Wars. The treatment of CANLOAN officers, especially those serving in Scottish regiments, was particularly enthusiastic, and Scotland was a favourite spot to spend leave. CANLOAN officers were grateful for the kindness and hospitality they received, and they admired the indomitable spirit of the British people. And finally, a surprisingly large number of CANLOAN officers had relatives in the United Kingdom, and visits with them did a great deal to counter any feelings of strangeness.

For the CANLOAN officers who had returned from leave and the others who had been posted directly to a battalion, there was an opportunity in the brief period before the landing in Normandy to become accustomed to life in an infantry regiment. For those whose military experience had been chiefly in training centres it was pleasant to discover how important and all-encompassing a regiment was. It was, in a real sense, a home as well as a repository of traditions and a source of pride. CANLOANs were immediately instructed in the history and unique customs of their regiments. They learned, for example, why the Middlesex Regiment was known as the "Die Hards," why the Royal Welch Fusiliers wore black ribbon on the backs of their collars, why some regiments wore roses in their hats on the anniversary of the battle of Minden, why the Wiltshire Regiment wore dented buttons, why the Oxfordshire and Buckinghamshire Light Infantry remained seated and continued to talk during the playing of "God Save the King" in their own messes, and much much more. They came to understand and share the affection and pride in a British regiment that often surpassed any loyalties they had hitherto experienced.

When CANLOAN officers were posted directly to battalions in 21st Army Group they realized that they were a part of a military formation that had attained a remarkable standard of efficiency and morale. Most of its divisions had been training for the four years since Dunkirk, first to defend the British Isles against invasion, and then in preparation for invading the Continent. They lacked, of course, recent battle experience, and for that reason several divisions were brought back from the Mediterranean to play a prominent role in the coming assault. The 51st

Highland Division, the 50th Division, and the 7th Armoured Division (the Desert Rats) had won impressive reputations in North Africa and Italy. They were brought home in November 1943 to prepare for the campaign in northwest Europe. Despite their recent and extensive battle experience, it was considered that they had much to learn about different terrain, new weapons such as PIATs and WASPs, and new tactics: infantry-tank co-operation in close country, river crossings, and other variations on familiar themes. Montgomery came back to Britain from Italy early in January 1944, and questioning the value of the training during his absence, he drove the 21st Army Group in realistic and strenuous exercises, tapering off to specialized training that included, in addition to practice landings for the assault troops, street fighting, field firing exercises, infantry-tank exercises, and naturally, emphasis on individual physical fitness.

Montgomery's first briefing of senior commanders on operation OVERLORD was on 7 April 1944, the day the first CANLOAN flight landed; his last briefing was on 15 May, by which time nearly everything was in readiness and exactly 500 CANLOAN officers had arrived. They took part in route marches and cross-country runs, in firing weapons on the range, in demonstrations of the fire power of 25-pounders and mortars, and in practising street fighting. There were also track and field meets from company up to division levels in which a considerable number of CANLOAN officers participated.

And there were visits from VIPs, including General Montgomery, who systematically visited all units. Other visitors were King George and Winston Churchill. When the King visited the 11th DLI the CO singled out a CANLOAN officer for presentation, which caused some jealousy among the Geordies. CANLOAN officers in the 43rd Division stood with their platoons on the roadside in Sussex to watch the passing of an open car bearing Winston Churchill, Field Marshal Smuts, and Mackenzie King, the Prime Ministers of England, South Africa, and Canada respectively. Nearly all divisional commanders briefed their officers on the coming invasion, so all knew what their roles would be, but not the magic date of D-Day. On 17 May 1944 the officers of 8 RS joined other officers in the 15th Scottish Division in the cinema in Worthing for an address by their Corps Commander, General O'Connor. On the 23rd they were visited by their Colonel-in-Chief, the Princess Royal.

During these final preparations for the invasion CANLOAN suffered its first casualties. There were several cases of illness and accidents, of which the one to Lieut. Earl Cloutier was particularly unfortunate. After trying every means to get overseas, including paratroops, he had welcomed the CANLOAN scheme. At Sussex he was singled out by Brigadier Gregg for his "special list." And then, while engaged in pre-invasion training with 1/7 Queens he suffered crushed spinal discs and spent the next year in a series of British and Canadian hospitals in Britain. Returned to Canada in June 1945, as a volunteer for the Pacific force, he remained in the regular army until his retirement after 32 years of service.

And it was on the day before D-Day (5 June 1944), that the first CANLOAN fatal casualty occurred. CDN/140, Lieut. Allen P. (Buster) Crabb was one of the American CANLOAN officers, a graduate of the University of Akron, who had enlisted in the Canadian Army in Toronto in August 1942 and was commissioned four months later. He was proficient in infantry weapons, particularly the 3-inch mortar. After volunteering for CANLOAN, he was posted to the 1st Battalion, the Border Regiment (Border), in the 1st Airborne Division. In a freak accident while supervising the firing of a PIAT on a range, he was hit by the projectile and killed. He is one of three CANLOAN officers who are buried in England.

In contrast to the long months, even years, of waiting for action in Canada, the time between arriving in the United Kingdom and landing in Normandy was one of intense activity. Surplus kit, such as service dress, Sam Browne, and great coats, was sent to storage depots at Aldershot. New flashes were sewn on battle dress sleeves – patches for the division, brigade, and battalion as well as the Canada flash and service stripes stretched from shoulder to wrist. New kit was issued and new duties were undertaken, and in some cases learned. Quite a number of CANLOAN officers recall their panic at being detailed to act as company paymaster with all the fractional NAAFI (Navy, Army, Air Force Institute) and other deductions – as well as sterling currency! And there was the beginning of what would always be a time-consuming but interesting and educational chore, the censoring of all letters written by members of their platoons. All was done in such a short time! CDN/142, Lieut. Alexander W. Cunningham realized that only 24 hours after he had expressed a regimental preference on board the *Cavina* in the harbour at Leith, Scotland, he was commanding his own platoon in 4 KSLI. in southern England. CDN/417, Lieut. John O. Levine, who landed in Normandy on D-Day with 2 Glosters. and was killed on 2 July, wrote:

> One thing about the British Army – it doesn't waste any time. Issued with regimental flashes, we shipped right into training as platoon commanders. A few days later our camp was sealed. Letters weren't allowed in or out. There we were, overseas about a week and waiting for the invasion to start ... but so help me, I was happy about the whole thing.[32]

5

Normandy:
The Bridgehead

IN THE HISTORY of the world 6 June 1944 will always be known as D-Day, the day of the launching of operation OVERLORD, the assault landing of Allied troops in northwest Europe. This operation had to be undertaken if the war with Nazi Germany was to be won. Such a return to the Continent had been an Allied goal since the evacuation of Dunkirk in 1940. It was not feasible before the spring of 1944, despite extreme pressure after the end of 1941 from the Americans, who, when they entered the war, wanted an immediate frontal assault on Germany; from the Russians, who wanted to reduce the pressure of the German campaign in the east; and even from the Allied media and civilian population, who spoke constantly of a "second front." Since the British, whose reserves of manpower were small, were reluctant to launch a premature attack that would result in heavy casualties, the assault was postponed until after the landings in North Africa and Italy in 1942 and 1943. Meanwhile, planning was undertaken for OVERLORD, which "called for more men, more ships, more planes, more equipment and matériel than had ever been assembled for a single military operation."[1]

The site of the assault landings was chosen early in 1943, and the secret was kept for more than a year. The number of assault divisions and the size of the initial bridgehead were dictated in large measure by the number of assault craft available. At first it was planned to have three divisions, but later, at Montgomery's insistence, the landing area was widened and the number of assaulting divisions increased to five: two American, two British, and one Canadian. Three airborne divisions were to seize and hold the flanks of the bridgehead. The assault plan incorporated lessons learned from earlier experiences, particularly the Dieppe raid of 1942, and included certain prerequisites which, it was hoped, would ensure success:

- air superiority so as to reduce, if not eliminate, the threat of the German fighter force;
- bombing of bridges to isolate Normandy from the rest of France and prevent German reserves from reaching the bridgehead quickly;
- massive bombardment, until the actual landing of troops on the beaches, by aircraft, naval ships, artillery, and rockets firing from assault ships;
- innovative means of dealing with beach defences by such devices as DD tanks, AVREs, armoured bulldozers, Flails, and so on;
- surprise, by keeping the time and place of landing secret and persuading the Germans that the main assault would be across the English Channel at the Pas de Calais; and
- protection of the flanks by airborne landings on both the east and west ends of the bridgehead.

Though the Germans did not consider Normandy a likely place for the invasion, it was part of the Atlantic Wall that had been ordered by Hitler in March 1942. Under Field Marshal Rundstedt's command, the emphasis was on a mobile reserve of panzer divisions to counterattack and destroy the invaders, wherever they should land. But because of Field Marshal Rommel's bitter experience in North Africa trying to move his reserves and counter-attack forces while under British air attack, during the winter of 1943–44, the emphasis was changed to a policy of preventing a landing and winning the battle on the beaches. This entailed strengthening the beach defences by building more concrete pill boxes and installing heavy guns, machine guns in enfilade and mortars covering every yard of the beaches, as well as by laying millions of mines in belts behind the beaches and building rows of obstacles, most with mines attached, between the high and low water lines. The area between the Vire on the west and the Orne on the east was defended by two German infantry divisions, the 352nd and 716th. The mobile reserve within a few miles of the coast consisted of three panzer divisions: the 12th SS Panzer (Hitler Jugend), the 21st Panzer Division, and the Panzer Lehr Division. This was the enemy the Allied invaders could expect to meet within hours of landing.

The general plan for the D-Day assault was to drop two American airborne divisions at the base of the Cotentin peninsula on the west and a British airborne division on the east to protect the flanks of the bridgehead. Five beaches were to be assaulted, each by an infantry division. The two American divisions on the right would provide beachheads through which follow-up forces would move to capture Cherbourg with its port and then move south and east towards Paris. The British 3rd Division was to capture Caen, which was considered vital to the Army plan. The British 50th (Northumbrian) Division was to capture Bayeux, push southward, and link up with the Americans. The Canadian 3rd Division in the centre of the three British beaches was to capture Carpiquet airport and seize the open ground south of Caen between the Orne and the Odon.

By May all of southern England from Cornwall to Kent had become a vast military encampment with huge dumps of guns, ammunition, mines, wire, food, clothing, and all kinds of supplies and equipment reaching to the horizon: roads and lanes were lined, and woods and open spaces filled with more than 50,000 tanks, armoured cars, trucks, jeeps, and ambulances. Masses of troops (20 American, 14

British, and 3 Canadian divisions, and hundreds of thousands of special forces) were packed into Nisson huts, Quonset huts, tents, and requisitioned civilian houses. And of course there were endless convoys as assault troops were moved into marshalling areas. One CANLOAN officer wondered why the island didn't sink from the weight!

Though most operational training had to cease when the assault troops were sealed in the marshalling areas, there was still a great deal of activity. Ammunition and grenades were issued, magazines loaded with the right number of rounds, and items issued for the cross-Channel voyage – life jackets, sea sickness pills, and (in case they didn't work) "bags, vomit," emergency rations, even French currency. Officers were kept busy with constant checks to see that the men in their platoons had all the required equipment; with practice dressing in full battle order, weighing 40–50 pounds, and full marching order, weighing around 90 pounds. The officers made sure that their men realized that *they* carried additional items that brought their full marching load up to 120 pounds. All officers were briefed on the objectives of their battalion, company, and platoon by means of maps, aerial photographs, and even plaster and sand models, and they in turn briefed their platoons. Until the time of embarkation fictitious place names were used.

In Canada many CANLOAN officers had expected they would be fighting for a foothold on some beach in western Europe. But when the time came they found that the only ones who would take part in the D-Day landings were those who had been assigned platoons in the two British assault divisions, the 3rd and the 50th, as well as those who would land with reinforcement units on D-Day. It was not a new experience for all the troops in the invasion forces. In the 50th Division two battalions – 1 Dorset and 1 R. Hamps. – would be making their third assault landing on an enemy shore within 12 months. Naturally there were rumours and speculation about the imminent assault. One was that the entire first wave was expected to be wiped out. Veterans of the North African campaign told grim tales about the fighting qualities of the German soldier. On the other hand, it was difficult not to be optimistic when one saw the buildup of troops and equipment and the relative ease of the practice landings, and was given detailed briefings about objectives and information about devastating firepower support and, especially, the low standard of the troops who were manning the beach defences in Normandy.

D-Day was set for 5 June, when weather and tides were expected to be favourable. The assault troops began to embark on 1 and 2 June in the craft called landing ships infantry (LSI), which were to take them to Normandy, where they would be transferred to landing craft assault (LCA), which would take them to shore. The ships in the vast convoy, a veritable armada, assembled in the Channel south of the Isle of Wight at a spot called Piccadilly Circus. Inspirational messages from Generals Eisenhower and Montgomery were read to the troops. In the early hours of 4 June, with a gale brewing, the Supreme Commander, General Eisenhower, postponed the operation for one day. Some ships, already on the way to Normandy, were brought back with difficulty. The rising sea and cramped quarters had brought waves of seasickness, and the sea was littered with "bags, vomit."

At midnight on 5 June the airborne landings began on time. On the eastern flank the 6th Airborne Division was successful in seizing the bridges across the Orne and the Caen Canal and in establishing a bridgehead across the Orne at Ranville. The joint firepower plan began at midnight with heavy bombing of Caen and the beach defences, followed by bombardment from battleships, cruisers, and destroyers and later by field artillery and rockets firing from assault craft. The invasion fleet left England early on 5 June, and for those who were in it it was an unforgettable sight: 5,000 ships, including more than 700 warships (battleships, cruisers, destroyers, frigates, and corvettes) and at least 1,500 landing craft stretched from horizon to horizon. The sea was rough, with waves five and six feet high, and most of the assaulting troops were miserably seasick. One said later that the chief reason the assault was successful was that the troops would do anything to avoid having to return by sea! Cornelius Ryan in *The Longest Day* describes the mood of the British assault force: "Lieutenant-General M C Dempsey's British Second Army was coming ashore with grimness and gaiety, with pomp and ceremony, with all the studied nonchalance the British traditionally assume in moments of great emotion."[2]

CANLOAN officers, who had been impressed by the attention given to history and tradition in the British Army, noted with interest the ways in which this memorable event was observed. The 2 E. Yorks. leading the 3rd Division on Sword Beach provided several examples. The battalion was being taken to Normandy by HMS *Glenhern*, the LSI whose captain and crew had worked with it in several practice landings. Before sailing, the Yorks.' Commanding Officer, Lieut.-Col. C.F. Hutchinson, presented Captain Hutchinson, Commander of the *Glenhern*, with a silver bugle inscribed with the regimental crest. In return Lieutenant-Colonel Hutchinson received a ceremonial pike bearing the regimental badge of the Royal Marines. As 2 E. Yorks. ploughed through the heavy seas towards Sword Beach, they passed the destroyer *Undaunted* and observed her commander, Angus Mackenzie, wearing a Highlander's bonnet and playing the bagpipes from his bridge. A bugler of the E. Yorks. sounded the General Salute as his LSI passed the British command ship, HMS *Largs*. Several American and Canadian as well as British officers had sought to conclude their final briefing with a statement worthy of the occasion, but none of them could outdo Maj. C.K. "Banger" King, Officer Commanding A Company 2 E. Yorks. Using a loudhailer as his LCA approached the beach he quoted from an account of an earlier invasion of France in Shakespeare's *Henry V:*

> He, that outlives this day, and comes safe home,
> Will stand a tip-toe when this day is nam'd

> And gentlemen in England, now a-bed
> Shall think themselves accurs'd, they were not here.

Two of Major King's three platoon commanders were CANLOAN officers: CDN/179, Lieut. Melbourne H. Neily and Lieut. Stirling Reid. C Company under Maj. D. Barrow also had two CANLOAN platoon commanders: CDN/118, Capt. James McGregor and Lieut. Leonard Robertson. Robertson has given a vivid account of the landing of a platoon on D-Day and the death of the first CANLOAN officer to be killed in action:

> The East Yorkshires were in. As C Coy moved in to land behind A Coy and to the right, we discovered that all the wire entanglements and beach obstacles which were to be cleared by the sappers hadn't been. Maj Barrow spotted an opening and made for it with 13 and 14 Platoons following in their LCAs. Not for me it wasn't. I figured that one or two

might get through and not be spotted by the Jerries but certainly not four craft. Gave the order for full speed ahead ... as I wanted to hit the wire hard and crash the entanglement with the mines without them going off. It was a chance to take but we didn't have all day to figure it out. The Marine corporal in charge of the LCA hesitated, and I really didn't blame him, but when I went to take the wheel he gave her the gun. Heads down! Here we go! The first wire parted like a string. The second wire jarred us and really gave us a scare as we just missed hitting an iron rail with a tellermine on top. Shells were falling all around us; a craft on our left received a direct hit and started to settle but on we went ... On the third wire we stuck and stayed. The corporal of the Marines thought we had hit the beach so he dropped the ramp and away I went with two of my men right behind me before we realized we were hooked on the wire. The three of us had gone right over our heads in water but we bobbed right up. I gave a yell to pull up the ramp and gun her while we got out of the way. The LCA broke loose and followed us and touched down and my men poured out. Bullets, shrapnel and what have you was flying around like a swarm of angry bees. Pte Woodhead was the first hit in our pl, stopping one in the arm. He was the one who the night before had said, "If you will lead I will follow you anywhere." Blood was flowing and bodies of other pls from A and B Companies were floating face down in the water here and there. Things were moving so fast that one had hardly time to think or be scared. Our main thought was to get the hell off the beach. While the rest of the pl made for dry land I grabbed Woodhead and his PIAT bombs and literally dragged him ashore. While doing so he was hit for the second time. Private Herbert simply disappeared – we never saw him again ... We were on the beach and soon organized and on the move. 15 Platoon was the first in the Coy to get moving as a unit and with the least casualties ... two killed and two wounded, the lightest in the battalion, I believe. We felt very lucky indeed. My men were just grand all the way, even finding time to joke now and then.

In the afternoon, after working our way inland, our Coy came upon an unknown enemy position and 15 Platoon got the job of clearing it up. Later on, 14 (McGregor) and 15 Platoons took on the Coy's main objective. All went well at first. Mac with 14 Platoon was on the left while we in 15 advanced on the right. Mac struck first and flushed five prisoners, which kind of cheered us up. We pushed on to cleared ground until we came in sight of the Coy's second main objective where we halted, then decided to turn to the left and help Mac and 14 Platoon. They had hit the enemy stronghold square on. It was a very large pill box, well concealed and well fortified. Mac had gone up to the entrance and called on them to surrender. They didn't give him a chance, but cut him down with a burst of gun fire hitting him in the chest and stomach. When we arrived his sergeant was in charge of the Platoon with Mac lying out in front of the pill box. The sergeant couldn't get near him nor blast the entrance with their PIAT for fear of hitting Mac. I took over this Platoon along with my own and surrounded the position. Later on I got close to Mac but couldn't get him away. Left a rear guard and reported back to Coy Headquarters. There I found that 13 Platoon with some Coy HQ had joined D Coy for the next objective and orders had been left for us to give covering fire from where I had left the rear guard. Promptly returned and again surrounded the pill box and covered the next objective at the same time. Went to see Mac again to see what I could do. Mac was dead.

Robertson covered him with his gas cape and, thrusting McGregor's bayonetted rifle into the ground, hung his helmet on the butt to mark the spot where the first CANLOAN officer had been killed in action.

Lieutenant Dickson, the British commander of 13 Platoon, was killed a few minutes later. Robertson concluded his D-Day account: "At 0200 hours on the morning of the 7th, after digging slit trenches and posting sentries we dropped into the trenches and slept. All objectives for us had been taken and the arduous training the Battalion had undertaken had proved its worth. So ended D-Day. At 0500 hours our second day began."[3]

Other CANLOAN officers landed on D-Day with regiments in the 3rd British Division. Two were in B Company, 1 R. Norfolk. CDN/45, Lieut. Robert Vezina commanded 11 Platoon and was wounded. 12 Platoon was commanded by CDN/171, Lieut. John A. Laurie, who won an MC before he was killed in action.

Despite the massive bombing and naval gunfire, only about 15 percent of the German coastal bunkers were knocked out and the rest had to be taken by infantry. Many landing craft were blown up on the mined beach obstacles, and where a beach was covered by German machine-gun fire, casualties were usually heavy. Reports by the commandos, who accompanied 2 E. Yorks., that they found E. Yorks.' bodies "stacked like cordwood on Sword Beach"[4] are somewhat exaggerated, but not all the platoons were as fortunate as Len Robertson's 15 Platoon. The battalion suffered approximately 200 casualties, mostly on the beach – five officers and 60 other ranks killed, four officers and 137 other ranks wounded. The other battalions in the brigade, the 1st Battalion, the South Lancashire Regiment (S. Lan. R.), and the 1st Battalion, the Suffolk Regiment (Suffolk R.), had somewhat fewer casualties, most of them later in attacks on strong points inland. By 0830 hours the 8th Brigade had cleared the beach, and during the day it made good progress inland, taking the strong points that were their objectives. 185 Brigade assembled for the critical advance to seize Caen, but the beaches were so crowded that it was late afternoon before the tanks that were to transport the 2 KSLI were able to get clear. It was late evening when the spearhead, within three miles of Caen, met the counter-attacking 21st Panzer Division and could get no farther. Two brigades (8 and 185) were ordered to dig in along the Perriers Ridge to meet 21 Panzer Division counter-attacks, and 9 Brigade was moved to the right to cover the gap between the 3rd British and 3rd Canadian Divisions. A few tanks of 21 Panzer Division attacked north in this gap during the evening; some reached the beach but were destroyed there. Even so, the assault on Sword Beach was considered a great success.

On Gold Beach the 50th (Northumbrian) Division had similar success. The 1 R. Hamps. and 1 Dorsets landed in the face of fire from German bunkers that had emerged unscathed from the bombardment. It took the R. Hamps. eight hours to knock out the le Hamel defences, and they suffered casualties of nearly 200, chiefly from machine-gun and mortar fire, before they were clear of the beaches. On the other hand the 1st Dorsets were off the beach in 40 minutes, and the 6th Battalion, the Green Howards, moved inland and captured their first objective within an hour. By the end of the day 50 Division had advanced inland against 352 German Division, reached Bayeux, eight miles from the coast, and firmly established a solid bridgehead. Actually Bayeux was captured the next day by an independent brigade, the 56th, which accompanied the 50th Division on D-Day and later became part of the 49th Division. The three battalions in the brigade, 2 SWB, 2 Gloster., and 2 Essex, eventually included approximately 20 CANLOAN officers, of whom five were in the D-Day landings. They are an example of how CANLOAN officers were sometimes able to stick together. They were part of a group of volunteers from A-14 Aldershot, Nova Scotia, where they had been instructors together. At Sussex they had been in the same barracks and training companies, and in the fifth CANLOAN flight they had shared accommodation on the *Empress of Scotland*. At the allocation to British units they had been assigned to the 56th Brigade: CDN/410, Capt. Ernest E. Cockburn and CDN/413, Lieut. Frederick H. Hatfield to 2 SWB; and CDN/408, Lieut. Glendon D. Bradshaw, CDN/416, Capt. Bernard Hudson, and Lieut. John Levine to 2 Glosters.

Though the D-Day casualties had been heavy, they were lighter than had been feared, and a substantial bridgehead had been established with its different sections joined up and reaching a depth of up to eight miles. It was the end of the beginning. Now the enemy's armoured counter-attacks must be dealt with. Only then could the breakout come and the drive that would knock Germany out of the war. In the euphoria of 6 June it could not be foreseen that it would be more than a month before the last of the D-Day objectives would be reached or that the battle for Normandy would be such a long, bitter, and bloody struggle, lasting two and a half months and at the cost of more than 200,000 Allied casualties. The majority of CANLOAN officers took part in this struggle; those who had not landed in Normandy on D-Day came with the follow-up divisions or RHUs. They were completely integrated into their adopted British battalions and rarely met any other CANLOAN officer. As platoon commanders their horizons were limited, usually to the men in their three sections and platoon headquarters and to the few hundred yards of ground that it was their responsibility to defend or attack or patrol.

For several days after the D-Day landings the British Army persisted in frontal attacks towards Caen, but the initial momentum had been lost and effective counter-attacks by panzer divisions prevented any significant gains. The 21st Panzer Division, which had been in Caen, had stopped the advance of the 3rd Division on D-Day; it continued to inflict heavy casualties on 7 and 8 June, when attacks such as that of the 2nd Battalion, the Royal Warwickshire Regiment (R. Warwick.), on Lebisey Wood were attempted. When the carrier platoon of 1 KSLI in the 8th Brigade attempted to push on to Caen on the evening of D-Day, all its carriers were knocked out as it approached Lebisey. Exactly one month later the carriers, with 1 KSLI bodies in them, were found in the final attack on Caen. One of the 3rd Division casualties at this time was CDN/52, Lieut. Allister Young, who had landed as a platoon commander with the 1st KOSB and was wounded on 9 June. Later he was awarded a rare decoration, the United States Silver Star. The citation noted that "he led his pl with courage and efficiency until being wounded during the attack on Cambes Wood" and "as a patrol leader he has shown himself to be quite fearless."[5] He recovered from his wound and rejoined his unit in late July. His experiences were typical of those of many CANLOAN officers in these first contacts with the enemy.

The 3rd Canadian Division became engaged in bitter fighting with the 12th SS Panzer Division (Hitler Jugend), which reached Caen on 7 June and prevented the Canadians from reaching Carpiquet. It was one of the most effective German formations during the Normandy campaign until it was almost exterminated near the end. Most CANLOAN officers who were in Normandy will remember this division as formidable and fanatical enemies. A third panzer division, the Panzer Lehr, reached the area of Villers-Bocage near the British-American boundary on 9 June. By that time a temporary stalemate had been reached on the Caen front and the first phase of the Normandy battle had ended. The next phase was to begin with a strong pincer attack intended to encircle Caen with left and right hooks from the flanks of the bridgehead.

Between the afternoon of D-Day and D plus two, the first of the follow-up divisions landed in Normandy. They were veteran divisions of the Eighth Army in North Africa and Italy, the 51st Highland Division and the 7th Armoured Division (the Desert Rats). Both divisions were famous for their fighting qualities, and in committing them to the battle for Caen Montgomery was going with his "first team." The plan was for the 51st Division to break out of the airborne bridgehead east of the Orne and attack towards Cagny, southeast of Caen. The 7th Armoured Division was to attack through the 50th Division on the west flank of the bridgehead to Tilly and Villers-Bocage and push across the Odon south west of Caen. Originally the 1st Airborne Division was to land south of Caen and link up with the 51st and 7th Armoured Divisions, but the drop was cancelled between the plan of 9 June and the attack two days later.

On 11 June the 51st Highland Division's attack east of the Orne was crushed within hours. The 5th BW alone had 200 casualties during the day. Counter-attacks by General Feuchtinger's 21st Panzer Division continued until 16 June, and the Highland Division did well to hold its ground against determined armoured and infantry attacks and heavy bombardment. The division remained on the defensive in the Bois de Bavent adjacent to the 6th Airborne Division for more than a month. This prolonged defensive role, with the troops dug in in a forest under constant shelling, was an unpleasant experience for the Highland Division, of whom it was said that "every nerve and fibre called out for offensive action." The morale of the division reached a very low ebb. CDN/29, Lieut. John McBride, a platoon commander in 7 BW, has reported a conversation with one of his "browned-off" Jocks who said he wanted to go "hame":

> I pointed to the German line and said, "Laddie, that's the only road hame." "It's aricht for you to say that, Surr-rr," he said. "Ye're a Canadian and ye like this sort of thing." I asked him where he got that idea. "From the Sergeant-Major, Sur-rr," he answered. "He says ye're a lot o' mad deevils." I told him that we weren't all "mad deevils," that some of us were quite civilized. "Well Sur-rr, ye volunteered, did ye no?" he replied, and that's where the matter ended.[6]

This incident illustrates the common view that Canadian officers were particularly adventurous and well versed in field-craft. In fact, there was a disproportionately high use of CANLOAN officers for patrolling, beginning with the landing of the 3rd and 50th Divisions on D-Day. Sometimes the only time CANLOAN officers met each other was during patrols for their battalions.

On 12 June the 7th Armoured Division launched its attack to encircle Caen from the west. Its infantry brigade consisted of the 1/5, 1/6, and 1/7th Queens, in which more than 30 CANLOAN officers served during the northwest European campaign. At first the armoured attack went well and drove south for several miles through Tilly and into Villers-Bocage. There it ran into an ambush and a counter-attack by Panzer Lehr. The County of London Yeomanry suffered losses of 25 tanks, 28 armoured vehicles, and many men. One CANLOAN officer was at the spearhead of the Desert Rats' advance. CDN/36, Lieut. Peter Pearce, 1/6 Queens, recalls:

> I was told to take my pl forward to a feature called Amaye sur Seulles. I blundered with the pl about half a mile ahead of the rest of the bn to this hilltop where we were joined by tanks of the County of London Yeomanry. We sat there in the afternoon enjoying the sunshine until the Germans counter attacked and really pulverized us and the accompanying tanks.[7]

CDN/3, Capt. Eric Hall of 1/5 Queens reported that his company was reduced to 13 men and one other officer besides himself in the next few days. The division was forced to withdraw.

Supporting attacks in the area by infantry divisions of XXX Corps had no more success. An attack on Cristot by 6 Green Howards on 11 June was met by the 12th SS Panzer Division and driven back in a counter-attack with the loss of 24 officers and a total of 250 casualties. Heavy casualties were suffered as well by other units in the 49th and 50th Divisions west of Caen. On 12 June 2 SWB lost the two CANLOAN officers who had landed with them on D-Day when Capt. Ernest Cockburn was killed and Lieut. Fred Hatfield was wounded. Two days later CDN/182, Lieut. Joseph A.C.A Noiseux was killed in the first attack by the Hallams., the York and Lancaster Regiment (Y. & L.).

After the failure of the pincer attacks on Caen, bitter fighting continued throughout the Normandy bridgehead, but there was a period of nearly two weeks before the next major offensive. Both British and German Armies were bringing in reserves and were fairly equal, at least in the number of divisions. The overwhelming Allied air superiority, their distinct superiority in weight of artillery as well as in numbers of tanks, and the support of naval bombardment seemed to have little effect on the stubborn resistance of the more experienced Germans and their ability to inflict heavy casualties.

The eastern flank of the Normandy bridgehead across the Orne River and the Caen Canal in the so-called airborne bridgehead consisted chiefly of flat ground overlooked by the thickly wooded ridge topped by the Bois de Bavent. From their slit trenches the Highland Division had only limited vision, and being under observation from higher ground west of the Orne and from observation posts in the factory chimneys of Colombelles near Caen, they were subjected to accurate mortar fire. The country between the coast and Caen was level farmland, dotted with tree-lined villages and stone farm buildings, all under observation from the height north of Caen and the Carpiquet airport. The most serious obstacle to attackers, though, was the *bocage* country west of Caen and south of Bayeux. Here small fields were enclosed by thickly banked hedgerows, woven with roots grown for over a thousand years, which were impenetrable to tanks and were adjoined by sunken roads below the level of surrounding fields. These provided a natural line of fortifications, ideal for defence and most difficult to attack. In addition, the trees in orchards and forest were a haven for snipers, and the stone farm buildings were miniature forts.

West of Caen the *bocage* was mixed with wheat fields, where the average range of vision was 100 yards, or rolling chalk uplands. These open spaces were covered by machine guns in well-prepared defensive positions and were under observation from higher ground south and west of Caen. There was ideal cover for Panther and Tiger tanks on the fringe of clearings or hull down on reverse slopes. When to the normal three-to-one advantage of defence over offence was added the natural defensive features that favoured the Germans, the resulting close fighting produced many Allied casualties.

Another advantage for the German defenders was a superiority in certain weapons. This was most apparent in the case of tanks. The German Panthers and Tigers, with their heavier armour and longer-range guns, could knock out the Allied Shermans, Churchills, and Cromwells before the latter got within their effective range. As previously noted, the breakthrough of the 7th Armoured Division at Villiers-Bocage on 12 June was blocked when the single Tiger of Hauptman Michael Wittman knocked out 25 Cromwell tanks and other armoured vehicles of the County of London Yeomanry in a few minutes. It was said in British armoured divisions that if you wanted to get a Tiger you should send four Shermans or four Churchills, and be prepared to lose three of them.

The 88-mm has been called the best gun produced by any combatant nation in the war. Its long barrel was a dramatic feature of the Tiger tank, and it had a formidable killing power against all Allied tanks. As a wheeled field gun it was used in an anti-tank role; time after time a screen of them stopped Allied armoured attacks dead. Originally an anti-aircraft gun, it could also be used with air bursts as a formidable weapon against infantry, as fragments still in the hide of the author can attest.

A weapon used most effectively and in great numbers by the Germans, and the one most feared by the infantry, since it caused up to 75 percent of their casualties, was the mortar. A similar weapon was the Nebelwerfer, a six-barrelled rocket projector. Its bombs were fitted with a siren that caused them to emit a wail which earned them the nickname "moaning Minnie." A mortar "stonk" could place hundreds of bombs in a company area, testing severely the endurance and sanity of those who were plastered to the bottoms of their slit trenches. It was usually followed by calls for stretcher bearers.

The German infantry anti-tank weapon, the panzerfaust, was superior in some respects to the British PIAT and the American bazooka and, though most British and Canadian troops were fond of the Bren light machine gun, which constituted most of a section's fire power, its rate of fire was only 500 rounds a minute compared to the demoralizing 1,200 rounds a minute of the German MG 34 and MG 42, collectively known as spandaus. The German schmeisser (submachine gun, MP 38) was far superior to the British Sten, "the plumber's nightmare." Even the German "potato masher" hand grenade was easier to throw than the British 36, the familiar Mills bomb of the First World War, although it was not as effective as the Mills bomb. Enemies of the Germans were tempted to use their small arms, such as schmeissers, Lugers, and P-38 pistols instead of the Stens and six-shooter pistols they had been issued. CANLOAN officers seem to have been particularly prone to such borrowing, for many of them are remembered by their troops and fellow officers for their use of German weapons, flashlights, and even boots and other articles of clothing.

The chief asset of the German Army in Normandy, however, was the quality of its fighting troops. The German fighting soldier has been called "courageous, tenacious, skilful, a formidable fighting man." Leaders of the British, American, and Canadian Armies have agreed that their troops were not equal to the battle-experienced German troops in Normandy. The elite troops were the panzer divisions, of which there were eventually 10 in Normandy, all except one on the narrow front of the 2nd British Army. Five of them were SS Panzer Divisions, which were regarded as "the most fanatical and effective battlefield forces of the Second World War." An example is the 12th SS (Hitler Jugend) Division. It was formed in 1943 from cadres furnished by the 1st SS Panzer Division. It had not fought before D-Day, but it contained a high proportion of battle-experienced officers and NCOs who had distinguished themselves on the Russian front. A photograph in the history of the British 43rd Division shows a group of prisoners from the 12th SS Panzer Division, each of whom had won the Iron Cross on the Russian front and had been wounded three times. The rank and file were chiefly youngsters from the military fitness camps of the Hitler Youth, full of Nazi ideology. In the words of the official historian of the Canadian Army, "The division was to show in action the characteristics which its composition might lead one to expect, reckless courage and determination combined with a degree of barbarity found, perhaps, in no other formation."[8] A British divisional historian wrote, "The young SS troops were detestable young beasts but like good infantry they stood and fought it out when overrun."[9] These troops carried on with 50 percent or even 75 percent casualties.

The calibre and experienced leadership of the German troops in Normandy was reflected in their tactics. They were effective in counter-attacks, which came instantly when a position had been lost. They showed a remarkable flexibility in attack, infiltrating boldly into and between Allied positions. Their co-operation between infantry and tanks, their teamwork between the tanks, and their "little brothers," the infantry, were better than the Allies were ever able to achieve. They were notable for disciplined fire control; in defence they usually waited until the attackers were only a few yards away and then cut them down with concentrated machine-gun fire, as they did the 10th Battalion, the Highland Light Infantry (HLI), south of Cheux on 26 June and many other units on other occasions. Sometimes they allowed patrols to probe their positions without betraying their presence, as in the case of Carpiquet airport before a Canadian attack. Their snipers were numerous, fearless, and accurate, concentrating particularly on picking off officers. The Germans were not supermen and they were defeated eventually, but they were a formidable enemy. There is no doubt that important elements in the Normandy campaign were the weight of airpower, the superiority in firepower, and the number of tanks, but it was essentially an infantryman's fight. Ultimately the battles were fought and won and the issue decided by tired, vulnerable, determined infantrymen in an adverse countryside against an implacable and experienced foe.

After the failure of the Villers-Bocage attack, Montgomery decided to launch a more powerful right hook nearer Caen, using an entire corps of three divisions to attack on a narrow front between Carpiquet and Rauray, to cross the Odon, and to exploit to the Orne south of Caen. Operation EPSOM was to be carried out by VIII Corps, consisting of divisions that were untried in battle but on the basis of their training record, morale, and leadership were considered three of the best divisions in the British Army: the 15th (Scottish) Division, the 43rd (Wessex) Division, and the 11th Armoured Division. The operation was intended to be launched on 22 June but had to be delayed because one of the assaulting divisions, the 43rd, which was embarking in London that day, was held up for several more days by a storm that has been called "the most famous gale since the Armada."[10] The storm wrecked as many as 800 ships, stopped all unloading over the beaches, and destroyed part of the floating harbour, Mulberry. The operation was eventually able to begin on 26 June. As a preliminary, the 49th "Polar Bear" Division in XXX Corps was to secure the right flank by capturing the high ground at Fontenay and Rauray. The attack of the 49th Division, led by the Hallams., 11 RS, and 1 R. Lincolns., began at 0415 hours on 25 June. They succeeded in taking Fontenay, but a counter-attack by the 12th SS Panzer Division prevented them from reaching Rauray. Thus the right flank of the Scottish Corridor was left open to observation and counter-attack.

Operation EPSOM, later known as the Battle of the Scottish Corridor or, in regimental battle honours, "the Odon," began early in the morning of 26 June. It was a powerful offensive by 60,000 men and 600 tanks supported by 700 guns, those of VIII Corps and neighbouring corps on the right and left, plus naval bombardment. A planned 250-bomber air raid was cancelled because of poor visibility, rain, and cloud. The opening barrage, which seemed devastating, was cheering to the Scottish troops in their first battle. They were piped to the start line and headed south, following the barrage. With the massive weight of manpower and firepower it was difficult to realize that the real attack was by the thin line of troops moving forward with five-yard intervals between men in the leading infantry sections. With the standard formation of a division in the attack being two brigades up and one in reserve, each brigade with two battalions up and each battalion with two companies up, the leading wave in an attack by 60,000 men in the three-division corps group consisted of no more than 500 men and 20 officers.

The 44th Brigade on the left, comprising 8 RS, 6 RSF, and 6 KOSB, was to capture the village of Saint Mauvieu on the first line of the German defences. The objective of the 46th Brigade on the right, which consisted of 9 Cameronians, 2 Glas. H. and 7 Seaforth, was the village of Cheux on the second defensive line. The 227th Brigade – 10 HLI, 2 Gordons and 2 A. & S.H. – was to cross the Odon and form a bridgehead from which the 11th Armoured Division would charge forward to the Orne.

In the first hours the 15th Scottish Division penetrated more than five miles on a three-mile front, occupying the ruins of Saint Mauvieu and then Cheux. "But then," wrote an historian of the Normandy campaign, "from out of the hedges and hamlets fierce German resistance developed. Some of the great Scottish regiments of the British Army – Gordons, Seaforths, Cameronians – began to pour out their best blood for every yard gained."[11] The attack stopped south of Cheux; it had been reached by dark, but counter-attacks from the west engaged 10 HLI in bloody conflict and pinned them down through the 27th. That day 2 Gordons reached Colleville, and 2 A. & S.H., ignoring the enemy on both flanks and rear, drove to the Odon and crossed. The 11th Armoured Division followed and occupied Hill 112 for the first, but far from the last, time.

Fierce fighting continued throughout the corridor on 28 and 29 June and no fewer than four fresh panzer divisions – the 1st, 2nd, 9th, and 10th – were identified as the Germans brought in all available reserves to stop the Allied drive. Their counter-attacks were beaten off, but on 29 June Montgomery, deciding that the narrow corridor was too vulnerable against such powerful opposition, closed down EPSOM and ordered the withdrawal of the 11th Division across the Odon. The 15th Division was relieved by the newly arrived 53rd Welch Division, and the 129th Brigade of the 43rd Division took over the tiny bridgehead across the Odon.

Troops of VIII Corps had lived up to their reputation and had fought well against the best German troops. They had driven a spearhead two miles wide and six miles deep into enemy territory and had held their ground against seven panzer divisions. But the operation was only half successful and the cost was alarming. VIII Corps lost more than 4,000 men, 2,500 from the 15th Scottish Division: in five days this division had one-quarter of the total casualties the division suffered in more than 300 days of the northwest European campaign. At the level of the rifle company such losses were devastating. The 2 Glas. H., for example, lost 12 officers and had a total of 200 casualties in the battle for Cheux on 26 June. This was a loss of 34 percent of the officers and 25 percent of the total strength of the battalion in a single day.

The CANLOAN officers who took part in EPSOM exceeded by a considerable number those who landed on D-Day. They were still few in proportion to the officers in their battalions, perhaps an average of 2 or 3 out of a complement of 37, but the effect of their activities in action was out of proportion to their numbers. For example, 7 Seaforth in the 15th Scottish Division landed in Normandy with two CANLOAN officers, CDN/18, Lieut. Charles B. Ewart and CDN/26, Lieut. Roderick C. Keary. In the attack on the morning of 26 June that launched EPSOM, Keary was wounded and Ewart's exploits earned him the first of many CANLOAN Military Crosses. His citation reads:

> At 1000 hours on Monday, 26 Jun, D coy was ordered to clear a wood at (map reference) 910686. The wood contained some 40 enemy, not a few snipers as expected. Owing to the exceptional dash and courage displayed by Lieutenant Ewart the wood was successfully cleared despite stiff opposition at close range. The whole action was performed under heavy fire.[12]

The 2 Glas. H. in the same brigade also had two CANLOAN officers for EPSOM, CDN/117, Captain Alexander M. Millar and CDN/42, Lieutenant Allan F. Smith. Both served with distinction in this and subsequent battles and were soon promoted to company commanders. Millar was wounded (with five other CANLOAN officers in 2 Glas. H.) on 30 September, but Smith commanded a company, and, at times in an acting capacity, the battalion, throughout the campaign in northwest Europe. He was eventually awarded a Croix de Guerre with Vermilion Star. The citation referred to his outstanding leadership, the earmark of a good officer: "He has proved himself to be a fearless and well-loved leader in whom his men have the utmost faith. At no time has he ever spared himself and in every operation can always be found where he can best influence the battle by his cool and inspiring leadership."[13]

CANLOAN officers were involved in the attack of the 49th Division on Fontenay and Rauray in support of EPSOM. One of them, CDN/165, Lieut. William A. James with B Company, 11 DLI, earned an MC in his first attack:

> On 28 Jun 44 at RAURAY Lieut James was commanding a leading platoon in the attack. Shortly after leaving the start line he was wounded in the head. He carried on and led his platoon, which had suffered many casualties, on to the objective. Later he was wounded again but did not go back to the RAP until his platoon was reorganized. He returned immediately he had had his wounds dressed and held the position against counter-attack. He displayed very fine leadership throughout the whole action.[14]

CANLOAN officers were also prominent among the casualties. On 26 June, the opening day of EPSOM, two CANLOAN officers in 9 Cameronians were killed in action: CDN/221, Lieut. George A. McDermott, MM, and CDN/37, Lieut. Lorne H. Paff. McDermott had served in the Royal Hamilton Light Infantry at Dieppe and had been awarded a Military Medal before returning to Canada for a commission in 1943. On 29 June no fewer than five CANLOAN officers in the 15th Scottish Division were killed in action, two of them as platoon commanders in the 10th HLI and the other three as platoon commanders in 8 RS. CDN/25, Lieut. Albert R. Harding and CDN/154, Lieut. David G. Hilborn had been among those who had been able to join affiliated regiments in England. In fact Hilborn had served overseas with the Canadian Highland Light Infantry from 1941 to 1943. The three CANLOAN officers who were killed on 29 June with 8 RS were CDN/129, Lieut. John Blackham, CDN/307, Lieut. Howard McAllister, and CDN/108, Lieut. Richard O. Young. Richard Young had joined CANLOAN and had been posted to the 8th RS with his younger brother Peter. As their father was dead, Richard was considered the head of the family. Their mother in Montreal was relieved that her sons would be serving together and assumed that Richard would look after his young brother. Both were killed in Normandy, Richard falling three weeks before Peter.

Another CANLOAN officer who was a fatal casualty with the 15th Scottish Division on the first day of EPSOM was CDN/105, Lieut. Dudley H. Wood, a platoon commander in 6 RSF. Four days earlier, on 22 June, this battalion had lost its first CANLOAN officer when CDN/130, Lieut. John E. Bowman was killed in action.

Casualties were suffered also by the three infantry battalions in 11th Armoured Division, 4 KSLI, 3 Mons., and the 1st Battalion, the Hereford Light Infantry (Hereford LI). The 11th Armoured Division was to have followed the 15th Scottish Division across the Odon and broken through to the Orne. In 3 Mons. were six CANLOAN officers, two of them, CDN/334, Lieut. C. Clifton Cassady and CDN/144, Lieut. James E. Davies, in C Company. This company was dropped off near Colleville about 0100 hours on 28 June with the intention of continuing to the Odon in daylight. Instead, dawn brought a panzer counter-attack in which the company was surrounded, and although they fought valiantly, the situation was hopeless. The company commander decided to fight his way out with the few unwounded troops. Only he and 14 men succeeded. Twenty-one were killed and the rest, including Cassady and Davies, were wounded and captured. It was their first and last battle, and their company ceased to exist.

The Odon was crossed on 28 June by 4 KSLI. This battalion helped to establish a bridgehead and held off the attacks by the panzer divisions. Among its casualties were two CANLOAN officers, CDN/336, Lieut. Pierre Duclos, who was killed in action, and Lieut. Alex Cunningham, who was wounded.

Casualties were also heavy in the 49th Division's sector at Rauray and Tessel Wood; 11 DLI, for example, lost all four of their CANLOAN officers within four days. They had all joined the battalion in England: CDN/62, Lieut. Charles T. Baker, CDN/146, Lieut. Elmer Fitzpatrick, CDN/165, Lieut. William A. James, and CDN/199, Lieut. Richard P.H. Sprague. One was assigned to each of the rifle companies. On landing in Normandy the 49th Division was to take over positions in the Tilly-Cristot area. The first major objective of 11 DLI was the village of Rauray. The first officer in the battalion to be killed in action was C Company's CANLOAN officer, Charles Baker, when he was on a night patrol on 25 June. On 28 June Elmer Fitzpatrick was sent, with a sergeant and a private, to patrol well into enemy territory east of Rauray. On their return they encountered an enemy position; the sergeant was killed and Fitzpatrick was wounded; he was picked up by the nearest Allied troops, the Tyneside Scottish (Tyne. Scot.). In a battalion attack the same day Sprague was wounded and James, who was wounded earlier and won an MC, later died of his wounds.

Another battalion of the DLI, the 8th, in 50 Division, also lost its CANLOAN officers but over a longer period of time. After landing on D-Day, it had heavy officer casualties near Tilly and on 22 June received four CANLOAN officers as reinforcements: CDN/392, Lieut. Francis E. Stewart, CDN/425, Lieut. George H. Luffman, CDN/426, Lieut. Harry Niznick, and CDN/419, Lieut. Carson E. Morrison. Stewart, who was ill, had to be evacuated; Luffman was killed by a mine while on patrol on 1 August; Morrison was wounded in an attack early in August after a spectacular performance as platoon and company commander; and Niznick, the last CANLOAN officer in the battalion, was killed in an attack at the Albert Canal on 9 September. A former company commander writes: "To the best of my knowledge we did not receive any further CANLOAN reinforcements, which was a pity because in our opinion the scheme had been very successful, producing very good officers."[15]

Whereas the "right hook" of Operation EPSOM was the main effort of the Second British Army in the 1st week in July, the divisions that had been on the defensive north of Caen since D-Day – the 3rd British, the 3rd Canadian, and the 51st Highland Divisions – were to make local advances as opportunity offered to keep heavy pressure on this flank. One of the resulting engagements concerned the 3rd British Division and the grounds of the Château de la Londe, which have been called "the bloodiest square mile in the whole of Normandy," although there are other candidates for that designation. On the night of 22 June the château was occupied in a silent attack by the 1st S. Lan. R. Just before dawn heavy enemy artillery and mortar fire was followed by a counter-attack by the troops of 21 Panzer

Division, which had lost the château together with more than 30 tanks and troops of the 22nd Panzer Regiment. One company of 1 S. Lan. R. was overrun, and the rest of the battalion, after holding the position all day, withdrew. On 27 June the S. Lan. R. returned to the assault and got into the château, were forced out again, but held the wood. It required a brigade attack to take the château on 28 June. It is described briefly in a history of the 3rd Division:

> The brigade attack by the East Yorkshire and Suffolk went in at dawn on 28 Jun. The determination of the assault is recalled by Major John Waring, commander, 454 Field Battery. The spirited attack on the Chateau started from a wooded area and continued over mainly open country covered in some two to three feet of growing corn in which many British infantrymen lay dead and wounded. As the advance reached the area of the Chateau the ground became rougher, there being ditches, hedge-rows and walls. It was here they met their stiffest resistance: all gaps in fences, hedge-rows and every conceivable place was booby trapped and mined and every yard of ground had to be fought for. Many men lost their lives or limbs pushing through hedges or climbing over ditches. The fighting inside the Chateau ground was bloody and confused. The Suffolk alone lost a total of 163 killed, wounded and missing on 28 Jun.[16]

Among the fatal casualties of 1 S. Lanc. R. were two CANLOAN officers, CDN/ 264, Lieut. David E. Edwards and CDN/401, Lieut. Harry F. Hughes. Hughes had been posted to 1 S. Lanc. R. in England and had landed with the battalion on D-Day. Edwards, too, had landed on D-Day with 50 RHU and had been posted to the 1st South Lancashires just two weeks before his death.

The Château de la Londe brought two more MCs for CANLOAN officers, James Fetterly and Leonard Robertson, both in 2 E. Yorks. The citations indicate the nature of company attacks, especially against enemy tanks. In the regimental history Lieutenant-Colonel Dickson is quoted as an eye witness to James R. Fetterly's exploits: "I watched this officer several times during the battle. He was quite fearless and previous to killing the German tank commander had already captured a machine gun post single-handed."[17]

On 4 July the 3rd Canadian Division attacked Carpiquet airport but were not successful in taking it, and the 5th Battalion, the Duke of Cornwall's Light Infantry (DCLI) of the 43rd Division in the Odon bridgehead, were exposed to view and fire from the airport and were obliged to withdraw across the river.

Montgomery decided to capture Caen in a frontal attack by three infantry divisions after a massive air raid. In a memorable attack by more than 450 heavy bombers on the evening of 7 July, 2,000 tons of bombs were dropped on Caen, reducing parts of the ancient city to rubble but inflicting little damage on German troops and their positions. It gave, however, a boost to the morale of the troops in the Normandy bridgehead who watched as wave after wave of bombers proceeded relentlessly to their target. They rose from their slit trenches to cheer.

In operation CHARNWOOD the 3rd British Division attacked on the left, the 3rd Canadian Division on the right, and in the centre the 59th Division, which had recently arrived and was in its first battle. In the two-day attack, on 8 and 9 July, the northern half of Caen to the Orne was occupied, but the cost was heavy – nearly 25 percent of the participating infantry. Among the attacking troops the 6th Battalion, the North Staffordshire Regiment (N. Staffs.), had particularly heavy casualties, including all the CANLOAN officers who had been posted to the battalion in England. CDN/87, Lieut. Brian Lynn died of wounds, CDN/363, Lieut. Raymond Thomson was killed in the attack on the battalion's objective, the village of La Bijude, and the third, Lieut. Arthur Stone, was wounded. Altogether in the two-day attack on Caen no fewer than six CANLOAN officers in the 59th Division were killed in action and many more wounded, almost equalling the casualties of the battle of the Scottish corridor. In addition to Lieuts. Brian Lynn and Raymond Thomson, they were CDN/112, Capt. Joseph A.R. Bourget, and CDN/197, Lieut. Thomas A.M. Smith, both of the 2/6 S. Staffords., CDN/44, Lieut. Henry G. Sheely of the 1/7 R. Warwick., and CDN/391, Lieut. Donald J. Smith of the 7 R. Norfolk.

It was Lieutenant Sheely about whom Hubert Campbell's father wrote to General McNaughton later, citing him as an example of the eagerness of CANLOAN officers to get into action. Captain Bourget was one of the more senior CANLOAN officers, having been a captain since May 1942 and having taken the field officers' course at the Royal Military College early in 1943. Both Donald Smith and Thomas Smith had married since their arrival in England. The courtship of Thomas Smith and a Red Cross nurse was one of the romances for which the SS *Cavina* was famous. The couple lost no time. The *Cavina* docked in Scotland on 23 April and they were married on 4 May. Donald Smith was married a month later, only days before embarking for Normandy. Both bridegrooms were killed in their first action.

During CHARNWOOD, the attack on Caen on 8 and 9 July, the 59th Division was in its first attack, whereas the 3rd British Division had been fighting continually in the area since D-Day. During the month the 3rd Division had sustained a seventh of all the British and Canadian casualties in the bridgehead. It had carried out a continuous series of attacks and patrols against the most solidly dug-in tanks, MGs, and troops of the 21st Panzer Division. Two CANLOAN officers in the 3rd British Division were killed in CHARNWOOD: CDN/423, Lieut. Lawrence Cohen, 2 R. Warwick., and CDN/191, Lieut. Leonard J. Richardson, 2 R. Lincs., both on 9 July. Lawrence Cohen had entered the active army from COTC and had qualified in both artillery and infantry before CANLOAN. He had been posted to 2 R. Warwick. on 1 July, just one week before he was killed in action. Leonard Richardson, like Cohen a graduate of the University of Manitoba, had enlisted as a private and worked up to a commission in 1943. From 101 RHU he had been posted to 2 R. Lincolns. on 28 June.

The capture of Caen and Carpiquet at the same time was followed immediately by renewed attacks west of the city in order to capture the high ground between the Odon and the Orne, to encircle Caen from the south, and above all to continue to engage the main German force so it could not block an American breakout to the south. This time the attack was on a broader front with no fewer than six divisions: the 49th and 50th attacked south to Hottot, the 59th attacked south to Noyers, the 15th Scottish was to attack Évrecy, an objective of EPSOM, followed by the 53rd, and in the first attack the 43rd Division was to capture Hill 112 and Maltot on 10 July.

The 43rd Division already held a bridgehead across the Odon, which it had taken over from the 15th Scottish and the 11th Armoured Divisions when EPSOM was terminated on 30 June. Since then it had held the panzer divisions that surrounded it on three sides, though the bridgehead was less than a mile wide, consisting of little more than the banks of the Odon and including Death Valley, so called because of the casualties from mortar bombs that burst in the narrow gorge of the river with its steep slate walls.

Hill 112 was an unimpressive stretch of country covered with wheat two or three feet high, and with a few wooded copses and several villages on its slopes. From this elevation the entire valleys of the Odon and Orne could be seen, and the Germans said, "He who controls Hill 112 controls Normandy." Certainly they clung to it desperately, and when they were driven off counter-attacked at once to regain possession. Between 29 June, when the 9th and 10th SS Panzer Divisions regained the hill, and 23 July, when they were driven from Maltot, the area around Hill 112 changed hands many times and thousands of Allied and German troops were killed or wounded on its bloody slopes. The 43rd Division alone lost more than 2,000 men in the first 36 hours of operation JUPITER to regain Hill 112. It was reported that the Odon River was dammed with corpses.[18]

The attack began before dawn on 10 July with an impressive artillery barrage. By 0630 hours 129 Brigade – 4 and 5 Wilts. and 4 Som. LI – had advanced through the waist-high wheat sprinkled with poppies. They reached their objectives at the crest of the hill, although for several hours fierce close-quarter battles continued in the wheat where SS troops manned concealed machine-gun nests and refused to surrender even when wounded.

The task of 130 Brigade was to capture the villages of Eterville and Maltot, after which 214 Brigade was to exploit with an armoured brigade to the Orne. From a firm base provided by 5 Dorset, 4 Dorset launched a successful attack on Eterville, and at 0815 hours 7 R. Hamps. attacked Maltot, initiating what has been called "a battle of shattering intensity even by the standard of Normandy."[19] SS panzer troops supported by dug-in and concealed Tiger tanks held an almost impregnable position, and even when the R. Hamps. were reinforced by 4 Dorset no progress could be made. Among the many casualties were five company commanders. From Eterville 5 Dorset and 7 Som. LI held off savage counter-attacks, as did 5 Wilts. and 4 Som. LI during the day. By 1500 hours it was clear that a fresh attack on Hill 112 was needed, but of the 214th, the reserve brigade, two battalions had already been committed, leaving only 5 DCLI. The CO was 26-year-old Lieutenant-Colonel James, who had been in command only 14 days, since the former CO had been killed in the first attack at Mouen on 27 June. With 4 Som. LI as a firm base 5 DCLI launched an attack at 2230 hours with two companies up. The crest of the hill was reached and the battalion consolidated in a wood, which was later called Cornwall Wood, in time to meet savage counter-attacks from the 9th SS Panzer Division. In fighting that continued all night, 10 counter-attacks were beaten off, but when Lieutenant-Colonel James was killed and most of the officers and NCOs killed or wounded, the remnants of the battalion withdrew. The CO of 4 Som. LI formed the survivors into two companies and sent them back to the wood for what has been called "the death struggle of 5 DCLI."[20] The final overwhelming attack left about 75 survivors, approximately 10 percent of the original strength of the battalion.

After the battle, all battalions of the 43rd Division required reinforcements, which, in effect, produced new battalions. Within two weeks 5 DCLI was back at full strength and in action on Hill 112, and 4 Som. LI required reinforcements of 19 officers and 479 other ranks. The enemy suffered equally. The next year when there was an opportunity to compare notes with the 9th SS Panzer Division, it was revealed that in the battle for Hill 112 casualties reduced their strength to five or six per company. It is appropriate that the 43rd Division's memorial is at Hill 112, the object of so much bloodshed in the Normandy campaign. On 29 July when Maltot was captured at last by 4 and 5 Wilts., the dead of the Dorset and R. Hamps. who had fallen on 10 July still lay in heaps around partly dug slit trenches and in streets and fields.

In the battle for Hill 112 CANLOAN officers played a prominent role; most were involved in patrols. 7 Som LI reported:

> Reconnaissance by Lieutenants [CDN/328, Walter] Tharp, [CDN/506, Hubert] Jones and [CDN/247, Pierre] Mercier, incidentally all Canadian officers, obtained information of the greatest value ... In one of these, Lieutenant Mercier was seriously wounded, to the great regret of the battalion, who had found in this young Canadian a patrol leader of genius.[21]

The regimental history adds that, when Lieutenant Mercier was wounded, "Private Evers, his escort, shot his assailants and carried his officer back to safety."[22]

For the attack on Hill 112 it was necessary to use two small bridges across the Odon near Verson that were in "no man's land" well outside the Odon bridgehead. Standing patrols sent to hold them against any opposition were commanded by CDN/ 198, Lieut. Wilfred I. Smith, 4 Wilts. carrier platoon. A particularly prominent role in the battle for Hill 112 was played by another CANLOAN officer, CDN/298, Capt. Joseph H.J. Gauthier. In an account written in March 1947 at the request of the Canadian Army Historical Section, Gauthier reported that, having arrived in Normandy with 33 Reinforcement Holding Unit several days before the 43rd Division, he was sent forward with reinforcements for 5 DCLI, which, in its first battle at Mouen, had lost its CO, two company commanders, four platoon commanders, and 60 other ranks. Captain Gauthier reported to Lieutenant-Colonel James with 80 other ranks and three other CANLOAN officers: CDN/279, Lieut. Mathew C.P. Rush, CDN/290, Lieut. Benoît D.J. Comolli, and CDN/300, Lieut. Marcel W. Hardy. Captain Gauthier was appointed OC Support Company, and the other CANLOAN officers were assigned to B, C, and D Companies respectively. Another CANLOAN officer, CDN/10, Lieut. Ralph B. Arthurs, was already in A Company. The next day Lieutenant Rush was killed by a mortar bomb as preparations for the battle for Hill 112 were being made. When 5 DCLI was ordered to attack at 2100 hours on 10 July, Captain Gauthier took the battalion to the concentration area and was with the CO during the attack. When the battalion retired from the wood at 0700 hours on 11 July, Colonel James and two company commanders had been killed and another company commander wounded. Only 150 men were left of the 500 who began the attack. Ordered back to the wood again at 1000 hours, the battalion was overrun by Tiger tanks when its anti-tank guns were knocked out. When the last rifle company commander was wounded, the adjutant informed Captain Gauthier that he was the senior surviving officer. As commander of the remnants of 5 DCLI, he withdrew with 75 men. In a few hours the battalion had suffered 425 casualties, including 20 officers, of whom two were CANLOANs. Lieutenant Arthurs, who was killed during the battle, had enlisted as a sapper in February 1940 and had been sergeant in charge of tunnelling at Gibraltar when he was sent back to Canada for a commission. Lieutenant Comolli had been particularly prominent in the attack. The divisional history reports: "Lieutenant Comolli, a Canadian officer, dashed ahead and pursued the enemy right into the valley beyond, only eventually to be killed with most of his men."[23]

The memory of the CANLOAN officers has not faded. A spokesman for the 5 DCLI Old Comrades' Association observed recently: "Three out of five killed on Hill 112 leading their platoons shows the gallantry they displayed, and the honour with which we remember them."[24]

Another fatal CANLOAN casualty at this time was CDN/506, Lieut. Hubert M. Jones, a platoon commander in 7 Som. LI. He was the son of Lieut.-Col. Hubert Jones, who, as chief training officer and second-in-command at A-34 in Sussex, New Brunswick, was well known to all CANLOAN infantry officers. A CANLOAN officer who was killed on 10 July with 4 Dorset was CDN/412, Lieut. Ronald M. Goddard. He was one of six CANLOAN officers who had come from the COTC contingent at the small Maritime university of Acadia. Lieut. John Levine had been killed on 2 July with the 2nd Glosters. Lieut. Fred Hatfield, CDN/316, Lieut. Archibald Street, and Lieut. Wilfred Smith were all wounded in Normandy, the last at Hill 112 on 10 July, with many other CANLOAN officers, including three from 4 Som. LI and four from 4 Dorset.

The only CANLOAN officers in 7 R. Hamps. were CDN/54, Capt. Frederick A.N. Chesham and CDN/123, Lieut. Harry J. Anaka; they survived the attack at Maltot, the first battle of the battalion, in which casualties were tragically costly: 18 officers and 208 other ranks, including 2 lieutenant-colonels killed and 3 majors, 6 captains, and many lieutenants killed or wounded. On 11 July Chesham was promoted to acting major and Anaka to acting captain.

Of similar ferocity was the battle for Esquay on 11 July. CDN/255, Capt. John W. Druhan, a company commander with 7 Seaforth, recalls, "On 11 Jul three companies, A, B and C, of 104 personnel each, 312 all ranks, went into a noon-day attack ... After one hour we were driven back, leaving 206 dead and wounded. Scott and Nelles were killed in the attack."[25]

Both CDN/310, Lieut. Larry D. Nelles and CDN/314, Lieut. Frederick Scott had served overseas with the Seaforth Highlanders of Canada from 1940 to 1943, before returning to Canada for officer training. Another CANLOAN officer, CDN/549, Captain Anthony de Serres, had also served with the Seaforth Highlanders of Canada. He was in charge of the Mortar Platoon, 7 Seaforths, and received a Croix de Guerre for his "high degree of skill and personal courage" throughout the Normandy campaign. On 11 July, "handling his mortars with great accuracy [he] brought down continuous and most effective fire on the enemy. He himself remained in a forward OP for the whole day under heavy mortar and shell fire."[26]

On the night of 15 July the 15th Scottish Division attacked Esquay and by the next day had consolidated and beaten off savage counter-attacks. In this battle 8 RS lost four CANLOAN officers. Two were wounded: CDN/175, Lieut. James A. Marshall and CDN/361, Lieut. Jackson Stewart. The latter returned to the battalion and was killed in action two months later. The CANLOAN officers who were killed on 16 July were CDN/107, Lieut. Peter B. Young, the younger brother of Richard Young, who had been killed three weeks earlier, and CDN/327, Lieut. Earl H. Harcourt, who had joined the Royal Scots only two days earlier.

On the night of 17 July the 53rd Welch Division, which had relieved first the 15th Scottish and later the 43rd Wessex Division, attacked towards Évrecy but was unsuccessful. Further progress was impossible as long as the enemy continued to hold the reverse slopes of Hill 112, and the 53rd Division did well to resist fierce counter-attacks and hold down three panzer divisions that otherwise might have been moved across the Orne to help block an Allied thrust towards Falaise.

In the attack on Évrecy on 17 July two CANLOAN officers in the 4th Battalion, the Royal Welch Fusiliers (RWF) were killed. They were CDN/205, Lieut. Allen W. Kuhl and CDN/284, Lieut. John R. Purchase. An entry at this time in the war diary of the 6th RWF indicates the intensity of the fighting and the resulting casualties in the 53rd Division: "Heavy casualties. D Coy strength of a platoon in no fit state to go into battle. Remnants of A coy approximately one officer and 10 ORs attached to D for the operation. OC D Coy killed and remnants of D Coy ordered to join Battalion HQ."[27]

Before the action at Évrecy the battalion had undertaken several fighting patrols led by CANLOAN officers. One, on 30 June, was led by CDN/174, Lieut. Harold W. Main. It had been ambushed but had given a good account of itself and was considered quite successful. A raid by D Company on 10 July had suffered casualties, including CDN/141, Lieut. Arthur D. Crighton, who was killed in action. In the attack on 17 July in which the commanding officer had been killed and there were severe officer casualties, the third CANLOAN officer in the battalion, CDN/485, Capt. Robert G. Marsh, had been wounded but rejoined the unit within a week. Both Main and Marsh were killed later in the campaign.

Further reference to the casualties at Évrecy is made in the citation of the Military Cross that was awarded to CDN/283, A./Capt. James M. Suttie of 4 RWF:

On the night of 17 Jul he led his platoon with great dash and vigour and only returned when his platoon had virtually been wiped out and all the officers of the coy had been killed. He did great work in finding and sending back wounded from the battlefield. On 19 Jul this officer took a patrol of two men into the enemy lines to try and contact a Pl of the Bn that was out of comm following the attack.[28]

The 53rd Division at this time lost three more CANLOAN officers. Two were from the 1st E. Lan. F.: CDN/557, Frederick A. Ells and CDN/355, Lieut. Thomas A. Phelps. The third, CDN/373, Capt. Hugh D. McLeod, was a platoon commander in the 1st HLI. He was wounded on 22 July and died four days later. Captain McLeod had gone overseas in 1940 with the Royal Canadian Regiment as a lieutenant. Returning to Canada in 1942 he had been promoted to captain in January 1943 and to major in July 1943. He relinquished the latter rank in order to join CANLOAN.

A final reference to the 53rd Division in mid-July is to a daylight raid by CDN/552,

Lieut. Burton E. Harper, a platoon commander in the 1st Battalion, the East Lancashire Regt. (E. Lan. R.), who was awarded the Croix de Guerre with Silver Star:

> At Bougy on 21 Jul Lieutenant Harper planned and executed a brilliant and most daring raid on an enemy strongpoint. It was strongly held by very active Spandau groups ... Lieut Harper personally led two of his sections in a dash across No Man's Land. The enemy position was penetrated and all the occupants killed or wounded ... The action was a model of daring, efficiency and inspired example by this platoon commander.[29]

Farther west the 59th Division launched its second attack on 16 July. Like its first action at Caen on 8 July, the battle for Noyers resulted in heavy casualties, including the deaths of three CANLOAN officers: Lieut. Justin Karls, 5 E. Lanc. R., CDN/424, Lieut. Peter Jeffries, 1/6 S. Staffords., and CDN/473, Lieut. Howard M. Stevenson, 5 S. Staffords. Lieutenant Karls was one of the American CANLOAN officers who had joined the Canadian Army and then the CANLOAN scheme in a spirit of adventure. His company commander, Maj. (later Lieut.-Col.) Charles Genese, recalls the battle of 16 July:

> We were attacking a prepared German position in the Bocage country near Vendes. Having reached the objective we faced an immediate counter-attack by the enemy with shell and mortar fire, tanks and infantry. The forward platoons were over-run. Later, when the situation stabilized slightly, I found the body of Lieutenant Karls, apparently killed by machine gun fire, in his platoon position. A detailed account of this action in the official regimental history contains the following relevant words: Lieutenant Karls, the American officer commanding 16 Platoon, broke into a run and with great shouts of encouragement led his platoon amid bursting shells up the last 50 yards to the objective.[30]

Another British company commander, Maj. John Evans, who won a DSO with the S. Staffords. in Normandy, recalls another of the CANLOAN officers who was killed on 16 July: "Oddly enough, the Canadian officer who stands out in my memory was Peter Jeffries, who was killed at Bactieville in France, serving with the South Staffords. He was a typical dare-devil Canadian who excited the admiration of the more stodgy conservative types like myself."[31] But, according to Capt. W. Gordon Chatterton, CDN/442, Maj. John Evans himself did not have a nerve in his body. When Major Evans went to 1/5 Queens as a company commander, he led a dawn attack on Susteren in which he lost a leg.

At the extreme west the 50th Division attacked Hottot on 11 July. One of the battalions that had landed on D-Day, 1 R. Hamps., had attacked Hottot nearly a month earlier and had been holding the line since. One CANLOAN officer, CDN/212, Lieut. MacIsaiah Dougherty, had been wounded in the first attack, and another, CDN/266, Lieut. Merle D.F. Florence, later. In the massive attack on 11 July one company was reduced from 93 to 30 in less than two hours; the casualties included two officers killed, one of them CDN/151, Lieut. Donald K. Hastings, and seven wounded, one of them CDN/551, Lieut. Arthur Connor, who was probably the only CANLOAN officer who was invading France for the second time, having been with the 1st Canadian Division in its brief expedition in 1940. Another CANLOAN officer in 50 Division who was killed at this time was CDN/545, Lieut. William J. Coll, 1 Dorset.

Other CANLOAN officers were active in the battles for Hottot. In his history of 1 Dorset, Brig. A.E.C. Bredin has referred several times to actions of CDN/397, Lieut. Hal D. Foster, including an occasion on 20 June when he, with three men, "was cut off during the action and returned the next day with valuable information." Again, on 11 July, when his company commander was killed he took command of the company. He and the company sergeant-major (CMS) "distinguished themselves and kept the company going in the most remarkable manner."[32]

Infantry units were pushed to the extent of their endurance, and the heavy casualties among officers had an adverse effect on morale. An example is 1/6 DWR in the 49th Division. The CO reported at the end of June: "In 14 days there have been some 23 officer and 350 OR casualties. Only 12 of the original officers remain and they are all junior. The CO and every rank above corporal in Bn HQ [battalion headquarters] have gone; all company commanders have gone. One company has lost every officer; another has only one left."[33] The unit was disbanded on 6 July 1944.

Two of the surviving officers of 6 DWR were CANLOANs who asked to be returned to the Canadian Army, as is related by CDN/68, Lieut. Hector J.B. Brown: "After the Bn was disbanded Don (Lieutenant Donald M Fraser, CDN/76) and I were a bit sour on the British Army. We put in our applications for transfer back to the Cdn Army. Gen Sir Miles Dempsey had us paraded before him in his caravan in order to find out what all this nonsense was about and possibly to find out anything further regarding the collapse of the Dukes. After hearing our story he agreed we had a legitimate complaint and phoned through to Montgomery's HQ. The upshot of the phone call was that Don and I were 'loaned' back to the Canadian Army. I don't know if any other CANLOANs were ever in this position or not but it struck us rather funny at the time. However, due to some clerk's error we were posted to the SWB and they never found out their mistake for over a month. During this time I found this lot entirely different from the previous Bn and signed a note saying I would finish the war with the British Army."

Shortly after joining 2 SWB Lieutenant Brown was awarded the United States Silver Star.[34]

6

Normandy:
Infantry Officers in Battle

EXCEPT FOR SUCH major offensives as the battle of the Scottish Corridor and the attack on Caen, most of the first two months of the Normandy campaign was a war of attrition that, in its static nature and extent of casualties, resembled the trench warfare of the First World War. Though only 14 percent of the troops in Normandy were infantry, they suffered 85 percent of the casualties.

Before considering the quite different conditions of the last few weeks of the campaign, let us look more closely at several features of the Normandy campaign before the breakout, which particularly affected CANLOAN officers.

By the end of July nearly all the CANLOAN officers who eventually served in the 2nd British Army in Normandy had been assigned to battalions in action there. Many of them, as noted, had gone to Normandy with their new battalions, mostly as platoon commanders, arriving between 6 June, when the 3rd and 50th Divisions assaulted the beaches at Lion-sur-Mer and Arromanches, and 27 June, when the 53rd and 59th Divisions landed. Many more CANLOAN officers had come with RHUs from D-Day on.

The British Army had an elaborate reinforcement system designed to ensure that troops of all ranks would be available to fill vacancies as they were created, usually as a result of casualties. Before the invasion of Normandy, personnel in each battalion, a cross-section of its composition (and designated first-line reinforcements) were selected and posted to the appropriate RHU, which would try to ensure that they were available when they were needed. For example, 5 DCLI in the 43rd Division, had a farewell party on 8 May for their first line reinforcements (R Company) who were being "posted away." When the CANLOAN officers first arrived and were posted to battalions, a number of them were assigned to fill existing vacancies in the war establishment of those battalions. The rest were posted to an

RHU for the division. In some cases arrangements were made for CANLOAN officers to spend several days getting acquainted with their prospective battalions before returning to the RHU. For example, several of the ex-Pictou Highlanders officers spent a week at the beginning of May with companies of 2 Glas. H. Since reinforcements would be needed as soon as the assault landings had taken place, some RHUs, which included a number of CANLOAN officers, landed on D-Day and set up operations near the beaches. From there they fed reinforcements forward to the units in action as they were needed. Ironically, in nearly all cases the reinforcements arrived in Normandy before the divisions and battalions they were intended to reinforce. For example, Capt. Joseph Gauthier and three other CANLOAN officers who were reinforcements for 5 DCLI arrived with 33 RHU two weeks before the 43rd Division. CDN/339, Lieut. Douglas G. Gage, a reinforcement officer for the 6th N. Staffs., also landed two weeks before his division, the 53rd Welch, and many other CANLOAN officers were early by several days or weeks.

The record of matching CANLOAN reinforcements with the right battalion was mixed. In some cases they were available to the battalion to which they had been assigned in England as soon as they were needed. For example, on the evening of 26 June, the first day of operation EPSOM, in which most battalions of the 15th Scottish Division suffered officer casualties, no fewer than six CANLOAN officers (Lieuts. Russ Parke, CDN/159, Stewart H. Cameron, CDN/344, G. Vernon Hurst, CDN/554, C. Roger MacLellan, CDN/407, Louis J. Boudreau, and CDN/259, Lorne A. Rice) arrived as reinforcements for 2 Glas. H. At the same time three other CANLOAN officers (Lieuts. CDN/331, Vernon E. Box, CDN/218, Philip A. Labelle, and CDN/313, Harold L. Schwark) came to fill vacancies in 6 RSF. Lieut. Archie Street had arrived a few days earlier. Two CANLOAN officers (Lieuts. James Marshall and CDN/228, Jack R. Stobo) arrived to reinforce the 8th RS on 27 June, and others came from 32 RHU as vacancies occurred: Lieuts. CDN/348, Hugh S. Mackenzie on 3 July, Jackson Stewart on 6 July, Earl Harcourt on 14 July, and CDN/519, Robert T. Collie and CDN/321, Donald K. Lee on 17 July.

Similarly, 4 KSLI in the 11th Armoured Division, which had suffered heavy casualties in the Odon bridgehead on 28 June, received on 30 June a batch of reinforcements from 33 RHU, who included CDN/353, Lieut. Georges Ouelette, who had been posted from 4 KSLI on 8 May. Among the first CANLOAN reinforcements were Lieuts. Lorne Ballance and James Fetterly, who had been designated as reinforcements for 2 E. Yorks. and were posted to that unit in Normandy on 8 June, only two days after it landed.

On the other hand, many CANLOAN officers who were posted to RHUs never reached the battalions to which they had been assigned originally, sometimes because they were posted by the RHU to other units that seemed to have a more urgent need, but often because the officers themselves insisted that they be sent to the first battalion that needed officers rather than wait for a request from the battalion to which they had been posted in England.

The 4 Wilts. was particularly unfortunate in regard to its CANLOAN reinforcements. Of eight CANLOAN officers who were posted to the battalion only two (Lieut. Wilfred Smith and CDN/360, Lieut. James H. Rutherford) saw action with the unit in Normandy. The remaining six went to 32 RHU, and eventually two, Lieut. John

Irwin and CDN/536, Capt. Donald J. Selvage, were posted to 2 Essex. Three, CDN/544, Capt. Jack E. Catley, CDN/446, Lieut. Gordon P. Cummings, and CDN/246, Lieut. Hector L. MacKenzie, went to 1/7 Queens, and Lieut. Vernon Good went to 2 Devon.

The 5 Wilts. was a little more fortunate. Ten CANLOAN officers were posted originally to the battalion. Of these, three went with the battalion to Normandy, and two joined later as reinforcements, but the remaining five were posted from the RHU, one each to 7 Som. LI, 1 Dorset, 9 Cameronians, 2 Essex, and 2 Glosters.

Some units received few if any CANLOAN reinforcements. For example, 7 S. Staffords. in the 59th Division went to Normandy with four CANLOAN officers in its war establishment. It received only one CANLOAN reinforcement (CDN/329, Lieut. Robert K. Robertson) before the unit was disbanded in August. Other units received CANLOAN officers in fairly large groups. The six who reported to 2 Glas. H. on 25 June have been mentioned. Another six, including several other ex-Pictou Highlanders, reported to 7 Seaforth as reinforcements on 7 July. The five who reported to 10 HLI in the 15th Scottish Division on 20 July included Lieuts. Stanley Rumble, Jack Owen, Delmar Struck, and Robert Jackson, officers who had returned from overseas for commissions, had been instructors together in Canada, and had managed to stick together as CANLOAN officers. In mid-June 2 Essex, which had landed in Normandy with no CANLOAN officers and had since had heavy casualties, received 131 ORs and six CANLOAN officers as reinforcements. All six had originally been assigned in England to other regiments – the Dorset, the Mons., and the Hereford Light Infantry (Hereford LI).

In view of the stories that are told about the tendency of armed forces to put square pegs in round holes, it is interesting to observe how efficient the British Army was in taking advantage of special talents of CANLOAN officers. Most of them were straight infantry officers, but some had specialist qualifications. For example, when 5 Dorset lost the commander of its Anti-Tank Platoon, the vacancy was filled by CDN/590, Capt. D. Kenneth Brown, who had a commission in the Royal Canadian Artillery before taking the infantry conversion course at Brockville. So too had CDN/666, Lieut. Jack A. Young, who was posted to the Anti-Tank Platoon of the 1/4 Battalion, the King's Own Yorkshire Light Infantry (KOYLI), and CDN/559, Lieut. Thomas E. White, who had anti-tank experience in Canada before obtaining a commission in the RCA. He served in the Anti-tank Platoon of 6 KOSB throughout the northwest European campaign.

Similarly, advantage was taken of the experience of CANLOAN officers in other support company platoons: carriers, mortars, and pioneers. Capts. Hank Henry and Arnold Willick, for example, had distinguished careers as commanders of the carrier platoons of 4 KSLI and 5 Wilts. respectively.

The four ex-Saint John Fusilier (machine gun) officers who had opted for their affiliated KOSB regiment in England but were destined as first-line reinforcements requested that they be posted instead to the reinforcement holding unit for divisional machine-gun battalions. This was approved, and nine days after D-Day they landed together with 34 RHU. Within a week, all had been posted to divisional machine-gun units. CDN/459, Capt. Donald R. Hartt went to the Manchester Regiment (Manch.) in the 53 (W) Infantry Division; CDN/439, Lieut. Douglas F. Bursey went to the 2nd Battalion, the Princess Louise Kensington Regiment (PLKR), in the 49 (WR) Infantry Division; and Mac McConaghy and Rex Fendick went together to 2 MX of the 3rd Infantry Division.

In some cases the basis for specialization was somewhat tenuous. Lieut. Leo Heaps would be the first to admit that his experience before he was appointed intelligence officer of 1 Dorset was very limited. He was more comfortable later as an officer in 1 Para. at Arnhem. Lieut. Norman Orr was posted to 2 Essex as signals officer on the basis of a single lecture he had given in England. He, too, was happier as an infantry platoon commander. Incidentally, both Heaps and Orr won MCs in their non-specialist roles.

Undoubtedly the managerial talents of Capt. Russ Waters were recognized in his appointment as OC 32 RHU, with which he landed on D-Day, setting up the holding unit near Bayeux and beginning to post reinforcements to units as they were needed. He deserves credit for his contribution to the smooth operation of the British Army's reinforcement system. Certainly there were few complaints about it from CANLOAN officers.

Naturally there were differences in the relationships of platoon commanders with members of their platoons. Some British Army subalterns had lived and trained with their men for months if not years. Some CANLOAN officers had been assigned to platoons in England and had come with them to Normandy, whereas others who came as reinforcements were immediately given platoons to command before, during, or after a battle. They seem, however, to have adapted well to these demanding situations and to have won the confidence of their NCOs and men. In fact, by the end of July in most infantry battalions, there remained only a relatively small nucleus of the original officers, NCOs, and men. The greater part of these battalions consisted of reinforcements of all ranks, and thus the CANLOAN officers did not seem at all out of place when they arrived.

Several references to patrols have already been made, but more should be said. Patrols are a normal activity of infantry battalions, and the conditions in Normandy resulted in almost constant patrolling by Allies and Germans alike. In the periods between battles they were a major occupation for platoon commanders, who were the leaders of most patrols. When CANLOAN infantry officers recall their experiences in Normandy, it is the frequency of patrols that comes first to mind, and there is an almost universal impression that CANLOAN officers were called upon to lead a disproportionate share of the patrols. The surviving British officers, however, tend to be surprised at this impression. Though they generously acknowledge the outstanding patrol work of CANLOAN officers, they would deny that there was a policy of deliberately over-using CANLOAN officers in this especially dangerous aspect of the Normandy campaign. It seems likely that, while all junior infantry officers were equally liable for patrol duties and most were called upon from time to time, there was a tendency (undoubtedly differing from battalion to battalion) for CANLOAN officers to be assigned a larger share of the patrol load. This was not because of any policy of discrimination, but because, generally speaking, the Canadian officers lived up to their reputation of being naturally good at that sort of thing. It seemed reasonable to take advantage of individual talents and experience, and though the CANLOAN officers may not always have volunteered they didn't seem to find this aspect of warfare particularly distasteful. One of them, in commenting on the frequency with which CANLOAN officers went on patrol, observed, "I had accepted that we were probably best able to carry them out."[1]

Another, who had been three times wounded on patrols and returned to his battalion, is reported to have respectfully asked his CO to be given a rest from patrol work. His CO, with an expression of surprise, replied that he thought "you Canadians particularly enjoyed that sort of thing."

CDN/17, Lieut. Joseph S. Craib reported to 1/6 Queens in mid-June as a reinforcement officer. Assigned to a platoon, he was sent on a reconnaissance patrol that same afternoon and encountered an enemy outpost. On his return his company commander said, "One more patrol." On his second patrol that day, all the members of the patrol – a sergeant, two privates, and Craib himself – were wounded, victims of a single mortar bomb. Thus ended his short campaign in Normandy.

The prevalence of patrols can be illustrated by many references in British regimental and divisional histories, such as the official history of the 43rd (Wessex) Division, which describes operation EPSOM:

> Lieut. Edward F. Larret [CDN/170], a Canadian officer attached to the 7th Somerset Light Infantry, had led no fewer than three patrols into Mouen and found it packed with tanks and infantry. The second time he had to fight his way out. Nevertheless he had gone in a third time and confirmed that in the evening the enemy still held the village in force.[2]

And a few days later in the Odon bridgehead:

> Further patrols from this battalion [7 SLI] on succeeding days continued to probe the enemy's positions around Jumeau and Carpiquet Aerodrome. Reconnaissance by Lieuts. Tharp, Jones and Mercier – incidentally all Canadian officers – obtained information of the greatest value, especially with regard to Tiger tanks dug in at the aerodrome. Clashes with enemy patrols in Verson became a daily event. In one of these Lieutenant Mercier was seriously wounded, to the great regret of the battalion, who had found in this young Canadian a patrol leader of genius. The Carrier Platoon of 4th Wiltshire Regiment under Lieutenant Smith, another Canadian officer, also took part in these skirmishes and encountered Tiger tanks in the tile-strewn streets of Verson.[3]

The author of the regimental history of E. Yorks. indicates the inadequacy of records of patrol activity: "Many actions took place in No-Man's-Land which have never been recorded. If the verbal reports of the patrol leaders to the Intelligence Officer could be recorded they would give many a wonderful example of gallantry and devotion to duty."[4]

Usually patrols were led by platoon commanders, who selected NCOs and men from their platoons to accompany them, but occasionally more senior officers were called upon to lead patrols. Among the more senior CANLOAN officers who regularly took out patrols in Normandy were CDN/86, Capt. C. Vincent Lilley, Second in Command and later OC of companies in 1/6 and 1/5 Queens, and Capt. Arnold Willick, Commander of the Carrier Platoon and later OC of Support Company in 5 Wilts.

Incidentally, Captain (later Major) Lilley had an unusual military background.

After serving from 1931 to 1934 in the Loyal Edmonton Regiment (Non-Permanent Active Militia), he enlisted in the permanent force, serving with the Princess Patricia's Canadian Light Infantry (PPCLI) in Winnipeg. In 1936 he and a friend travelled 6,000 miles by "riding the rods" and working their passage on a cattle boat to enlist in the Loyal Regiment (North Lancashire) in the British Army. After two years of courses they were qualified as officer candidates, but as they could not afford British peacetime commissions they volunteered for overseas service with a battalion of the regiment that was in Shanghai. There, Lilley was promoted through all the ranks from lance corporal to regimental sergeant-major (RSM). After serious attacks of malaria he was posted to the United Kingdom. There he accepted an offer from the Commanding Officer of the Loyal Edmonton Regiment (his former militia regiment), then in England with the Canadian 1st Division, to be his RSM. Back in the Canadian Army, Lilley was sent to Canada for a commission and was an early volunteer for the CANLOAN scheme. In Normandy he was first second in command and then OC of a company in 1/6 S. Staffords. When the 59th Division was disbanded he went with remnants of his company to 1/6 Queens in the 7th Armoured Division, where he had two of his best friends, CDN/83, Lieut. Harvey Langstaff and Lieut. Lester Stilling, as platoon commanders in his company. Lilley was eventually reunited with the friend with whom he had joined the Loyals, when they were both company commanders with the RCR in Korea in 1950.[5]

There are several types of patrols. One, sometimes called the contact or liaison patrol, was intended to establish physical contact with friendly troops on either flank. This was particularly important in the initial stages of the Normandy bridgehead. Despite the element of danger in all patrols, there was sometimes a lighter side. For example Lieut. John McBride, of 7 BW, in a contact patrol to a flanking Canadian unit, the Queen's Own Rifles of Canada, was greeted fraternally with Calvados and had a Canadian Volunteer Service Medal (CVSM) and clasp (to which he was entitled but had not yet received through regular channels) pinned to his unadorned breast. His explanation of the purpose of this distinctively Canadian medal evoked from his company commander the comment, "My, you Canadians are an odd lot."[6]

Contact patrols to the Americans on the right flank were usually met with good-natured enthusiasm and generosity, and members of British patrols were amazed at the boisterous informality, the quantity and variety of food, and other characteristics of their American allies, who, while greeting a Canadian as one of themselves, nevertheless demonstrated distinct differences. Sometimes the Americans were unpredictable. One morning 2 E. Yorks. was surprised to discover that a neighbouring American unit had disappeared during the night without warning, leaving the E. Yorks.' flank exposed.

The most frequent type of patrol, constituting probably 70 percent of all patrols, was reconnaissance. Its purpose was to obtain information by stealth without fighting for it. Typical missions were to find out if a natural feature or buildings were occupied by the enemy, and if so, in what strength. The following report of a typical reconnaissance patrol was made after the war by a CANLOAN officer, Elmer Fitzpatrick, who was asked by the War Office to account for a sergeant in 11 DLI who was still listed as missing:

On the night of 27 Jun 44 I was ordered by Lieut-Col M Hamner, 11 Bn DLI, to take a Recce Patrol, consisting of myself and two men, into German territory in order to obtain information regarding German positions, MGs etc. Sgt Critchley and Pte J R Metcalfe volunteered to accompany me on this patrol. We set out at approximately 2400 hrs. We proceeded up one side of a designated road, circled around a cross roads and started back down the opposite side of the a/m road as we had been instructed to do. About half way back to our own lines we encountered a slight rise in the ground. There was a hedge running along the crest of this rise and when we came within approx 200 yds of this crest we were fired on by 10 Spandaus. We could also hear German patrols closing in on us from the road. I saw that we had to get out of there and since it was impossible to go head on through the hedge I attempted to by-pass it by going further left through what appeared to be a break in the hedge. I made off towards this break, the two men following immediately behind me. Just as I was about to go through the opening I was halted by a German sentry. I immediately fired and either killed or wounded this sentry. However, we must have passed right over a silent Spandau position because as soon as I fired this Spandau opened up on us from about five yds distance. Pte Metcalfe and I immediately dashed to one side but Sgt Critchley, according to Metcalfe, was about to throw a grenade and did not move fast enough. He was definitely hit but I cannot say whether he was killed or not. We attempted to get back to him but he was surrounded by Germans and we were therefore unable to do so. There was a heavy concentration of German troops in this area. Pte Metcalfe and I eventually got back to our own lines details of which are immaterial to you. I was wounded and picked up by the Tyneside Scottish later. I gave a major there all details I could but he possibly was unable to relay them to the 11th Bn DLI as I believe they (the Tyne Scots) were counter-attacked almost immediately. Pte Metcalfe I understand did reach 11 DLI. I sincerely hope that I have outlined the above so that it may be of some assistance to you.[7]

Another incident recalled by Lieut. Leonard Robertson shows why at least some CANLOAN officers acquired a reputation for boldness on patrols:

It was while here that I first met up with CDN/267 Jim Fetterly. It was late one evening and the Cpl in charge of the duty guards for the evening came to report that a patrol was coming through our area and heading towards enemy lines. I went to meet them and found a Canadian officer taking them out. It was Jim, wearing a German Luger and German holster and, I swear, wearing German high boots. I told him he was crazy and if caught he would be shot. His only answer was a laugh and the remark, "They'll have to catch me first." Well, anyway, they didn't catch him for he came back through our lines later on, said he had found a German machine gun post and went back to report to Bn Headquarters. By golly, didn't he come back the next night. "Where to now," I asked. "Hell," he said, "the CO doesn't believe me and wants me to bring back a prisoner or something." I understand he brought the machine gun back and told the CO the gun wasn't out there any more.[8]

The information acquired through reconnaissance patrols was important and could be obtained in no other way. Aerial photographs, reports from the French underground, and other sources were important, but the regular on-the-spot eye-witness accounts obtained by patrols were invaluable for the planning and execution of military operations, since they provided accurate locations for air strikes and mortar and artillery targets as well as for the operations of companies, battalions, or divisions. The importance of patrols was shown by the attention they received. Requests for information may have originated at the battalion, brigade, or even divisional level. Though it was usually the battalion intelligence officer who briefed the patrol commander before he set out and who questioned him when he returned, the commanding officer was always involved and was frequently waiting for news when the patrol returned. When certain officers acquired reputations for success it was not surprising when they were called on with more frequency by anxious COs. Some patrols were particularly important. One of them was led by CDN/180, Lieut. Robert Newstead of 7 S. Staffords., who, on the night of 6 August, discovered a place near Thury Harcourt where the Orne could be forded. The attack next day by the 59th Division was thus greatly assisted, for it was able to establish a bridgehead on the east bank of the Orne.

Sometimes a reconnaissance patrol was asked to bring back a prisoner if one could be captured without undue noise or force. An example has been related by Lieut.-Col. E. Jones, who in late July 1944 was Battalion Intelligence Officer (IO) of 1 S. Lan. R.:

> I think it must have been during the 48 hours we spent there (in an orchard near Escoville) that (CDN/454) Lieutenant Eric Fryer went out on his first night patrol. On his return he reported to me, as the newly-established IO of the Bn, more or less carrying under one arm a German NCO he had captured. His account went something like this: He knew we were in very close contact with the enemy, and he had gone forward less than a hundred yards when he stepped cautiously across a ditch. As he stood with one foot on either side of this ditch, he happened to look down and there, between his legs, were two German soldiers asleep in a fox-hole. He was wondering what he should do, when he heard a slight noise and looking to one side saw a dim, wavering light approaching. Surmising, quite correctly as it transpired, that this was a German NCO going his rounds, he stood stock-still until the figure almost cannoned into him. Then he clapped one hand over the German's face, encircled his body with the other arm, pinioning his arms to his sides, and so carried him back to our lines! ... I clearly remember how delighted he was at the success of this his first patrol.[9]

When Lieut. Donald Diplock returned from his first patrol he was told cheerfully that in a day or two he would have "a nice fighting patrol." As the name implies, the members of a fighting patrol might have to fight in order to accomplish their mission, which ranged from obtaining information, such as the identity of the enemy, by capturing one or more prisoners, to destroying an enemy post. Depending on the task, the strength of fighting patrols could be as little as a section but was more often a platoon and could be as large as a company, when they were comparable to the trench raids of the First World War. Fighting patrols were usually rehearsed and often had the advantage of supporting artillery and tanks. One example is the raid on an enemy position by Lieut. Burt Harper of 1 E. Lan. R., which has been described earlier.

Fighting patrols were strong in 6 RWF. On 30 June a fighting patrol under Lieut. Harold Main "was nearly ambushed but gave a good account of itself." On 10 July Lieut. Arthur Crighton was killed in a D Company raid when a house occupied by the enemy was attacked. Near Évrecy between 29 and 31 July both CANLOAN officers in the battalion were engaged in fighting patrols. On 29 July Lieutenant Main led one, and on 30 July both he and Capt. Robert Marsh led fighting patrols. Following is a typical report by a fighting patrol:

> Date: 30 Jul 44 Unit: 6 RWF Type of Patrol: Fighting Time Out: 0300 Patrol Comd: Lieut. MAIN. Time In: 0530 Strength: 1 Offr 18 ORs Object: To destroy Tks in orchard 006616 Answer to object: Tks not destroyed because of ambush but three enemy killed and some wounded. Route: SP 003621 – along hedge from 003619-006617- returned same route. Visibility and Weather: Poor (overcast) misty. Narrative: I followed route to area 006617 when I placed a fire section in posn along hedgerow. With remainder of patrol I went through and around the hedgerow. When we were partly round I saw what I thought was the fwd part of my patrol. I then realized they were Germans and they threw grenades. We got down and opened up killing three definitely and wounding a Spandau team. Grenades were still being thrown along hedge and we had to withdraw as four of our automatic weapons had been knocked out. We returned by the same route. Own cas – four wounded and two missing. Special points of interest: Enemy dug in SOUTH of line of trees along hedgerow 006617 to river. Enemy heard in orchard 005616.
>
> Date: 31 Jul 44 Time: 0645 Lt. MAIN i/c Patrol[10]

In other battalions also, certain officers were considered specialists in fighting patrols. In 5 Wilts. such specialists for a time were CDN/330, Lieut. Everett O. Baker and CDN/493, Capt. J.G. Gerry Robichaud.

Finally, there were standing patrols, usually between a section and a platoon in strength, which occupied a protective position forward of the main defensive line to give early warning of an impending attack or to observe enemy activity. An example is the occupation, by 2 RUR in the 3rd Division, of a stone farm building in advance of the battalion position every night. It was suspected that the enemy might have occupied the same building at other times.

Another example of a standing patrol was one mounted by 4 Wilts. in the 43rd Division, before the attack on Hill 112 on 10 July. It was commanded by Lieut. Wilfred Smith and is described in detail in the regimental history:

> Preparations for the big attack were much in evidence. The Carrier Platoon was ordered to send out standing patrols to hold the Odon bridges south of Verson. The task was to make sure that the two bridges, though they lay well outside the Odon Box, were held intact in preparation for the attack southward (they were the only bridges capable of supporting armoured vehicles). Each bridge was to be held by a Carrier Section reinforced by a section of B Company. The easterly bridge was to be held to the last round and the last man. Verson and Fontaine both lay in No-Man's-Land and were believed to be thick with German patrols and outposts.[11]

Despite difficulties with German patrols and an encounter with Tiger tanks the patrol held the bridges until relieved on the eve of the attack by 5 DCLI.

Though not, strictly speaking, standing patrols, a similar and frequent task for infantry platoons was to form a protective screen while pioneers or engineers lifted or laid the mines in front of the battalion position. Pioneers were known to finish and slip away without notifying their protectors!

There is no doubt that patrols were especially dangerous. Among the CANLOAN officers who were killed on patrols in Normandy were Lieuts. Charles Baker, 11 DLI; Alfred Cope, 1 S. Lan. R.; Arthur Crighton, 6 RWF; and George Luffman, 8 DLI. Others were killed and many more wounded by a variety of hazards: mines, mortar and shell fire, machine guns, including those firing on fixed lines, and, a particular danger in proximity to enemy positions, grenades.

Still, there were some advantages to patrolling, in contrast to set-piece attacks in which platoons advanced across open fields towards the enemy, following an artillery barrage in extended line or V-formation towards the objective. Patrols permitted some freedom and initiative within the limits of the task: freedom from the tedium of the slit trench and the dangers of daylight movement and from the usual marching burden with pack, pick, and shovel. Each patrol was an absorbing task from the time when the patrol leader was called to battalion HQ for briefing. There was the study of maps and aerial photographs if available; a reconnaissance to see as much of the ground as possible; the selection of other members of the patrol; some rest if possible before a night patrol; the preparation of clothing – trousers, sweaters, berets, and running shoes; the provision of maximum firepower with Bren, Stens, and grenades; and, a final touch, the blackening of faces and hands. Upon return a sense of achievement in accomplishing a difficult mission in enemy territory – and an indelible CANLOAN memory of Normandy, 1944.

It is neither feasible nor profitable after more than 40 years to attempt to compare the relative participation in patrols of CANLOAN officers and their British counterparts, but one can say that patrolling was a very frequent task of CANLOAN officers in the Normandy campaign, as, indeed, it was in all stages of the campaign in northwest Europe.

Though the Germans had not heard about CANLOAN, their reports of operations in Normandy sometimes revealed an awareness of their presence. On the evening of 26 June, 10 HLI, leading the attack of the 15th Scottish Division at that time, was pinned down in the orchards southwest of Cheux by a counter-attack by the 12th SS Panzer Division. The Company Commander of 8 Company SS Panzer Regiment has described an attack by a British patrol while he was standing beside his tank talking to the division's Artillery Commander:

Dark figures rose up out of the bushes and came crashing forward, firing from the hip and shouting, "Hands up." The Company Commander dived at the nearest one and they went down in a tangle together, the British soldier's Sten gun firing as it hit the ground. He also had a bayonet or a knife but got the point entangled in the overalls of the German, who tried to grab the Sten. In the confusion the Artillery Commander was killed and the gunner of the Company Commander's tank was captured and ordered out of the tank. He reported that he was grabbed and bundled off towards the British lines when a burst of machine gun fire sent his captor diving for cover and he was able, by lying motionless in a small stream, to escape. He heard two soldiers whom he judged to be American, searching for him, one of them trailing a series of "God Damns."[12]

Alexander McKee, quoting the German commander's report, commented, "A number of young Canadian officers were seconded to British infantry battalions under a scheme called CANLOAN; the accent, the words and the absence of Americans in the vicinity make it almost certain that at least one of these soldiers was a Canadian officer."[13] Does any CANLOAN officer who served in the 15th Scottish Division wish to confess to the attempted kidnapping?

There was similar confusion for the Germans later near Hill 112 when aggressive patrolling drew their attention to soldiers who didn't sound British, although they knew that no Americans were in the area. It is possible that they were from the 3rd Canadian Division, but it is more likely that they were CANLOAN officers, since several of them were actively engaged in patrols in the area at the time.

French-speaking CANLOAN officers were particularly valuable in Normandy because they were able to obtain information from the French civilian population. The Commanding Officer of the Hallamshires (a battalion of the York and Lancaster Regiment) reported that CDN/181, Lieut. J.L. Fern Nobert had obtained valuable information from civilians, including the fact that Fontenay and Tessel Wood were held by two German companies instead of "the odd sniper, as was thought by Bn HQ"; consequently the attack on these positions was made with adequate artillery support. The war diary of 4 KSLI in the 11th Armoured Division reports that, on 28 June, "Lieutenant Duclos (Canada) of B Coy, who had been our indefatigable interrogation officer up to date was badly wounded and died later in the day ... In the assembly area a few hours earlier he had discovered Norman civilians who were related to his own ancestors who had come from that region."[14]

Another element beyond the usual capacity of infantry officers was illustrated by the activities of Capt. J.H.J. Gauthier. The official history of the 43rd Division notes that on 12 August Captain Gauthier passed through the enemy lines, met the leaders of the French Resistance in the area, and established and maintained valuable and close contact with them. This liaison produced an "intimate knowledge of local roads and tracks and the location of enemy mines."[15] Several of the British fellow officers pronounced their French-speaking CANLOAN comrades to be vivacious and delightful companions. Lieutenant-Colonel Le Mesurier, who served with the 7th Battalion, the Duke of Wellington's Regiment (DWR), in Normandy with CANLOAN officers said of one of them, CDN/82, Lieut. Dominique Lambert: "He was quite the most splendid man you could wish to meet. Quiet with a lovely sense of humour and courageous ... When the going was so slow that it was a mite depressing he would put on an old top hat he had found some place and cheer us up."[16]

It has been said that warfare is 90 percent boredom and 10 percent sheer terror. That is not a completely accurate description of the life of an infantryman in Normandy, but it is a reminder that pitched battles account for only a small proportion of the time. In fact, those who served in battalions of the British Second Army in Normandy, spent most of their time in small holes in the ground.

Slit trenches, of course, were familiar to all infantrymen. Digging them was one of the least pleasant aspects of realistic training exercises; even carrying picks and shovels was sometimes considered a nuisance, if not a burden. But the first time an infantryman came under fire, it became apparent to him that the alternative to the protection of a slit trench was almost certain death. Though officers and senior

NCOs continued to say, "A soldier's best friend is his rifle," it was generally accepted that his best protection was his shovel. This was particularly true when an objective had been taken, since a German counter-attack, preceded by saturation mortar or artillery fire, was usually immediate. No matter how tired the attackers were, they had to dig in quickly; the casualties resulting from failure to dig fast enough provided an object lesson that was forgotten at one's peril.

The textbook dimensions of the slit trench – 1 1/2 feet (the width of shoulders) by 6 feet (more or less according to height) by 4 feet deep – were generally satisfactory and usually complied with. Slits for two were slightly longer but no wider or deeper. A great deal depended on the soil. Sandy soil was easy to dig but posed problems of falling gravel from movement or even collapse from near misses. Clay soil or chalk was difficult and slow to dig, requiring vigorous use of a pick, but it was good and solid when completed. The most hated was stony soil, which resisted the shovel and required the removal of stones. The siting of slit trenches was an important responsibility of the platoon commander, and since their location was based on tactical considerations, such as fields of fire, it was seldom possible to select spots just because they were favourable for digging.

During the time between moves, which could be days or even weeks, the improvement of slits was a constant preoccupation. They were made deeper, lined and strengthened, and provided with overhead cover against rain and shrapnel. Few of them achieved the standard of one occupied by CDN/153, Capt. Harold J. Hihn after his company had discovered cases of cigarettes, wine, and glasses in a farmhouse: "I enlarged my slit trench, digging out little alcoves for the wine, glasses and cigs. The slitter was named 'Cafe Anglaise by Major' 'Digger' Tighe-Wood after an A Coy O Gp [Orders Group] was held there. The 'moaning Minnies' that landed close by only shook a little clay about as the walls were quite firm."[17]

Since it was demonstrated constantly that slit trenches would provide protection against anything except a direct hit, infantrymen felt safe in them or, to put it another way, they never felt safe out of them. When they were obliged to be in the open they always kept an eye on the nearest cover, as is illustrated by a story related by Capt. Hal Foster. He was attending an O. group called by Lieut.-Col. A.E.C. "Speedy" Bredin, CO, 1 Dorset:

> Rather than have us come to Battalion HQ he had set up a chair with a small umbrella to protect against the sun ... As we gathered round most, I think, noted one single three-foot deep slit trench nearby ... The O Group had just nicely started when the first Jerry "range" shot came in, followed by a pretty fair stonk of the area. In my own case I was second from the top as we hit the one trench. When the stonk lifted we sheepishly crawled out of our cover to find "Speedy" sitting under his umbrella (a little paler) and saying, "Well, gentlemen, now that is over shall we resume?"[18]

The conditions of occupancy of slit trenches depended on circumstances. There were two extremes. When a platoon was in slits on a forward slope and thus in constant view of the enemy, no movement was permitted in daytime. Food was brought up at night and eaten during the day. Sometimes crawl trenches permitted some movement between sections, platoon HQ, and latrines. Perhaps the greatest hardship was that there was almost no chance to make tea. The other extreme was in positions, especially in reserve, where periods of fairly free movement were feasible but all ranks when in the open kept an ear cocked for the whistle of a mortar bomb and an eye on the nearest cover, as in Hal Foster's tale. The standing or running broad jump to the nearest slit was developed to a fine art.

To appreciate fully the experience of living in a slit trench 24 hours a day for weeks on end, one must have endured it. As an example of static warfare it resembled trench life in the First World War, but the slit trenches of Normandy were very primitive and confining compared to the elaborate First World War trench systems. They had several unpleasant features. One was discomfort. Healthy and tired bodies soon grew accustomed to lying on the hard bottom of a dry slit trench, but it was different when it rained. CANLOAN officers who were there at the time will remember the period in mid-June and again in July when it rained for days at a time. Rain capes were unable to keep out the rain, and trenches seemed likely to fill. In the case of a stonk there was no alternative to the slit no matter how full it was. One CANLOAN officer recalls that in his platoon each person stripped, had his clothing twisted and wrung out, and then put it back on after a quick towelling. Another CANLOAN officer observed that despite living in cold, saturated clothing for long periods nobody ever caught a cold!

Added to discomfort was the dirt, for there were no adequate washing facilities, and often the same clothing and boots were worn for weeks at a time. Moreover, battle dress, when impregnated with wet mud, was abrasive as sand paper. Eventually however, arrangements were made for periodic visits to mobile baths and changes of clothing.

The need to remain in slit trenches also meant isolation, which was particularly hard for troops who had become accustomed to life in a group, to communion with their "mates." Except in cases where slits were shared, it was virtually solitary confinement. A CANLOAN officer writing to his parents mentioned that his best friends, officers in the same company, were in the same field about 50 yards away but that he rarely saw them. It was not considered reasonable to risk death just for a chat.

The infantryman's knowledge of the progress of the war was limited to his section and platoon; he had only a vague idea about his company or battalion. On one occasion men in Lieut. Len Robertson's platoon found a badly wounded officer in front of their position. It was a fellow CANLOAN officer, CDN/541, Lieut. Norman A. Brown, who had been in the same battalion a considerable time, unbeknownst to Robertson. Earlier, Len had met in the field another CANLOAN officer from an adjoining company but had never seen or heard of him before or since. News about the war (except that given in O. group briefings) was usually obtained from the crews of supporting tanks or the drivers from B Echelon who brought up the rations and had access to wireless sets. Sometimes letters from home, even from Canada, revealed that civilians far from the battlefield knew more about the progress of the campaign than the most active participants.

The periods of enforced inactivity spent in trenches could not be regarded as rest because there was constant stress. The danger from enemy fire was real. Casualties mounted and the strength of units in static positions at the front diminished rapidly. Most positions were noted by the enemy, who regularly shelled crossroads and any place when there was movement of vehicles or troops. A full-scale stonk, which usually preceded a counter-attack, was a terrifying experience. One such experience has been related by Lieut. John McBride of 7 BW:

> There was a shattering explosion as a bomb hit the parapet, showering the sergeant and me with earth. Part of the trench wall caved in ... During the next 50 minutes my platoon suffered the most severe mortaring it was to experience in the war. It is impossible to describe the horror. Bombs fell on the position like rain and tore it to pieces ... I had to order that no casualties be evacuated. There was no way without adding to their numbers. I did see a corporal running to another trench against my orders. In an instant his face was covered with blood. He was screaming that his eyes were gone ... My sergeant and I huddled as far down as we could in our little damaged trench. With each salvo the sergeant would exclaim, "In the name of God!" while I held my arms closely across my face to protect my eyes and quietly echoed his sentiments. There came a dreadful moment when I no longer wanted to live. To survive only meant that at another time, in another place, this would all happen again – and again – until I would inevitably take my place in the ranks of the dead.[19]

McBride estimated that something like 3,000 mortar bombs landed in the platoon area in the 50 minutes. Despite the protection of slit trenches all except six in his platoon were either killed or wounded.

Such experiences resulted in troops becoming apprehensive about anything that would provoke enemy shelling, such as being relieved by inexperienced troops. Capt. Eric Hall of 1/5 Queens in the 7th Armoured Division recalls being relieved by an American unit: "Lots of yelling and whooping; cries of 'Where are the Goddamned Krauts?' and telling them to keep quiet and not let the Jerries know what was happening."[20]

Other causes for alarm included supporting arms, such as 3-inch or 4.2-inch mortar sections that came to do a "shoot" from a company area, provoking automatic "return shit" (counter-battery fire, from the enemy). Similar annoyance was evoked by tanks and other vehicles, which caused the dreaded movement, noise, and dust that meant enemy fire. Signs reading "DUST MEANS DEATH" and "DUST DRAWS FIRE" were often erected by the engineers along tracks and were literally true. Nor did the enemy neglect meal times. Food was usually brought to a platoon position by a 15-cwt. truck or the company carrier. The troops, who came with their mess tins to get their food and tea, often had to dash up one or two at a time and run back to their slit trenches to eat between mortar salvos.

Life in slit trenches took its toll, not only in casualties but also in morale. A CANLOAN officer in the 51st Highland Division, on relieving another unit in the same division, was struck by the effect on the troops of two weeks at the front: "What kind of war could have turned them into so many blank faces? It was as though they were living in a twilight zone – neither dead nor alive." And there was no reason to think that his own battalion would not look the same after two weeks.

The lives of troops in defensive positions revolved around a regular routine. There was the 100 percent stand-to at dawn, when troops faced the enemy and were inspected by the officers and senior NCOs. If conditions were bad enough there could be a rum ration, but this was rare in Normandy. Capt. Gordon Chatterton recalls:

> Once, early on, when I was temporarily i/c of the coy, the CSM (coy sergeant major), knowing a soft touch, suggested that we "splice the main brace." I agreed – and it was done. When Maj Geoff Ball, the coy commander, returned and heard about the alcoholic distribution, he asked on whose authority it was done and I replied "On mine." He said we needed authority from the bde [brigade] or at least the bn (I forget the exact details). One result was that for some time thereafter I was called "Splice."[21]

Then came breakfast in mess tins, followed by washing and shaving. It was a sign of good discipline and morale that all ranks shaved, even when water was severely rationed – in the dregs of breakfast tea as a last resort. During the day there was usually one-third alert, improving the trenches, working parties, preparation for patrols, and so on. At dusk there was 100 percent stand-to again followed by 50 percent alert during the night. During long periods of sitting or lying in slit trenches, the troops wrote letters, which were censored by the platoon commander (who was thus deprived of the opportunity for daytime naps), smoked, and talked, if they were fortunate enough to share a trench, in which case the partners got to know each other more intimately than their families and so the shock was greater when one of them was killed or wounded.

By the end of June arrangements were made for units to be relieved if circumstances permitted. Sometimes troops of all ranks were sent back a short distance from the front, a few at a time, where they could sleep in a bed, change their clothing, and eat in peace. Eventually whole units were relieved and given short periods in leave centres such as Bayeux, where there were mobile baths, restaurants, and such luxuries as Camembert cheese in the town market. By mid-July there was even entertainment, for example George Formby in an ENSA troop. But however pleasant these breaks were, troops were usually glad to get back to the cocoon of their platoon.

Though the enemy was usually invisible, the Allied troops became familiar with the sounds and smells of the battlefield. Silence was unknown. In the medley of sounds they could distinguish those of many weapons, the enemy mortars, especially the moaning Minnies, the '88s, the spandaus, and even the schmeissers; and among the Allied weapons the trusty Brens, the 3-inch and 4.2-inch mortars, Vickers MMGs, the 25-pounders, the medium and heavy artillery, and the boom of the naval guns, which were within range for the first two months in Normandy. Although ammunition was rationed for a period after the severe storm in June that wrecked the Mulberry harbour, a CANLOAN officer, Lieut. Norman Orr of 2 Essex, was impressed by the unlimited supply of artillery ammunition in the 50th Division: "I think their motto was 'better fire it before Jerry hits it.' One shell from Jerry and they would open up for the day. My battalion history says it was 10 for 1, but I'm sure they were being very conservative."[22]

Those who served in the Normandy campaign have indelible recollections of the smells – the odour of cordite, the acrid smell of burned buildings, the overpowering stench of dead cattle lying in dozens in the fields, legs sticking up, smelling to high heaven. Nearly a quarter century later a CANLOAN officer visiting Normandy exclaimed, "Look, the cattle are right side up!" Sometimes there were smells from humans, when the unburied bodies of friends or enemies were found long after their deaths. A more subtle smell betrayed the presence of the German troops. There has been speculation about the cause of this odour. It is most likely that the sickly, sweet smell was from the smoke of Turkish cigarettes, which came to permeate clothing and shelter. Perhaps the Germans could detect Allied troops by the odour of their Player's, Woodbines, or Sweet Caps!

An observant British commentator on the war, Major-General Essame, has written:

> Only those who have some first-hand knowledge of it can begin to appreciate the incessant dangers and discomforts, as well as the cumulative stresses and strains which the front line soldier is called upon to endure for weeks or months on end ... for most of the front-line soldiers the bleak rule was that you normally continued to fight on, either until you were killed or so severely wounded as to be unfit for further active service in the line.[23]

Infantrymen are *always* tired. They march with heavy loads of equipment, weapons, and ammunition, they are awake from morning to evening "stand-to," they do sentry duty night and day, they get uncomfortable "rest" in wet and/or cold slit trenches, they dig in, they endure the constant stress of shell fire, mortars, and MGs, they run, fall, crawl, and get up, they are either too hot or too cold or too wet, or thirsty, or hungry. When "resting," apart from working (mining, wiring, digging), they clean themselves and their weapons, and, if part of carrier crews (who transport machine guns, anti-tank weapons, and mortars), they must fuel and do regular maintenance on their vehicles and weapons. Furthermore, every platoon was usually short-handed. Amazingly, physical breakdown was rare; mental breakdown was more common.

One historian has noted that though the popular memory of the Normandy campaign is of

> the dramatic and heroic invasion of 6 June and the great breakthrough and pursuit emanating from COBRA at the end of July, yet most of the campaign was a grim struggle and those who fought there are more likely to remember the dreadful bocage, the heat, mud and dust, the terror of unseen mortar and sniper fire, the incessant artillery and aerial bombardments, and the loss of many comrades to an enemy who was rarely seen.[24]

Another refers to

> the path of the advance marked by the rifles of the fallen, the dead, the wounded, the bloated cattle, the burning farm, the dust, the deadly corn, the Panthers and Spandaus, the whine of bullets, the mines and booby traps, the shell that screamed before it thunderclapped amid the grass. Certainly those participants will agree with Rommel's judgment that "it was one terrible blood-letting."[25]

From time to time officers in the Canadian Army, including several CANLOAN officers, have expressed the view that the leadership aspect of an officer's role was not given sufficient emphasis during formal officer training. This is the nature of comments by two CANLOAN officers in the first flight to the liaison officer at CMHQ about the refresher course at A-34 SOTC, Sussex. They insisted that the training at Sussex, like that at Brockville, consisted chiefly of basic training subjects, such as foot and arms drill and weapon training, "treating officers like recruits." There were, of course, subjects that were purely for officers, such as map reading, military law, tactical exercises without troops, and practice in commanding platoons and companies.

The justification for the emphasis on basic training that would have been given by Brigadier Gregg or Colonel Jones, for example, was threefold: First, the more battlefield elements, from care of weapons to sequence of orders, that could be reduced to drills and done automatically, the easier it would be to operate effectively in an atmosphere of noise, crisis, and confusion. Second, it was assumed that if officers were to instruct other ranks in a wide range of basic subjects they should be superior to them in knowledge and performance. And finally, this knowledge and ability in infantry skills were particularly important in the Canadian Army, where egalitarian principles were so firmly entrenched that officers received little automatic respect by virtue of their rank alone. Respect was accorded when officers were considered to deserve it on the basis of knowledge, performance, and leadership.

Some of the most important elements of military leadership are personal qualities that are often innate and not easily taught. During the training and selection of officers, those qualities were recognized and recorded. In these extracts from the records of future CANLOAN officers, the emphasis on innate leadership qualities is evident:

"Excellent in all categories: leadership, attitude, instructional ability, infantry skills."

"As a leader he is confident with very good powers of command."

"Ability in man-management of all types of soldiers."

"Has the makings of a good platoon commander."

"Excellent prospects of good leadership, should make a first-rate infantry officer."

"Ready to accept responsibility and inspires others to do his will."

"Well above average ability and will make a splendid reinforcement officer."

"Definite leadership qualifications and good officer material."

"More than average intelligence, a fighter, should have ability to inspire confidence."

"Leadership ability and initiative."

"Aggressiveness, enthusiastic leadership to a high degree."

"Will be a very effective officer, has a high standard of military efficiency and is a fast-moving hard-hitting combatant with the ability to obtain the last ditch loyalty of his men."

"A young western Canadian of the best type who will make an excellent representative for the British Army."

"Has confidence in his ability to carry the responsibility of leadership."[26]

Despite any weaknesses in their training, the CANLOAN officers who served in Normandy seem, on the whole, to have arrived with the basic elements of leadership, the right attitude, a reasonable standard of infantry skill, and a concept and understanding of the role of the junior infantry officer, which were then refined in the crucible of the Normandy campaign.

The infantry skills that had gained the respect of troops in Canada proved to be important in action, for lack of confidence in the knowledge and ability of one's officer was a most serious matter for any platoon. It has been suggested that in modern warfare the role of junior infantry officers is less to kill the enemy than to provide inspiration and direction to their men. Though this may be true there are many examples of platoon commanders, including CANLOAN officers, who demonstrated skill in the use of all infantry weapons – rifle, Bren, mortar, PIAT, and grenades. This ability, evident in most citations for gallantry, for example, was a definite asset.

It was important for the platoon commander to set a good example for his platoon at all times. In Normandy, from the moment he led his platoon ashore or took command of a platoon in the field, he was constantly checking for stragglers, keeping spirits up, setting an example in matters which affected pride and morale such as by shaving when water was scarce, maintaining reasonable levels of smartness when living in muddy trenches, keeping cheerful even when conditions were bad, and steadying the men when they were badly shaken.

It was said of some infantry officers that their men would follow them anywhere. The admiration and respect of their men were accompanied by a desire not to let their officers down, which resulted in high morale and spirited performance. It also imposed on officers a constant awareness that they must set a good example and not yield to impulses that might be normal in other circumstances. An example of such leadership was reported by a CANLOAN officer who, at the time, was a liaison officer at the headquarters of the 51st Highland Division, which was commanded by the immensely popular Maj.-Gen. Thomas Rennie, known to the troops as "Mad Rennie." On the eve of an attack by the division the General was looking over the ground while exposed to enemy artillery fire. When it was suggested that he take cover he asked, "What do you see behind you?" "The Black Watch, sir, coming up to the attack." "Then it wouldn't do for them to see me hiding, now, would it?"[27]

This awareness of the consequences of one's actions was with a platoon commander constantly, but especially in times of crisis. Many CANLOAN officers will remember the moment, usually during the first big mortar stonk or just before the first attack, when they realized that regardless of their own fear, shock, or alarm, they must never betray such emotions to their platoons. Sometimes the inspirational role resulted in casualties. Observers of the Normandy campaign have noted "the insistence by the British soldiers on leadership by example from their officers." Certainly a high percentage of officer casualties were among junior officers who were at the front to direct advances by their troops. For platoon commanders such actions were almost instinctive, but a considerable number of the casualties among company commanders and even more senior officers were a result of awareness of what Lord Moran, in *The Anatomy of Courage*, has called "the electrifying effect of an act of coolness and courage on the part of an officer."[28] An example of this occurred during the terrible night of 10 July on the slopes of Hill 112. 5 DCLI had been nearly wiped out by a succession of counter-attacks by the 9th Panzer Division, in which nearly all the officers were killed or wounded. As the remnants of the battalion were withdrawing through 4 Som. LI, a corporal in the battalion observed his commanding officer and the commander of 129th Brigade sitting in the open on their shooting sticks chatting calmly. This apparently foolhardy act probably prevented a general panic.

On the other hand, an officer could be too brave as far as his platoon was concerned. Liddell Hart, a British writer and war expert, has observed that a basic condition of effective leadership is the feeling that it will not be used recklessly.[29] Certainly in Normandy men tended to become uneasy when their platoon commander acquired a reputation for daring, and there was a mixture of pride and apprehension when this reputation appeared to be the reason for an unusual number of patrols, leading position in attacks, and other dangerous missions in which they had to be involved with their courageous commander.

An element in leadership that is particularly important for junior infantry officers is a genuine concern for the welfare of the men whom they command. In training, this was shown in such ways as inspecting feet after route marches, seeing that the men were fed before the officers, and taking action on behalf of individuals. In the field it was even more important that the officer be perceived as considerate, that he be considered a father figure, even though he may have been younger than many of his men. Since the platoon commander censored all outgoing letters, he was known to be aware of the domestic situations of those in his platoon and was in a favourable position to be consulted when the need arose. He knew the meaning of the initials on the envelopes, from the familiar SWALK (sealed with a loving kiss) to more unusual ones such as ITALY (I truly always love you), and GUTS (get up them stairs), the latter sometimes supplemented by remarks in the letter such as, "Take a good look around the flat 'cos when I get home you won't see anything but the ceiling." CANLOAN officers seem to have been particularly successful in establishing direct contact with their men in such cases instead of dealing with them through the platoon sergeant. In protracted periods in defensive positions when troops became terrified to leave the shelter of their slit trenches and were inclined to brood, visits from their officer and the awareness of the risks they involved were good for morale. One CANLOAN officer who was wounded slightly and was away from his platoon for a couple of weeks, noticed on his return that there had been a distinct drop in morale when he was not there to visit them regularly.

In the isolation imposed by the battlefield in Normandy it was not the division or the battalion (though regimental pride and spirit had been inculcated in the original members), or even the company that formed the community or group of which the soldier felt an integral part. It was the platoon or even the section that provided the nucleus of kinship and identity. The ultimate test of leadership for a platoon commander was his ability to identify completely with the group he commanded, to be the living personification of it, and to weld it into an effective, cohesive fighting unit with good morale, confidence in him, and pride in serving in his platoon. In the relationship between a young officer and his men two important elements were consistency and sincerity. "You know where you are with him" and "You can trust him to do the right thing" were comforting thoughts. One of the most remarkable features of the CANLOAN scheme was the extent to which officers whose backgrounds were so different from those of their platoons and who were imposed on them so abruptly were able to develop a team spirit. This development of a team spirit was greatly assisted by the natural philosophy of the British soldier – to "muck in" and "not let the side down," as they put it.

Given the logistics of the battlefield, a platoon commander's most frequent contacts were with those who constituted platoon headquarters and so were part of his immediate personal team. Two of those members were especially significant: the platoon sergeant and the batman. The platoon sergeant was his right-hand man. The standard of NCOs in the British Army being what it was, the platoon sergeant was almost invariably well trained, competent, and reliable. He was particularly important for most CANLOAN officers because, in addition to being directly responsible for weapons and ammunition, dress, equipment, records and discipline, and for commanding the platoon in the absence of the officer, he was the one person with whom the officer could share the burdens of leadership and was the chief tutor to his Canadian officer in the ways of the British Army.

The batman, often a volunteer for the position, was officially a servant and looked after his officer in many ways. In barracks a batman was primarily a valet, but in action he was an indispensable part of the HQ team. In theory he looked after his officer so that the officer could devote all his attention to the men in his platoon or company. In practice the batman was the platoon commander's constant companion, acting as bodyguard during reconnaissance and as the platoon runner. He often shared a slit trench with him. One CANLOAN officer admits that he spoiled his batman outrageously, insisting, for example, on taking turns in making tea in the morning. Sometimes the batman was platoon signaller, carrying the platoon's #38 wireless set. Allowing for individual differences, the officer-batman relationship was usually a very special one.

Also part of platoon headquarters were the teams responsible for the platoon's special weapons: the 2-inch mortar, which was used for high explosive, illumination, and smoke, and the PIAT, which was the platoon's sole anti-tank weapon. Each weapon had a team: No. 1, responsible for firing, and No. 2, responsible primarily for the bombs. The Mortar No. 1 was usually a lance corporal (L./Cpl.) and a member of the platoon O. group, or command team.

Each platoon had three sections, each consisting of two junior NCOs and eight privates. The section was commanded by a corporal and had a rifle group and a Bren group. The Bren group was commanded by a L./Cpl., the section's second in command, and had a No. 1 and No. 2, the former known as "the Bren gunner." The

Bren gunner was an essential man, because the Bren provided most of the firepower of the section and, indeed, of the platoon and company. Though platoons were each supposed to have a lieutenant and 36 other ranks, they were rarely at full strength. Since it was difficult to reduce platoon HQ to fewer than five, or Bren groups to fewer than two, the rifle groups in sections sometimes had only three or four members, and a platoon might be reduced by casualties to two weak sections.

The platoon commander was issued with a revolver (a Smith and Wesson .38 calibre six shooter), the three section commanders with 9-mm Sten submachine guns, and all others with rifles (SMLE [small magazine Lee Enfield] No. 4, Mk 1, .303, 10-round bolt action). In Normandy, because of the deadly aim of snipers, whose primary target was officers, most officers removed their rank shoulder badges (pips) and other signs of rank and carried a rifle or a Sten. For the same reason, other ranks were often forbidden to salute.

For platoon commanders an ominous summons was for an O. group, called by the company commander to give orders for an imminent attack or other operation. Often these meetings were the only chance to meet the other platoon commanders as well as the officer commanding (OC) and the second in command of the company. The O. group, with all the officers in a company present as well as commanders of supporting arms, was usually held in less than secure forward locations. There is a story about Brigadier Cass commanding 8 Brigade of the 3rd Division, whose O. group received a direct hit knocking out every member of the group except the Brig., who, although badly shaken, immediately ordered, "Send for the seconds in command."[30]

After the company O. group came the platoon commander's O. group, consisting of the platoon sergeant, section commanders, and the mortar NCO. At this the platoon commander passed on his superior's orders and detailed his own orders. This, too, was vulnerable. The death of Lieut. Jack Levine, 2 Glosters., by a direct hit during an O. group was one of a number of such incidents.

The O. group was usually followed by a reconnaissance (or recce) in which officers, sometimes accompanied by their junior commanders, made their way to the most suitable place from which to observe the ground over which the planned operation was to take place.

One of the most difficult duties of the platoon commander was what Gen. Sir John Hackett has called "the management of fear."[31] All the stresses of the battle-field that contribute to fear – noise, loneliness, insecurity, pain, and the prospect of immediate death – had an effect on everyone who was exposed to them. By the time of the Second World War it was recognized that each person had a limit of endurance which, if exceeded, would result in some sort of breakdown, which was referred to in various terms: battle fatigue, shell shock, or "bomb happy." This breakdown was recognized as a type of casualty rather than a crime of cowardice and constituted perhaps 20 percent of all battle casualties. One of the most difficult tasks for a platoon commander was to decide whether an apparent psychiatric breakdown was real or faked. There were also the problems of deciding whether self-inflicted wounds were accidental or deliberate, and of what to do about stragglers in a patrol or attack.

As the Normandy campaign dragged on during July the duties of the platoon commander became more and more demanding. First, it became more difficult to keep up morale, reduce fear, and head off breakdowns. Second, the drain of casualties meant that there were fewer soldiers to carry out the duties required of a platoon. Third, reinforcements needed a great deal of individual attention and usually were not up to the standard of those who had landed with their divisions. CANLOAN officers still recall with pride the cheerful enthusiasm, fighting spirit, and high level of training of troops who were going into battle for the first time with their British divisions. By the end of July few of these troops were left and the survivors were subdued, tired, more dependent on self-discipline and stubbornness than enthusiasm, and outnumbered by relatively inexperienced reinforcements who had never felt the original elation. One platoon commander said at the time, "Look, all I can do with my men, the sort of men I have, is to persuade them to get out of their holes in the ground, march up to the objective, dig a hole in the ground and get into it."[32]

There was similar deterioration in the ranks of the NCOs, all of which made the platoon commander's burden of leadership heavier. He had also to cope with his own fear and the steady approach to the limit of his endurance. Though he could become inured to the occurrence of casualties, to dealing with the dead and the wounded, it was nevertheless a recurring shock to observe what enemy weapons could do to those with whom he had developed a bond of friendship and fraternity.

What was perhaps most difficult to bear was the unceasing fatigue. Two CANLOAN officers, Lieuts. Russ Parke and Roger MacLellan in 2 Glas. H., were wounded at the same time and found themselves on adjoining stretchers. They calculated the average amount of sleep they had had during the Normandy campaign. It came to two hours and thirty-five minutes a day. Another CANLOAN officer wrote to his parents that in the 100 hours before he was wounded he had had barely five hours of sleep. This aspect of warfare in Normandy has been described by Max Hastings:

> Battles are not fought by keen-eyed, bright-faced young heroes but by drugged men walking in a daze, jumpy from noise and strain and lack of rest. The destiny of them all is determined by the battalion commander who gives out his orders having had two hours sleep in the last 24, then the company commanders trying to awaken the young platoon commanders from their death-like slumber, all of them heavy and drained of energy. Thirty minutes to make plans, then they lead the dog-weary men against the Spandau and everlasting mortar to the first, second and third objectives.[33]

For a CANLOAN officer who survived the first two months of the Normandy campaign, there was an improvement in infantry skills, which were, however, performed more and more as a routine than as a challenge. His feelings were mixed: resignation to the idea of becoming a casualty, but a fierce devotion to his platoon and a determination to behave so as to justify their faith in him, as well as to maintain the honour and traditions of the regiment and live up to the sometimes unrealistic expectations for CANLOAN officers. But inevitably there was a slow deterioration of spirit and a loss of spontaneity and humour as the insidious effects of battle fatigue took their toll.

7

Normandy:
The Breakout

THOUGH THE ATTACKS west of Caen had served the main purpose of pinning down the bulk of the enemy forces in Normandy, they had not made significant gains of ground and, perhaps more important, they had incurred excessively heavy casualties, which could not be replaced. As already mentioned, Sir Ronald Adam, the British Adjutant-General, made a special trip to Normandy to discuss the reinforcement crisis with Montgomery. It was evident that if infantry casualties were to continue at the same rate it would be necessary to cannibalize some divisions to maintain others.

There were several reasons for the ultimate defeat of the Germans in Normandy, but an important one was the skill with which Montgomery influenced the movements of the most effective German troops, the panzer divisions.

Since the German High Command expected the Allies to take the most direct route from Caen to the Seine and Paris, their major strength was built up east of the Orne. Recognizing this, the Allied strategy from the beginning was to attract as many German troops as possible to the Caen area in order to facilitate a breakout by the Americans from the Cotentin peninsula south and then in a right hook to the Seine. The Second British Army had the unenviable task of fighting and holding the most and best German forces for nearly two months on the east of the beachhead in Normandy to clear the way for an American breakout in the west and then, when it came, of hearing reports of how the Americans were winning the war while they, the Brits, sat on their fannies at Caen.

The only way the Germans might have repulsed the Allied landing in Normandy would have been to hold the line with infantry reinforcements while the panzer divisions withdrew to organize a massed armoured counter-attack at the weakest point in the Allied front. But the Germans were prevented from doing this by Montgomery's strategy of choosing the timing and location of Allied attacks in the Second Army sector so that the German panzers had to be used defensively and piecemeal to plug gaps and were kept tied down on the front of the British Second Army.

Operation EPSOM, the spearhead of the Scottish Corridor, was part of this strategy and it required all the available panzer divisions to contain it. At the end of EPSOM and for some time after, no fewer than eight of the nine panzer divisions were west of the Odon between Hill 112 and Villers-Bocage. After the British attacks in the area were halted between 10 and 18 July, however, two panzer divisions began to move towards the American front.

By mid-July it became important for the British Army to launch an attack south of Caen that would tie down the bulk of the available German forces, prevent transfers to the west to oppose the imminent American breakthrough, destroy or severely weaken the panzer divisions, gain open ground south of Caen for use as airfields, and, by the use of tanks, of which there was a plentiful supply, reduce casualties among the dwindling numbers of infantrymen. Lieut.-Gen. Sir Miles Dempsey, Commander of the British Second Army, devised a plan that seemed to meet all these objectives: a massive attack led by three armoured divisions. This plan was operation GOODWOOD. General Dempsey said later in a letter to General Eisenhower, "I was prepared to lose a couple of hundred tanks as long as I didn't lose men."[1]

While operation GOODWOOD was being organized between 10 and 18 July, XXX and XII Corps were ordered to maintain enough pressure west of the Orne to prevent the withdrawal of the II Panzer Corps either to the American front, where the long-awaited breakout was being prepared, or across the Orne south of Caen, where operation GOODWOOD was to be directed.

These attacks west of the Odon were more than feints. They were large-scale attacks on strongly held locations, and they were resisted fiercely. More often than not the objectives could not be taken and casualties were heavy. In two days, 15 and 16 July, there were 3,500 British casualties.

CANLOAN officers were active in all these actions, as is evident from their casualties. It has already been noted that on 16 July alone five CANLOAN officers were killed in action. During the period 15 to 30 July between GOODWOOD and BLUECOAT, the last great effort to hold the German armour in the east and the main contribution by the Second Army to the breakout in the west, no fewer than 14 CANLOAN officers were killed in action, all except one of them west of the Odon. Of these fatal casualties five were from the 53rd Division, four from the 59th, two from the 15th, and one each from the 43rd, 50th, and 3rd Divisions.

There were also heavy German losses. By the end of July several divisions had lost up to 75 percent of their men but continued to fight fiercely.[2] Though the British had gained little ground, they had been successful in pinning down at least four panzer divisions during a critical period.

Operation GOODWOOD was an attack on Bourguébus Ridge on the road to Falaise from the port of Caen east of the Orne. An armoured corps, the VIIIth, consisting of three armoured divisions, the 11th, the 7th, and the newly arrived Guards Armoured Division, with a total of 750 tanks, was to deliver the main attack, supported on its left by I British Corps and on its right by I Canadian Corps. The operation, which began on 18 July, was preceded by what has been called "the greatest air-raid of all time,"[3] more than 2,000 heavy bombers and 2,000 fighter-bombers and fighters, supplemented by massed artillery – 720 guns with 250,000 rounds of ammunition. While this overwhelming firepower aroused optimism in senior commanders and the men in the armoured divisions who observed it, the results of the two-day battle were disappointing. The Germans, who knew 36 hours before the attack where and when it would take place, were able to mount effective anti-tank defences with Tigers and 88s, and even to summon the only available reserves, the remnants of the 12th SS Panzer Division. The German defences, well prepared in belts to a depth of up to 10 miles, were armed with 272 "moaning Minnies," one hundred 88s, several hundred tanks, and thousands of infantry.[4]

After the air attack and artillery barrage that were intended to obliterate the German defences, the armoured attack began at 0530 on 18 July, when the 11th Armoured Division threaded its way through gaps in a minefield and drove south towards Bourguébus Ridge. At first it made good progress, advancing 12,000 yards before being stopped by the German anti-tank defences, which filled the corn fields with knocked-out and burning Sherman, Cromwell, and Churchill tanks. The attack continued the next day, but all three armoured divisions had ground to a halt. At the same time heavy rain turned the tank tracks into rivers of mud. The losses in the two days of GOODWOOD were nearly 400 tanks and more than 5,000 troops. To prevent further casualties Montgomery halted the operation, although the 2nd Canadian Division continued to attack the nearby Verrières Ridge for the next two days.

During operation GOODWOOD, a number of CANLOAN officers were serving in the lorried infantry battalions of the 7th and 11th Armoured Divisions, and others in the British 3rd Division, which attacked villages on the left flank. A few days later, on 23 July, four British divisions, the 3rd, 49th, 51st, and the 6th Airborne, were transferred temporarily to the new First Canadian Army, which assumed responsibility for this sector.

Two CANLOAN officers were killed in GOODWOOD. One was CDN/483, A./Capt. Bernard J. Kelly of the 2nd KSLI in the 3rd Division. Kelly was born in Ireland but grew up in the Canadian west, where he obtained a commission in the militia before enlisting in the active force. He had gone to Normandy with 4 KSLI in the 11th Armoured Division and had later transferred to 2 KSLI in the 3rd Division, arriving approximately 24 hours before he was killed. CDN/78, Lieut. James H. Gilmour, 1 Gordons, 51 Highland Division, had enlisted in July 1940 and served as a sergeant in the 2nd Canadian Parachute Battalion and as an instructor at Brockville OTC before obtaining a commission in 1943. A fellow officer observed later, "Lieut Gilmour was one of our best platoon commanders, brave as a lion and well liked by the Jocks."[5]

In the 11th Armoured Division the first CANLOAN officer who had joined 4 KSLI in April, CDN/28, Lieut. Colin M. Patch, was wounded in GOODWOOD. The unit's war diary noted that he was shot in the foot but continued to command his platoon as long as he could communicate with it. It was in this battle that Capt. Harold (Hank) Henry established a reputation as a dashing commander of 4 KSLI Carrier Platoon. The war diary notes that in GOODWOOD the carrier platoon "was sent over to the left flank under Lieut. H.F. Henry (Canada) where they did good work in killing or routing the Boche machine gunners who had caught the Bn in the flanks."[6]

A fellow officer recalls that Captain Henry "was incredibly brave in action and appeared to show no fear. It was an inspiration to be close to Hank's carrier in the heat of battle, seeing his broad grin and the impression he gave of almost enjoying the fighting."[7] Both Patch and Henry were mentioned in dispatches.

The advances south of Caen and transfers of German troops as a result of

GOODWOOD had a beneficial influence on at least two battlefields west of the Odon that had been bitterly contested for weeks. On 20 July the 50th Division finally captured Hottot, which had been a divisional objective shortly after D-Day and had been the scene of constant fighting ever since. The village of Maltot, near Hill 112, which had been attacked by the 43rd Division on 10 July and had been held by the Germans in the subsequent two weeks in bloody attacks and counter-attacks, was finally taken in a night engagement on 22 July. An active participant in the struggle was Lieut. James Rutherford, the only remaining CANLOAN officer in 4 Wilts. His platoon's position on the forward slope of Hill 112 came to be known as "Hank's Strip." In the final assault on Maltot both Rutherford and his platoon sergeant were wounded in the house clearing at night in Château Maltot. As was noted earlier, daylight revealed the many bodies of Dorset and R. Hamps. who had been killed in the assault on 10 July. They could be buried at last.

Finally the American breakout in the Cotentin peninsula, which the British Second Army had done so much to assist and which had been postponed several times, was ready to be launched. A drive from Saint Lô towards Avranches, which bore the code name COBRA, was to begin on 25 July and on 30 July the British Army would launch operation BLUECOAT, a drive from Caumont towards Vire. Montgomery ordered General Dempsey to "throw caution overboard and to take any risks he likes and accept any casualties and step on the gas for Vire."[8]

With the benefit of hindsight it is apparent that the three major thrusts around the beginning of August by the American, Canadian, and British Armies were vital preliminaries to the long-hoped-for breakthrough and the successful conclusion of the Normandy campaign before the end of the month. At the time, however, that was not apparent to the participants. For the British Second Army, operation BLUECOAT involved fighting in the heart of the *bocage* country, which became increasingly difficult and culminated in the capture of Mont Pinçon, 1,200 feet above sea level in "la Suisse normande." Mont Pinçon had been designated as a major objective by Montgomery in his briefing in St. Paul's School weeks before the landings in Normandy and later was assigned as an objective to 1 Dorset in the 50th Division. Until the last few days of the Normandy campaign the enemy proved capable of inflicting heavy casualties. Among CANLOAN officers there were as many fatal casualties in this period as in June, and more decorations for gallantry. The bitter struggle and constant drain of losses persisted to the end in Normandy.

For the troops who took part in operation BLUECOAT, particularly the infantry divisions, such as the 15th Scottish and the 43rd Wessex, there was none of the excitement and enthusiasm of their first battles a few weeks before. Coming from the fierce Odon battles they were tired. One of those who took part in this offensive summed up their attitude:

For two months they [the British] had pinned down most of the enemy's divisions. When the offensive (BLUECOAT) began they were already weary with the endless routine of marching and fighting, they were already punch-drunk with battle, so that for them there was no elation, no feeling of the great and wonderful day that had come at last, only the determination to stick it out a little longer, to conquer the numbing weariness, the fear that grew suddenly a hundredfold at the prospect of dying at the moment of victory.[9]

The dogged courage and determination of the British foot soldier that was a constant feature of this campaign was never displayed more fully than during BLUECOAT.

Operation BLUECOAT involved the concentration of three corps, most of the British Second Army, west of the Orne. For the three armoured divisions it meant a fast move from Caen, where they had been engaged in GOODWOOD, to the western portion of the Normandy bridgehead. One infantry division, the 3rd British, which had been in the Caen area since D-Day, was ferried in vehicles to the extreme west next to the Americans, while the 49th Division, which had been in the Villers-Bocage area since landing in Normandy, was transferred to the airborne bridgehead east of Caen. Responsibility for the GOODWOOD-Caen sector east of the Orne was handed over to the newly formed First Canadian Army, with the British I Corps under its command. The chief purpose of operation BLUECOAT was to draw the Germans' attention from the American breakout while still keeping the pressure east of the US sector. The transfer from a sector where the bulk of the German panzer divisions were concentrated to one where there were none was calculated to give the divisions in XXX, VIII, and XII Corps an advantage. Considering the difficult *bocage* country, they needed all the advantages they could get.

On the right, VIII Corps, now consisting of the 15th Scottish Division and the 11th Armoured Division and soon to be joined by the 3rd Division, had as its objective Vire while protecting the American left flank. In the centre, XXX Corps (43rd and 50th Divisions and 7th Armoured Division) were to capture Mont Pinçon. On the left was XII Corps, consisting of the 53rd Welch Division and the 59th Staffordshire Division. They were to clear the west bank of the Odon and establish a bridgehead across the river. Like Mont Pinçon this was a long-term objective that had been identified in England before D-Day.

The assault began on the morning of 30 July. Despite the difficult country, which was ideal for ambushes, the 15th Scottish and 11th Armoured Divisions made rapid progress, gaining up to six miles in the first day of BLUECOAT. By 1 August the 11th had reached Le Bény-Bocage on the way to Vire, after which the drive was halted by German troops rushed from south of Caen. Having finally realized that OVERLORD was the main invasion, the Germans were now rushing infantry divisions from the Pas de Calais to Normandy, relieving panzer divisions around Caen, which now began to move west.

Progress was slower on the fronts of XXX Corps towards Mont Pinçon and XII Corps towards the Orne because of more difficult country, extensive minefields, and increasingly fierce German resistance. On 4 August Montgomery reported to Churchill, "I fancy we will now have some heavy fighting on the eastern flank, especially on that part from Villers-Bocage to Vire which faces the east. The enemy has moved considerable strength to that part from the area south and south-east of Caen."[10]

It has been suggested that the 48 hours beginning on the afternoon of 6 August settled the fate of the German armies in Normandy.[11] First, Mont Pinçon, the highest point in Normandy and the key to the German defences, was captured by the 43rd Division. Meanwhile the Germans had retreated from Villers-Bocage and Évrecy to the Orne and were determined to hold that line to protect their flank and rear. On the same night that Mont Pinçon was captured, the 59th Division forced a crossing over the Orne north of Thury Harcourt and established a bridgehead. And on 7 August the Germans, on Hitler's orders and against the better judgment of the military commanders, and using panzer divisions released from the eastern area, launched the Mortain counter-attack in an attempt to cut off the American drive to the south and to reach the sea in Brittany. The failure of this effort resulted in the encirclement of two German armies in the Falaise pocket and the dramatic conclusion of the Normandy campaign before the end of August.

CANLOAN officers were active in all aspects of BLUECOAT. More of them were in the 15th Scottish Division than in any other. On 5 August the 10th Battalion, the Highland Light Infantry (HLI) had no fewer than nine CANLOAN officers on strength, four of whom were wounded on that day. Nine CANLOAN officers were also in 2 Glas. H. during BLUECOAT, of whom, fortunately, only one, Lieut. Stewart Cameron, was wounded, on 11 August. One CANLOAN officer in the 15th Scottish Division earned a Military Cross in the bitter fighting at Estry. His citation reads in part:

On 6 August Lieut. [CDN/81, John H.] Hitchcock was commanding the leading platoon of C Coy 2 Gordons which was acting as advanced guard company in the battalion advance on Estry. On approaching the cross roads just NW of Estry Lieut Hitchcock's platoon and the tp of tanks supporting it came under heavy fire, the exact position of which was difficult to locate. Lieut Hitchcock carried out a right flank attack and succeeded in reaching the cross roads. From there the enemy strong point containing machine guns and an A/Tk gun was located and Lieut Hitchcock himself led a party armed with grenades and a PIAT forward to try and deal with it. He succeeded in getting within grenade throwing distance of one machine gun and killed four Germans but was then forced to withdraw owing to intense enemy fire. He and his platoon continued to hold the position on the cross roads (a position further forward of which a subsequent attack by two battalions failed to make any progress) until forced to withdraw. Lieut Hitchcock by his action showed great courage and sound leadership, attributes which he has shown in all previous actions.[12]

In the infantry brigade of the 11th Armoured Division, Hank Henry continued his imaginative direction of the Carrier Platoon of 4 KSLI, with its Vickers machine guns and flame throwers. In the 1st Hereford, CDN/270, Lieut. William J. (Kotch) Kotchepaw, who had been wounded on Hill 112 at the end of June and had left all the platoons in C Company commanded by sergeants, returned in time to resume command of 15, his former platoon in the attack on Flers, which became the site of the 11th Armoured Division's memorial. The reunion was short-lived, unfortunately, for Kotch was killed in action on 10 September.

In the 11th Armoured Division's attack on Vlers on 6 August, 3 Mons. suffered heavy casualties. Of 550 men who started the battle, 160 were killed or wounded. Platoons became little more than sections; one, with 15 men, was commanded by a lance corporal.

The 3rd Division, which had been transported from Caen to the extreme western boundary of the Second Army next to the Americans, arrived after the capture of Vire. It attacked south towards Tinchebray, southwest of Falaise, where it was soon squeezed out by the Canadian Army on the left and the Americans on the right.

On 1 August, 3 Infantry Division had joined VIII Corps and begun relieving 11 Armoured Divisional units in the area of Le Bény-Bocage. On 6 August near the village of Burey, the Germans counter-attacked, and Cpl. Sidney Bates of 1 R.

Norfolk won, posthumously, 3 Infantry Division's third VC of the war and the first in Normandy. Pushing south towards Vire, which was included in the neighbouring US sector, 3 Recce Regt. was stopped short of the Vire-Vaudry ridge. The same day, 6 August, 1 KOSB of 9 Brigade was involved in fierce fighting attempting to cross the Allière River. Two CANLOAN officers in the battalion were killed; Lieut. Willard Caseley and CDN/502, Lieut. Malcolm R. Rose. Caseley was the first fatal casualty of the "600 group" who had converted to infantry in order to join the CANLOAN scheme. He had served in coastal artillery for more than two years. Posted to 1 KOSB on 23 July, he was killed in his first attack. Rose was one of the battle drill instructors who had been recruited by Brigadier Gregg to instruct the other CANLOAN volunteers at Sussex. He had been posted to 1 KOSB as a reinforcement on 1 July and joined the battalion a week later. When leading a patrol across the Allière he bumped into a German position and was killed in the resulting fire fight. A third CANLOAN fatality in the 3rd Division at this time was Lieut. Norman Brown of 2 E. Yorks. As noted earlier, he was picked up badly wounded in front of Len Robertson's platoon position and died two days later.

At first the progress of XXX Corps was slower than that of VIII Corps, but the 43rd Division pressed a vigorous attack through the heart of the *bocage* against an enemy which had been reinforced by three panzer divisions within a day or two of the beginning of BLUECOAT. In the first attack, on 30 July on the village of Briquessard, a CANLOAN officer in 4 Som. LI, CDN/50, Lieut. Gordon V. Wright, earned the first of his two MCs. The citation notes:

> This officer led his platoon with conspicuous success through a field of AP mines and small arms fire to the assault on their final objective in the village. His platoon's success was entirely due to his leadership and enthusiasm. Lieut Wright was wounded during the action but stayed with his platoon until they had captured their objective. This action is typical of this officer, who has served continuously with the Bn since the opening of its Normandy campaign, and throughout it he has commanded his platoon with the greatest bravery and determination.[13]

Gordon Wright recovered from his wounds, rejoined 4 Som. LI, and earned a bar to his MC in the spring of 1945. A few days later, on 5 August, another CANLOAN officer in the 43rd Division, CDN/60, A./Capt. Ellis G. Andrews of 4 Dorset, earned an MC. His citation reads:

> During the battle for the village of Ondefontaine on 5 Aug his company was completely cut off from the rest of the battalion. Two self-propelled guns and approximately 100 infantry attacked his company which, at that time, had been reduced to a total strength of 31. For two hours he moved from post to post encouraging the remnants of his company, cheering and heartening the men. It was entirely due to his example and leadership that all attacks were repelled and the position held until they were able to join up with the rest of the Battalion ... Throughout the action this officer displayed exemplary courage and devotion to duty in the face of the enemy.[14]

Andrews had served overseas with the Carleton and York Regiment from 1940 to 1942 before returning to Canada for a commission. He went to Normandy with 4

Dorset, was wounded at Hill 112 on 18 July but returned to his battalion in time for BLUECOAT. Three days after the action that won him the MC he was killed in action.

A third MC was earned at the same time by yet another CANLOAN officer in the 43rd Division. He was CDN/475, Lieut. Harry A. Taylor of the 7th R. Hamps. His citation is unusual, since it recounts four separate examples of gallantry, illustrating

> outstanding courage and leadership since the start of operations. As leader of a fighting patrol in the Rauray sector when his platoon was caught in the open by enemy machine gun fire he [Lieut. Taylor] advanced with three others, dislodged the enemy with hand grenades and captured the machine gun. On the night of 17 Jul he led his platoon with great dash and vigour and only returned when his platoon had virtually been wiped out and all the officers of the company had been killed. On 19 Jul this officer took a patrol of two men into the enemy lines to try to contact a pl of the Bn which was out of commission following an attack. He carried out the patrol with great boldness and complete disregard for his own safety. Finally, on 6 August when commanding the leading platoon of his company in an attack the company was held up by heavy fire from well placed enemy MG posts. He observed one of these MG posts and led his front section across the stream to deal with it. Moving 150 yards in advance of the coy position under heavy fire he killed two of the enemy and captured the remainder. He showed great skill, initiative and daring throughout the action.[15]

Harry Taylor's company (B Company) in 7 R. Hamps. was commanded by another CANLOAN officer, Maj. Frederick Chesham.

It has been said that the capture of Mont Pinçon by the 43rd Division "may well be considered among the finest infantry actions in the war."[16] Certainly it was a bitter struggle, as is attested by the casualties in 129 Brigade. One platoon of 4 Som. LI was reduced to five men,[17] and the 5. Wilts. was almost exterminated. After the first day's assault the remnants of two companies were combined to form one; at the end of the second day there were only 60 survivors of the 800 in the battalion.[18] The CO, Lieut.-Col. J.H.C. Pearson, set an example of gallantry and inspiration when the battalion was pinned down at a river. Walking calmly forward, he picked a rose by the roadside to put in his hat and swung his walking stick as he crossed the bridge. He was killed, but, inspired by his example, the Wiltshires stormed across the stream and up the slopes ahead.

Also part of XXX Corps were the 50th Division and the 7th Armoured Division. In BLUECOAT the 50th Division finally captured Villers-Bocage and then were placed in reserve for the first time since they landed on D-Day. They returned to action, however, in time to continue the push towards Falaise. At this time a CANLOAN officer who was to have a most distinguished military career earned a Military Cross. CDN/59, Roland A. Reid had joined CANLOAN as a captain and had been posted to 2 Devons at the end of June as second in command of a rifle company; he was promoted to company commander while the battalion was in reserve. His citation, in part, reads as follows:

> On 11 August when commanding a company in action for the first time he was given the task of clearing the village of Rousseville en route to his first objective. The village was

surrounded by thick hedges and orchards which limited visibility and made control almost impossible. The enemy were holding the area in some strength, particularly heavy fire coming from the right flank. Disregarding this fire during which the rifle he was carrying was hit, Capt Reid displayed great dash and initiative, personally supervising the clearing of the village. He then reformed his company, still under heavy fire, and led it on to the objective ... Although the company had suffered heavy casualties he was able to lead his men into the next phase of the attack, which was again successful. He maintained a high standard of skill and leadership throughout the whole operation.[19]

Roland Reid retired from the Canadian Army in 1976 as a major-general.

The third division in XXX Corps was the 7th Armoured Division. It was involved in changes of command when, two days after the beginning of BLUECOAT, Major-General Erskine, the Divisional Commander, and Brigadier Hinde, Commander of the Armoured Brigade, were replaced, as was Lieutenant-General Bucknall, Commander of XXX Corps. Such changes, however, were beyond the ken of junior officers in the 131st Infantry Brigade, consisting of the 1/5, 1/6, and 1/7th Queens. Back in the *bocage* after GOODWOOD, these units took part in a night attack on 3 August, which was followed by a vigorous counter-attack in which several companies were overrun. Alexander McKee has described the condition of the Queens on 6 August:

> The infantry brigade of the 7th Armoured had been virtually used up, the worst hit battalion being 1/6 Queens. As the four rifle companies trudged forward that day one only was respectable, numbering 55 men, approximately half strength. There were 40 men in the next company, 15 in the next, and a pathetic little group of eight men represented the last company.[20]

At that time there were five CANLOAN officers in 1/6 Queens, three in the same company: Maj. Donald Findlay, Lieut. Peter Pearce, and CDN/289, Capt. Eric Brown. A few days later, on 12 August, Findlay and Pearce were wounded. In the attack on 3 August another of the American CANLOAN officers, CDN/28, Lieut. William J. Lalonde, was killed. Born in Brooklyn, New York, he had enlisted in the Canadian Army in 1940. He had been posted to the 1/7 Queens when he arrived with the first CANLOAN flight.

On the left flank in BLUECOAT was XII Corps, which comprised the 53 Welch and the 59th Staffordshire Divisions. Though they had the shortest distance to travel, moving from the Odon up to the Orne, their advance was contested fiercely.

The 59th Division had three costly battles in Normandy: Caen on 8 July, Noyers on 16 July, and the Orne bridgehead on 7 and 8 August. Their 176 Brigade, consisting of 7 R. Norfolk, 7 S. Staffords., and 6 N. Staffs., advanced to Villers-Bocage on 4 August and to the Orne on the 5th. The brigade crossed the Orne on the 6th to establish a bridgehead, which it held against furious counter-attacks by the 12th SS Panzer Division on 7 and 8 August. A CANLOAN officer who served in the 59th Division at this time has noted that "the battle resulted in the nearly complete loss of the Division as well as that of the enemy, an SS Division on its way to attack the Americans at Mortain."[21]

CANLOAN officers played an important part in this action. There were five Canadian lieutenants in 1/7 S. Staffords.: George Beck; CDN/158, Hubert Hollier; CDN/

275, William B. Mottram; Robert Newstead; and Robert Robertson. It was Robert Newstead who, on a patrol on the night of 5 August, found a spot where the Orne could be forded to establish a bridgehead at Grimbosq. In the battle of the bridgehead 1/7 S. Staffords. had 14 officer casualties (five killed and nine wounded), including four CANLOAN officers. Beck, Hollier, and Newstead were wounded and Robertson, who had joined the battalion a week earlier, was killed.

In addition to Robertson in the 1/7 S. Staffords, two other CANLOANs in the 59th Division were killed in the Grimbosq bridgehead: CDN/441, Capt. Aubrey C. Cawsey, 5 S. Staffords., and Lieut. Andrew Bushell, 7 R. Norfolk. Captain Cawsey was one of those who had reverted from major to captain in order to join CANLOAN. Lieutenant Bushell's death has been described by his batman:

> We were against the 12th Hitler Jugend Panzer Div and the 25th and 26th Panzer Grenadier Regiments who threw in a number of counter-attacks. Our anti-tank sergeant knocked out three German tanks practically single handed I had just gone into the dug-out and Lieut Bushell and the platoon corporal went out. A German tank appeared and the sergeant tried to train on it but the tank fired an 88 mm shell which hit the gun and killed the sergeant and the gunner and the blast killed the corporal and Lieut Bushell. That was when I lost Andy.[22]

The 6 N. Staffs. fared no better. By 9 August the battalion was reduced more or less to its headquarters and D Company. According to the battalion's war diary A, B, and C Companies were skeletons – 202 men were dead, wounded, or missing and there were no replacements. The only remaining CANLOAN officer in the battalion, Lieut. Doug Gage, was wounded at the bridgehead.

The 53rd Welch Division, which had been fighting in the Hill 112 and Évrecy area for nearly a month before BLUECOAT, continued to fight forward against stiff opposition. The idea of a breakthrough was foreign to their experience. The division suffered fatal casualties to four CANLOAN officers during the campaign in addition to the many who were wounded. On 1 August CDN/395, Lieut. James P. Day, 1 E. Lan. R., was killed. He had served overseas with the Cameron Highlanders of Ottawa 1940–42 before returning to Canada for a commission. On 8 August CANLOAN lost another of its American members with the death of CDN/24, Lieut. William G. Hartman, 1 Oxf. Bucks. Hartman was commanding the battalion's carrier platoon when he was killed by a bomb from an RAF Typhoon aircraft. On 12 August Lieut. Maurice Trudeau, 1/5 Welch, was killed in action, and on 19 August, in the last stages of the battle of the Falaise pocket, Lieut. Harold Main, 6 RWF, who had such a distinguished record of commanding fighting patrols for his battalion, was finally killed in an attack on a village when the grenades he was carrying were exploded by machine-gun bullets.

Like the 59th Division, the 53rd was concerned with the crossing of the Orne. A patrol on the evening of 5 August in search of a suitable crossing site earned a Military Cross for CDN/380, Lieut. Gordon J. Booth, 4 Welch. The citation says,

> Lieut Booth, a Canadian officer, was detailed for the task ... with an RE sergeant, a corporal and six ORs. He had completed the western end of his assignment and was working to the eastern end when the patrol came under heavy machine gun fire. Booth ordered his men to

take cover. He then ran forward over an open stretch to obtain a better view of a demolished bridge. He had rejoined his patrol when the enemy opened up accurate mortar fire, forcing him to split the party. Both were heavily mortared and machine-gunned throughout the withdrawal and the RE sergeant and another man seriously wounded. Lieut Booth, in full view of the enemy, crawled out with a stretcher-bearer and carried back the sergeant, then went back for the other wounded man. His courage, determination and utter disregard for personal safety were an inspiration to his men.[23]

Earlier Booth had been commended for courage and leadership in a raid on 23 July. Another CANLOAN in the 53rd Division, CDN/145, Lieut. Frederick Evans, 2 Mons., earned a Croix de Guerre with Silver Star on 15 August near Falaise. His citation reads:

On Aug 15 the Battalion attacked the village of Leffard, west of Falaise. Lieut Evans was in command of the leading platoon of his company. Soon after crossing the start line the platoon came under very heavy and accurate fire from a strong force of Germans concealed in the houses and dug in on the outskirts of the village. With great determination and dash Lieut Evans led his platoon on to his objective. Casualties were heavy and on reaching the objective the platoon consisted of only seven men. Very shortly afterwards the platoon was counter-attacked by a force of 40 Germans. Inspired by Lieut Evan's cool leadership and determination the platoon repulsed this attack, inflicting heavy casualties and held the objective under heavy and sustained mortar fire until relieved. Lieut Evan's courage, determination and inspiring example undoubtedly contributed greatly to the success of a hard fought action.[24]

The spectacular events that resulted in the encirclement of the German Seventh Army and Fifth Panzer Army have been related by others. CANLOAN officers in the British Second Army advanced with their divisions "up the bottle" to the pocket and then proceeded to the crossing of the Seine. One of the best descriptions of conditions in the "pocket" was given by a CANLOAN officer who passed through the gap as a prisoner of war on 17 August and escaped two days later.[25] Eisenhower's brief comment that "it was literally possible to walk for hundreds of yards at a time stepping on nothing but dead and decaying flesh"[26] is as graphic a description as any.

While the British Second Army was pushing painfully through the *bocage* country, there were more dramatic advances on both its flanks. On the right the Americans had swept south and east and then turned north to cut off the Germans in the "Falaise pocket." At one point General Patton telephoned his superior, General Bradley, to say, "We have elements in Argentan. Shall we continue and drive the British into the sea for another Dunkirk?"[27]

On the left the First Canadian Army in two successive hard-fought operations, TOTALIZE 7–10 August and TRACTABLE 14–16 August, drove down from south of Caen to Falaise. CANLOAN officers in the British I Corps, which was part of the Canadian First Army, participated in TOTALIZE and TRACTABLE on the eastern flank. This corps consisted of the 51st Highland Division, the 49th Polar Bear Division, the 7th Armoured Division, and the 6th Airborne Division. A CANLOAN officer, Lieut. Jack McBride, 7th BW, who commanded a platoon in operation TOTALIZE, has expressed the feelings of an infantryman after a successful battle:

There is something about a big battle that is both terrifying and glorious at the same time. Perhaps because it is so tragic it seems to take on some inexplicable romantic aura. And as the battle runs its course the soldiers, who at first credited their opposing numbers with too much of everything, rose above them. For a few frightening, glorious hours they were super men, caught up in a terrible excitement from which they no longer wanted to withdraw. It was "Up the Highland Division" and "Scotland Forever" all the way. The infantryman with his own two feet beat his own path straight to the enemy. He knows it is axiomatic that his own supply columns will soon hammer his little path into some sort of highway. Whether it becomes "HD up" or "the road to the front" is of no consequence. What is of consequence to him is the knowledge that when he made those little tracks it was on sacred ground. And in some curious way he may even resent those who follow him ... for the ground is no longer sacred.[28]

In the breakout operations in Normandy, three CANLOAN officers in the 51st Highland Division were killed in action. The first was CDN/518, Lieut. Frederick J. Dynes of the 1st BW, who was killed on the first day of TOTALIZE. Born in Northern Ireland, he grew up in Montreal and served in the Black Watch militia before enlisting in the active force. Another CANLOAN officer in the 1st BW had been seriously wounded on 14 July and died of his wounds in hospital on 23 August. He was CDN/16, Lieut. Kenneth W. Carstairs.

On 15 August, at the beginning of TRACTABLE, Lieut. Edward Glass of 1 Gordons was killed in a rare German bombing attack. Another officer and 20 men were wounded at the same time. Glass had served with the 48th Highlanders of Canada in the militia and overseas from 1939 to 1943 and had been given a warm welcome by an affiliated regiment, the Gordon Highlanders.

The last fatal casualties of CANLOAN officers in Normandy were in the 15th Scottish Division at the crossing of the Seine on 27 and 28 August. Lieut. John Aitken, 2 Gordons, was killed with the second in command of his company and 37 other ranks. A former artillery officer, he had taken the extensive Canadian infantry conversion course at Brockville and the battle course at Barnard Castle in England and had joined 2 Gordons only four days before he was killed. On the same day Lieut. Harold Schwark, 6 RSF, was seriously wounded in the crossing of the Seine; he died later in No. 7 Canadian General Hospital. He had been with his battalion since the beginning of EPSOM, in the Scottish Corridor.

Though several CANLOAN officers had joined the 6th Airborne Division before D-Day, they arrived too late to be included in the D-Day landings by that division. It was expected to return to England shortly after the landing but instead continued to fight as infantry until the very end of the Normandy campaign. At least one CANLOAN officer was able to join a battalion in the division as a reinforcement officer. He was CDN/409, Lieut. James Cochrane, of the 2nd Oxf. Bucks., who, in the closing stages of the Normandy campaign, earned a Military Cross:

On August 18 at Marville-Franceville Plage he showed great courage and initiative in leading his platoon round by a flank over enemy minefields to dislodge some enemy snipers who were holding up the advance. On August 25 close to Manneville la Rouat Lieut. Cochrane led his platoon with such dash and vigour that a large force of the enemy who had been holding the bridge over the River Rorelle were completely disorganized and prevented from counter-attacking. He captured many prisoners and assaulted and captured an enemy MG position which overlooked the bridges.[29]

The Normandy campaign is usually considered to have ended on 25 August, when the Falaise pocket was completely closed, although immediately after came the crossing of the Seine by the 43rd Division on 26 August and by the 15th Scottish Division on 27 August, followed by the astounding dash to Belgium and Holland, which was such a contrast to the bloody slogging match in Normandy. But of course the war was not over. There remained eight months and many hard battles, but the most important battle had been fought and won in Normandy.

The first reaction was the realization of the extent of the German losses. When the campaign ended on 25 August the Germans had lost 400,000 men killed, wounded, and captured. Of these 200,000 were prisoners, most of them captured in the last month. The 10 feared German armoured divisions had a total of fewer than 70 tanks left. In fact, when the losses were added up, the Panzer Lehr and the 9th Panzer were not even counted, since they had been virtually destroyed in the Mortain counter-attack. The 12th SS Panzer Division, which on D-Day had had 20,000 men and 150 tanks, had been reduced to 300 men, 10 tanks, and no artillery.[30]

The Germans had, however, proved to be formidable fighting men and had inflicted severe casualties on the Allies, whose losses were 207,000 men – 124,000 American and 83,000 British and Canadian.

For CANLOAN officers the Normandy campaign was most significant for several reasons. In the first place their numbers were greatly reduced. The 77 who were killed in action or died of wounds in the three months between D-Day and the end of August constituted 60 percent of the total fatal CANLOAN casualties during the entire 11 months of the campaign in northwest Europe. And there were three times as many wounded, a clear majority of the CANLOAN officers who served in Normandy. The official casualty statistics at CMHQ in London showed that the effective strength of CANLOAN at the end of the Normandy campaign was approximately 200. Of the 673 CANLOAN officers, approximately 500 had served in Normandy. Of the 500, 208 were wounded, 65 had been killed in action, and 12 had died of wounds. In addition 11 were missing and 3 were prisoners of war.

The second important effect of the Normandy campaign on CANLOAN officers was the development of an esprit de corps, for those who had volunteered for the CANLOAN scheme and had endured the crucible of the Normandy bridgehead became a band of brothers. In hospitals, reinforcement holding units, and anywhere else from that time on, they had three sources of pride: their Canadian identity, which was never in danger of being diluted; their regiments, to which they had pledged lifelong loyalty and affection; and their membership in the CANLOAN family.

Thirdly, the Normandy campaign established a CANLOAN reputation for infantry leadership and courage. While the number of CANLOAN officers was small, the fact that one or more served in almost every battalion of the Second Army made them conspicuous. In fact, a kind of mythology grew up, which helped to establish in fighting units of the British Army a reputation for CANLOAN that was greater than the numbers warranted. This reputation in turn became a benchmark against which CANLOAN officers felt they must measure their performance on the battlefield.

8

Hospitals and Reinforcement Holding Units

UNLIKE MEMBERS OF the Air Force and Navy, who lived and fought in relative comfort, the vulnerable foot soldier could be killed or disabled in innumerable ways. Since 75 percent of the CANLOAN infantry officers were battle casualties, their experiences as casualties are an important part of the CANLOAN story.

Infantrymen were vulnerable to all enemy weapons. There were the dreaded mortars, the moaning Minnies, and the artillery, especially the 88-mm, against which, admittedly, slit trenches offered a measure of protection much of the time. There was the whole range of small-arms fire, from the sniper's bullet that could pick off an officer without warning to the sustained bursts of machine-gun fire that could cut down an advancing platoon like a scythe. There were the mines, anti-tank and anti-personnel, sown in minefields and along the verges of roads, as well as booby traps and trip wires, an ever-present danger when entering buildings, walking between hedges, or even moving dead bodies. In close-quarter fighting there were grenades, machine guns, rifles, bayonets, submachine guns, and even pistols. There was also danger from the bombing and strafing, sometimes by one's own planes, as the 51st Highland Division discovered several times. Disease, however, which had decimated British armies all over the world for centuries, was rare in Normandy, except for the occasional recurrence of malaria among troops who had served in the Mediterranean or Far East. Nor do many CANLOAN officers seem to have met with accidents, which in most armies account for a high proportion of casualties. Training accidents in England, which had led to the death of "Buster" Crabb and the serious injury to Earl Cloutier, and accidents during operations in the field, such as that to CDN/548, Capt. John E.D. Davies, who reported that he "toppled from a tank onto a bayonet," were fairly rare.

Generally speaking, high-explosive projectiles – moaning Minnies, mortars, and artillery – accounted for up to 75 percent of battle casualties, bullets for up to 10 percent, and mines and booby traps for up to 10 percent.[1]

The procedure for handling casualties was, on the whole, very efficient, the chief difficulty being to get the wounded person into the hands of medical staff as quickly as possible. The initial treatment was first aid. For example, when Jack Levine was hit by shrapnel during a platoon "orders" group early in Normandy, the commander of an adjoining platoon, Capt. Frederick H. Burnaby, was able to apply a field dressing before returning to prepare his platoon for an imminent counter-attack.

A first field dressing, a small bandage package, was carried by all ranks buttoned into a special pocket on the right leg of the battle dress trousers. In addition, a shell dressing, a larger version of the first field dressing, was usually carried under the camouflage net that covered the steel helmet. These would be applied when needed by the wounded man himself or a comrade.

After a mortar "stonk" (heavy concentration of shelling) or during an attack, calls for stretcher bearers were heard. These platoon and company medical orderlies did a remarkable job of finding casualties, and giving first aid to, and evacuating, all those they could reach. They were brave men and saved many lives. Walking wounded were directed to the regimental aid post (RAP), whereas the more seriously wounded were placed on stretchers and carried or transported by carriers or jeeps to the RAP, where, under the direction of the battalion medical officer, a preliminary medical diagnosis was made and emergency treatment, such as bandages, splints, and shots, was given. From there casualties were evacuated from the battalion area, usually by ambulance to the field dressing station, where emergency surgery could be carried out, and on to the casualty clearing station. In Normandy, in the early days before field hospitals were in operation, casualties was usually evacuated immediately by sea or air to hospitals in England.

The rate of survival of the seriously wounded depended greatly on how much time elapsed before professional medical treatment could begin. In Normandy this could be as little as an hour, compared to many hours in the First World War. Equally important were three medical innovations: penicillin and sulphanilamide (sulpha) to combat infection, and blood transfusion (plasma) to reduce shock. The results were remarkable. For example, in the First World War two-thirds of abdominal wounds were fatal, whereas in the Second World War there was a 75 percent recovery rate in such cases. It was estimated that penicillin and sulpha drugs reduced the time spent in hospital by half. Amputations were one-half the rate of the First World War. In fact, if one was not killed outright in Normandy, the chances of recovery were twice as good as they would have been in the First World War.[2]

The attitude of CANLOAN officers towards wounds tended to differ somewhat from that of their British comrades of all ranks. For the latter a wound, particularly the famous "Blighty," usually meant not only survival but reunion with family, sweethearts, and friends in the United Kingdom. This was rarely true of CANLOAN officers, whose emotional attachments overseas were to their regiments and, particularly, to the companies or platoons, which were in effect their families. An example of this attitude is the reaction of a CANLOAN officer who, with a British fellow officer, was a casualty in the 10 July battle for Hill 112:

[In a carrier on the way to the RAP] all I could think of was the Carrier Pl – 50% killed or wounded today – and now Bobby and I leaving just when they needed us most. I wanted, more than I ever wanted anything in my whole life, to stay with them. A Blighty to most meant home but to me it just meant leaving my men ... They took Bobby off and then helped me out and laid me on a stretcher. The MO told me that Bobby was dead. He wanted to cut my sleeve off but I insisted that I had to get my arm out as it was my only suit of Canadian battle dress ... I gave orders to Stockley and Windsor and when they left me tears were flowing down their cheeks, and mine weren't dry ... Finally an ambulance arrived and I was taken away. I have never felt as miserable as I did alone in the back of that ambulance bumping over the shell-pocked roads. Not from pain but something inside that kept saying, "Poor Bobby! Poor old Carrier Platoon!"[3]

It was not unusual for wounded CANLOAN officers to be reluctant to be evacuated. In fact there are many examples of ones who insisted on staying with their platoons until the objective was secured, and then going reluctantly to the regimental aid post. For one thing there was the danger that they might not get back to their unit, even in the case of relatively minor wounds. That this was not an idle notion is shown in two examples: Len Robertson, 2 E. Yorks., had a series of minor injuries: shrapnel scratches first on his lip, then on his wrist, and finally a chunk in the groin. He proved to be allergic to the drugs administered in the battalion – his lip swelled and eyes closed – and he was packed off to a field hospital and from there to an RHU. He reluctantly parted with his Canadian battle dress (this was an issue with all CANLOAN officers, particularly those who were wounded);[4] he considered himself fortunate to get back to his own battalion in a couple of weeks, since he knew that other CANLOAN officers had been sent to different regiments.

Rex Fendick, 2 MX in the 3rd Division, was blown up in his carrier by Teller mines and he too was sent to a field hospital. He refused to part with his tattered Canadian battle dress, and later, the men in his platoon patched it and sponged the blood out of it. Posted to an RHU, he wrote to his CO to ask if he could get back to his unit. Two days later, the CO, on receiving the letter, sent his Humber to pick him up.

On the other hand, some CANLOAN officers were able to return to their units without difficulty. Capt. Arnold Willick, with 5 Wilts., who got shrapnel splinters in his back at Maltot, was away from the battalion only five days before being returned to his company.

Early in July the CO of 4 KSLI inquired about members of his battalion who had been wounded and was informed that "most of them, even those only very slightly wounded, seemed to be back in England."[5] This was certainly true of many CANLOAN officers. One example is the experience of Lieut. Arthur Stone, who led a platoon in 6 N. Staffs. in the attack on Caen on 8 July: "I walked forward until I received a blow behind my left knee which buckled my legs and I went down. In exploring, it turned out to be only a gash which did not cripple me. Not bothering to waste a field dressing on it I tied a handkerchief around it."

After the battle his company commander urged him to go to the regimental aid post to get the wound properly dressed. There he was given a shot of tetanus antitoxin, a sprinkle of sulpha, and secure bandages. As he rose to leave the MO insisted that he get into a jeep to be taken to the casualty clearing station, saying he would be gone only three or four days. Later, on finding that he was being sent to the evacuation point, he protested and demanded to see a doctor. Stone continues, "The doctor eventually came and looked at it. He grew quite short and angry and told me to get used to the idea that I was going back to England. Over-patiently he explained that there were facilities on this side for only extremely bad cases who were too serious to risk moving to England. However trivial my wound seemed it had to be taken care of or it would become gangrenous."[6]

Stone was driven to the shore and loaded on a landing ship, tank, fitted with bunks for the cross-Channel voyage, and then spent months in and out of hospitals in England, sometimes on leave, while waiting for a medical board. He was eventually sent back to the Continent and posted to a different unit in a different division on 9 February 1945, exactly seven months after having been evacuated from Normandy.

There were many similar cases of CANLOAN officers who were evacuated when they did not believe their wounds were serious enough to warrant it. CDN/429, Lieut. Anderson Rodger, 1/6 S. Staffords., was evacuated with a bullet through his right calf; he spent the next seven months in England. In the same hospital in Liverpool was CDN/335, Lieut. Paul Cofsky, 2 Devons. He had been on a patrol all one night, pinned down on one side of a hedgerow while Germans tossed grenades over the hedge. Fortunate to survive, he returned exhausted to his company and was told to be ready for an attack later in the day. His company commander suggested that he try to find a quiet place for a nap. After falling asleep on a stretcher in the regimental aid post, he awoke to find himself on the way to England. Both Cofsky and Rodger returned to the Continent to fight in the battle of the Rhineland. Andy Rodger was killed at the Rhine crossing on 24 March 1945.

At the other extreme were CANLOAN officers who were so seriously wounded, often with limbs amputated, that it was clear that they could fight no more and should be returned to Canada. In many cases, however, months of treatment in hospitals in England were necessary before they could be repatriated. By the end of October 1944, 29 cases of medical repatriation of CANLOAN officers to Canada were recorded.[7] Many of the more seriously wounded had been evacuated by air from Normandy to England.

CANLOAN officers were sometimes amazed at what they or others were able to do when they were wounded so seriously that one would expect that pain alone would be incapacitating. The reason, apparently, is that in addition to the increased flow of adrenalin in the heat of battle, the shock of a wound tends to inhibit the awareness of pain. Even when they were settled in a hospital bed, the strongest impression was often not discomfort or even pain, but the luxury of clean sheets and, especially, sleep. CDN/51 Lieut. Kenneth J. Wilson, 1 R. Norfolk, who was wounded in July 1944 and again in April 1945, recalled, "When wounded it was a relief because one could get some sleep." It was not unusual for CANLOAN officers to sleep for 24 hours at a stretch at the first opportunity.

Incidentally, Kenneth Wilson's two wounds were not unusual. It was an experience that was shared by many CANLOAN officers. In fact, several, including Hank

Henry, 4 KSLI, CDN/217, Lieut. Alfred T. Kirby, 7 Cameronians, and CDN/94, Maj. Alexander A.R. McIntosh, 5/7 Gordons, were wounded three times.

In England CANLOAN officers were sent to both Canadian and British hospitals. These were usually military hospitals, but quite a number of British civilian hospitals were used. For example, one of the younger CANLOAN officers, Alex Cunningham, 4 KSLI, was evacuated by air from Normandy to a civilian hospital in Wolverhampton, where he celebrated his 20th birthday.

There seemed to be no logical reason why particular British or Canadian hospitals were selected to receive CANLOAN officers. Sometimes they understood that they were sent to Canadian General Hospitals because they were Canadians. On the other hand they were sometimes told that they must go to British hospitals because they were in the British Army. CANLOAN officers had few complaints about their treatment, and they always got along famously with the nurses in any hospital. But they felt more at home in Canadian hospitals, particularly 4 and 19 Canadian General Hospitals, whose staff had been at Sussex, New Brunswick, with the CANLOAN officers and had been the travelling companions of nearly half of them on the *Empress of Scotland*. It was very pleasant to receive special treatment from Canadian nursing sisters who were old friends. Sometimes, too, CANLOAN officers met other nurses who came from their home towns or had mutual friends and were a welcome reminder of home. But CANLOAN officers were, on the whole, well treated in British hospitals and by British visitors. CDN/337, William T. (Bill) Edwards recalls, "I shall never forget Lady Astor entering our ward and greeting us with 'Well, what some people won't do to get some tender loving care!'"[8]

Often CANLOAN officers found themselves reunited in hospital wards with other CANLOAN officers and saw members of their own battalions of all ranks, with whom they could exchange news and stories about their experiences in Normandy. Usually they found others who were in worse condition than they. Ken Wilson recalls, "In hospital I was most impressed that fellows who were in the worst shape were the most cheerful. One had lost a leg, an arm, one eye and was waiting to find out if he could see with the other eye. He was cheerful!"[9]

CANLOAN officers were required to remain in hospital as long as they were undergoing treatment or had to have bandages changed or casts and stitches removed. Gradually they were able to move about the countryside, and many of them have pleasant memories of visits to picturesque villages, favourite pubs, and sometimes to the homes of new-found friends. Eventually many were sent to convalescent hospitals or homes. One of the favourites was Garnon's Castle near Hereford, the country residence of Vincent Massey, the Canadian High Commissioner. Joe Craib recalls that life there was quiet, since good behaviour was a requirement of continuing residence, but those who were fortunate enough to stay there enjoyed the luxury of a country house with their comfort attended to by a butler and hostess, a marked contrast to their slit trenches in Normandy.

When the patients were released from hospital, they were usually given leave, which was an opportunity for visits further afield. Some CANLOAN officers, for example, took the opportunity to visit the homes of their British regiments. Stewart Cameron, ex-Pictou Highlanders and 2 Glas. H., happened to be discharged from hospital at the same time as CDN/256, Capt. Harold C. Long, a fellow officer in both the Pictous and the Glasgows. Meeting by chance in London, they decided to go to Glasgow. Cameron recalls, "The hospitality there was beyond imagination. The sight of Canadians wearing the Glasgow Highlanders' patches was something they couldn't understand and we were wined and dined during our stay, to say nothing of many other hospitable gestures."[10]

Sometimes leave was quite long. Arthur Stone, despite his reminders to the authorities, was on almost continuous leave from mid-August to early November 1944. Actually, it was recognized at CMHQ that CANLOAN officers, not having homes in the country, could not usually profit from extensive leave. Major MacLaren, CANLOAN Liaison Officer at CMHQ, wrote on October 13, "It is British practice to grant lengthy sick leave but for Canadians it is better to spend sick leave at a convalescent hospital."[11] Convalescent facilities for CANLOAN officers were made available at the Roman Way Convalescent Hospital at Colchester and the Convalescent Depot at Hindhead.

The disposition of CANLOAN casualties was covered by a memorandum of 31 July 1944 from the Director of Medical Services at CMHQ to the CANLOAN Liaison Officer:

a) Officers obviously unfit for further service will be boarded [reviewed by a medical board] in Canadian hospitals in the usual manner and repatriation effected immediately;

b) CANLOAN officers who are in our hospitals and who are fit for further service will be directed into British channels for reconsideration of category.[12]

Later, on 16 August, the Director of Medical Services was more specific in a further communication, saying that CANLOAN officers would be treated as British officers except when unfit for further military service (i.e., having five in any PULHEMS heading, including M or S) and that repatriation certificates would be prepared in such cases, but "if fit for further duty in any category the officer would be discharged to No 3 Infantry Depot, Kirkee Barracks, Colchester and will not be boarded in a Canadian Medical Installation."[13]

From August 1944 on, 3 Infantry Depot, Kirkee Barracks, Colchester, was the depot for all CANLOAN officers who were evacuated wounded to the UK, as well as for several British regiments. They were carried on the strength of the depot from the time they were discharged from hospital. At any one time there could be as many as 150 CANLOAN officers on strength, although as few as 50 might actually be present, the others being on leave, on temporary assignments, or in convalescent establishments, such as Roman Way.

Some of the officers, who were medically unfit for further duties and slated for repatriation to Canada, were waiting for a medical board or a draft. Others, whose PULHEMS had been lowered temporarily because of their wounds, were waiting for complete healing or for a medical board to restore them to an operational category. This was the case, for example, with Arthur Stone's knee. Others, who had had a non-fighting category confirmed, were waiting for assignments that they were fit to perform, usually in the UK but sometimes staff positions on the Continent. Finally – and this was a majority – there were those who had been declared fit for operational duties and were waiting impatiently for postings back to regiments in the British

Second Army in northwest Europe, preferably to those in which they had served in Normandy. In the meantime many of them were engaged in tasks such as training reinforcements or supervising prisoners of war. Alex Cunningham, for example, while stationed at 3 Infantry Depot, took 100 to 150 German POWs to London to build a reception centre for POWs from northwest Europe and the Mediterranean. Art Connor had a similar assignment with POWs, but whereas Cunningham was eventually returned to his regiment in Germany, Connor's wounds did not permit him to be restored to full operational status.

An officer who was "reboarded" to battle status was not guaranteed a return to his regiment in northwest Europe. In the first place there was a demand for infantry instructors, particularly those with battle experience in Normandy, to train, as infantry reinforcements, personnel who were being converted from the RAF, the RN, or other Army elements, as well as to provide conditioning for troops who had been wounded in Normandy or the Mediterranean. After being assigned to such duties, CANLOAN officers had great difficulty getting postings abroad.

Troops who had been wounded and had been released from hospital and declared fit were posted to training centres for refresher courses in infantry weapons and tactics as well as conditioning. Since such troops were sometimes scornful of instructors who had not seen action, there was a demand for instructors who had been wounded in action. These included a number of CANLOAN officers who, once caught in the net, found it very difficult to escape. At one time two CANLOAN officers in Northern Ireland, after exhausting every legal method of getting back to action, virtually staged a mutiny and were posted back to their regiments as punishment!

Even when officers were posted to the Continent there was seldom any assurance that they would get back to their former units. Alex Cunningham recalls, "Each day we longed to return to our units, and that was the desire of all CANLOAN officers who were fit. Posting abroad was usually as conducting officers for drafts of reinforcements. One could usually only hope that they could somehow get to their units once they got across the English Channel."

Sometimes there were other possibilities for waiting CANLOAN officers. For example, John Druhan, who was training reinforcements while waiting for upgrading by a medical board, was tempted to apply to the War Office for a transfer to India as a brigade major, but when the opportunity came to return to the 7th Seaforths he didn't hesitate.

After No. 3 Infantry Depot, Colchester, was designated as the depot for all CANLOAN officers who were returned to the UK from units in 21st Army Group,[14] it became a place for CANLOAN reunions or initial meetings, a place where experiences were recounted and news of other CANLOAN officers was exchanged. Writing from Kirkee Barracks after hearing many reports of deaths and injuries, a CANLOAN officer observed, "Soon CANLOAN will be just a casualty list and a memory."[15] A feeling of camaraderie and distinct identity emerged at Colchester. This was noted by those at CMHQ who, in a six-month report on the CANLOAN scheme in October 1944, observed,

> Generally speaking the morale of CANLOAN officers is high and over the last six months an esprit de corps has developed which is very desirable. CANLOAN officers, feeling that they are "a race apart," have come to regard themselves as an operational entity and take

great pride in the achievements, awards, promotions and decorations of other CANLOAN officers.[16]

This esprit de corps and sense of distinct identity led to a proposal that a CANLOAN association be formed. An account of the origin of the idea was published many years later in the *Canloan Review* of March 1977:

> In the venerable Red Lion Inn of the High Street of Colchester a group of wounded CANLOAN who were convalescing at nearby Roman Way Hospital met for their customary evening pints. Morale as always was running high as comments were made concerning a certain major who was our rather ineffectual LO at CMHQ. At once the idea of forming our own network and association was raised. One of those present, CDN/237, Lieutenant James M Buchanan, 2 Gordons and 7 KOSB, who was a commercial artist, deftly sketched the Red Lion pub sign, florally entwined with maple, thistle, shamrock and rose. "Voilà!" said Jimmy, "Our badge." He added, *sotto voce,* "the lion rampant sinister on a rouge field screwing the beaver couchant surmounted."[17]

This report should be supplemented by a couple of eye-witness accounts. Don Diplock, one of the participants at the CANLOAN gathering in Colchester, visited James Buchanan, whom he had known in Canada.

> Sitting up in his hospital bed he was producing a drawing in colour. On poster-size paper was the British lion copulating with a Canadian beaver. It was splendid and bright and carried the message without the need of a caption. I never did find out what happened to that magnificent sketch but it became the inspiration for the Canloan insignia, which reversed, with admirable good taste, the positions of the two animals and avoided the earlier intimacy.

Don was also present when the first CANLOAN party was organized:

> One day while lounging in the US Red Cross gathering place a few of us were asked by a staff member to examine some ears of sweet corn purchased from a local farmer. When we approved, a corn feed was arranged and we were provided with a private room where the corn was served and devoured. I suppose that at least 15 of us gathered and actually convened a meeting for the first time as a group.

He recalls that CDN/125, Lieut. Bart A. Bartholomew was chairman of the meeting and insists that it was at the US Red Cross canteen, not the Red Lion Inn.[18]

On the other hand, a letter written by the author to his parents in Canada two days after the meeting reported:

> Friday evening all the CANLOAN officers got together at the Red Lion in Colchester. There was a piano in the room and about 35 of us sang and talked and compared notes and then ate 200 ears of corn on the cob. Lovely! We decided to form a club of CANLOAN officers with Brig Gregg as honorary president and one of the lads who can't go back to France as secretary.[19]

The beaver and lion crest later caused a tempest in a teapot at NDHQ in Ottawa. Major MacLaren sent it on a card at Christmas to his friend, Brig. R.E.G. Roome, DAG, who showed it to Maj.-Gen. A.E. Walford, Adjutant-General, as evidence of the high morale and esprit de corps of the CANLOAN officers. The AG sent it to CMHQ in London with orders to find out more about it and to determine if it should be submitted for official approval. Major MacLaren replied that the crest was unofficial and the College of Heralds had ruled that if it was not intended for use on the cap or the sleeve it need not be registered. He requested that notification of the existence of the crest be sent to all CANLOAN officers who had been returned to Canada for medical or other reasons. This was done, and the 47 CANLOAN officers who had been repatriated by the middle of February 1945 must have been surprised to receive from NDHQ a copy of a crest which, they were informed, they were allowed to use "on cigarette boxes and other souvenirs." CANLOAN officers overseas heard nothing about this![20]

Life at No. 3 Infantry Depot also had some less pleasant features, in particular the boredom of enforced idleness and the frustration of not getting a medical board or a posting abroad without long waits. Kirkee Barracks and Roman Way became a focal point for complaints which, under the circumstances, loomed larger than would normally be expected.

As noted earlier, it was decided during the development of the CANLOAN scheme to appoint an officer at CMHQ who would be a liaison officer between the CANLOAN officers and the War Office and 21st Army Group as well as CMHQ and, through it, NDHQ in Canada. The officer who was selected was Maj. A.B. MacLaren, Deputy Assistant Adjutant-General Liaison (DAAG(L)) – who began his duties on 10 April 1944. He was part of the welcoming committee for most of the CANLOAN "flights," and it was he whom CANLOAN officers were expected to contact regarding mail, pay, promotions, kit storage, leave, and any other problems. In his reports Major MacLaren always gave the impression that CANLOAN officers were happy with and grateful for the efficient manner in which they were being looked after. His reputation among CANLOAN officers who knew of his existence, however – whether justified or not – tended to be unfavourable. One said bluntly that he had never heard one good word said by CANLOAN officers about the liaison officer at CMHQ.

From the beginning of August 1944, Major MacLaren was involved in a contentious matter for which he could not be blamed. It was the "three-months issue," the impression of many CANLOAN officers that they would or could be returned to the Canadian Army after three months in a British regiment. On 15 August Major-General Montague of CMHQ wrote to NDHQ, enclosing letters from the War Office and 21st Army Group concerning statements by CANLOAN officers that the CANLOAN agreement provided for return to Canadian control after three months in the British Army:

[That] such an interpretation of the agreement does exist in the minds of these officers is evinced by the fact that three months after the arrival of CANLOAN drafts, almost to the day, many verbal applications for return have been received by the CANLOAN liaison officer. Several written applications also have been received. Many CANLOAN officers are now serving in Normandy and it would appear that applications for return, passing through normal channels, have now reached such a proportion that the War Office and 21st Army Group seek official guidance in the matter.[21]

The War Office had received a letter from the father-in-law of a CANLOAN officer in which he inquired if, since the three-month period of the loan had expired, the officer, father of children, aged 3 months and 18 months, would be returned to the Canadian Army. He wrote, "We in civilian life understand that after the length of time was up, men would be returned to their own units before any [battle] action. For if you borrow anything you usually take good care of it, use it, then return it in good condition, not to put it in danger while the borrowed term was on."[22]

Unfortunately, Lieut A.D. Crighton, 6 RWF, was killed in action in Normandy on 10 July, the very day his father-in-law wrote to the War Office.

It seemed reasonable to find out what CANLOAN officers understood about the time period of the loan to the British Army. Since they were most accessible at Kirkee Barracks, on 22 August 1944 Major MacLaren went to Colchester, assembled the CANLOAN officers there ("about thirty officers at the Depot though possibly three times that number on paper strength"), and led a discussion on the three-months issue. MacLaren tended to support those who had the impression that CANLOAN officers would be recalled after three months or, at least, that requests for recall would be considered, and he felt that the terms of the agreement were open to that interpretation. He quoted remarks of individual CANLOAN officers at the meeting. One said that a captain from NDHQ had told him he could return to the Canadian Army if he wished. Another said that a board had told him the same: "You are only going to the British for battle experience." A third was told that the loan was for the duration, but "You are subject to recall by the Canadian Army after three months." Others at the meeting had no complaints about the issue. MacLaren concluded, "The general feeling is that CANLOAN officers are not dissatisfied with the British Army but they feel promises made to them in Canada have not been kept."[23]

General Letson, the Canadian AG, responded personally and immediately to MacLaren's report. He denied that the agreement could be interpreted as giving the right to apply for return to the Canadian Army after three months. He said that the only reason for mentioning three months was to ensure that CANLOAN officers would have an opportunity to prove themselves before being rejected by the British, that mass returns would be embarrassing, and that Gen. Sir Ronald Adam had agreed the Canadians would have three months to make good. Letson insisted that every opportunity to clarify the issue had been seized: his cable to CMHQ on 22 February 1944; question 8 and reply in the information pamphlet; and his orders to all district officers commanding in Canada to circulate the appropriate information, all of which had said clearly, "Individual requests for return to the Canadian Service will not be entertained." He hoped that his explanation would permit a fair response to applications for return.[24]

General Letson's hopes were fulfilled. Altogether there were 45 applications for return to the Canadian Army, most of which were withdrawn when the conditions were explained. A few weeks later, on 16 September, an officer from NDHQ, Capt. D. Ivor, visited Kirkee Barracks with Major MacLaren and was able to report, "The matter of the three months clause is practically a thing of the past and I don't think that anything further will be heard of it."[25] He had got the impression that the CANLOAN officers were generally satisfied, though there were some complaints about the slowness of mail and the return of kit from France. He reported that morale was excellent and that the officers had become thoroughly identified with their British regiments and were proud of their distinctive patches.

Though it was clear that CANLOAN officers could not request a return to the Canadian Army after three months, such a return could be initiated by the British. A report from CMHQ in February 1945 on those officers who had been struck off the strength of CANLOAN included those who were "returned to Canadian control." The total was then 49, broken down as follows: (1) at request of CMHQ – 1; (2) at own request – 4; (3) at request of War Office – 44, for (a) medical reasons – 22, (b) adverse reports – 12, (c) language – 10."[26] The medical reasons seem to have included not only physical injuries but also disabilities such as battle fatigue. The adverse reports, which were varied, included such phrases as "has difficulty in adapting" or "too old for a Platoon Commander." The language category meant that 10 French-speaking CANLOAN officers were considered to have difficulty in communicating in English. Although those officers were bilingual, it was noted that there was a difference between giving orders on a parade square and communicating with a Highlander or Cornishman over a radio net in the middle of a battle. Altogether, the percentage of CANLOAN officers who were considered expendable was remarkably small and did not reflect badly on any of the individuals concerned.

Around the end of September Major MacLaren paid a liaison visit to Rear Headquarters of 21st Army Group to discuss CANLOAN matters. His general impression of the CANLOAN officers whom he encountered (which must have been remarkably few) was most favourable. The DAG Rear HQ said that "they were not only pleased but very pleased with the CANLOAN material," and General Dempsey himself was reported to have said that he was very well satisfied with the Canadian officers under his command and would welcome all the Canadian officers who could be posted to the Second Army.[27]

During his visit, MacLaren discussed many administrative matters with his chief contact, a Major Anderson, including individual cases, airborne pay, letters to next of kin, non-delivery of letters and parcels, compassionate leave, Canadian Press news, kit and effects of fatal casualties, reporting of CANLOAN casualties, burials and grave registration, reversion to Canadian service, staff appointments, and temporary ranks. All concerned were pleased with the results of the visit and felt that personal contact was much more effective than correspondence.[28]

After returning from the visit to 21st Army Group, Major MacLaren made several liaison visits in England to deal with CANLOAN problems. One visit was to GHQ 2nd Echelon in Oxford to discuss many administrative matters, including delays in publishing in Part II Order entries concerning CANLOAN officers, errors in reporting casualties, delays in the publication of General Routine Orders (GROs) and in forwarding letters to next of kin, hospitalization, parachute and airborne pay, acting and temporary ranks, reversion of ranks on hospitalization, and allowance for food rations on leave.[29]

Another visit was to the Military Forwarding Officer in Liverpool concerning the personal kits of casualties. Yet another was to the postal depot in Nottingham concerning delays in the delivery of letters and, particularly, all parcels, including cigarettes and tobacco, and the disposal of those addressed to units for officers who had become casualties. Poor postal service was one of the most annoying problems for CANLOAN officers. Lieut. Fred Hatfield, for example, had had 150 letters and 100 parcels sent to him over a period of several months and had received none of them.[30]

At the end of October 1944 a comprehensive report was prepared at CMHQ (probably by Major MacLaren) and sent by Major General Montague, Chief of Staff, to the Secretary, Department of National Defence, Ottawa. Part I, entitled "Infantry Officers," described the warm welcome given to each CANLOAN draft on arrival and the period of settling into British regiments. The three-months issue was mentioned as "due to misunderstanding." The report continued:

> Even without battle inoculation or intensive training they [CANLOAN officers] acquitted themselves extraordinarily well in the early stages of the invasion of Europe, according to the favourable comments heard by the liaison officer during a visit concerning the standard of leadership displayed by CANLOAN officers in action.

The report noted that "casualties were high but not excessively so," that a number had been returned to Canada on medical grounds, that there had been many promotions of CANLOAN officers, and that a considerable number of Military Crosses had been awarded and more were expected. It concluded: "On the whole the infantry officers have acquitted themselves well and the favourable impression they have made and their conduct in action is no small contribution to British/Canadian postwar relations."[31]

Part II, which concerned the ordnance officers, reported that on arriving in England they had been enrolled in special ordnance officers' courses and had obtained good results, that none had yet been posted to a theatre of operations because of the RAOC reinforcement situation. Though they were "100 percent anxious to get into action," they were still employed in static ordnance depots.

Part III of the report, entitled "General," noted that there had already been inquiries, especially by ordnance officers, about service in India, Burma, and elsewhere in the Far East and that the current restrictions might have to be relaxed if the war against Japan continued. Generally speaking, the report concluded, the CANLOAN scheme could be considered a success. The morale of the CANLOAN officers was high and an esprit de corps had developed. The report concluded on a self-congratulatory note: "Everything has been done to foster this esprit de corps ... all individual inquiries, problems and complaints are heard with the utmost despatch. CANLOANs have come to realize that their point of contact, one with another, centres around this headquarters."

A great deal of information about CANLOAN was contained in the appendices of the report: a copy of the letter of welcome from the Adjutant-General, Sir Ronald Adam; a list of the dates and numbers of the nine CANLOAN drafts; a report on the current strength of CANLOAN, including casualties; a list of promotions; a list of the six MCs that had been awarded to date; and a detailed list of the distribution of CANLOAN officers showing the names of those in each unit.[32]

In March 1947 a CANLOAN officer, Capt. Joseph Gauthier, who was then serving on the staff of NDHQ in Ottawa, was asked to comment on the October 1944 report. He was rather critical, questioning, for example, the observation that casualties were not unduly high. He claimed they *were* unusually high, not because CANLOAN officers were given so many difficult tasks, but because, in his opinion, "they were always ready to go on any mission." He was critical of the liaison officer, noting that in 18 months he had never seen any Canadian publication or orders or notices relating to CANLOAN. He insisted that urgent requests sent to the liaison officer were not even acknowledged and that he had seen few, if any, CANLOAN officers on his visit to the Continent. In short, he disagreed with the statement that the CANLOAN officers were well looked after.[33]

To mark six months' service by CANLOAN officers in the British Army, a reception was organized by the liaison staff at CMHQ. Held on 4 November 1944 at the Royal Empire Society in London, it was attended by approximately 160 CANLOAN officers, most of whom had been wounded in Normandy and were in hospitals, convalescent establishments, or training depots, together with British officers from the War Office, infantry depots, and Eastern and Southern Commands, and Canadian officers from CMHQ. At about noon on the day of the reception, Russell Parke arrived at 19 Canadian General Hospital, where two nurses who recognized him asked if he was going to the CANLOAN party that evening. After examining his swollen hand, which was in a cast, the CO refused to let him out of the hospital, but the nurses persuaded the CO himself to give Parke a new cast and let him attend the party. The organizers considered that the CANLOAN party was very successful and that "the personal contact established there did much to cement further the happy relationship existing between CANLOAN officers and British authorities."[34] It is doubtful if many of the CANLOAN officers had ever attended a party at which there were so many generals.

Shortly after the CANLOAN reception in London, No. 3 Infantry Depot was disbanded in a reorganization of Southern and Eastern Commands. It was suggested by the War Office that CANLOAN officers stationed there be held at their regimental depots, and probably a majority of CANLOAN officers would have agreed if they had been consulted. But it was decided they should be kept together and transferred to No. 6 Infantry Holding Battalion at Southend, a summer resort town on the north side of the Thames Estuary. During the winter it was deserted, most of the hotels and boarding houses empty. One, the Westcliffe, was assigned to CANLOAN officers. Because of the distinct nature of the group and the decentralized location, Maj. Sandy Millar was put in charge of them. He had been conducting officer for the third CANLOAN flight and later an able company commander in 2 Glasgows in Normandy. Major MacLaren reported to Brigadier Fleury: "In effect this means that this HQ will have an officer to deal with who speaks our language and since Maj Millar is category C for some time it is requested that authority be obtained to attach him to CMHQ for one week in order that he can be put in the administrative picture."[35]

There were, however, factors beyond Major Millar's control that made the Southend set-up less than satisfactory. Since at all times there were up to 100 CANLOAN officers en route to or from northwest Europe, the Westcliffe Hotel was frequently crowded, the quarters were not as comfortable as at Kirkee Barracks, and a coal shortage added to the discomfort. The CO of No. 6 Infantry Holding Battalion was described by Major MacLaren as unco-operative and having "little knowledge or interest in CANLOAN." Little effort was made to find employment for CANLOAN officers because there were also several hundred British officers at No. 6 who needed jobs to occupy them. Major MacLaren reported, "[As a result] there has gradually developed a lack of discipline and training with a consequent weakening of moral and physical fibre of some of the officers concerned ... [It is] common practice for some CANLOAN officers to remain in bed half the morning, play cards most of the afternoon and go their own way at night."[36] This rather prissy description seems to be confirmed by an account which appeared many years later in the *Canloan Review* under the heading "South End Escapade":

There was really nothing to distinguish this particular February morning from any other February morning of 1945 at the Westcliff Hotel. The matter of rising for breakfast had been considered the night before but CANLOANs had decided to avoid the mess table as an egg had been served for breakfast the month previous and there was no enthusiasm for cold kipper or partially warmed Brussells sprouts which would have soured since being first cooked.

The events proceeded according to plan. About tenish the majority of CANLOAN were to be found assembled at Garron's tea and crumpet emporium on High Street. Tea and toast and comment from Stu Townshend were mixed up in proper proportion after which the group paraded to the Palace Hotel. En route Dunc MacDougall [CDN/273, Lieutenant Duncan] paused briefly at Barclay's counting house to draw his daily ration of five pounds.

Billiards, lunch, picking up laundry, acquisition of ersatz fuel and arguments with the PMC [President, Mess Committee] occupied most of the hours until evening. The day's mail, however, had been received and posting away from the unit had arrived for Dunc MacDougall and Jack Brown. It was this news that disrupted the usual pattern. The boys decided that a farewell should be staged at the Railroad Inn. It seems that even the publican was pleased to see the end of this pair and, good soul that she was, set aside a few bottles of excellent whiskey. Stu Townshend acted as MC and decreed that the treatment was to be a double whiskey and a pint of bitters repeated as required.[37]

At the beginning of February there were 60 CANLOAN officers at No. 6. Nineteen were category A waiting for postings; 19 more were waiting for medical boards; 11 in employable categories other than A were waiting for postings in the UK; 4 who had been "boarded" were waiting for confirmation; 3 had been requested by the War Office to return to Canadian control for medical or language reasons; 3 more were waiting for admission to hospital; and one was waiting for a court martial. Sixty-seven other CANLOAN officers had been posted to No. 6 and might arrive at any time, and 37 low-category officers were being posted away.[38]

Though No. 6 Infantry Holding Battalion was about to be moved to another location, Major MacLaren recommended that the CANLOAN officers continue to live at the Westcliffe Hotel but be under the administration of No. 1 Infantry Holding Unit, two miles away, whose CO was "taking a great interest in CANLOAN officers and their problems."[39]

These CANLOAN problems were considered serious enough for a Brigadier Stainer to be instructed by the GOC Home Forces to investigate the situation. He visited Southend with Major MacLaren, and together they made several recommendations:

a) as above, CANLOAN officers to stay at the Westcliffe but report to No. 1 Holding Unit;
b) to confirm that a CANLOAN officer would be in charge of the group and act as intermediary between the OC No. 1, CMHQ and the War Office;
c) the transfer of all CANLOAN officers in British hospitals to Canadian hospitals and in future CANLOAN officers to be sent to Canadian hospitals as soon as possible; and
d) to set up immediately a special CANLOAN medical board for those awaiting boards, including the 19 at No. 1 Infantry Holding unit at Southend, and in future to grade CANLOAN officers on Canadian medical standards.[40]

The adoption of these recommendations meant that CANLOAN officers would be under Canadian control from the time they were hospitalized until they reported to No. 1 Infantry Holding Unit as Category A, ready for posting abroad. If they were lower than A category (or the equivalent in PULHEMS) they were to be moved to a Canadian medical establishment for rehabilitation or treatment. Of particular concern at one time were the cases of psychiatric casualties from Normandy. The total number, 30, was not excessive, but the chief Canadian neuropsychiatrist was concerned because the CANLOAN officers were not being treated according to the same standards as other Canadian officers.[41] Such concerns were satisfied by the new policy, which meant generally that all CANLOAN officers in the UK were to be treated in Canadian medical installations and examined by Canadian medical boards.

These recommendations would appear to have been beneficial, for a month later Major MacLaren, reporting on liaison visits to seven ordnance units, 16 infantry units, and four Canadian hospitals, noted that he had interviewed 140 CANLOAN officers and had not heard one complaint about conditions or continuance in the British service. He attributed this favourable situation to several factors:

a) Officers have definite jobs to do in which they take a real interest;
b) Commanding Officers on the whole are interested in CANLOAN officers;
c) Officers are capable and well-trained and have demonstrated a capacity for hard work; and that
d) there was a feeling of pride and *esprit de corps* in CANLOAN and a desire to uphold the short traditions and achievements of these Officers.[42]

This rosy report of the transformation of the undisciplined layabouts whom Major MacLaren had described a month before into hard-working paragons may stretch the reader's credulity. The fact is, however, that by March circumstances had changed considerably. Most of the CANLOAN officers who were able had returned to battalions on the Continent, most of those who were medically unfit for operational service had returned to Canada, and most lowered-category officers had been assigned tasks that kept them busy.

The chief goal of those who had been wounded in Normandy and had recovered from their wounds was to get back into action, preferably with the regiments with which they had served. Eventually most of them did get back into action, a surprising number of them with their old battalions. The method of returning to the Continent was quite efficient. It usually took the form of posting an officer to a military installation, usually an RHU, where he would be appointed to serve as a conducting officer for a draft of reinforcements. Several officers were assigned to each draft, and sometimes two or more of them were CANLOAN officers. The drafts were shipped across the Channel and escorted to an RHU, where the draft was taken over by others and the conducting officers made their way through RHUs to an eventual posting to a battalion at the front. In a number of cases CANLOAN officers short-circuited the system and, on arriving in the general area of their former battalions, hitchhiked the rest of the way. An account of one example follows:

> We arrived in about three hours at 105 CRC [Corps Reception Centre] in an imposing mansion. There I found a room full of officers writing letters or reading or re-reading old magazines. Many had been there for weeks and were still waiting for a posting to their Bns. At lunch I met three 5th Wilts officers who had been at the nearby Field Court Martial Centre. I decided to be unorthodox and asked if I could get a lift back to the 4th Wilts. They said "OK" so I put my kit in their 15 cwt and went off with them. It was actually weeks later before they discovered that I was missing and inquired about me at my Bn where I was then in action![43]

The feelings of CANLOAN officers on returning to action after being wounded were akin to those in the following description:

> Being wounded had now ended. It had been an interlude of unreality. Now he wanted impatiently to get back to the Battalion. For better or for worse that was where his war was, where he had grown used to it being. Not that he wanted to fight again. He wasn't thirsty for action. It was simply that it seemed the most natural thing to do: to go back where he belonged. It was his whole existence. For him there could only be the Battalion. Now it was tugging him umbilically and he was glad.[44]

This sentiment was shared by most returning CANLOAN officers who, even when they did not return to their former regiments, felt that they were fulfilling the purpose for which they had volunteered in Canada.

9

The Canals and Arnhem

THE CROSSING OF the Seine marked the end of the Normandy campaign, and for all the survivors there was a great sense of relief. It has been described by Jack McBride, a CANLOAN officer with 7 Black Watch:

> The breakout had pulled things together again. The men were happier now and morale was good. And yet I knew that many more were to fall on the long road ahead. But at least for a time a man could breathe air into his lungs instead of the foul, stinking stench of that little bridgehead. The advance now started would never again turn back.[1]

The advance, known as the "great swan," was indeed spectacular. Because supplies had to be brought by road from Normandy and transport vehicles were in short supply, it was not possible for four armies to advance on a broad front towards Germany at the same time. In the 21st Army Group sector, the First Canadian Army, which included several British divisions, was to advance up the coast, capturing successive Channel ports. For the British Second Army, VIII Corps and nearly all the medium and heavy artillery were grounded at the Seine to enable XXX Corps, under the inspired leadership of Lieut.-Gen. Brian Horrocks, to undertake an armoured drive through France, Belgium, and Holland, followed, as transport became available, by XII Corps. The Guards, 7th and 11th Armoured Divisions, followed by the 50th Division, had orders from Horrocks to "keep going like mad," and averaged 50 miles a day from their start on 29 August. Often travelling day and night, the Guards Division sped from the Seine on 31 August to Brussels on 3 September. The 11th Armoured Division was in Antwerp on 4 September, and the 7th Armoured Division covered a similar distance.

This exhilarating drive, coming so soon after the often static warfare in Normandy, made a deep impression on all the participants, particularly the infantry, whose feet were being rested in vehicles for a change. All were nearly overcome by cheering civilians welcoming their liberators. Lieut. Arthur Stone, who arrived from England six months later, has told about it:

> A captain in 50 Div had been on the long and now classic chase across France to Brussels and Antwerp. This large-scale chase or "swan" was looked back on with affection by all who took part in it. All the Infantry and Armour piled into every vehicle available and drove eastward at all possible speed, their limits determined by the gasoline. The men enjoyed this easy advance immeasurably and almost wept when it had to stop for lack of petrol. Those who reached Brussels and Antwerp loved to recall the wild celebrations in packed streets and the hysterical exuberance of the populace, who swamped the liberators, stopping the vehicles in the choked streets and dragging them out amid hugs and kisses to carry them off to their homes.[2]

CANLOAN officers in the infantry battalions of the armoured divisions and the 50th Division participated in the "great swan." In fact, a CANLOAN officer was in the leading tank in the leading battalion of the 7th Armoured Division as the "swan" was launched. Maj. Eric Brown, 1/6 Queens, tells the story:

> Lisieux. I recall the beautiful cathedral there and the fact that it was from there that "the great Swan" started. That I have indelibly stamped because my platoon was to lead and the tank upon which I was standing was first in line in a laneway off the main road. We were surrounded by Officers to see us started (our battalion CO, Company Commander, 2 i/c and the other Platoon Commanders) but as our tank pulled onto the concrete road a Teller mine blew under us, blasting many of the Officers with bits of concrete and me up into the air. Because we lost our company OC and other officers I had to take over even though I had to pop off every few minutes with a bad case of the trots. The Queens were nice enough to give me a third pip dating from that time. That night, to compound my misfortune, while poking about in an abandoned barn for a place to locate company headquarters I fell into a cess-pit in the dark ... This was well-aged stuff and reeked to high heaven. Because the swan was on there was no chance to change clothes. I had a tank to myself for several days. Would have been a luxury except I didn't like myself either![3]

For the divisions that were temporarily grounded there were useful activities. One was the reception of reinforcements to bring depleted battalions up to strength, often for the first time since landing in Normandy. The 1/6 Queens in the 7th Armoured Division, for example, at about half-strength after crossing the Seine, was pleased to receive reinforcements from the 1/6 S. Staffords. of the 59th Division, which had been disbanded. Especially welcome for one company were three CANLOAN officers, Capt. Vince Lilley as company commander and two platoon commanders, Lieuts. Lester Stilling and Harvey Langstaff. Shortly thereafter, incidentally, Stilling was awarded a Mention in Dispatches and Lilley a Military Cross and eventually two MIDs.

At this time the 1st Battalion, the Grenadier Guards (Gren. Gds.), received its first CANLOAN officer, Lieut. Larry Fazackerley. The 5th Dorset welcomed three

CANLOAN officers in three days   CDN/629, Lieut. William J. Hudson and CDN/672, Lieut. Harold G. Matthews on 6 September and Capt. Ken Brown on 8 September. CDN/652, Lieut. Harry C. Roper joined 5 Wilts., and CDN/507, Lieut. Gerald A. Hebb, 2 E. Yorks. Capt. Len Robertson, then Acting Company Commander with 2 E. Yorks., 3rd Division, recalls that he was informed that reinforcements, including two officers, were available and his company could have one of them: "So, while the runner was handing out the mail to the men I explained to them that I was going to HQ to pick up some reinforcements including an officer, one of whom was a Canadian and who did they want. 'Bring us the g——d—— Canadian,' they shouted. And I did. It was Hebb. A good choice."[4]

Another activity for the temporarily stranded divisions was maintenance, particularly a thorough overhaul of all weapons and vehicles. And, of course, there was training, including long route marches with full equipment, which raised blisters on feet that had become soft in the bottoms of the slit trenches in Normandy.

It is not surprising that the opportunity was seized for both authorized and unauthorized trips. An example of the former is the several truckloads of troops which Arnold Willick and Gerry Robichaud of 5 Wilts. took to Paris "for a little R and R"; an example of the latter is an unauthorized jeep ride to Paris by Ken Brown and a couple of other 5 Dorset officers.

CANLOAN officers continued to learn about the history of their regiments, and occasionally some Canadian history at the same time. Len Robertson of the 2nd E. Yorks. was surprised at orders for band practices and the blancoing of all equipment for "the 13th." His platoon sergeant explained that 13 September was Quebec Day, the anniversary of General Wolfe's defeat of General Montcalm on the Plains of Abraham. On the 13th the battalion was transported to the nearest city, where they marched through the streets with fixed bayonets and blancoed equipment, the band playing, and were later inspected by the Divisional Commander. Robertson commented, "Leave it to the British to put on a show in the middle of a war." The regimental history notes that the customary Quebec Day dance had to be cancelled because of the lack of female partners. "The suggestion of the unit's Canadian officers to put out a big notice 'Quebec Day,' so as to attract partners was ruled out as rather tactless in France."[5]

An earlier anniversary that was celebrated by several regiments in Normandy under more difficult conditions was Minden Day on 1 August at the beginning of operation BLUECOAT. At the battle of Minden during the Seven Years' War, as the British infantry went into battle on 1 August 1759 against 10,000 French cavalry, they "plucked wild roses and decorated their headgear," a practice that is perpetuated by the descendants of those regiments to this day. In 1944 the commemoration ranged from full-scale treatment by 7 KOSB at Airborne Headquarters, Bulford, to the plucking of wild roses (much like the originals) in the Normandy *bocage* by the 6th KOSB (when the roses ordered by the quartermaster sergeants were not delivered), to a "booze-up" by officers of 1/4 KOYLI in a dugout within a few yards of the enemy.

CANLOAN officers in the 51st Highland Division were privileged to share in an emotional event on 3 September when the division returned to Saint-Valéry, where the parent division had been eliminated in 1940. As the massed pipes and drums of the Highland Division, perhaps 400 in all, beat retreat, none present could fail to be moved. Equally appropriate during the liberation of the Channel ports by the First Canadian Army, which included I British Corps, was the capture of Dieppe by the 2nd Canadian Division on 1 September. The 49th Division encountered fierce resistance in capturing Le Havre; later Dunkirk was by-passed and besieged as the German Fifteenth Army, which had been defending the Pas de Calais, retreated up the coast to the Breskens Pocket near Antwerp and the Scheldt Estuary.

On 1 September Eisenhower assumed direct command of all Allied land forces and Montgomery became commander of 21st Army Group, which comprised the First Canadian Army and the Second British Army. He was promoted to Field Marshal. A great deal has been written about "the great argument" between Eisenhower and Montgomery concerning post-Normandy tactics. Eisenhower favoured a broad front, an advance by all four armies towards the Rhine: the First Canadian to clear the Channel ports, the Second British to capture Antwerp, essential for supplies, the First American to advance towards Aachen and the Ruhr, and the Third American to continue towards Metz and the Saar. Montgomery argued for a "single full-blooded thrust" by the British Second Army, assisted by the First American Army, on a northern route to the Rhine and into the North German Plain, a strategy which he believed would end the war in 1944. While Montgomery was given a degree of priority in supplies because of the urgency of opening the port of Antwerp, the single-thrust proposal was frustrated by Eisenhower's preference for a broad advance and to some extent by the ability of Patton, who commanded the Third Army, to obtain enough gasoline to keep going, regardless of the overall policy.[6]

The German troops who escaped from Normandy were handicapped in every way in their preparation of defence lines. Especially serious was the loss of mobility because of the lack of tanks. Of 2,300 German tanks and assault guns that had been committed in Normandy, only 100 to 120 were brought back across the Seine.[7] The Seventh Army, fleeing on foot or in horse-drawn carts, could barely keep ahead of the advancing British and were often overtaken. An attempt to form a defence line on the Somme was frustrated when the 11th Armoured Division captured Amiens and three of four bridges over the Somme on the night of 30 September. The only natural line of defence before the Rhine was the series of rivers and canals northeast of Antwerp, beginning with the Albert Canal. For a time there was an important 75-mile gap between Antwerp and Maastricht, but the Germans were quickly able to convert it into a strong defence line: because of the desperate need for troops to halt the Allied advance, the Luftwaffe released 20,000 paratroops to form the First Parachute Army on 4 September. The next day the paratroops were digging in on the north side of the Albert Canal.[8] On the same day Field Marshal Karl von Rundstedt, who had been dismissed by Hitler in Normandy, was reinstated as Commander-in-Chief, West. Taking charge immediately, he welded all available troops, regardless of unit, age, or physical condition, into a surprisingly effective defence. Finally, the German Fifteenth Army, 80,000 strong, was able to escape.

When Antwerp was captured by the 11th Armoured Division on 4 September and the port was secured intact, it was considered a major achievement. But later it was realized that if the division had continued 15 miles northward it would have cut off the South Beveland peninsula and blocked the escape of the German Fifteenth Army. Instead these troops retreated and were fed into the defence line of the Albert and Meuse-Escaut Canals. Two days after the triumphant "swan" had reached Brussels and Antwerp, the British Second Army was engaged in bitter fighting to gain crossings over the canals.

As the "swan" approached Brussels and Antwerp, the first serious opposition was encountered at Ghent. Even there the initial contact by the 7th Armoured Division was encouraging, as is described by Maj. Vince Lilley (now with 1/6 Queens):

> Enemy resistance did not stiffen until we were in the south-eastern suburbs of Ghent. After a bit of street fighting we consolidated our defensive positions in houses overlooking the river ... Two days later A Coy with my Recce Section under command were ordered to circle Ghent to the north-east in the hope of cutting off the retreating enemy. After a by-pass of 10 miles we headed west to Ghent and I couldn't believe my eyes – marching down the street in column of route were the remnants of a German Bn headed by a colour party prominently displaying white flags. Luckily all they wanted to do was surrender and get out of the war ... The Bn then established a firm bridgehead and several days later, after a few counter-attacks were put in, we handed over to the Polish Division.[9]

At the same time 2 Glas. H. of the 15th Scottish Division encountered more difficulty in street fighting and house clearing along the Canal du Nord in Ghent. The platoon of Lieut. Roger MacLellan, while clearing houses, was assisted by troops from the Queens, who called across the canal to tell them which buildings were occupied by the Germans. The entire battalion was heavily engaged all day on 10 September before it, too, was relieved by the Polish Division. Later the CO of the 2 Glas. H. singled out three CANLOAN officers for special commendation in the fight for Ghent: Lieut. Louis Boudreau, Lieut. Russell Parke, and Lieut. Roger MacLellan. MacLellan was awarded a Military Cross, the citation for which follows:

> On 10 Sept 44 Lieut MacLellan's pl was engaged in the street fighting and clearing north of the Canal of Ghent. He was ordered to advance to a forward position and clear the enemy whose strength and positions were unknown. Lieut MacLellan led his pl with great coolness and ability. 50 yards from the enemy intense fire was met, the left flank sec being particularly exposed. This sec had two men wounded and the Bren gun out of action. The pl commander, realizing the true situation, decided to change his pl's position; during this he showed an utter disregard for his own personal safety, and by his initiative and ability he successfully extricated all his men, including five wounded. His courage and coolness steadied and calmed his men, and by his example he enabled his pl to move in good order to a better position and finally to clear the enemy. During two days fighting his pl captured a total of 207 prisoners of war.[10]

Fighting on a larger scale occurred along the Albert Canal, and then the Meuse-Escaut Canal. A small bridgehead was established over the Albert Canal on 6 September, but there was a strong counter-attack, and it was another four days before the Irish Guards of the Guards Armoured Division advanced 10 miles and captured a bridge over the Meuse-Escaut Canal near Neerpelt on 10 September. The terrain between the Albert and Meuse-Escaut Canals with its sandy heath, streams, and swamps made advance difficult, and the defenders "fought with fanatical bravery and were dislodged only when their village strongholds were demolished house by house."[11] Even though a bridgehead had been made over the canals, fighting continued for the establishment of other bridgeheads and against counter-attacks for nearly two more weeks.

From 12 to 18 September the 15th Scottish Division was engaged in fighting at Gheel on the Escaut Canal. During this period several CANLOAN officers were wounded, including CDN/357, Lieut. Alfred H. Pierce of 2 A. & S.H. At Gheel Lieut. Jack Stobo, one of the few surviving CANLOAN officers in 8 RS, earned an MC:

> During the relief of another company in Gheel on 12 Sep Lt Stobo was wounded in the stomach. Though in considerable pain he refused to be evacuated and continued to command his platoon for the next four days. After crossing the canal his platoon was ordered to hold a position vital to the bridgehead. On the evening of 14 Sep several counter attacks on his position were defeated by the well directed fire of his platoon, but all his full rank NCOs were wounded. A final attack just after dark penetrated into his platoon position. Lt Stobo, armed with a Bren gun, went forward single handed and engaged the enemy with such success that this attack was dispersed.
>
> All day during 15 September Lt Stobo's platoon was in a most exposed position where digging was impossible. Strong enemy attacks supported by heavy arty fire continued all day, but Lt Stobo, though now with only one L/Cpl left, directed the fire of his platoon with such effect that every one was defeated with heavy loss to the enemy. On 16 Sept, now on the west flank of the Bn line, under almost equally heavy fire, he continued to fight his platoon with the greatest courage and success.
>
> Throughout this action, lasting 72 hours, under continuous enemy shelling and counter attacks, Lt Stobo showed great personal courage and leadership of the highest order. Suffering from a painful wound he withstood all strain of battle and inspired his tired soldiers to renewed efforts. The action of his platoon vitally affected the success of the Bn in establishing and holding the bridgehead.[12]

By mid-September other divisions were closing up to the Escaut Canal. In the 53rd (Welch) Division, Capt. R.G. Marsh of the 6th RWF, who had been so prominent in leading fighting patrols in Normandy, continued his exploits in Belgium and Holland. The regimental history notes that in a night patrol across the canal the company sergeant-major accompanying him was shot in the stomach during an ambush by the Germans. "Capt R.G. Marsh, tossing a grenade among the enemy managed to pick him up and brought him back to the boat and to safety."[13] The account continues, "This was one of the many brave acts performed by Capt Marsh, a Canadian officer who was later killed in Holland commanding A Company."[14]

In this fighting another CANLOAN officer in 6 RWF, CDN/661, Lieut. Philip G. West, died of wounds. The regimental history reports, "C Coy had fierce fighting and one of their officers, a Canadian, Lieut P. West, was badly wounded and though, despite well-aimed German machine gun fire, members of his platoon succeeded in rescuing him he died the next day from his wounds."[15]

The fighting for the canals was not devoid of humour as can be seen from the following account by Burt Harper of 1 E. Lan. R. in 53 Division:

About nine PM we moved up to an assembly area some 600 yards from the [Meuse-Escaut] canal, and then the long wait began. Waiting for imminent action is always trying, especially for the men in the sections who have little to do but wait. It had started to rain at dusk and now, in the pitch black night, with no smoking, no noise, and no sleep possible, there was plenty of time for contemplation. Some time before ten PM the CQMS arrived with great containers of hot tea, and despite these somewhat miserable surroundings this was enjoyed every bit as much as a fine English tea served in comfortable surroundings. This before-battle tea, which had become a tradition in the E Lan R, was a supplement to the need for the inevitable nervous pee which, in this case, in the darkness, resulted in a few muffled curses and threats because of badly directed streams.

At 2300 we moved up towards the canal, guided by white tapes laid by the Intelligence Section, and stopped at a marker 100 yards from the canal. Then the artillery began to beat a drumfire on the far bank, and as it lifted I led the first boat through the gap in the bund [embankment].

Suddenly and almost unexpectedly we were at the very edge of the stone-faced, very steep, and slippery canal bank, with the water about eight feet below, about twice the distance expected. Our drills hadn't catered to this.

In haste I scrambled clear of the path of the fast-following boat and shouted to those carrying it to hold everything. I can only assume that with the noise and in the darkness they thought I was exhorting them to greater effort because the forward motion seemed to speed up, and as each boat carrier reached the edge he had to let go or be carried into the canal below. The bow of the boat dipped down to the water and, propelled by the pushers at the rear, took on a momentum of its own. I realized that we were about to lose the boat and, in desperation, as the stern went by, I leaped aboard. With this added boost and the steep slope down which it slid, boat and I shot off into the darkness and disappeared, leaving behind a startled platoon, no doubt marvelling at the enthusiasm of their Canadian officer.

Boat and stowaway skimmed across the canal. I struggled to my feet only to be knocked flat as it hit the enemy side – fortunately out of sight of both friend and foe. When I did manage to grab a paddle, few athletes, Olympic or otherwise, ever expended more energy than I did in recrossing that fifty or so yards of water.

I embarked my platoon, and as each one slid down the bank to the boat, I couldn't resist a few sarcastic comments about how nice it was to have them join me.

Another adventure began after we cleared the bund on the far side – but that is a separate story. My hurt feelings were softened somewhat when I learned that at the other crossing site, two boats capsized and two soldiers had drowned.

But the E Lan R had established its bridgehead.[16]

During the week before the Arnhem operation, five CANLOAN officers were killed in action in the attacks on the canals. Lieut. Harry Niznick of the 8th DLI was killed on 9 September. A fellow officer, Maj. I.R. English, reports, "Soon after the battalion had launched a successful attack across the Albert Canal in the area of Steelen, Niznick's company was moving forward but ran into heavy shell and machine gun fire and he was killed. At the time he was the last remaining Canadian."[17]

Lieut. William Kotchapaw, 1 Hereford, 11th Armoured Division, was killed on 10 September. Posted to the battalion on 13 May, he had been wounded at Hill 112 on 1 July but rejoined his battalion and resumed command of 15 Platoon on 14 August, just before the attack on Flers, where the memorial to the 11th Armoured Division is located. A fellow platoon commander recalls the circumstances of his death:

> Driving forward in TCVs [troop carrying vehicles] the company came under attack. 13 and 15 Platoons launched an attack with 14 in reserve. When, after a short but furious battle the reserve platoon was sent for the platoon commander discovered that both Lieutenant Kotchapaw and his sergeant had been killed and the remnants of his platoon were being gathered together and reorganized by a l/cpl, who later was awarded a DCM. Lieutenant Kotchapaw was held in the highest esteem by 15 Platoon, who mourned him as front line soldiers do – deeply, but not on the surface.[18]

On 15 September Lieut. Jackson Stewart of 8 RS was killed at Gheel. Posted to the 8th RS in May, he had joined the battalion as a reinforcement officer in June and was wounded on 8 July. After being released from hospital he managed to rejoin the battalion by the end of the month in time for the breakout in Normandy.

Two CANLOAN officers were killed on 16 September, both of them from the 15th Scottish Division. Lieut. Wilfred Brownlee-Lamont has been referred to earlier. The young American scholar, who left a position as researcher for the Imperial Economic Commission in London to join the Canadian Army as a private, had completed the infantry courses at Brockville, in Canada, and at Barnard Castle. Posted to the 2nd Gordons in Normandy on 23 August, he was wounded in the crossing of the Seine five days later. On release from hospital he rejoined the Gordons on 1 September, two weeks before his death at the Escaut Canal.

CDN/233, Lieut. Kenneth Coates had served overseas with the Carleton and York Regiment in the 1st Canadian Division from 1940 to 1943, rising from private to sergeant before being sent to Canada for a commission. As a CANLOAN officer he had been posted to the 2/5 Battalion, the Lancashire Fusiliers (LF). Wounded in Normandy on 17 July, he was in hospitals and reinforcement holding units in England before being posted on 25 August to the 6th KOSB in the 15th Scottish Division. He was killed three weeks later at the Albert Canal.

The battles for the canals and particularly a secure bridgehead over the Meuse-Escaut Canal were important because the bridgehead was to be the starting line for a major operation which was scheduled to begin on 17 September.

Montgomery's proposal for "one powerful and full-blooded thrust towards Berlin"[19] required the halting temporarily of General Patton's Third Army and the full support of Bradley's First Army, but though Eisenhower approved in principle a drive on the northern route to the Rhine, he was not prepared to stop the Third Army or insist on the support of the First Army for Montgomery, who was thus left to depend on his own resources. Given the other commitments of the First Canadian Army and the Second British Army, only General Horrocks's XXX Corps was in a position to continue the advance into Holland.

Montgomery realized that this was an opportunity to use the Allied Airborne Army for which both he and Eisenhower had been seeking a role and devising plans that had been dropped for various reasons. On 10 September he put to Eisenhower a proposal that would, if successful, bring a penetration deep enough to get the Second Army over the Rhine in a single bound, outflank the Siegfried Line, and reach the North German Plain north of the Ruhr. It was a combined operation called MARKET GARDEN. In the MARKET phase the Airborne Army would drop over the Maas at Grave, the Waal at Nijmegen, and the Rhine at Arnhem. The GARDEN phase would be an armoured and infantry drive by XXX Corps to link up the airborne bridgeheads and form "a carpet to the Rhine."[20] Though Eisenhower approved the plan, he still refused to halt or redirect the operations of the American armies. Consequently Dempsey's right flank would be left exposed and less armour and infantry would be available for MARKET GARDEN; nevertheless, Montgomery was confident that his bold stroke would succeed. The operation was set to begin on 17 September, leaving less than a week to plan "the greatest paratroop and glider borne infantry operation ever conceived."[21] There would be 35,000 men, twice the number of airborne troops used in Normandy, 3 1/2 airborne divisions – two American and one British – and a Polish brigade. The 101st Airborne Division under Maj.-Gen. Maxwell Taylor and the 82nd Airborne Division under Brig.-Gen. James Gavin were to seize crossings over the Maas and Waal Rivers while the 1st British Airborne Division under Maj.-Gen. Robert Urquhart with Maj.-Gen. Stanislaw Sosabowski's Polish Brigade under command was to capture the most important objective, the 2,000-foot, three-span highway bridge over the Rhine at Arnhem. One-third of this airborne force would be carried to its targets by 2,500 gliders; the rest would drop by parachute. The attacking force would be escorted by more than 1,500 planes. The 52nd Division would be flown into the Arnhem bridgehead as soon as airstrips were available.[22]

The ground attack by XXX Corps was to be supported by a 350-gun artillery barrage. The Guards Armoured Division would "blast down the main road,"[23] followed by the 43rd Division and the 50th Northumbrian Division. General Urquhart reluctantly agreed to drop zones six to eight miles from the Arnhem bridge to avoid heavy anti-aircraft fire. A few days before the operation was to begin, intelligence reports were received from Dutch observers who reported that elements of the 9th and 10th SS Panzer Divisions were at Arnhem. Field Marshal Model, Commander of German Army Group B, had established his HQ in Arnhem, and the HQ of II Panzer Corps, which comprised the 9th and 10th SS Panzer Divisions, was nearby. These reports were not taken seriously. It was noted afterwards that "nothing was allowed to mar the enthusiasm for the airborne operation."[24] There was a belief that this might be the last chance to get the Allied Airborne Army into action before the war ended.[25]

Impressed by the peacetime exploits of Russian paratroops and the effective use by the Germans of paratroops and glider-borne troops in the Netherlands, Winston Churchill on 22 June 1940 had ordered that a corps of paratroops be established.[26] In November of 1941, Maj.-Gen. Frederick "Boy" Browning was appointed GOC Airborne Forces. In November 1942, the 1st Airborne Division undertook its first operations, in North Africa; others followed in Sicily. The 6th Airborne Division was formed in May 1943. Its dramatic D-Day landing in Normandy and subsequent defence of the left flank of the bridgehead until the end of August have been noted.

Between 6 June and 17 September the 1st Airborne Division lived in a state of constant anticipation. No fewer than 16 airborne operations were planned, but all came to naught, usually cancelled because of the rapid advances of ground troops over the objectives of the airborne divisions. From the beginning, airborne troops were required to attain the highest standards of training and performance and were justified in considering themselves an elite force. They were ready for action, and the summer of 1944 was a frustrating time. Sharing this frustration were the CANLOAN officers who joined the division between April and August 1944.

There seems to have been no particular desire by CANLOAN officers to serve in airborne forces; several of those who asked for a Scottish regiment discovered only later that the one to which they were assigned was airborne. More were interested in keeping together, either with one or more friends or as a group. A group of six volunteers from the Battle School at Vernon, British Columbia, was pounced upon by Brigadier Gregg at Sussex and persuaded to be instructors until their flight left. Five of the six went to airborne units, one, CDN/489, Lieut. James W. Taylor, to 7 KOSB and four others to parachute battalions in the 6th Airborne Division.

Though the airborne divisions were proud of their reputation for high standards, there was no special selection procedure in the recruiting of CANLOAN officers. But since there was a shortage of platoon commanders, many of the CANLOAN officers who did not have a strong preference for other British Army regiments were assigned to airborne battalions. Nowhere was there a greater concentration of CANLOAN officers than in the Air Landing Brigade of the 1st Airborne Division, which ultimately listed 23 in 7 KOSB, 13 in 2 S. Staffords. and 11 in 1 Border, a total of 47. In C Company in 7 KOSB, three of the four platoons were commanded by CANLOAN officers, and of the 27 platoons in the battalion eight were commanded by CANLOAN officers and one company had a CANLOAN second in command.

CANLOAN officers were informed that, since parachute training was long and arduous, and since both the 1st and 6th Airborne Divisions must be ready for immediate action, they would be limited to glider-borne units. There were, however, some exceptions. In the 1st Airborne Division CDN/203, Lieut. Harry H.D. Barons, Lieut. Leo Heaps, and CDN/449, Capt. Maurice Duhault managed to get into 1 Para. and CDN/639, Lieut. James L McKenna into 11 Para. More CANLOAN officers joined parachute battalions in the 6th Airborne Division: there were no fewer than eight in five different parachute battalions, and 15 were in the glider-borne battalions of the division: 2 Oxf. Bucks., 1 RUR, and 11 and 12 Devon.

Generally the CANLOAN officers assigned to airborne units were well received and fitted easily into those units. They were popular with their men, who found their informality refreshing. Some of them had heard of the reputation of Canadians as assault troops in the First World War and thought that the arrival of so many of them meant that the unit was "really in for something big." There seems to have been no thought that the Canadian officers were not ready for battle as airborne platoon commanders. Some, indeed, who were experienced instructors, did more work than their British colleagues, as Lieut. Jim Taylor recalls:

> I, along with CDN/167 Kaufmann, Martin L, worked 11 and 12 Platoons many more hours weekly than other platoons. Because my platoon was instilled with the need for their being properly prepared for battle, particularly in an airborne role, they accepted the extra hours of hard work. It is my belief that the only reason 12 Platoon was still functioning as an effective fighting force after other platoons had ceased to exist, was due to those long hours of training and their belief in their invincibility.[27]

The majority of the CANLOAN officers in the 1st Airborne Division joined their battalions in April or May and remained with them until the launching of MARKET GARDEN in September. Quite a few, however, were in the 600 group (those who converted to infantry) and came to the division at the end of July or early August after completing the excellent course at Barnard Castle. Still others had served in infantry battalions in Normandy, had been wounded, and had joined the 1st Airborne Division from the RHUs to which they had been posted after their convalescence.

One of these officers, who showed remarkable persistence in getting into a parachute battalion, was Leo Heaps, who has told the story in his books, *Escape from Arnhem* and *The Grey Goose of Arnhem*. He had served in Normandy with the 1st Dorset, 50 Division, was wounded near Villers-Bocage, and was evacuated to a hospital in England. Released and posted to an RHU, he applied for a posting to a paratroop unit but was rejected by a selection board. Refusing to give up, he eventually marched into the office of Major-General Crawford, who was in command of airborne training at the War Office. He told him of the boredom in an infantry holding unit after being discharged from hospital and of his desire for action. The general was sympathetic. Although over 50 years of age, he had parachuted into Normandy on D-Day, unbeknownst to his superiors, rather than miss a great event. He told Heaps he would look after the details:

> A week later the florid faced colonel of my holding unit who had threatened to court martial me for conduct unbecoming to an officer (I had on occasion disappeared when wanted for orderly officer duty), handed me my transfer. He was glad to get rid of me. Colonel Dobie, Commanding Officer of the 1st Parachute Battalion, 1st Airborne Division, couldn't understand why a strange Canadian lieutenant should join his battalion a few weeks before they left for Holland.[28]

Leo Heaps's first parachute jump was at Arnhem.

As was noted earlier, between 6 June and 17 September, 16 airborne operations had been planned for the 1st Airborne Division and all had come to naught, either because the ground troops had not gone far enough or because they had gone too fast. The Allied First Airborne Army had been formed at the end of July. Headed by an American, Lieut.-Gen. Lewis H. Brereton, it included all Allied airborne forces in Europe and had been held in reserve for just such a strike as MARKET GARDEN.

Operation MARKET was to be carried out in three lifts on three successive days. The first left England at 0930 hours on Sunday, 17 September. The vast armada of 4,700 aircraft, 10 miles across and 100 miles long, took more than two hours to pass.[29] The American 101st Airborne Division (the Screaming Eagles) dropped north of Eindhoven with the task of capturing bridges over the Wilhemina and Willems Canals. Then the 82nd Airborne Division (the All-American) dropped north of the Maas River with the ambitious tasks of seizing bridges over the Maas at Grave, the Maas-Waal Canal, and the main bridge over the Waal at Nijmegen. Both divisions expected to complete these tasks on the 17th to permit XXX Corps to reach Arnhem and relieve the 1st Airborne Division in 48 hours.

Cornelius Ryan has made famous the comment to Field Marshal Montgomery by Lieut.-General Frederick Browning, Deputy-Commander of the First Allied Airborne Army: "But, sir, I think we might be going a bridge too far." There was no such thought in the minds of the "Red Devils" of the 1st Airborne Division as they landed on Renkum Heath, eight miles west of Arnhem, shortly after 1300 hours. Nearly 95 percent of the parachutes and gliders landed in the right spots. The units were piped to the assembly point to the tune of "Blue Bonnets over the Border" and moved off briskly to their appointed tasks.

The 1st Air Landing Brigade under Brig. Philip "Pip" Hicks was to set up a defence of the landing zone for the second lift, which was expected the next morning. It consisted of 7 KOSB, the 2nd S. Staffords., and the 1st Border. All but two of the CANLOAN officers in the division were in these battalions.

The 1st Parachute Brigade under Brig. Gerald Lathbury, consisting of the 1st, 2nd, and 3rd Parachute Battalions, was to capture and hold the bridge at Arnhem. The 2nd, summoned by the hunting horn of Lieutenant-Colonel Frost, followed the road nearest the river and fought its way to the north end of the bridge, which it reached and captured by 2030 hours. It then had a strength of around 500. Meanwhile the 1st and 3rd Battalions, following parallel roads to reach the bridge from the north, found their way blocked by the 9th and 10th SS Panzer Divisions. Pinned down, along with Brigadier Lathbury, who was wounded, and the Divisional Commander, Major-General Urquhart, who had moved forward to urge the paratroops on, the two battalions were slowly cut to pieces, although individuals and small groups managed to make their way to the bridge, where Lieutenant-Colonel Frost's strength rose to more than 600 before being reduced by casualties. An American glider carrying the entire plan for MARKET GARDEN had been captured, and so the Germans were able to anticipate the Allies' moves and their drops of troops and supplies.

The only CANLOAN officer in the 1st Parachute Brigade on 17 September was Leo Heaps. His very first parachute jump was successful. As he had no platoon to command or a position on the establishment to fill, he was free to undertake special missions on orders from superior officers or on his own initiative. On the morning of 18 September he was sent with a jeep, ammunition, food, and a wireless set towards the Arnhem bridge. When the steering wheel of the jeep came off, Heaps commandeered a passing Bren gun carrier and continued. On the way he encountered his CO, Lieutenant-Colonel Dobie of 1 Parachute Battalion, and Brigadier Lathbury and Major-General Urquhart, who sent him back to Divisional Headquarters with messages. Years later General Urquhart described the encounter to Cornelius Ryan:

> Urquhart and his officers were dumbfounded to see a British Bren gun carrier clatter down the street as though unaware of the German fire and pull up outside the building. A Canadian, Lieut Leo Heaps, who in Urquhart's words "seemed to have a charmed existence," leaped out of the driver's seat and raced for the building. Behind Heaps was Charles "Frenchie" Labouchère of the Dutch resistance who was acting as Heaps' guide. Now for the first time in hours Urquhart learned from Heaps what was happening. He decided to break out but meanwhile sent urgent messages by Heaps to Divisional Headquarters at the Hartenstein Hotel in Oosterbreek.[30]

During the night of 17 September and the early morning of the 18th, the 1st Air Landing Brigade had been attacked and had suffered heavy casualties, among whom were several CANLOAN officers. In 7 KOSB, part of D Company had been overrun, and both CANLOAN officers in the company became casualties. CDN/169, Lieut. Albert E. Kipping was killed on the 18th, and CDN/176, Lieut. Peter B. Mason was wounded and captured with the remnants of his platoon. CDN/477, Lieut. Albert E.F. Wayte of C Company was seriously wounded and died two days later. At the same time CDN/535, Captain Basil W.H. Hingston of 2 S. Staffords. had been killed in the defence of the dropping zones.

The second lift from England, which was five hours late arriving, comprised the three battalions of the 4th Parachute Brigade under Brigadier Hackett, and the 10th, 11th, and 156th Parachute Battalions. In the absence of General Urquhart, Brigadier Hicks had decided to send the 11th Para. with the 2nd S. Staffords. to the relief of the bridge. In exchange the 7th KOSB was assigned to the 4th Brigade to attack the enemy on the high ground north of Oosterbeek and protect a dropping zone for the third lift, which was to come the next day. The desperate efforts to reach Arnhem bridge to reinforce the dwindling 2nd Para. were unsuccessful. Cornelius Ryan says that in the attempt four battalions were "shredded" – the 1st, 3rd, and 11th Paras. and the 2nd S. Staffords. By the morning of 19 September only 20 percent of the S. Staffords. remained.[31]

When the 48 hours that had been allowed for the relief of the 1st Airborne Division by XXX Corps elapsed on 19 September, the ground troops had barely reached the Nijmegen bridge, which was to be attacked the next day by the 82nd Airborne Division. From the beginning there had been delays. The ground attack, led by the Irish Guards had begun at 1435 hours on the 17th after a massive barrage but was stopped almost immediately when nine tanks were knocked out, blocking the road. The advance on a single road through marshy land unfit for armour was slow and had to proceed at the speed at which infantry of the 43rd Division could knock out the anti-tank defences ahead and fight off attacks from the flanks that kept cutting the narrow corridor.

General Urquhart was able to reach Divisional HQ at the Hartenstein Hotel on the morning of the 19th. Because of bad weather in England the drop of the Polish Parachute Brigade had to be postponed to the 21st and was then directed to the south side of the Rhine, since the original drop zone was in the hands of the Germans. After all efforts at reinforcement had failed, General Urquhart asked Leo Heaps to try to get through to the bridge on the night of the 19th, but it was impossible. On 20 September Lieutenant-Colonel Frost learned there was no hope of relief, since the 82nd US Division was only then attacking the Waal bridge at Nijmegen, 11 miles away. His force of defenders was reduced to about 140, and he himself was wounded. Early on the 21st the 2nd Parachute Battalion, having done all that was humanly possible to hold the Arnhem bridge, was driven off, and German tanks began to roll across it towards Nijmegen to bolster the defences against XXX Corps.

The Nijmegen bridge was captured on the 20th, and the Irish Guards were ordered to "go like Hell for Arnhem." Earlier, in the attack on Nijmegen the CANLOAN officer in the 1st Gren. Gds., Larry Fazackerley, was wounded. The regimental history describes the attack:

No 4 Company's attack in the centre started badly. Major Stanley, Company Commander, decided to advance on a two-platoon front, each platoon supported by a tank. At 3:30 the left-hand platoon commanded by Lieut L W Fazackerley led off, fanning out across the open ground known as Kelfkensbosch. They had not advanced more than a hundred yards before the Germans opened up with the most withering fire from the area of the bridge. Lieut Fazackerley was shot through the stomach, Lieut Prescott's tank was hit by an enormous shell and blew up, L/Sgt Heawood and his section were mown down and pinned down by fire and casualties started to mount all around at a most alarming rate.[32]

Even when the Guards were on the last stretch to Arnhem they were stopped at Elst, a frustrating six miles from the Rhine.

On 20 September a decision was made to withdraw all surviving troops to a perimeter around the Hartenstein Hotel at Oosterbeek. By that time few platoons were operating as such. Officers were assigned so many men for particular tasks or gathered any survivors, regardless of their regular units. The war diary of 2 S. Staffords., for example, notes that CDN/452, Lieut. James S. Erskine was wounded and that "about 50 Staffords together with certain details of other units were under the command of [CDN/476] Lieut. P.H. Turner in the church area" of the perimeter. On the day before, Turner's leadership had earned an unusual award, the United States Distinguished Service Cross:

> Lieutenant Philip Hart Turner, British Army, for extraordinary heroism in connection with military operations against the enemy on 19 Sep 1944 during the Battle of Arnhem. Lieutenant Turner led his platoon with great gallantry in the attack on the wooded hill at Der Brink. The skill and courage with which he handled his platoon were decisive factors in the success of the attack. During the subsequent reorganization he behaved with great coolness under very heavy mortar fire and with complete disregard for his own personal safety. Later he commanded a sector near Oosterbeek church where his platoon was constantly shelled and mortared, and harassed by enemy tanks and guns. During the entire period of the defence of Oosterbeek he gave a splendid example of fearless devotion to duty and set an example to his men which contributed largely to their success.[33]

All the officers in the tight and contracting perimeter were subjected to the most severe tests of leadership; under constant mortar and artillery fire, surrounded by snipers, attacked by tanks and SS panzer grenadiers, without food or rest, and with decreasing supplies of ammunition and dwindling numbers, they not only defended their areas and fought off counter-attacks, some of which got within 25 yards of their positions, but to the end continued aggressive patrols and counter-attacks.

At 0430 hours on 20 September, Lieut. Martin Kaufmann of 7 KOSB led a patrol beyond the perimeter with a section of machine guns to ambush the enemy at a railway embankment. From 0001 to 0430 on the 21st, fighting patrols under Lieuts. Jim Taylor of C Company and Erskine Carter of B Company were sent out to ambush enemy tanks. Later a full-scale enemy attack on the battalion's position threatened to overwhelm it. Carter describes this attack:

> The Hun, having recovered from the jar which our patrols had given him in the morning, mounted a full scale attack. From the vicinity of the white house numerous heavy calibre machine guns chattered supporting fire and more than a hundred shouting SS troops

charged over the 40 yards towards our positions. Our front position casualties were heavy and we fell back 50 yards but the Vickers gunners stuck to their guns and, reorganized by the Colonel, we prepared to assault the Hun, who now occupied our trenches.

Led by the Colonel, who ran ahead tossing grenades, and ably supported by our machine guns, whose devastating fire kept the Jerry machine gun replies to a minimum, we fixed bayonets and went after the Hun. It was a costly business; enemy bullets ripped around us but still we pressed on. After covering about half the distance to the enemy the Colonel ordered us to the ground and the Vickers swept the woods to our front; then, having tossed a few more grenades, we followed in for the kill. Many of the SS elected to stay in their trenches and fight to the end. These were swiftly dealt with and the trenches filled with German dead. Others, unable to stand the prospect of steel, took to their heels and soon the whole area which we had to give up at various stages during the previous 12 hours was in our hands ... We quickly consolidated ... There were our wounded to be attended to. Never before in the battle had we suffered so many casualties in one assault. There were about 15 dead and many more wounded. Some of our bravest had died leading the charge.[34]

Among the wounded was Martin Kaufmann; this left Jim Taylor and Erskine Carter as the remaining CANLOAN officers in the battalion. Taylor was particularly aggressive in regard to patrols. The activities of his platoon at Arnhem were summarized later:

We were the vanguard in C Coy's battle; we were the rear guard coming out; we cleared woods, did house clearing, fighting in built-up areas, counter attacked, using only machine guns for covering fire, and we repelled tank attacks with stealth and determination using PIATs and 36 hand grenades. One Mark 4 tank was put out of action within five feet of my slit trench. We were also involved in day and night patrols, digging out snipers and generally forming the backbone of the Company. Two of our platoons were destroyed on 17/18 September and 1 Platoon commanded by Martin Kaufmann was reduced to a few leaderless men by shellfire which severely wounded Martin and killed or wounded many of his men. Finally, to my knowledge, only one member of 12 Platoon survived to be evacuated across the Neder Rijn. The remainder of C Company was either killed, wounded or taken as prisoners of war.[35]

In the attack on 21 September, Jim Taylor acquired the nickname, "the Arson" from his use of Molotov cocktails and fire to rout out three German snipers from haylofts during the morning.[36]

It would be difficult to improve on the vivid and detailed account of the struggle of the 1st Airborne Division at Arnhem by Cornelius Ryan in *A Bridge Too Far*. Some things, however, can be told best by those who were there. An example is a description of the battlefield at Oosterbeek by Erskine Carter:

After the casualties had left our area we moved in small groups to the new positions. Before we left, the ground was thoroughly searched for anything which might be of value. All that we discarded were smashed guns and irreparable transport. Here we fought for nearly 48 hours; when we had entered it had been a green and fertile plantation, spotted with very trim and quaint houses. Now there was scarcely a leaf on the trees. The trees themselves were smashed and splintered; the fields were a mess of shell holes, while the buildings, if not demolished, were blazing with fire. The ground was strewn with our dead and many more of the enemy; shell cases were piled high around the gun positions; supply parachutes hung from the branches; broken equipment littered the trenches. Everywhere hung the smell and picture of battle and death.[37]

And this is a description of the defenders on 22 September, after five days at Arnhem:

In the gloom we could see tanks attacking C Coy, and their anti-tank and Vickers guns were in continuous fire. The silence around our positions was tense. Haggard faces, some with six days growth of beard, others hardly recognizable because of the dirt, filled the trenches; exhausted bodies, tired minds and shaken nerves vied to overcome the ever-pressing desire to sleep. It began to rain.[38]

In the tank attack on C Company Jim Taylor was finally put out of action: a German officer riding on a tank machine-gunned him while he was attending to a wounded glider pilot who had joined his platoon as a volunteer.

Another CANLOAN casualty on 22 September was Lieut. James McKenna of the 11th Para. who was killed in the defence of the bridgehead at Oosterbeek. McKenna was probably the only CANLOAN officer in the 1st Airborne Division who had trained as a paratrooper in North America. After qualifying for a commission in the RCA in May 1942 he received parachute training in Montana. He continued artillery training at Petawawa, Ontario, and Shilo, Manitoba, and converted to infantry to join CANLOAN.

By 21 September the small bridgehead around the Hartenstein Hotel in Oosterbeek, called the perimeter, had been reduced to a width of less than two miles at its widest and only a mile on the Rhine. On the west of the perimeter was a party commanded by Brigadier Hicks of the Air Landing Brigade and consisting of remnants of the Border Regiment and stragglers from several other regiments. On the east, under the command of Brigadier Hackett of the 4th Parachute Brigade, were the survivors of 10 and 156 Parachute Battalions with a few artillery and other troops. On the north were 7 KOSB and an independent parachute company, and on the south was a group consisting of remnants of the 1st, 3rd, and 11th Parachute Battalions and 2 S. Staffords.

On the night of 21 September the Polish Parachute Brigade finally dropped on the south side of the Rhine. It was hoped that this brigade, together with reinforcements from the 43rd Division, could reinforce the 1st Airborne Division and enable it to hold the foothold over the Rhine until the main force of XXX Corps arrived. There were, however, frustrating delays. Although some elements of the Guards Armoured Division and of the 4th Dorset did reach the Rhine on the 22nd, the Guards were ordered back towards Nijmegen to reopen the route, which had been cut by German tanks, and there was difficulty in getting assault boats up to the Rhine for a crossing. That night about 50 Poles were ferried across in rubber dinghies. They joined the Border Regiment in the perimeter, but most became casualties. Leo Heaps, on his own initiative, crossed with a returning dinghy and

Maj.-Gen. H.F.G. Letson, the Canadian Adjutant-General. (Courtesy of National Archives of Canada, PA 141499.)

The Hon. James L. Ralston, Minister of National Defence. (Courtesy of National Archives of Canada, PA 47702.)

Brig. Milton Gregg, Commandant 34 SOTC, Sussex. (Courtesy of CANLOAN Army Officers Association [CA].)

A graduating class at Brockville OTC in 1943, which includes a number of future CANLOAN volunteers. (Courtesy of Maurice Carter.)

Training at Sussex with Brig. Gregg and the Hon. J.L. Ralston. (Courtesy of CA.)

Number Volunteer To Serve In British Army

Shown in the accompanying pictures are ten officers from provincial centres who have volunteered for service with the British Army, as members of a group of officers being loaned by the Canadian Army. All ten are lieutenants. They are, left to right:

TOP ROW—Wilfred Irvin Smith, John Thompson Irwin, Malcolm Rudolph Rose and Lloyd Murray Huggan.

CENTRE ROW—Leonard Bowman Robertson, James Andrew Hislop, Lawson Mitchell Smith and Melbourne Hugh Neily.

BOTTOM ROW—Stewart Howey Cameron and Warren Thompson.

Lieut. Irvin Smith was born in Port Latour, on May 20, 1919, and was a teacher there prior to his enlistment in June 1943. His father, A. Claude Smith, resides in Shelburne.

Lieut. Irvin is a native of Port Morien, born on Aug. 2, 1924. He was a student in Halifax prior to his enlistment in October, 1942, his mother, Mrs. J. T. Irwin, residing at The Bower, Tower Road, Halifax.

Born in Yarmouth, June 24, 1918, Lieut. Rose was a resident of that town at the time of his enlistment as a private. Prior to joining the Army Lieut. Rose was employed by the Irving Oil Company, and was active in athletics, sailing and riding. His mother, Mrs. G. E. Rose, lives at Yarmouth North No. 1.

Lieut. Lloyd Murray Huggan, was born at New Glasgow, Dec. 29, 1918, and was still living in that city at the time of his enlistment as a private on Aug. 26, 1940. He was a commercial traveller prior to joining the Army and was a sports enthusiast. His father, Duncan Huggan, lives at 527 Nelson Street, New Glasgow.

Lieut. Robertson was born at Stellarton, Oct. 19, 1918, and was a resident of Faulkland Street, Pictou, at the time of his enlistment on July 25, 1941. He was an accountant prior to joining the Army. His mother Mrs. L. B. Robertson, lives at Pictou.

Lieut. Hislop is a native of South Ohio, born on April 24, 1918. He was a farmer there prior to his enlistment in October 1942. His wife and his two children reside at South Ohio.

Lieut. W. Thompson was born in Westville, on Aug. 10, 1923, and resided there until enlisting in September, 1939. His mother, Mrs. Hiram Thompson, resides at Church Street Westville. Lieut. Thompson has two brothers in the service, one with the R.C.N.V.R. and another commissioned officer in the R.C.A.F.

(Canadian Army Photos)

Lieut. Lawson Smith was born in New Glasgow, Sept. 27, 1919, and was a student there until his enlistment in January, 1940. Since joining the Army he has seen 14 months service in Bermuda. His mother, Mrs. L. E. H. Smith, resides at 495 Pleasant Street, New Glasgow.

Lieut. Neily was born in Middleton, Sept. 14, 1921, and farmed there until his enlistment in March 1941. His mother, Mrs. Evelyn Neily resides in Middleton; one brother is in the R.C.A.F. and a sister is serving with the C.W.A.C.

A native of Pictou County, Lieut. Cameron was born at Scotch Hill, on July 30, 1918, and was a resident of Stellarton, prior to his enlistment. He joined the Canadian Army as a private on Sept. 1, 1939. His wife resides at 106 Windmill Road, Dartmouth. Lieut. Cameron has two brothers in the R.C.A.F., both commissioned officers.

Malcolm Rose K/A 1944
Lawson Smith K/A 1944
James Hislop Died 1954

Contemporary newspaper clipping. (Courtesy of Evelyn Smith.)

Most battalions had group photographs of officers taken before leaving for Normandy. The 4th Battalion, Wiltshire Regt., included (extreme left, back row) CDN/198, Lieut. Wilfred Smith and CDN/164, Lieut. John Irwin. (Author's collection.)

Officers of C Company, 2 East Yorkshire Regt. In England closely knit teams of company officers were formed. Second from left is CDN/172, Lieut. (Capt.) Len Robertson, who earned an MC in Normandy. Second from right is CDN/118, Capt. James MacGregor, who was killed on D-Day. (Courtesy of Leonard Robertson.)

In England groups from Canadian regiments were often split up. Of this group of Saint John Fusiliers, two officers, CDN/453, Capt. (Lieut.-Col.) Rex Fendick (far right) and CDN/464, Lieut. F.A. McConaghy (second from left), managed to stay together in the 2nd Middlesex MG Battalion in 3 Division. Also in the photo are CDN/459, Don R. Hartt (far left) and CDN/439, Douglas F. Bursey. (Courtesy of Rex Fendick.)

Digging in. (Courtesy of National Archives of Canada, PA 137989.)

A platoon in the 15th Scottish Division preparing to attack. (Courtesy of National Archives of Canada, PA 145675.)

Officer briefing a patrol. (Courtesy of National Archives of Canada, PA 133104.)

Troops in the 43rd Division at Hill 112 on 10 July 1944. This was a hotly contested battlefield that saw many CANLOAN casualties. (Author's collection.)

Decorations for the 4th Battalion, King's Shropshire Light Infantry. Capt. H.F. Henry (front row left) and Lieut. C.M. Patch (front row right) are CANLOAN officers who were mentioned in dispatches. (Courtesy of Lieut.-Col. J.E. Taylor.)

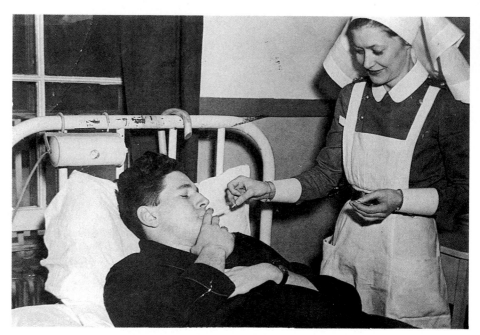

One of the 310 CANLOAN officers who were wounded. The patient is CDN/339, Lieut. (Maj.) D.G. Gage, now president of the Canloan Association. The nurse, Lillian Noble, married CDN/630, Lieut. Hugh Ingraham. (Courtesy of Douglas Gage.)

A few of the CANLOAN officers who were wounded in Normandy and who attended a CANLOAN reception in London, England, on 4 November 1944. (Courtesy of Department of National Defence.)

CANLOAN officers at South End awaiting posting. A crap game. From left to right, CDN/249, Lieut. Norm J.N. Orr, CDN/207, Capt. Norm A. Barnes, CDN/168, Capt. Sydney A. Kemsley, and CDN/461, Lieut. Jack A. Howe. (Courtesy of Norman Orr.)

CANLOAN officer Lieut. (Capt.) G. Smith Macdonald with his platoon in the 7th Battalion, King's Own Scottish Borderers, which landed at Arnhem with the 1st Airborne Division. Macdonald and most of his platoon were wounded and captured. (Courtesy of G. Smith Macdonald.)

158

Of the 20 CANLOAN officers at Arnhem only two were evacuated: CDN/150, Capt. W. Alex Harvie and CDN/476, Capt. Philip H. Turner, both 2nd Battalion, South Staffordshire Regt. Turner was presented with a distinguished Service Cross by General Eisenhower. (Courtesy of National Archives of Canada, PA 169958.)

CANLOAN officer CDN/590, Capt. (Lieut.-Col.) D.K. Brown briefing the Carrier Platoon of the 5th Battalion, Dorsetshire Regt., at Bauchem, Holland, November 1944. (Courtesy of Imperial War Museum.)

CDN/267, Capt. James R. Fetterly, 2nd Battalion, East Yorkshire Regt., being presented with a Military Cross by Field Marshal Montgomery in November 1944. (Courtesy of James Fetterly.)

A Belgium family celebrates with officers of the 1st Battalion, Highland Light Infantry, in the 53rd Welch Division, which liberated their town, Wervicq. CANLOAN officers are CDN/366, Capt. E.A. Watson (fourth from left) and CDN/4, Major Joseph Hemelryk, MC (on extreme right). Hemelryk was later killed in action. (Courtesy of Edward Watson.)

53rd Division in the Reichwald, February 1945. (Courtesy of the estate of the late Brian Horrocks.)

German prisoners at Calcar, February 1945. (Courtesy of National Archives of Canada, PA 145761.)

Buffaloes moving up to cross the Rhine. (Courtesy of National Archives of Canada, PA 137734.)

Gliders of 6th Airborne Division across the Rhine, 25 March 1945. (Courtesy of the Imperial War Museum.)

After the Rhine crossing, Field Marshal Montgomery presented Military Crosses to five CANLOAN officers in the 51st Highland Division at the same ceremony. They were CDN/543, Lieut. (Lieut. Col.) Maurice Carter, 2 Seaforth; CDN/14, Capt. Richard Coates, 1 Black Watch; CDN/115, Capt. (Maj.) Robert Gelston, 7 Black Watch; CDN/56, Maj. (Lieut. Col.) Roderick MacKay, 2 Seaforth; and CDN/677, Capt. (Maj.) William Mitchell, 1 Black Watch. (Courtesy of Maurice Carter.)

A typical scene of liberation in Holland (Doesburg 1945). (Courtesy of National Archives of Canada, PA 131040.)

With British Units

CITY OFFICERS SERVE IN ITALY

Four Vancouver officers, Captains Jack Chambers and Maurice J. Crehan, and Lieutenants Alastair McLennan and "Gus" Lefevre, the first Canadian officers to go to Italy for service with British Army units, arrived there recently among reinforcements for infantry, armored and artillery regiments.

Pte. Lorrie Chalmers, C.W.A.C., Vancouver, is among another mixed concert group which arrived with the first C.W.A.C. detachment assigned to permanent duty in the Italian theatre.

CHOSE FUSILIERS.

The Canadian officers, all members of the Irish Fusiliers (Vancouver Regiment) volunteered under the government scheme for making trained Canadian leaders available to Britain. They chose the Imperial Irish Fusiliers, of which the Vancouver Regiment is an affiliate, as their unit.

Capt. Maurice J. Crehan, former well-known city sportsman, who was lieutenant-colonel and officer commanding the 3rd Battalion Irish Fusiliers, reverted to the rank of captain to serve overseas with the British Army.

FORMERLY AT OTTAWA.

Captain Crehan was formerly with the directorate of organization at Ottawa. His wife and three children reside at 1849 West Forty-first.

Lt. Gus Lefevre.

Lieut. Lefevre, whose wife resides in Vancouver, is the son of Mr. and Mrs. A. Lefevre, 3161 Turner. He enlisted at the outbreak of war and was commissioned in June, 1942. He was formerly with A. E. Jukes & Co. Lt. Alastair Hamilton, son of Mr. and Mrs. A. L. McLennan, 1426 Southeast Marine, enlisted in May, 1942, with the Fusiliers, and was later posted to the Prince Albert Volunteers.

Pte. Lorrie Chalmers, C.W.A.C., was formerly employed with the pay office at Little Mountain

CAPT. J. CHAMBERS

LT. A. H. McLENNAN

CAPT. M. J. CREHAN

Barracks and joined the army show last year. A brother, Sgt. Walter Chalmers, resides at 2844 Main.

CANLOAN officers in the Royal Irish Fusiliers. Contemporary newspaper clipping. (Courtesy of Gus Lefever.)

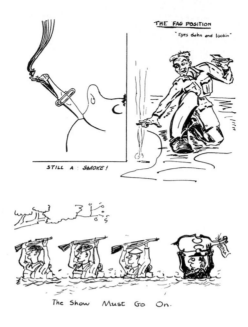

Sketches from the POW journal of CDN/334, Lieut. (Capt.) C.C. Cassady.
(Courtesy of C.C. Cassady.)

Liberation of POW camps.
(Courtesy of G. Smith Macdonald.)

First detachment of CANLOAN ordnance officers at the Royal Army Ordnance Corps Training Establishment, Leicester, 1944. (Courtesy of Roger Smith.)

CANLOAN in Italy. More than 20 of the RAOC CANLOAN officers served in Italy, most of them in the Eighth Army. One of them, CDN/574, Lieut. Thomas T.A. Parker (far right) (500-AOD), is shown here with two of the Royal Irish Fusiliers CANLOAN officers, who also served in Italy, CDN/463, Capt. F.A. Lefever (far left) and CDN/178, Lieut. A.H. McLennan. (Courtesy of Tom Parker.)

A group of CANLOAN officers returning to Canada. (Courtesy of CA.)

CANLOAN national reunion, Montreal, 1977. From left to right: Brig. Milton Gregg, VC, PC, OC, CBE, MC, ED, CD, LLD, Honorary President of the Canloan Army Officers Association; former nursing sister Eileen Smith, wife of CDN/42, Major Allan Smith; and CDN/494, Maj., the Rev. Fr. John Brayley, MC. (Courtesy of CA.)

An early Maritime CANLOAN reunion, Moncton 1947. (Courtesy of CA.)

First national CANLOAN reunion, Toronto, 4–6 June 1954. (Courtesy of CA.)

Unveiling of the CANLOAN memorial in Ottawa by Governor General Vanier, 1961. (Courtesy of CA.)

CANLOAN overseas pilgrimage, 1968. The Red Lion Inn, Colchester. (Courtesy of Frederick Burd.)

The Gregg Memorial, Camp Gagetown, June 1987. (Courtesy of CA.)

The British High Commissioner, Sir Derek Day, laying a wreath at the CANLOAN memorial, 11 November 1985. At right are Brig. Mike Addison, British Defence Liaison Staff, and CDN/218, Lieut.-Col. Philip Labelle, Parade Commander. (Courtesy of CA.)

discussed the critical situation with the commander of the Polish Brigade and the CO of the 4th Dorset. Heaps went back with messages for General Urquhart but volunteered to return to act as a guide for the Dorsets when they were ready to cross.

On the night of 23 September more Poles were ferried across the Rhine, but of the 250 who set out only 150 reached the Hartenstein perimeter. 4 Dorset was to cross the next night.

Meanwhile the situation in the perimeter was critical, for the defenders were reaching the limits of human endurance. Remnants of 1 Border, for example, were defending the area around a hotel at Westbouing. Three CANLOAN officers had landed with 1 Border at Arnhem: CDN/285, Lieut. Clifford M. Aasen; CDN/139, Lieut. George W. Comper; and CDN/318, Lieut. John A. Wellbelove. The last of these was observed, during the final stages of the defence of the bridgehead, by A. Wilson, a section commander of an adjacent platoon; in a letter to the author he has described the death of the Canadian officer, whom he regards as "the bravest man at Arnhem":

> Lieut Wellbelove's platoon was on our left. We were attacked by the Herman Goering Officer Corps behind four German tanks. The only way the tanks could get at us was up the short road to the restaurant but coming through the trees were hundreds of Germans. Four of us were on the left hand side of the restaurant and Lieut Wellbelove approximately 50 yards to our left. When they got to about 30 yards of us our Bren jammed and Lt Barnes' batman was shot between the eyes. To our left we could hear Lt Wellbelove encouraging his lads and hear his Sten firing. We jumped over the parapet as the Germans came round the other side. We could still hear Lt Wellbelove shouting, "Come on you Heine bastards!" It was the first time I had ever heard him swear. He was a perfect gentleman and it must have upset him seeing his lads being slaughtered. He kept firing his Sten until he was overrun. You can't do any more than that. God knows how many Germans he killed before they got him. Over the years I've told my sons about him and what a brave chap he was. No braver man ever came out of Canada. He was a credit to his country and his regiment.[39]

On the night of 24 September the Dorsets of the 43rd Division sent 250 men to reinforce the airborne bridgehead. But there were no assault boats for the Poles and only four for the Dorsets, and as they had no oars the Dorsets were obliged to use their reversed rifles as paddles. Only a handful reached the perimeter.

Both of the CANLOAN officers then serving in 4 Dorset were in the crossing. Capt. Thomas King recalls the experience: "I ended up with a group of five or six including the CO and the IO. We managed to get to our designated position just before first light and dug in. By 0830 we had been completely overrun and although we accounted for a large number of Germans we were out of action by 0900."[40]

The other CANLOAN officer in the battalion was CDN/621, Lieut. John Foote, who had joined the battalion from 32 Reinforcement Holding Unit on 16 September, the day before the start of MARKET GARDEN. He was in B Company, which was commanded by Major Mike Whittle, who recalls, "He was with me most of the 30 hours or so we spent across the river and although wounded quite badly he behaved magnificently throughout."[41]

The remarkable luck of Leo Heaps finally ran out. Accompanying the Dorsets to guide them to the Hertenstein perimeter on the night of 24 September, he found the way blocked by Germans. He returned to the river but was captured in the early morning of 25 September.

It was decided to evacuate the 1st Airborne Division, by then reduced to 2,500 men, during the night of 25 September. During the day final O. group instructions were issued, including such information as the order in which groups would leave, the marking of the route to the river, and so on. Evacuation was to begin at 2100 hours and end at dawn on the 26th. Erskine Carter of the 7th KOSB has described the final stage of the Battle of Arnhem:

> We passed hurriedly down the path towards the Battalion RV [rendezvous]. The shelling was increasing and the bullets coming uncomfortably close. We were less than a mile from the river when the shells began to drop in our midst. The line broke, the wounded groaned, the shells tore the path to shreds. I ducked into a hollow, shouted to see if anyone was still with me and got several answers ... Only six of us were unhurt of the twenty who had set out. The barrage did not stop, the house in which we had taken shelter received several hits, shattered trees had practically obliterated the route. After making the wounded as comfortable as possible we set out for the river. It was nearly impossible to make our way over the torn ground. It was growing light. We crossed an open patch and entered a wood. There a company of Huns awaited us. The escape route had been cut off. This was the end.[42]

One who took part in the relief of the 1st Airborne Division at Arnhem was CDN/505, Lieut. J.L.P.H. Boucher, who, as a Royal Engineer officer in the 43rd Division, was in charge of assault boats. Boucher was an officer in the Royal Canadian Engineers who nevertheless had taken the battle school course at Vernon, British Columbia, and so had come to the attention of Brigadier Gregg, who, when planning the course at Sussex, New Brunswick, asked Boucher to lecture on engineering subjects. Later Boucher accepted the Brig.'s invitation to join the CANLOAN group, inspiring a complaint from the RCE that other RCE officers with a higher priority had been refused since the CANLOAN plan did not include engineers. By 15 June Boucher was in 33 RHU in Normandy, where his engineering qualifications were discovered, and he was promptly posted to the Royal Engineer establishment of the 43rd Division. He was awarded a Military Cross for his part in the Battle of Arnhem:

> He has consistently set a high standard of gallantry and leadership of which there were several examples from Normandy to the end of the war in Germany. These examples included the ferrying of troops across the Neder Rijn to the relief of the 1st Airborne Division at Arnhem when he was in charge of the assault boats with the leading company.[43]

The 1st Airborne Division that landed at Arnhem numbered 10,000. When the evacuation ceased at dawn on 26 September, only 2,400 had been brought back across the Rhine: 2,163 of the 1st Airborne, 160 Poles, and 75 Dorsets. Casualties included 1,130 killed and 6,000 taken prisoner, nearly half of them wounded.[44]

Several hundred who were in hiding eventually found their way back across the river. The 1st Air Landing Brigade, in which most of the CANLOAN officers served, had gone to Arnhem with around 100 officers and 2,000 men. Approximately 20 percent of them returned: 7 KOSB – 4 officers and 72 men; 2 S. Staffords. – 6 officers and 133 men; 1 Border – 10 officers and 225 men.

Of the 20 CANLOAN officers who were at Arnhem only two were evacuated: Philip Turner and CDN/150, Lieut. W. Alex (Doc) Harvie, both of 2 S. Staffords.

Many tributes have been paid to the men of the 1st Airborne Division who, in holding a bridgehead for nine days instead of the 48 hours that had been expected, and under most adverse conditions, tested the extent of human endurance and inspired the admiration of both friend and foe. Field Marshal Montgomery said, "In years to come it will be a great thing to be able to say 'I fought at Arnhem.'"[45] An official British account of airborne operations goes further:

> With an enemy growing ever stronger, pressing them on all sides but one – and that a wide swiftly flowing river – they fought on. Without sleep, presently without food or water, at the end almost without ammunition, they fought on. When no hope of victory remained, when all prospects of survival had vanished, when death alone could give them ease, they fought on. In attack most daring, in defence most cunning, in endurance most steadfast, they performed a feat of arms which will be remembered and recounted as long as the virtues of courage and resolution have the power to move the hearts of men.[46]

The CANLOAN officers who were there were worthy members of this gallant force, a credit to the proud British regiments that had adopted them and to their homeland.

10

Stalemate

ALTHOUGH THE ATTEMPT to capture the bridge at Arnhem had not been successful, eight other bridges had been captured in operation MARKET GARDEN, and a salient nearly 60 miles long had been opened up in German-occupied territory. Field Marshal Montgomery still believed, at the end of September, that the Second British Army with strong support from the American First Army and without waiting for the opening of the port of Antwerp, could launch a successful attack from the Reichwald into the Rhineland and perhaps even cross the Rhine before winter.[1]

During September the strength of the enemy had doubled and on the 24th the Second British Army was opposed by 14 German divisions.[2] Since the large-scale attack by General Hodges and the American First Army on the Siegfried Line at Aachen had not been successful, there was no prospect of American help for Montgomery. Moreover, General Eisenhower was not prepared to support a "full-blooded drive" on the Reich until the port of Antwerp was open for shipping and supplies could be received. This view prevailed. A directive by Montgomery on 16 October 1944 ordered that operations to open the port of Antwerp would be given "complete priority over all other offensive operations in 21 Army Group, without any qualification whatsoever."[3] Even though Antwerp was taken at the end of November, the weather and terrain prevented a major offensive towards the Rhine. On 4 December 1944 General Eisenhower wrote to General Marshall, "The enemy should be able to maintain a strong defensive front for some time assisted by weather, floods and muddy ground."[4] In fact, from the upper Roer east of Aachen to the mouth of the Maas north of Antwerp, the 21st Army Group was held in check by rivers, in a stalemate that extended into 1945.

Although the major attack on the Rhineland, which was intended to follow the completion of MARKET GARDEN, did not materialize, the units of the 21st Army

Group in which CANLOAN officers served were fully engaged in military activities with more limited objectives. While the divisions in XXX Corps – the Guards Armoured, 43rd, and 50th – were to join up the three airborne bridgeheads between the Escaut Canal and the Neder Rijn at Arnhem, those in VIII and XII Corps were to provide flank protection, expand the corridor, and prevent it from being cut. This proved to be a difficult task. The 15th Scottish Division, for example, was to occupy the area north of Eindhoven, which had been the dropping zone of the American 101st Airborne Division. The 2nd Glas. H. attacked the town of Best at noon on 22 September. In the next two days no fewer than six of the eight CANLOAN officers in the battalion were wounded: Lieut. Louis Boudreau, CDN/254 Lieut. Lloyd Greene, Capt. Harold Long, Lieut. Roger MacLellan, Maj. Alexander (Sandy) Millar, and Lieut. Russell Parke.

Two days later, on 26 September, two CANLOAN officers in 10 HLI were wounded in the same area near Don Derdonk: CDN/467, Capt. Roy A. McCabe and CDN/456, Capt. Donald L. Graham. A third CANLOAN officer, Del Struck, earned an MC in this action, the citation for which reads in part as follows:

On 26 Sept 44 B Coy 10 HLI was clearing a portion of the wood northwest of Don Derdonk when they came under heavy machine gun fire followed by shell and mortar fire. The company was pinned down and the flanking company suffered many casualties. Lieut. Struck, who was pl comd of the leading pl of B Coy immediately started to work his way forward along with nine other ranks to locate the enemy fire. He crawled for a distance of 300 yards along a ditch under fire until he located the enemy posn. He then discovered that he had been spotted by the enemy who were at both ends of the ditch. With complete disregard for his own safety he attacked the main enemy position with four other men, charging the posn with fixed bayonets and firing from the hip ... This determined display resulted in not only casualties being inflicted on the enemy but in addition Lieut Struck took 35 prisoners without loss.[5]

At this time three CANLOAN officers in the 15th Scottish Division were killed in action. Lieut. Gordon Beaton, 2 Gordons, was killed on 25 September. Three days later, on 28 September, Lieut. Donald Lee, 8 RS, was killed. Another CANLOAN officer in the division, Capt. Phil Labelle, 6 RSF, came upon a Bren carrier of the 8 RS in which he found Don Lee's body and that of one of his men. He buried them along with one of his own men in a small garden in front of a farmhouse and held a burial service there, not far from the road to Arnhem, which had come to be called "Hell's Highway."

On the same day CDN/227, Lieut. Fernie B. Stewart, 9 Cameronians, was killed. He had served overseas with the Cameron Highlanders of Ottawa from 1940 to 1943 and had gone to Normandy with the 9 Cameronians.

In MARKET GARDEN, the British 3rd Division provided right flank protection for XXX Corps's advance, starting from the Meuse-Escaut Canal. Here in a few hours, 1 S. Lan. R. lost both its CANLOAN officers, as has been recounted by a fellow officer:

After digging-in, vigorous patrols were sent out and on one of these, Lieut Cope, the CANLOAN officer who had taken over my 8 Platoon, was killed ... Moving forward on a dusk reconnaissance patrol accompanied by two of his platoon, Lieut Cope entered a sparse wood where they surprised two German soldiers who immediately ran away. One of them, however, paused long enough to hurl one of the "potato masher" grenades in the direction of the patrol. A portion, by ill fortune, struck Lieut Cope in the throat and by the time help had arrived he was dead.

At dawn on the 19 Sept 1 S Lanc R was to create a diversion while an adjacent brigade attempted to secure a bridgehead across the canal. We had been supplied with assault boats and the other Canloan officer, Lieut E Fryer, serving with B Coy, took his platoon across the canal in these boats as a fighting patrol to keep the enemy occupied ... When Lieut Fryer's boats were almost across, the enemy opened intense small arms fire at close range, holing all or most of the craft and wounding or killing many of the troops in them. Those that did struggle to the far bank were taken prisoner including Lieut Fryer.[6]

Later, on 24 September, a CANLOAN officer in 2 R. Warwick. of the 3rd Division was killed. CDN/387, Lieut. Robert E. (Bob) Inman, fellow CANLOAN officer in the division, was told that CDN/388, Lieut. Robert J. Keast had been mortally wounded while trying to bring in one of his wounded men who was lying in the open. Inman himself had been wounded for the first time four days earlier.

Meanwhile 49 Division was to extend the Arnhem corridor to the west. Crossing the Antwerp-Turnhout Canal on 24 September, the division launched an attack on Ryckevorsel, which involved 4 R. Lincolns., 2 Essex, and the Hallams. A CANLOAN officer in the Hallams., CDN/495, Capt. Wilfred A. Pearce, was killed in action on 25 September. On the next day two CANLOAN officers in the 49th Division earned MCs: Lieut. Norman Orr, 2 Essex, and CDN/102, Lieut. William J. Stainton, 4 R. Lincolns. Their citations read in part as follows:

Lt Orr was in command of the right hand platoon of A coy during the enemy counter attacks on Ryckevorsel during the action on 26 Sept. At frequent intervals his area was under enemy artillery and 20 mm gunfire from close range. His platoon was repeatedly attacked by the enemy who at times were within 20 yards of his platoon and on the afternoon he himself was wounded by shrapnel but refused to be evacuated. Throughout this period he was amongst his sections rallying his men and directing fire. His courage and leadership were of a very high standard and played a great part in the defeat of all the counter attacks.[7]

Also on 26 Sept Lieut Stainton was ordered to take a fighting patrol to the area of some houses and destroy the occupants of the position adjoining those houses. Covered by members of his patrol he cleared the house with grenades and then rushed a nearby Spandau position. Throughout the patrol was under heavy fire from Spandaus on either side. The complete success of this patrol was entirely due to Lieut Stainton's skilful planning, thorough briefing and superb leadership throughout the execution of this task.[8]

The fighting at Arnhem did not cease with the evacuation of the 1st Airborne Division. For nearly two weeks British troops across the river were subjected to fierce counter-attacks from Arnhem and the Reichwald forest. The exploits of several CANLOAN officers during these attacks were recorded in the history of the 43rd Division. On 27 September an attack from Arnhem was countered by 7 Som. LI at a village west of the town:

On the right the vanguard of A coy, commanded by a Canadian officer, Lieut W B Mottram, hugged the hedgerows and under heavy fire from 88s at last entered the maze of houses of Randwyk where lively and confused fighting now developed.

On 1 October a major counter attack intended to recapture Nijmegen was launched from the Reichwald. At one time it was estimated that 100 88s were pouring shells into the area occupied by two companies of the 5th Wilts in "one of the most bitter defensive battles of the campaign." Lieut Harry Roper was killed in this attack. Capt Kenneth Brown of the 5th Dorsets estimated that at one time 200 German mortar bombs landed in a company area in a few minutes.

During another counter attack Capt Harry Anaka, the Canadian second-in-command of D Coy, attacked a machine gun single handed and was mortally wounded.[9]

Capt. Fred Chesham, a company commander in 7 R. Hamps., was slightly wounded in these attacks but refused to be evacuated.

After a German counter-attack was repulsed by 5 DCLI and an American parachute regiment, the CO of 506 Para. reported to General Taylor, commander of the 101st US Airborne Division, "The gallantry of the British officers and men was outstanding and instilled in the men of the 506 Para infantry the highest regard for the fighting ability of the British infantry."[10] This admiration was reciprocated by Vince Lilley of 1/6 Queens, 7th Armoured Division, who has referred in glowing terms to the 101st Airborne Division: "I found them to be well trained and disciplined troops who impressed me especially with their patrolling ability. This was one of the elite forces which I was proud to be associated with."[11]

The 7th Armoured Division played an active part in the fighting on "the Island"; CDN/664, Lieut. Richard N. Wilson of the 1/7 Queens was killed there on 2 October.

A number of events resulting from the Battle of Arnhem involved CANLOAN officers. One was the months of incarceration in German prisoner-of-war camps that was the fate of most of the CANLOAN officers who were at Arnhem. This will be described later. Another was the commemorative ceremonies that followed the evacuation of the remnants of the 1st Airborne Division. One of these was the presentation by Lieutenant-General Browning of the 1st Airborne's flag to the 4 Dorset, which had suffered so many casualties in coming to its aid. There were also presentations of awards at Buckingham Palace to the heroes of Arnhem. A special ceremony was held for the presentation of the American Distinguished Service Cross to Lieut. Philip Turner. When General Eisenhower and his party arrived, only the CANLOAN officers seemed to notice that the American flag was upside down!

Finally, throughout the fall and winter there were the clandestine activities in the marshes and waterways of western Holland of the "escapers" from Arnhem and the gallant Dutch who were hiding and helping them. Prominent in these activities was CANLOAN Leo Heaps, one of the few who managed to escape from the Germans. He had jumped off a train on the way to a prison camp and made his way to England, where he reported to the War Office and was interviewed by General Urquhart. He was authorized to return to Holland to assist the Dutch underground in helping the hundreds of "escapers" still in hiding behind enemy lines, including such distinguished officers as Brigadiers Lathbury and Hackett. Heaps has told in this story in his two books on Arnhem.[12] The initiative and courage displayed in these operations combined with his exploits at Arnhem earned Leo Heaps a well-deserved MC.

Field Marshal Montgomery's directive of 16 October 1944 ordered all offensive operations of Second British Army to be shut down, with the exception of "a strong thrust westward on the axis s'Hertogenbusch-Breda," to which all available resources were to be directed. This thrust, designed to cut off the Germans in southwest Holland, involved the CANLOAN officers who were serving in XII Corps: the 15th Scottish, the 53rd Welch, and the 7th Armoured Divisions. Two CANLOAN officers in the 53rd Division were killed in the latter part of September: CDN/400, Lieut. Joseph Brais, 1/5 Welch, on 30 September and Lieut. Philip West, 6 RWF, on 24 September. Lieutenant West's death is referred to in the regimental history of 6 RWF: "C Coy had fierce fighting and one of their officers, a Canadian, Lieut West was badly wounded and although members of his platoon succeeded in rescuing him despite well-aimed German machine gun fire, he died next day of his wounds."[13]

The regimental history also contains a detailed account of the action of a CANLOAN company commander in the westward thrust to Breda:

A Coy under Capt R G Marsh advanced along the s'Hertogenbusch road capturing many prisoners as they went. Reaching its objective it dug in in an area vital to the enemy. During determined enemy counter attacks a night and morning of fierce and bitter fighting ensued during which A Coy, under the magnificent and inspiring leadership of Capt Marsh, although completely cut off from the rest of the battalion, defied every effort to drive them from their position and inflicted heavy losses on the enemy. A Coy had infiltrated right into the main German position covering s'Hertogenbusch, firmly astride the main line of withdrawal of strong enemy forces further west. Throughout the night A Coy was continuously attacked in a pitched battle with hand-to-hand fighting and direct enemy fire into Coy HQ by an SP gun. Inspired by the bravery of their gallant commander the coy hung on despite heavy casualties. Capt Marsh was severely wounded but refused to leave his post. At last about 1000 hours the gallant A Coy was relieved by the advance of 7 RWF. A Coy's magnificent fight at Hintham added a new and well earned battle honour to the records of the Regiment. Unfortunately a heavy price was paid, Capt Marsh dying of his wounds shortly after his coy was relieved. In his death the Bn lost an officer of outstanding gallantry and merit whose cool bravery in action was the inspiration of his men. Capt Marsh was recommended for the Victoria Cross and received a posthumous Mention in Despatches.[14]

Two days earlier another CANLOAN officer in the 53rd Division, Capt. James Suttie of 4 RWF, had been killed in the same area. James Suttie had served overseas with the PPCLI in the 1st Canadian Division from 1940 to 1943. After joining CANLOAN he was posted to 4 RWF and served with that battalion throughout the Normandy campaign, during which he was promoted to captain 25 July and awarded the MC.

Among the other battalions in the attack on s'Hertogenbusch was 2 Mons. Lieut. Bob Newstead, a CANLOAN officer in that battalion, recalls the support of tanks with flame throwers and a protest from the enemy: "A German officer, black from head to toe, with his hands up saying in perfect English as he passed by, 'Why don't you bastards fight fair?'"[15] This protest might have carried more weight if Bob had not recently seen Germans in action with portable flame throwers.

In the operations designed to drive the Germans out of southwest Holland and clear the approaches to Antwerp, the 51st Highland Division was involved in the heavy fighting. On the outskirts of Vught the 7 BW overran one of the first concentration camps to be encountered by the Allies. Two CANLOAN officers were present: CDN/115, Maj. Robert J. Gelston, a company commander, and CDN/21, Lieut. Robert L. Hunter, Carrier Platoon Commander. They found evidence of atrocities, including a roomful of childrens' boots, instruments of torture, and a crematorium containing human ashes.

The bitter struggle for the port of Antwerp, the Battle of Scheldt, began on 2 October and lasted until 4 November. Since it was the responsibility of the First Canadian Army, CANLOAN officers were not directly involved unless they were serving in battalions in the 52nd Lowland Division. This division, whose officers had been such genial hosts to the third CANLOAN flight on its arrival in Edinburgh, had been held in reserve for a special purpose. Like the 1st Airborne Division, it had lived in anticipation as various missions were proposed and then cancelled. Though it had been trained in mountain warfare with mules and portable artillery, when it finally went into action it was below sea level on Walcheren Island in the approaches to the port of Antwerp.

CANLOAN officers served in several battalions in the 52nd Division, including 4 KOSB and 6 and 7 Cameronians. When the division arrived at the Scheldt to attack South Beveland with the 2nd Canadian Division, it was discovered that the British troops were not as well equipped as the Canadians for the mud and water of polder warfare. One CANLOAN officer used his Canadian connections to provide for his platoon, as recounted to Lieut.-Col. Denis Whitaker, co-author of *Tug of War: The Canadian Victory That Opened Antwerp:* "What really bothered us, said Lieut George McRae, was that the Canadians had been issued knee high rubber boots, while the British had never been issued any. Finally I went over and scrounged enough for my platoon – and got in trouble for it."[16]

McRae, with Lieut. Glen Harrison and Maj. James Duncan, made up a trio of CANLOAN officers from Winnipeg who had been together at Sussex with their wives (in fact, for the newly married MacRaes it was a honeymoon). They had managed to be posted to the same battalion, 7 Cameronians. In Europe Harrison was wounded almost immediately, and George McRae a little later. Jim Duncan was unharmed to the end of the war and earned the Military Cross and a Mention in Dispatches.

Another CANLOAN officer in the 52nd Division was CDN/558, Maj. Beverley R. Howard, the artillery officer who had been squeezed into CANLOAN at the last moment by Brigadier Gregg. He lost a leg at Walcheren in the assault by 6 Cameronians. CDN/517, Lieut. Ernest Thirgood was in the same battalion. As an NCO he had earned an MM and had been wounded in the Dieppe raid in 1942. Shortly after the capture of Walcheren he wrote an account of his second assault landing, a portion of which follows:

My platoon was given a huge area to patrol – mopping up procedure ... We were dismayed to learn that we had to make an assault boat landing, this time in paddle boats across a large stretch of water on the Walcheren ... The RAF had bombed some dykes and half of the island was reported flooded. The attack on Walcheren was slated for the early hours of the following morning which would be Thursday, 2 Nov. Clem McCallin and I got some sleep from five o'clock till nine in the evening. Then we had a hot meal ... I cannot remember what time we set off but it must have been about 2230 hours. We had to march a few kilometers and on the way we passed a huge fire burning. Jerry had planted some bombs smack on a building used by us as a petrol dump and garage ... At the time we were only about 500 yards from Jerry's forward defence position so everything had to be done most carefully ... We learned that the assaulting companies were to be A and B, which was the same as the previous attack. This simply meant if the brunt of the assault had to be borne by somebody, we, 12 Platoon, had bought it again ... While waiting for H-hour behind a dyke near the water's edge we erected the boats and took our last drags at our cigarettes. Some of the lads even settled down for a sleep. I sat shivering in the bottom of our boat. C Coy pushed off but with great difficulty, the dyke was high and steep and getting the boats over it was no easy job, especially with everybody loaded down with arms and ammunition ... Our paddling across was very good and we were about third to land, having passed most of C Coy's boats. The platoon was in two boats and after collecting them and putting them into battle order we set out along the tape. I will never forget that thousand yards – it was wet, muddy, slippery and well-nigh impass-able. It took us the best part of an hour to reach the dyke, all wet and dripping with mud ... As in our previous assault landing we had not gone far before we found Jerry all along the dyke, cowering in his slit trenches. We started to winkle them out and it wasn't as easy as our last operation. Jerry would not play in some cases – some were shot and many were sent back as prisoners.

The Platoon's first objective was a group of buildings and a farm at a dyke junction. As we got to it there was some firing from it so I ordered my mortar crew to lay down four quick rounds on the farm. Then our Brens opened up and at this moment I chanced to look round and saw two explosions and a couple of my lads started to scream and moan. Thinking Jerry was using a small mortar on us I ordered everyone to open up on the buildings. But as our own lads were near them we had to stop and I ordered everyone to go over the dyke and clear the buildings. This we did and in a few minutes dozens of Jerries came streaming out. I learned later on in the day that we had captured over eighty of them.

Our next objective was about five hundred yards further inland ... I was in the lead of my platoon and used hand signals to have them follow ... It was difficult to find out what was happening. Jerry was pounding the position with everything he had and there was a good deal of confusion ... Finally Stanley had gathered the set-up and called for me. I was ordered to go along the left flank. We dragged ourselves over the road and into an even larger and deeper ditch filled with dead horses and men. I arrived at my position and called the platoon up. They came on, what was left of them, and we strung out along the ditch. The cold water was uncomfortable but not as dangerous as on top. Most of us stayed in the water – the ones who did not lived only a short while, as one of Jerry's SP guns was landing shells about 50 yards away. My platoon sergeant reported to me that Corporal Carrigan and Rifleman Frewin had been killed coming up. Apparently there was a desperate battle going on on the other side of the dyke but we could not see it ... It was a tricky business as we were being sniped at and mortared and the self-propelled gun kept hammering at us. One of the shells landed short and I felt a pain in my back. I thought,

"Well, I've got it now, too." So I called Sergeant McGhie up to me and he took a look. He said I was lucky and that the shrapnel had cut the surface skin and was not bleeding too badly, so I stuck my sweater in the wound and started to take notice once more ... I kept asking the OP if he could observe anything but he said he could see nothing ... I did send Sergeant McGhie back to D Coy's position to try to find out what was happening. It was nearly an hour before he came back. He said there was no one there. I took a count of the platoon and found there were only thirteen of us left, and as we were wet, tired, muddy and our weapons in a useless state, I figured the position was growing desperate. But still we stayed on ... By this time we had been in the water at least four hours and it was bitterly cold. Finally, after summing up the situation, I said we would withdraw to our original position, the one we had captured that morning.[17]

Lieut.-Col. Denis Whitaker, Commanding Officer of the Canadian Royal Hamilton Light Infantry during the battle of the Scheldt, wrote, "For the 52nd Lowland Division no battle could have been tougher than their first one, nor fought with greater valour."[18]

For most of the Second Army the period from the end of operation MARKET GARDEN, on 26 September, until the beginning of operation VERITABLE, the battle for the Rhineland, on 8 February, was spent in a so-called stalemate along a front extending from "the island" at Nijmegen south along the Maas and Roer Rivers to the boundary with the American First Army north of Aachen. Though there were few significant operations or territorial gains during the period, there was no lack of activity. Troops were occupied with training, constantly patrolling, shelling, refitting, and absorbing reinforcements, and there was no lack of battle exhaustion and casualties.

The experiences of CANLOAN officers during this period have been summarized by John Anderson in a single sentence: "The usual patrols, water crossings, overtaking and passing through other units, getting soaked, late meals, long tedious moves, more water crossings culminating in the big one at the Rhine."[19] Most CANLOAN officers recall the fall and winter campaign as long, uncomfortable, and depressing. Eric Hall recalls, "The weather turned cold and foul, loads of rain, sheets of it, made it all very uncomfortable. In all it was a monotonous and depressing period of routine activity."[20] To which Rex Fendick has added, "Mortar fire, wet, wet heavy skies, raw winds, mud, streams, mines, battle exhaustion."[21] Even the ebullient Lieut.-Gen. Brian Horrocks has observed, "During the rest of October and on into November there ensued in north western Belgium and southern Netherlands some of the dreariest campaigning of the war."[22]

The terrain where this part of the war was fought was low, flat, water-logged, unsuitable for vehicles, and void of cover. Consequently, movement during daylight by either British or Germans was not feasible, and most action took place at night. Because the land was sodden, the slit trenches ranged from plain mud to water-filled holes that had to be bailed out after the heavy and frequent rain. Several areas were deliberately flooded by the Germans, who controlled the upstream waters.

Another consequence of the low, wet terrain was that tank support for the infantry was difficult, and wheeled transport carrying rations and other supplies often could not reach the forward troops. The evacuation of wounded, which in

Normandy had made extensive use of vehicles from the most forward positions, was adversely affected by the mud and the lack of cover. The experience of Arnold Willick is an example: "From the forward position where I suffered a shattered humerus I had to walk and crawl about a mile to my own HQ. There I had my sergeant put a better dressing on my arm and after a morphine ampoule and the top half of a bottle of Johnnie Walker Scotch he helped me onto a bicycle and we went another mile to the RAP."[23]

The weather, which seemed to lack sunshine for the entire period, ranged from cold, dank, clammy fog to days of pouring rain and increasing cold. The first snow came on 9 December, and by then life in the slit trenches was most uncomfortable and becoming worse, until in January the cold was considered the worst enemy, more to be feared than the Germans. Fortunately, in most company positions, the essential slit trenches were supplemented by the shelter of houses, which added a dimension to infantry life that was a contrast to the experiences in Normandy, where only division and corps commanders lived in houses, if they were lucky.

The routine of life at the front varied little from division to division. CDN/651, Lieut. Harold F. (Moody) Richards, 6 Green Howards in 50 Division, recalls the routine on "the island" near Nijmegen:

> In the line the routine included stand-to at first light in the morning and at dusk, periodic night patrols (an officer often leading several in one night), some village clearing, scrounging fresh vegetables and occasionally a chicken or two from the local farms to supplement the army rations, maintaining contact patrols at night, and the occasional flurry of making or repelling a local attack. Within a couple of weeks of going onto the Nijmegen island we were down to two officers in the Coy.[24]

Although there were few large-scale offensive operations on the front of 21st Army Group between October 1944 and February 1945, it was far from inactive. The program was for "aggressive local activity" to dominate no-man's-land, and watch for signs of enemy movement, counter with artillery, mortars, and machine guns, but above all, by reconnaissance, fighting, and standing patrols, to keep informed about the enemy and prevent his preparations for attack. Trip wires attached to tin cans or booby traps were set up in front of platoon positions to warn of infiltrating German patrols, and the many gliders left by the American 101st and 82nd Airborne Divisions served as observation posts, while the parachutes were useful as gifts. Many young Dutch women were soon wearing underwear made of parachute silk.

The Germans made extensive use of mines and booby traps, and in raids on German-occupied buildings it was assumed that every one was booby-trapped. Mine fields were very dangerous, especially those with the new Schu mines, which, being made of wood instead of metal, could not be located by normal mine detectors. CANLOAN officers who were there can sympathize with Rex Fendick, who, on finding himself in a minefield, "tried to suspend [his] feet a little above the surface as [he] walked."[25]

On another occasion, during the winter, a CANLOAN officer, Elmer Fitzpatrick, 11 DLI, led a section of his platoon through a minefield to cut off a German patrol:

"The next morning we looked over where we had gone. There were several inches of snow and there was only one set of foot prints through the mined area. Not one person in the section had stepped out of my tracks."[26]

Given the nature of the 21st Army Group's activities during the fall of 1944, it is not surprising that most of the awards for bravery for CANLOAN officers during this period were for fighting patrols. One of those who were honoured, CDN/633, Lieut. J. Ross LeMesurier, was virtually a full-time patrol officer in the Scout Platoon of the 5th Battalion, the Queen's Own Cameron Highlanders (Camerons), as the citation for his Military Cross notes:

> Whenever there has been a dangerous and unpleasant task he has volunteered for it and carried it through with skill and daring.
>
> South of the Maas in October Lieut LeMesurier led 10 patrols and raids against enemy positions in the woods near Pest(?). On one of the fighting patrols Lieut LeMesurier met strong MG and grenade opposition from an enemy strong point at 30 yards range. Under withering fire and with grenades being thrown at him from three sides he charged the nearest post and personally accounted for the machine gunners in it. Again, crossing the Zig Canal bridgehead he showed the same bravery and his patrol accounted for 20 enemy snipers and machine gunners.[27]

Three CANLOAN officers in different divisions earned MCs on the same day, 17 October 1944, two of them on fighting patrols. One was CDN/468, Lieut. John A. McIntosh, 10 RSF, 49th Division. He was in command of a fighting patrol of two sections, who were ordered to destroy all enemy in the vicinity of a particular house. With one section he cleared the house and captured two Germans. With grenades he then disposed of eight enemy in four nearby weapon pits and withdrew under heavy machine-gun fire. His citation concludes: "Throughout this operation Lieut McIntosh showed outstanding leadership and initiative. With no regard for his own personal safety he was entirely responsible for the great success of the patrol."[28]

Also on 17 October CDN/624, Lieut. Bruce F. Harley, 1/7 Queens, 7th Armoured Division, was in command of a fighting patrol attempting to contact the enemy. After passing through the German outposts he was attacked from two sides by enemy patrols. He rallied his platoon and while they were deploying he himself shot six of the attackers with his Sten. Continuing with the patrol, he was again attacked from the rear. His citation, in part, reads, "Lieut Harley immediately led his men in a charge and fought his way out, inflicting many casualties on the enemy and by his personal bravery and fine courage he was able to bring his patrol safely back to our lines."[29]

The third CANLOAN MC on 17 October was awarded to CDN/466, Lieut. Vernon L. MacDonald, 2 A. & S.H., 15th Scottish Division. His citation refers to him as "one of the outstanding patrol leaders in the Bn." It continues:

> On a daylight patrol at Ospeldyk on 9 Nov he led a reconnaissance patrol forward across flat ground dominated by enemy observation and fire, where the only cover was provided by ditches, which were known to be thickly strewn with mines. Having established his patrol in a good covering position he went forward alone to within 30 yards of a house where enemy movement could be seen and successfully completed a valuable recce.

The gallantry and coolness displayed in these and many similar occasions and the shortage of experienced junior leaders led to his being given at times an unfairly large share of difficult and dangerous ops. He tackled them all with unflagging courage and cheerfulness, and was always able to inspire his tps with the same qualities and with absolute confidence in his ability to lead them.[30]

The extensive use of houses has been noted. Although they were regularly shelled, the cellars provided shelter as well as the space needed for platoon and company headquarters. They were often used as sleeping accommodation for whole platoons, supplementing the nearby slit trenches, which were essential for defensive and stand-to positions. Unfortunately, a number of houses were set on fire by the Germans or accidentally. An example has been related by Lieut. Hugh W. Ingraham, 3 Mons.:

It was a forward position on the Maas and we were occupying three houses on one side of the lock with Jerry on the other side. The position was manned on a 24-hour basis and platoons were changed at different hours during the night because Jerry kept up an almost constant machine gun strafing of the fronts of the three houses and the houses were across a 300–400 yard open field with the last 100 yards through a Jerry mine field. During the daylight hours we were confined to the basements except for sentries and the house I was occupying with one of my sections contained a large supply of Jerry hand grenades and small arms ammunition. One day one of my men fell asleep on a feather mattress on a large four-poster bed and dropped a cigarette on the mattress. With the resulting fire and no water available we all lined up and proceeded to leak on the smoldering mattress. The stench, without a doubt, was beyond description and the instigator was cursed by one and all as we strained for that last drop. Unfortunately we ran out of water before we ran out of fire so we had no alternative but to get the mattress out of the house or have the house blow up around us. No time for caution, we dragged it up the stairs and out the back door to a water filled ditch behind the house.[31]

The conditions which prevailed on the front were not, however, without their benefits, for they enabled the officers to get to know their men and to develop a platoon esprit de corps. This was particularly important because a large proportion of each platoon consisted of recent reinforcements. By this time the 3rd British Division, for example, estimated that the rifle companies had gone through two complete replacements in total numbers. In fact, there was a striking contrast between the keen, well-trained, confident troops who had gone to Normandy as cohesive fighting teams, imbued with devotion to each other and their regiments and anxious to prove their fighting ability, and the reinforcements who came to replace them. Most were very young, usually barely 18, and had had only the basic training of the training centres and no opportunity to absorb the regimental spirit. Others were transfers from units that had been disbanded, such as those in the 59th and 50th Divisions and the 1/6 and 1/7 Queens, the Tyne. Scots., and the 7 DWRs. Even those who had been wounded in Normandy and had returned to their former regiments were inclined to be more apprehensive than before and to miss the "mates" who had not survived. It was a challenge to officers and NCOs to weld these human elements into a cohesive team. The opportunity to serve together for a considerable time without extensive casualties, to live together in accommodation other than in the isolation of slit trenches, were steps in the right direction. And it worked. An example of the esprit de corps that developed is a poem entitled "The Boys of 18 Platoon," which was sent by a wounded Jock to his Canadian platoon commander, Lieut. John Anderson, 5/7 Gordons; a few lines of it follow:

Le Havre you joined us I remember quite well
Of our gallant deeds we used to tell
To learn later on that we had found
The best platoon commander safe and sound.

May you all be together and keeping well
And if I come back may your stories tell
Each man there is worth all the gold
That the biggest of vaults could e'er hold.[32]

When a unit was not in contact with the enemy, there was vigorous training in weapons tactics, route marches, and even arms drill.

Some officers, including several CANLOAN officers, were seconded to training activities; at least two were assigned to sniper training. After the Normandy campaign CDN/260, Capt. Robert M. Barr, 5 BW, had been asked to form a team of snipers for the 15th Scottish Division. This was so successful that a similar task was undertaken for the 53rd Welch Division, and then a 21st Army Group Sniper School was formed, with Captain Barr second in command to Maj. the Hon. Tony Wills, later Lord Verulam.

The task of Lieut. "Moody" Richards was more limited. When it was discovered, while his unit, 6 Green Howards, was in the line near Nijmegen, that he was a product of the "Johnson Musketry Course," he was called upon to form a sniper section. He recalls:

It took about two hours for a Johnson coach to turn a rifleman from a miserable shot to a marksman who could score at least 20 out of 25 on the range. I applied the coaching technique to about 10 selected privates and from them selected 6 or 8 of the best and turned them into a sniper section ... The corporal of the section over a period of about 4 weeks had some 32 confirmed kills, some at a range as great as 500 or 600 yards, and earned a citation – great stuff for the IO to put in the twice daily SITREP that had to be submitted to Bde.[33]

Sometimes officers were themselves sent on courses. CDN/153, Capt. Harold J. "Harry" Hihn, for example, commander of the mortar platoon of 2 RUR, went to the School of Infantry at Barnard Castle for a mortar officers' course, where he was informed that his was one of the four best mortar platoons in the 21st Army Group.

Since the forward companies and battalions were relieved and billeted in private houses, many CANLOAN officers had an opportunity to become acquainted with Dutch and Belgian civilians. They were surprised to see how quickly the British troops could "get their feet under the table" and become adopted members of families. But the CANLOAN officers also shared in the kindness and open-armed welcome of the Dutch and Belgian families, who insisted on sharing their meagre rations. Occasionally, when whole divisions were relieved, they returned to their favourite spots, often those they had liberated, like Tilburg for the 15th Scottish Division and Brunssum for the 43rd Wessex. Del Struck, for example, recalls that the massed pipes and drums of the 15th Division played in the square at Tilburg during one such relief.

By November arrangements had been made for short leaves, and a 48-hour visit to Brussels was a favourite for CANLOAN officers. Seventeen good hotels had been placed under the supervision of NAAFI, and the free travel on trams that the Germans had demanded was extended to British troops. As General Essame, historian of the 43rd Division, has observed, "It was good to be a British soldier in Brussels in the autumn and winter of 1944. You felt and were treated like a conqueror."[34]

On these occasional leaves CANLOAN officers were able to become acquainted or reacquainted with each other. Small informal reunions were held as CANLOAN officers who had been wounded returned to active service in the Second British Army. In November Lieut. Fred Hatfield, who had been wounded in Normandy, returned to 2 SWB, where he joined CDN/68, Lieut. Hector J.B. Brown, who had been posted to the battalion after earlier service with 6 DWR in Normandy. Brown was awarded a rare decoration, the United States Silver Star. A portion of the citation follows:

> On the 6 Nov 44 at the fording of the River Mark considerable opposition was met from the enemy holding a small village. The leading company was pinned down by accurate Spandau fire. The only approach was a road, as the fields on either side were flooded. Manoeuvre was impossible. Lieut. Brown's company was ordered to attack; without hesitation this officer, who was commanding the leading platoon, ordered his men to fix bayonets and at their head charged down the road, overran the enemy posts and secured the village.
>
> This is but one example of Lieut Brown's resource, courage and speed of action. He was an officer who inspired the greatest confidence and trust in all with whom he had dealings, both his superior officers and the men under his command. In short, one of the best types of junior officers who with their sound judgement, great experience and bold leadership often played an unspectacular but always invaluable part in winning battles.[35]

On the same day, 6 November 1944, another CANLOAN officer in 2 SWB was killed, as is related by a local Dutch historian, Johan Van Doorn:

> Some small rear guards of the famous German 6th Parachute Regiment had taken defence positions in an old fort called De Hel. This regiment had been able to pin down the 2nd Canadian Infantry Division for two weeks in the battle for the Scheldt in October.
>
> When resistance was encountered D Company of the 2nd South Wales Borderers received orders to move forward. They had to pass Fort De Hel. When Lieut Harris with his men nearly reached this old fort with their carriers the paratroopers opened fire with a heavy machine gun and a mortar. Lieut Harris was killed together with three of his Welch comrades.[36]

Mr. Van Doorn has noted that CDN/79, Lieut. Alfred J. Harris is the only CANLOAN officer buried in the Bergen op Zoom war cemetery.

The capture of bridgeheads over waterways in the southern Netherlands produced battles on a platoon or company scale that tested the initiative and courage of junior officers and were recognized in some cases by decorations. Two such incidents involved the 51st Highland Division, which shared this battlefield with the 49th Division. CDN/494, Capt. John A. Brayley, the popular instructor at Brockville and Sussex, who was commanding a company of the 5/7 Gordons, was awarded a Military Cross:

> At first light on 25 Oct Capt Brayley's company was consolidating its flank position on the Esche bridgehead when a force of 80 Germans delivered a surprise attack. Almost immediately a platoon commander was shot up, a platoon position penetrated and an anti-tank gun overrun. Capt Brayley ran up through streams of Spandau fire to stabilize the situation. He ran from section to section cheering on the men. He brought up fresh supplies of ammunition wherever the fire was hottest. But in spite of his efforts the enemy continued to make progress. He then took the considerable risk of bringing down SOS fire to within 25 yards of his position. This made the enemy waver. Seizing this opportunity he drove in a counter attack. The Germans retired in great disorder, leaving in our position many dead, 24 prisoners and the enemy commander. His utter disregard of danger and his fierce offensive spirit was a wonderful inspiration to all and not only wrested from the enemy all the advantages that their surprise had given them but [also] caused their complete defeat.[37]

Also at this time Lieut. Richard Coates, a platoon commander in 1 BW, earned an MC when his company was expanding a bridgehead:

> His Pl suddenly discovered several well dug in, previously unlocated, German positions in thick scrub country. Without a moment's hesitation Lieut Coates dashed forward and cleared up the first of these positions and later so skilfully handled his platoon that the whole area was cleared of a number of enemy who considerably outnumbered his platoon ... Throughout his courage and leadership and complete disregard for his own safety were beyond praise.[38]

In the skirmishes for possession of the water-logged fields in "the island" near Nijmegen, a CANLOAN officer, CDN/421, Maj. John W.G. Hunter, 7 Green Howards, 50 Division, earned an MC only a few days before the famous Tees and Tyneside Division was disbanded:

> On 15 Nov Major Hunter was commanding A Coy in a forward position at Haalderen, very close to the enemy and very exposed. When the enemy put down heavy shell and mortar fire and launched an attack supported by a tank, Major Hunter moved from post to post encouraging the men and directing fire. Finally he himself engaged a party of enemy which had reached within 30 yards of his position, causing them to retire in disorder. He then assisted to carry back a wounded man under heavy fire. Throughout the engagement he showed exceptional courage and powers of leadership.[39]

On 23 November a CANLOAN officer in 2 Essex, 49th Division, Capt. Donald Selvage, who was second in command of B Company, earned an MC in another incident that illustrates the opportunities for initiative and leadership offered by the terrain and circumstances:

> Although wounded in two places he took charge of the company when the company commander was wounded and the CSM [company sergeant-major] killed and other casualties suffered. Under heavy fire he directed the reorganization and digging in of the company showing coolness, steadiness and good leadership at a critical time before being relieved and having his wounds looked after.[40]

The activities on the Second Army front during the fall were not limited entirely to defensive action and company or platoon operations. Between October and January several major offensives were undertaken in the Venray area to eliminate a strong German bridgehead west of the Maas and Roer before the massive assault on the Rhineland could begin. The first of these attacks was by the 3rd Division at Overloon and Venray in mid-October.

The attack on Overloon was postponed two days because of rain, and when it was finally launched, by 2 E. Yorks. and 1 Suffolk R., there were heavy casualties. Two of the three platoons in Maj. John Baker's B Company, 2 E. Yorks., were commanded by CANLOAN officers Lieuts. Jim Fetterly and Bob Inman, when this company captured the objectives of D Company, which had lost all its officers.

On 17 October an attack on Venray involved house-to-house fighting under terrible conditions of terrain and weather. In this battle Bob Inman of B Company was wounded for the second time when he was hit by shrapnel from an 88 gun. When the tanks bogged down, the infantry was deprived of their support. Len Robertson, who had been left out of battle, was called upon to command D Company when all the company officers were killed or wounded. Lieut. Gerald Hebb was cut off with his platoon, which suffered heavy casualties in an action for which he was awarded the Military Cross:

> He commanded the leading platoon in the right assault company attack and pressed forward when the left assault company was held up. For two hours the platoon held its position in the face of repeated counter attacks and heavy shelling. His personal example held the platoon together after it had suffered numerous casualties and advanced in spite of heavy machine gun fire. Lieut Hebb himself was the first man to reach the objective and his actions throughout the day with a platoon already much depleted were worthy of the highest levels of personal courage and junior leadership.[41]

In this battle another CANLOAN officer in the 3rd Division, CDN/320, Capt. Georges A.J. Bellavance of 2 KSLI, also earned the MC:

> He had shown outstanding courage and leadership throughout the campaign since D plus 1. In the battle for Venray Lieut Bellavance's platoon was the leading pl and suffered heavy casualties advancing through the woods. Despite this he rallied them and got his

men right amongst the enemy posns and caused so much confusion that the coy was able to capture 85 prisoners.

The 3rd Division history reports that in the first six months of the northwest European campaign the division recorded 127 cases of battle exhaustion but that in the one week of the Overloon-Venray battles they had twice that many.[42]

Equally bad conditions were encountered in a joint attack on the enemy bridgehead at Geilenkirchen by the 43rd Division and the American 84th Division on 18 November. The divisional history refers to "the sordid horror of Dorset Wood," where the 5th Dorsets wiped out an entire German battalion, the "unspeakable discomfort," the appalling conditions in slits that had to be bailed out continuously, and being "raked by shells from the Siegfried line."[43]

A major offensive to capture the Roer Triangle, where there was a large German bridgehead, with the 7th Armoured, 43rd, and 52nd Divisions was postponed. With the coming of winter came instead the struggle to keep warm and to keep weapons functioning. General Horrocks observed, "This was warfare at its most beastly – continuous cold, driving rain turning the ground into a sea of mud and constant counter attacks from experienced German troops."[44]

In times of extreme discomfort troops tend to compare their conditions with those of senior officers. Elmer Fitzpatrick recalls a story along such lines:

> We were in the Nijmegen-Arnhem area in a static position. The area was water-logged from heavy rain and damaged dykes. We moved into position to relieve another unit one evening. As Bn HQ sat down to dinner the Colonel asked the Intelligence Officer if the men were all in their positions. The answer was, "Yes sir, but it is bloody awful out there." The comment from the Colonel was "Oh well, the men have got their ground sheets. Pass the port." This comment leaked and everywhere you went it was, "Pass the port. The men have got their ground sheets."[45]

With no major operations the entire British Second Army was determined to have as pleasant a Christmas as possible. In some cases the Christmas festivities were to be at the battalion level, but elaborate meals and parties were planned by several companies and even platoons. These plans were rudely interrupted by the surprise attack by the Germans in the Ardennes, where a breach 20 miles wide and 25 miles deep was made in the American lines in the "Battle of the Bulge." The attack began on 16 December, three days after XXX Corps had been withdrawn from the front to prepare for the coming attack on the Rhineland. Field Marshal Montgomery immediately ordered these divisions to prevent the Germans from crossing the Meuse and to protect Brussels. It was said that General Horrocks was disappointed that the Germans didn't get far enough to be defeated on the battlefield of Waterloo.

None of the battalions in which CANLOAN officers were serving actually fought in the Battle of the Bulge, although several of them moved into a position from which they could support the Americans if the need arose. On 23 December the 6th Airborne Division arrived by sea from England and did their full share in the defence of the line of the Maas. In their frequent patrols one CANLOAN officer in 2 Oxf. Bucks., CDN/370, Lieut. Philip Bordinat, was captured when he was unable to return from across the Maas. On 24 February the division was flown back to Bulford to prepare for an airborne landing across the Rhine.

On 23 December Field Marshal Montgomery announced that Christmas would be celebrated on 25 December after all and that a Christmas message from him was to be read to all troops in 21st Army Group.

During the Ardennes affair it was reported that teams of German suicide troops, speaking English, dressed in American uniforms, and driving American jeeps, were infiltrating Allied lines to assassinate Eisenhower. Road blocks were manned and arrivals were asked questions designed to find out if they were Germans. One such question was "Who won the last world series?" One of the very few who could answer that question was Ross LeMesurier, who even knew the names of the pitchers, but he was still regarded suspiciously with his Canadian flashes, British uniform, and Scottish kilt.

In January the unfinished business of the Roer triangle was again taken up in operation BLACKCOCK from the 20th to the 25th. The assaulting divisions were the 7th Armoured, the 43rd, and the 53rd. Since the ground was frozen enough to take advantage of the 79th Division's special equipment known as "the Funnies" – Kangaroos, Flails, Crocodiles, and Crabs – the attack was successful and the divisions concerned were relieved. It was not, however, a bloodless affair, and several CANLOAN officers will recall the Roer triangle as a major battle. One of them was Vince Lilley, 1/5 Queens, 7th Armoured Division, who commanded D Company in an attack in the Roer salient. Just after last light the two forward platoons of his company at Bakenhoven were overrun by a German counter-attack. His reaction resulted in the award of the the MC. The citation reads in part as follows:

> Major Lilley immediately collected all the available men – fifteen in all – and dashed forward at the head of his small force. The enemy were all dressed in white and very difficult to see as by then it was completely dark, but in spite of this and the complete confusion in the whole area, this officer recaptured his lost positions which were still holding out. The extraordinary courage and dash of this officer in the face of almost overwhelming odds were entirely responsible for restoring the situation and an example of outstanding bravery to all his men.[46]

Two days later the Germans broke through B Company and mauled one of D Company's platoons, but the attack was repulsed. Lilley noted that the second in command of his company, Capt. Gordon Chatterton, "had the unenviable task of taking prisoners and wounded back over a circuitous route that could hardly be considered safe. He made it." During operation VERITABLE, Lilley at different times commanded three of the four companies in the 1/5 Queens, in which three CANLOAN officers were serving: Lieut. Joe Craib; CDN/43, Lieut. John Surtees; and CDN/418, Lieut. Hugh W. Macdonald.

At this time an MC was earned by another CANLOAN officer, CDN/287, Capt. Maxwell L. Baker, 1/5 Queens, 7th Armoured Division, for his leadership in repelling a violent counter-attack at Paarlo:

> The counter attack went on for four hours during which time this officer went from position to position pointing out targets and inspiring his men to greater efforts ... This

officer was the dominant figure during the very long and heavy counter attack and it was largely due to his personal bravery and magnificent example that his platoon was able to hold on to their positions until relieved.[47]

In the same month CDN/445, Lieut. Harry S. Crowe, 4 Welch, 53 Division, earned the MC for "numerous actions in which he has engaged, his display of courage, disregard for danger and devotion to duty have become a pass word with the men of his platoon to whom he was always an inspiration, culminating in a heroic crossing of a river in full daylight to obtain information."[48]

An attack in which a platoon in 9 DLI had taken part during the battle of the Roer triangle was described and illustrated by several full-page drawings in the *Illustrated London News* of 17 February 1945. The 9th DLI was commanded by Lieut.-Col. John Mogg, later General Sir John Mogg; the platoon commander, whose platoon was shown fighting Panzers and Tiger tanks at the Schilberg crossroads, was CANLOAN officer Elmer Fitzpatrick. He had been wounded with 11 DLI, 50 Division, in Normandy and had recently returned to the Continent and rejoined his regiment, then in the 7th Armoured Division. He was wounded again in the action illustrated in the *Illustrated London News*.

From the beginning of November 1944 to the end of January 1945 there were, fortunately, only eight fatal CANLOAN casualties, an indication of the nature of the winter campaign. In the 43rd Division CDN/163, Lieut. William G. Hunt of the 1st Battalion, the Worcestershire Regt. (Worc. R.), was killed at Mook on "the island." In the 49th Division CDN/644, Capt. William E. Nicholas was killed in the 2nd Battalion, the Gloucestershire Regt. (Glosters.).

In the 15th Scottish Division three CANLOAN officers in the 7th Seaforth Highlanders were killed during this period. Capt. Lawson Smith, a former Pictou Highlander, had applied for service in the British Army when he was serving in Bermuda before the inception of the CANLOAN scheme. He had served in the 7th Seaforths throughout the campaign in northwest Europe, where he established a legendary record as a fearless patrol leader. CDN/659, Lieut. Raymond F. Thoreson and CDN/668, Lieut. Leland A. Young were both former RCASC officers who joined the 7th Seaforths in Holland. Young's grave was adopted by a civilian family in Venray, who undertook to give it perpetual care.

During the winter, three CANLOAN officers in the 51st Highland Division were killed in action: CDN/615, Lieut. William M. Cowan in 5 BW, CDN/640, Lieut. Hugh D. McKibbon in the 5/7 Gordons, and CDN/594, Lieut. Evatt F.A. Merchant in 5 Camerons. Merchant was killed in the battle for a bridgehead over the Zig Canal on 18 November. McKibbon was killed during the Battle of the Bulge when his vehicle, in a convoy to relieve the Americans, received a direct hit from a mortar bomb. The death of two of a group of three CANLOAN officers who had been together at Sussex prompted the following poem, "Lest I Forget," by the sole survivor of the group, CDN/635, Lieut. D. Lewis C. Miller:

LEST I FORGET (Respectfully dedicated to Capt. Ev Merchant, Cameron Highlanders and Lieut. Dave McKibbin, Gordon Highlanders, both killed in action while fighting as CANLOAN officers with the 51st Highland Division.)

Just looking at my will today –
The will required by Army rules
For every man, despite his wealth
or lack of wealth, before he fought –
Recalled the day I made my will,
When Dave and Ev and I were hunched
Together on a folding form
Pretending to respect a chap
Who bored us with his Army law,
When luckily – we thought so then –
Another officer came in
Who brought with him a sheaf of forms.

"These forms," he said to us, "are wills,"
And Dave and Ev and I just laughed –
What sense in pessimism then?
"Just fill them in with pen and ink,
and don't forget the witnesses –
Two signatures are all you need."
We took the forms and made our wills.
My friends were witnesses for me,
And Dave and I then signed for Ev,
And Ev and I then signed for Dave.

A year went by since my return,
My useless will came back to me;
And looking at the names today
Of Dave and Ev recalled with awe
The day we laughed unthinkingly,
For in THEIR wills my name is used,
And mine alone remains unused;
And all I think is "Why? – Why?"[49]

CANLOAN officers continued to be friendly with all ranks. An officer in the 79th Division made the following note in his diary concerning a Canadian officer who was probably in the infantry brigade of the 7th Armoured Division:

> Very cold weather. Rain, sleet and snow. As darkness came on pulled into an abandoned brickworks near Susteren. As night fell we were joined by a British infantry platoon commanded by a young Canadian officer who was obviously very popular with his men. He chatted away with great good humour and treated everyone with unfailing courtesy, regardless of rank.[50]

During the winter senior officers visited the troops to keep up their spirits, and in each division recipients of awards were gathered for presentations by Montgomery on his visits. In some cases CANLOAN officers were presented with the same decorations more than once in the field and later, if opportunity permitted, one again at Buckingham Palace. On that momentous occasion each recipient was allowed two guests. Gordon Booth was accompanied by two brothers who were officers in the RCN and RCAF respectively. Len Robertson was presented with his MC first by Major "Banger" King, 2 E. Yorks., again, together with Jim Fetterly and others in 3 Division, by Field Marshal Montgomery, and finally by the King at Buckingham Palace. Jack Brayley, in characteristic fashion, managed to hitch a plane ride to London in order to receive his MC from the King.

With the closing of the Roer pocket, which brought the front line of the British Second Army up to the Maas and Roer Rivers, several divisions were withdrawn to Holland to prepare for operation VERITABLE, by which 21 Army Group would reach the Rhine in a major step towards victory in Europe.

11

To the Rhine and Beyond

AFTER LONG DELAYS, operation VERITABLE, the assault on the Rhineland finally began on 8 February 1945. It was to be a powerful attack commanded by HQ First Canadian Army with the greater part of the Second British Army placed under the command of General Crerar. The assault was to be by no fewer than five divisions of the XXX Corps supported by three armoured brigades and eleven regiments of specialized armour (to breach the fortifications in the Siegfried Line); two more divisions would be in reserve. The attack was to be preceded by the most concentrated artillery bombardment up to that time in the war in the West – from more than 1,000 guns and 500,000 shells on a seven-mile front.[1] After the initial break-in II Canadian Corps would move into the left sector. In the planning of operation VERITABLE several optimistic assumptions had been made. The first was that once the attackers were clear of the Reichwald forest they would have "good tank going," and if the ground remained frozen it would be difficult for the Germans to stop armoured thrusts. Second, a simultaneous drive by the American Ninth Army across the Maas towards the Rhine should keep the German reserves in the south.

Neither of these assumptions, as it turned out, was justified. In the first week in February there was a thaw, and 8 February saw the beginning of five days of rain that turned the ground into a quagmire. Within an hour of the assault every tank had bogged down. Second, the drive of the US Ninth Army in the south had to be postponed when the Germans blew up the Roer dams. It was more than two weeks before the American assault could begin. In the meantime, just as in Normandy, 21st Army Group attracted all the available German reserves and was soon faced with nine divisions instead of the one division that they had attacked on 8 February. In addition, the Germans had had five uninterrupted months to improve their defences in the Rhineland. Finally, when the Allied attack began, the Germans opened the dykes along the Rhine to flood the area north of the single main road from Nijmegen and thus reduced by one-half the width of the corridor for the advance of XXX Corps. For all these reasons the Battle of the Rhineland was a more bitter struggle with heavier casualties than had been anticipated by the planners. The postponement of VERITABLE until the Rhineland had changed from a frozen path on which tanks were expected to reach the Rhine in 48 hours to a morass of mud resulted in a 31-day struggle and nearly 18,000 British and Canadian casualties.

On 7 February, the eve of VERITABLE, Field Marshal Montgomery issued a "Personal Message from the C in C" which was to be read to all troops. In it, he said, "We are going into the ring for the final and last round; there will be no time limits; we will continue fighting until our opponent is knocked out."[2]

For CANLOAN officers in 21st Army Group, operation VERITABLE was an exciting prospect. Most of the units in which they served had been relieved after the battle of the Roer triangle and sent to locations well back from the front in Holland, ostensibly to train for the forthcoming operation but incidentally to have a welcome break from the discomforts and frustrations of the winter stalemate. For a few days they luxuriated in the comforts of warm houses, with clean and comfortable beds, and enjoyed the company of friendly and grateful civilians who adopted them into their families and whose children attached themselves to their platoons and companies; the cap badges they scrounged read like a roll call of British Army regiments. Clean uniforms and baths were welcomed. The mail delivery had so improved that letters from England took a few days instead of several weeks. One CANLOAN officer was the subject of surprise and envy when he obtained 75 letters and four parcels, the accumulation of more than two months.

A feature of this period was the return to action of a large number of CANLOAN officers who had been wounded in Normandy. Several had come as early as November: Fred Hatfield and Hector Brown in 2 SWB have been mentioned, as has John Druhan of 7 Seaforth. Others, such as CDN/236, Lieut. John A. Bannan of 2 Essex, 49th Division, had returned in December, but many more came in January and February in time to take part in the Battle of the Rhineland. Among them were Alfred Kirby and CDN/106, Lieut. Thomas H. Cunning, who both returned to 9 Cameronians in the 15th Scottish Division on 2 January; and Edward Larrett and Walter Tharp to 7 Som. LI and Gordon Wright to 4 Som. LI in the 43rd Division. Several CANLOAN officers joined the 1/5 Welch in the 53rd Division in January: CDN/106, Lieut. Joseph C.M. Veronneau, who was returning, and Jack Catley and Paul Cofsky, who had served in other units. Also in January several CANLOAN officers joined or rejoined 1 BW in the 51st Highland Division: CDN/653, Hyman Rosenthal, CDN/663, Lieut. Donald Wilson, Richard Coates, CDN/677, Lieut. D. William Mitchell; and later Peter Pearce, formerly 1/6 Queens. CDN/349, Lieut. John B. Matthew rejoined 2 Glas. H. in the 15th Scottish Division, and Wilfred Smith, 4 Wilts. in the 43rd Division. Others returned in February in time for the later stages of VERITABLE and also for the Rhine crossing. Alex Cunningham returned to 4 KSLI, 11th Armoured Division and several joined 1 Gordons, 51st Division, after having been wounded with other regiments in Normandy: Arthur Stone, Jimmy Marshall, Anderson Rodger, and CDN/33, Lieut. Alistair K. MacDonald. For every officer able to return to the same battalion at least two were posted to new ones.

If the returning CANLOAN officers felt any apprehension about returning to battle after being wounded, it was offset by the relief at having been released from the boredom of holding units by the pleasant familiar associations within a platoon, company, and battalion, and above all by the satisfaction of doing what they had volunteered for.

The massive barrage with which operation VERITABLE began, at 0500 hours on 8 February, was designed to destroy the first line of enemy defences. It introduced what Lieut.-Gen. Brian Horrocks, Commander of XXX Corps, has called "twenty-eight horrible days."[3] On the extreme right the 51st Highland Division attacked the southern part of the Reichwald. The division battle in this area lasted nearly three weeks. It involved close-quarter fighting, sometimes with bayonet charges, and, according to the regimental history of the BW, was "some of the bitterest fighting of the whole war."[4] The battle was described by Field Marshal Montgomery:

> The enemy parachute troops fought with a fanaticism unexcelled at any time in the war and it is interesting to note that the Germans had available against Canada's Army some 700 mortars and over 1000 guns of all types; the volume of fire from enemy weapons was the heaviest which had been met so far by British troops in the entire campaign.

General Horrocks said of this battle, "At the start ... we had been faced by one division approximately. Now nine divisions had been drawn into battle against us. It was a soldier's battle fought by the regimental officers and men under the most ghastly conditions imaginable."[5]

CANLOAN officers were involved at once. On 9 February A Company of 1 BW was sent to help the 5/7 Gordons. In this action Hyman Rosenthal of 1 BW was killed and Capt. Bill Mitchell was wounded. On the same day, Ross LeMesurier, whose role in fighting patrols on the Maas had been prominent, was wounded in spectacular fashion while commanding a platoon of 5 Cameron Highlanders in the Reichwald. The regimental history reports, "LeMesurier (Canloan) having fired all his ammunition charged the enemy with a shovel, the only weapon he had left."[6] His company commander reported, "I put him up for an MC. It should have been a VC."[7]

Another CANLOAN officer in the 51st Division who was killed on 28 January at the end of the Reichwald battle was CDN/656, Lieut. Richard N. Stewart, 5 BW. The regimental history contains the following account:

> An officer who saw it [the attack] go in tells how, waiting near Thomasof [where the attack was launched], he saw a group of seven German prisoners shuffling back, covered by a single Jock, holding a captured Luger so covered with mud that he could never have fired it. As he walked behind his prisoners he was weeping: Dick Stewart, the Canadian platoon commander for whom he was batman, had been killed.[8]

On 10 February 5 BW captured Gennep on the Maas, thereby securing the right flank of the attack.

The centre of the Reichwald was assigned to the 53rd Welch Division, which, in the opinion of General Horrocks, was "the division which suffered most."[9] In fighting its way through the Reichwald between 8 and 18 February it suffered

5,000 casualties, 50 percent of all its casualties in northwest Europe.

The key to a successful breakthrough in VERITABLE was the Materborn feature, a piece of high ground at a narrow gap between the Reichwald and the city of Cleve that was to be seized by the 15th Scottish Division. The city had been demolished by the RAF to prevent the rapid movement of German reserves, and the leading troops were transported in Kangaroos to ensure a rapid seizure of Cleve. The 43rd Division was to pass through the Materborn gap and seize the cities of Goch and Udem to the south.

When the 15th Scottish reached the outskirts of Cleve, General Horrocks, commanding XXX Corps, committed the 43rd Division prematurely. In his own words, the arrival of the division in the middle of the night "turned out to be one of the worst mistakes I made in the war. It caused one of the worst traffic jams of the war."[10]

The history of the 43rd Division relates how the CO of the leading battalion, 4 Wilts., followed a secondary road leading into Cleve and at dawn the Germans found a British brigade superimposed on their headquarters:

> With a troop of 15th Scottish Reconnaissance Regiment and one of his own platoons Lieut Col Corbyne personally led the head of the column forward into the darkness ahead, finding the road blocked by a Spandau ... Lieut Col Corbyne's bold action at the road block outside Cleve has a parallel with that of Ludendorff at Liege in 1914.[11]

The history of 4 Wilts. reveals that the platoon that led the way into Cleve riding on tanks was commanded by a CANLOAN officer:

> Lieutenant W Smith led 13 Platoon up to the road block. The platoon had been much reduced owing to a tank having broken down and consisted of platoon headquarters and one section commanded by L/Cpl Miller. Lieut Smith himself had been forced to release his grip on his Sten when it became entangled in branches in the dark rather than be swept off the turret of his tank. He was armed with a pistol in addition but had no ammunition for it. This did not prevent him doing a true "Wild West" draw on a young German parachutist, frightening him into surrender before he fired a shot.[12]

The confused occupation of Cleve, followed by fierce attacks and counter-attacks in and near the city were as violent as any battles that the 43rd Division fought during the war. This, and fighting elsewhere in the Rhineland, produced scenes like the following:

> The first shell landed in the street, killed the medical sergeant and a stretcher bearer and smashed the MO's car. Another hit the RAP, another our house; every one was within 100 yards. At the first shell L/Cpl Miller, Skilton and Hewitt dashed into Pl HQ. There was a pause and Skilton decided to make a dash for his section billet across the street. He had just left when three shells in rapid succession burst all around us and we were sure that he must at least be wounded. Sgt Stacey, L/Cpl Miller and I went to look for him, calling his name ... We found no trace of Skilton until we reached the house across the street and there in the doorway was what was left of him after a direct hit from an 88. His scalp was stuck on the wall two feet over the door; his head was hanging by the skin on the back of his neck; one leg and one arm were missing and the remaining leg shattered and his wrist

hanging by a bit of skin. His intestines were in a heap covered by his body. All we could do was scrape the pieces into a blanket and carry it away, leaving a pool of blood in front of the door and drops spattered all over the front of the house, a truly gruesome sight.[13]

Farther south the 15th Scottish Division encountered fanatical resistance. It has been observed that "the brigade's bitter struggle for Moyland [was] the worst experience it had endured since the campaign began."[14] It lasted four days and was followed by stiff fighting in another attack northeast of Weeze, in which two CANLOAN officers were killed on 22 February: Lieut. Vernon Box of 6 RSF and CDN/ 667, Lieut. Everett E. Young of 7 Seaforth.

Vernon Box was one of the large group of Pictou Highlanders who had joined CANLOAN as soon as it was announced. Posted to 6 RSF in Normandy, he was wounded in July, and after being released from hospital in England managed to return to his old regiment in October. Everett Young, too, had been wounded while serving with 7 Seaforth. After being released from hospital he, too, rejoined his regiment only a few days before he was killed in action.

Among those who were wounded on 22 February was CDN/359, Lieut. Ralph Russell, who had joined 9 Cameronians only two days before. On 18 February two CANLOAN officers in 6 KOSB were wounded: CDN/73, Lieut. Neil Compton and CDN/ 674, Capt. George E. Sweeney.

After the advance of the 43rd Division from Cleve to Goch, which General Horrocks regarded as "the turning point of the battle,"[15] Goch was captured by the 15th, 51st, and 52nd Divisions between 17 and 21 February. This marked the end of operation VERITABLE, which brought the advance of the First Canadian Army up to a line between Gennep on the Maas and Xanten on the Rhine. VERITABLE was followed immediately by operation BLOCKBUSTER, which removed the last of the German troops west of the Rhine.

In BLOCKBUSTER other divisions played a prominent role after the 51st and 15th Divisions were squeezed out by the end of February. For example, the 3rd Division relieved the 15th Scottish at Goch and drove south with the 11th Armoured Division on its left and the 53rd on the right flank of the 21st Army Group. A CANLOAN officer in the 3rd Division, CDN/171, Lieut. John A. Laurie of 1 R. Norfolk, earned the MC at this time:

On the capture of Kervenheim on 28 Feb this officer was a pl comd. On his coy comdr becoming wounded and the 2 i/c being killed he immediately assumed comd of the coy. With great skill and under perpetual enemy sniper fire he organized his coy and was personally instrumental in beating back an enemy counter attack. Not content with defensive fighting he led fighting patrols against the Boche counter attack force and by his forceful leadership and skilful use of fire wrought havoc amongst the opposition. During the whole of the operation his leadership and disregard of danger were most conspicuous and the manner in which he accepted his new responsibilities and discharged his duties as coy comdr were commendable beyond words.[16]

Another MC was earned by CDN/4 Maj. Joseph Hemelryk of 1 HLI in the 53rd Division during its advance towards the Rhine between 4 and 8 March. His citation reads in part:

This officer was in command of the right forward company of the 1st HLI when the battalion was ordered on the night of 4 Mar to gain part of a bridgehead astride the main road in the woods n.e. of Issum to cover a bridging operation to allow the armour to advance towards the Rhine. In order to reach this objective he had to advance uphill over open ground swept by MG fire from Spandau posts in the forward edge of the wood. In spite of the fact that both flanks of his company were exposed to heavy and accurate MG fire ... he put in a well-organized assault on the enemy positions in the wood and succeeded in breaking through to his objective. Although this position became almost untenable by daylight as a result of an enemy counter attack ... Major Hemelryk kept his company in good heart by his personal coolness and disregard for his own safety. It was largely due to his tenacity in holding such an isolated position, fine leadership and skill in directing fire under most difficult and dangerous conditions that the bridgehead achieved its purpose and the armour was able to get through.[17]

Both Hemelryk and Laurie were killed in action during the last few days of the war, on 14 and 16 April, respectively.

For the final drive to the Rhine, from 8 to 10 March, the 53rd Division was relieved by the 52nd, which encountered determined enemy resistance at Alpen and suffered heavy casualties. In the attack by 7 Cameronians Maj. James Duncan, commanding D Company, earned the MC:

On 9 Mar 45 the Coy under Maj. Duncan's comd was ordered to attack an enemy position in the rly stn area covering the main rd NE of Alpen. It was considered essential to clear this area in order to open the road. The leading pl seized the first fortified building but was then stopped by intense automatic fire from the next building 30 yds in rear. Several men were killed or wounded by this fire and by enemy panzerfausts. Maj Duncan personally led in a second platoon and remained directing this and subsequent assaults on the building under close-range enemy fire. Without his magnificent example and leadership at this critical time the attack would most undoubtedly have been held up and the position not captured.[18]

Whereas it was Canadian divisions that were primarily engaged in the bitter fighting in the Hochwald forest, the British 11th Armoured Division was engaged in several attacks, in one of which 1 HLI had more than 150 casualties. Among the CANLOAN officers who were wounded at this time was Wally Ingraham, 3 Mons., who, while alone on a reconnaissance patrol, was hit by shrapnel. He was reported missing and believed killed but had managed to make his own way to an ambulance and was safely evacuated. Another CANLOAN officer in the 11th Division, Alex Cunningham 4 KSLI, who had been wounded in his first battle in Normandy and managed to return to his old battalion in the Hochwald, was wounded again in his first attack in the Rhineland.

By 10 March the First Canadian Army and the Ninth United States Army were occupying the west bank of the Rhine from Nijmegen to Dusseldorf. The Battle of the Rhineland had been a fiercer encounter than had been expected. The First Canadian Army had suffered around 15,000 casualties, 10,000 of them British. The Germans had suffered more, with 22,000 killed and wounded and 22,000 prisoners of war.[19]

On 26 March General Eisenhower wrote to General Crerar, commander of the

First Canadian Army: "Probably no assault in this war has been conducted under more appalling conditions of terrain than was this one." Crerar replied, "I believe that no troops could have put up a finer exhibition of enduring gallantry and determination than was demonstrated during those weeks of bitter, bloody and muddy fighting."[20]

Nevertheless, the Battle of the Rhineland contained moments of humour that helped to preserve the sanity of the troops. Prominent among their memories are the unofficial supplementary rations. A cartoon at the time showed the road from Cleve to Calcar strewn with chicken feathers. In addition there were the tasty contents of the well-stocked cellars of the prosperous Rhineland farms whose owners had been evacuated. These unofficial rations were described in a letter from a CANLOAN officer to his parents:

> Our meals today: bacon, fried egg, sausage, bread and tea for breakfast; roast chicken, mashed potatoes, peas and plum pudding for lunch; fried egg, ham, potato chips, fruit salad and cream – apples, pears, peaches, cherries, strawberries for tea, and dinner with the company commanders and the CO, consisting of an hors d'oeuvre, roast chicken, etc and another fruit salad, cake and coffee – the result of German farms having such well-stocked cellars.[21]

There remained only one major natural obstacle to victory in the west – the Rhine. As he had on the eve of VERITABLE, Field Marshal Montgomery issued a "Personal Message to be Read to all Troops" before they crossed the Rhine. After describing the plight of the enemy, which since his last message on 7 February had lost the Rhineland and suffered 250,000 casualties, he concluded, "21 Army Group will now cross the Rhine ... and having crossed the Rhine we will crack about the plains of Northern Germany chasing the enemy from pillar to post ... Over the Rhine, then, let us go. And good hunting to you on the other side."[22]

The plans for the crossing had been drawn up under General Dempsey's direction during the Battle of the Rhineland, and equipment had been stockpiled near the banks of the river during the two weeks before the assault. It included 22,000 tons of assault bridging, 2,000 assault boats, 650 storm boats, and even 80 miles of balloon cable. The assault was to be preceded by the biggest artillery bombardment of the war – 3,411 guns (three times the number used in VERITABLE) and more than 1,000,000 rounds of ammunition.[23] A continuous smokescreen was put down along the river bank to hide the preparations.

The initial assault was to be made by the 51st Highland Division, followed immediately by the 15th Scottish Division and the 1st Commando Brigade. As early as the end of February the 51st Division had been pulled out of action in order to practise assault crossings on the Maas River; other divisions were released for rest and training as their tasks west of the Rhine were completed.

It had been a welcome break. Depleted platoons were brought up to strength with reinforcements who seemed to be younger and younger. There was weapons maintenance and firing, tactical training, foot and arms drill, and conditioning – route marches and physical training. One CANLOAN officer in a Scottish unit recalls, "It was customary in the evenings for the officers to assemble in a hall where we were to learn Highland dancing under the instruction of the pipers."[24]

There were also other forms of relaxation: football games were organized at company, battalion, and even divisional levels, and ENSA troops came to entertain – and were entertained, as usual, in the sergeant's mess. And there was leave. Almost every CANLOAN officer in the 21st Army Group got a 48-hour leave in Brussels. For some it was their last leave. Wilf Smith, 4 Wilts., recalls sharing a hotel room with a fellow Maritimer, Jack Matthew, 2 Glas. H. Earlier, they had shared command of a draft of reinforcements; now they shared a date with two Canadian nurses, one of them Jack's fiancée. Jack observed calmly that he would not survive the Rhine battle – and he did not. Arthur Stone shared a room with Andy Rodger. They, too, had been together in a reinforcement draft and had then joined 1 Gordons in time for the Rhine crossing, in which Rodger was killed.

Some CANLOAN officers were afraid they would miss the Rhine crossing. Ross LeMesurier, 5 Cameronians, and Bill Mitchell, 1 BW, had been wounded in the Reichwald and were in hospital, but they went AWL and hitched rides back to their units in the assaulting 51st Division, arriving less than a week before the assault. Another CANLOAN officer, Del Struck, had been on a course at Barnard Castle in Scotland and while there had got married, missing part of the Battle of the Rhineland. But he managed to get back to his unit, 10 HLI in the 15th Scottish Division, in time for the Rhine crossing.

The river crossing during the night of 23 March was supplemented by an airborne drop by the 6th Airborne Division and the 17th United States Airborne Division on the morning of the 24th. The barrage, which began at 1700 hours and continued until 2100 hours, when the crossing began, made a deep impression on all the troops in the area. John Anderson, a former RCA officer, observed, "Never to be forgotten was sitting under the barrage waiting to cross the Rhine. It seemed to go on for hours and hours and with the tracer lead it was a brilliant display, frightening in its power."[25]

The artillery was supplemented by machine guns and mortars. Rex Fendick of 2 MX in the 3rd British Division, recalls firing medium machine guns for 36 hours non-stop in support of the assault and subsequent buildup. There were also batteries of rockets called flying mattresses.

The assault crossing, which had been given the code name Operation PLUNDER, was almost an anti-climax. Two brigades of the 51st Highland Division were loaded into Buffaloes which, beginning at 2 minutes to 2100 hours on 23 March, began to lumber down the near banks, following taped routes, and to lurch into the dark waters of the Rhine. Six minutes later at 2104 hours a message came back: "Black Watch has landed safely on the far bank."[26] 5 BW was followed quickly by the rest of the division.

A CANLOAN officer, CDN/543, Lieut. Maurice (Mo) Carter, 2 Seaforth, was in the leading Buffalo in his battalion and the first man on shore. Sure that he was the first Canadian officer, if not the first British soldier, to get across the Rhine, he was startled to hear a familiar voice from the darkness as he climbed the bank: "What kept you, Mo?"[27] It was an old friend, Hubert Campbell, a fellow instructor at Brockville, and long-time friendly competitor. Campbell, not Carter, had been the first to cross the Rhine, as was reported in several British and Canadian newspapers:

ON THE RHINE MAR 26 (CP) TRENTON OFFICER FIRST OVER RHINE

Scottish troops of the 51st Highland Division, singing *Annie Laurie,* crossed the Rhine Friday night under a terrific barrage from Field Marshal Montgomery's guns ... The Highlanders took three and a half minutes to cross the Rhine. The first man ashore was Lieut Hugh J Campbell of Trenton, Ont. on loan to the British Army.

VALUABLE LOAN

First man across the Rhine was a Canadian officer on loan to the 51st Highland Division. That lad certainly upheld the honour of Canada because you have to be a man to be first in the 51st.[28]

A CANLOAN officer in a follow-up division observed to a Scottish soldier on the bank of the Rhine that it seemed very peaceful. He was informed that he was standing where the commander of the 51st Highland Division had been killed not long before. The death of Major-General Rennie from a mortar bomb was a great loss to his division. An historian of the Black Watch has observed, "He was a great Jock-lover, and they in turn adored him."[29]

Though casualties were lighter than had been expected, there was fierce fighting in two places on the front of the 51st Division: at Rees on the banks of the Rhine, where 1 Gordons were held up for 48 hours by ferocious opposition from a battalion of German paratroops, and at Speldorp one and a half miles inland, where 1 BW had to fight off fierce counter-attacks supported by SP guns.

The Rhine crossing has been described by Arthur Stone, a CANLOAN officer who was a platoon commander in 1 Gordons:

The anticipation: Everyone was keyed up to a high pitch and I was walking about two feet off the ground.

The barrage: The 25-pdrs were bamming and rippling away all around us as we followed the tapes and coloured lights ... We watched the MMG tracers soaring over in gigantic rafts rising from the darkness and sailing off to the horizon in an arc amid the measured rattle of the machine guns. Flying mattresses of rockets rushed over with a great gathering whoosh. These were fired electrically from a rack or rocket bank which could hold hundreds.

The crossing in Buffaloes: They were like huge prehistoric monstrosities and just as awkward while out of the water. The roar of the engines was so great that a shout could be heard only with difficulty ... We had moved up in boat loads which required splitting the platoon. We were directed to one of these leviathans and clambered up the lowered ramp at the tail. We immediately lumbered off, steeply rising over the first bund or dyke, violently lunging down, then over a flat stretch to cross the next dyke and enter the water. Then everything was calm and quiet as we smoothly forged across the broad calm Rhine, looking beautifully serene in the dim light of the moon, fireworks and reflected search-lights. We touched gently on the other side without being under fire at any time during the crossing and all scrambled over the bow onto the land.

The objective: To capture a town which had been by-passed by 5 BW, advancing through Spandau and sniper fire.

The willing but inexperienced troops: I was extremely worried about the platoon as I had to personally place every man and personally get them to do things which should have been automatic with proper training. Not that they weren't willing – just that they had no idea of proper procedures and safeguards. By personally directing the firing of six sections (two platoons) I got some fire going in the direction of the sniper. At the same time I had to keep dashing around to place the men so they were keeping a lookout in all directions ... Two were caught in the open. One was killed and the other wounded and taken out by stretcher bearers.

CANLOAN casualties: I found the B Coy platoon commander was Alistair MacDonald and just had time to greet him while passing. It was the last time I saw him as he died of wounds the next day after being shot with a burst of Spandau. I subsequently learned that Andy Rodger, the third Canadian, had been killed by a direct hit by an 88. He was killed with his platoon sergeant in a German trench near the water's edge. Of the CANLOAN reinforcements who had joined 1 Gordons a month earlier only I survived the Rhine battle.

The speed with which the front line became the rear: After capturing a position and taking many prisoners and 36 Spandaus I laid out my bedroll on a table in the cellar of platoon HQ, took off my boots and outer clothing for the first time in three days and was instantly asleep. I awoke with a strange feeling of bucolic peace. The guns across the river were silent ... I looked out the cellar window and saw the back of a recce car parked outside the house on which were strapped crates of live chickens. Our square, so deserted and sinister before, was lined with vehicles and periodically others roared up the grade from the river and passed through the square. The bridge was up already and the armour freely on their way.[30]

After crossing the Rhine the 1 BW pushed inland and captured the small town of Speldorp but was driven back by fierce counter-attacks: "Houses had to be cleared at the point of the bayonet and single Germans made suicidal attempts to break up our attacks ... Trapped elements of the Black Watch were relieved by the Highland Light Infantry of Canada."[31]

The war diary of 1 BW for 24 March notes:

Withdrawal only at the cost of leaving platoons commanded by Coates MC [Capt. Richard B., CANLOAN] and Henderson completely cut off. Another attack and withdrawal. Again a platoon had to be left behind from A Coy under Lieut D W Mitchell. All the platoons were released having held out against every nature of attack from SP guns at point-blank range to pole charges and eventually being reduced to holding one room of a house only. In spite of this they brought back some 25 prisoners and had killed a large number of the enemy. First class junior leadership had saved much from what had threatened to be a mass of wreckage. [CDN/49] Lieut Raymond Watson was among the wounded.[32]

For his part in this action Capt. Bill Mitchell was awarded the MC:

The tireless energy and courage shown by this young officer throughout the siege are worthy of the highest praise and his cheerful leadership inspired his men to hold out under what appeared the most desperate situation. He showed soundest judgement in the careful way in which he husbanded the meagre stock of ammunition which thereby enabled the pl to prolong the defence against heavy odds which included at least three tanks or SP guns.[33]

The commander of the other platoon that was cut off, Lieut. J.R. Henderson, was awarded the DSO. Another CANLOAN officer in the 51st Division who earned an MC in the crossing of the Rhine was Capt. Robert Gelston, 7 BW. The citation reads in part as follows:

> On the night of 23/4 March 45 the Bn was the left fwd assaulting bn of the Division ... Capt Gelston's coy was rt fwd coy of the bn. His coy captured the first objective assigned to it, taking a number of prisoners. Later a second objective, after considerable battling against determined opposition and under heavy shelling, was captured. During the whole of this period Capt Gelston's leadership and determination were very largely responsible for carrying out this intricate and complicated move ... The following morning a determined enemy counter attack under cover of thick mist was launched against Capt Gelston's coy and this was most decidedly beaten off, only one of the enemy escaping, the remainder being either killed, wounded, or taken prisoner. Capt Gelston's coy position was one of such importance that had this enemy counter attack succeeded the whole crossing of the Rhine by subsequent formations would have been seriously jeopardized. The throwing back and defeat of this counter attack was again largely due to Capt Gelston's initiative and he set a very fine example to his coy.[34]

Among the CANLOAN casualties in the Rhine crossing were two in 5 Cameron Highlanders, Lieut. Ross LeMesurier and CDN/61, Lieut. Francis L.J. (Lou) Arnett. LeMesurier had had a spectacular career with the Cameron Highlanders in Holland and the Rhineland and, as noted earlier, had gone AWL from hospital to rejoin his unit and take part in the Rhine crossing. On the first day across the Rhine he was hit by a mortar bomb and had to have a leg amputated. On the next day his friend Lou Arnett, who had been wounded at Sainte-Honorine in Normandy, died of wounds received in the Rhine battle. Maurice "Mo" Carter, a fellow instructor of Arnett's at Brockville, who was in 2 Seaforth, was pleased to see his friend pass by as the 5 Cameron Highlanders moved up. A few minutes later Arnett was wounded; he was killed when the ambulance in which he was being evacuated was hit by a shell.

The 15th Scottish was the second assaulting division in the British sector, crossing the Rhine just north of Wesel between the 51st Division and the Commando Brigade. Its task was to secure a bridgehead and push on to link up with the airborne landings five miles inland. At 0230 hours on 24 March the 6 RSF on the right and the 8 RS on the left crossed the river in Buffaloes. By 0400 hours the battalion had achieved all its objectives and had captured several hundred prisoners. Following in storm boats, 6 KOSB cleared Bislich after heavy fighting. The airborne landings came at 1000 hours. At 1400 hours the 6 KOSB linked up with the 17th US Airborne Division, and by 1600 hours the 8 RS had reached the 6th Airborne Division.

The next task for the division was to seize the bridge over the Issel River, ten miles from the Rhine. At first light on 26 March a heavy counter-attack on 6 KOSB resulted in a desperate hand-to-hand struggle in which the battalion was eventually victorious. In this battle CDN/671, Lieut. Ian M. Macdonald earned the MC:

> On 26 Mar 45 C Coy 6 KOSB attacked a large farm near Dingden. Lieut Macdonald was in command of 15 Pl. After about half the objective had been cleared a violent enemy

counter-attack developed and bitter hand-to-hand fighting took place in the darkness. With ammunition almost entirely expended the coy was ordered to withdraw to a firm base and Lieut Macdonald was left with his pl to cover this withdrawal.

Under the determined leadership of Lieut Macdonald 15 Pl fought to the last round, incurring very heavy casualties but enabling the withdrawal to be successfully completed. Only when their task was finished and their ammunition exhausted did the survivors rejoin their coy. During this period Lieut Macdonald displayed great courage and a complete disregard for his personal safety. He moved from one post to another encouraging his men and directing their fire with the greatest effect. In the confused fighting that took place he succeeded in holding up immensely superior forces and was personally involved in hand to hand fighting with the Germans.[35]

On 27 March Lieut. Jack Matthew, 2 Glas. H., 15th Scottish Division, was killed in action. He, too, had been wounded in Normandy and had returned to his old battalion in time for the Rhine crossing. All 15 CANLOAN officers in 2 Glas. H. were wounded, but Jack Matthew was the only fatal CANLOAN casualty in the battalion.

Whereas the Rhine assault by water took place in darkness, the airborne assault was in broad daylight, a spectacular event that filled the sky with aircraft, parachutes, and gliders – 1,795 parachute aircraft and 1,305 gliders. The plan for the airborne crossing of the Rhine was conceived as early as October 1944, and a great deal of thought, preparation, and practice had occurred in the subsequent months. The 6th Airborne Division was withdrawn from the western front in February to prepare for the drop.

On 24 March the 6th Airborne left England at 0615 hours. They had reached the Rhine by 0930 and were landing by 1000 hours. The landing of the gliders of the Air Landing Brigade was especially successful. Ninety percent touched down in the landing zone, and before noon all objectives were taken.

There was, however, considerable damage to the gliders of the Air Landing Brigade – the 1 RUR, 2 Oxf. Bucks., and 12 Devon. Of the 416 gliders that reached the battlefield only 88 were undamaged – 37 were completely burned out, some came down in flames, and the rest were hit by light flak and small-arms fire. CANLOAN officers in the gliders that landed safely included Lieut. Tom Anstey, 2 Oxf. Bucks., who has a copy of a photograph from *Life* magazine showing glider No. 155 just touching down with him in it. Less fortunate was his friend Jim Cochrane, who had won an MC in Normandy. His glider came down in flames, and he was killed instantly. The other CANLOAN officers in 2 Oxf. Bucks. were wounded the same day: CDN/431, Lieut. Morgan G. Allcroft in the landing and CDN/474, Lieut. John Stone on a patrol that evening.

One of the three CANLOAN officers in 12 Devon, CDN/204, Lieut. Hubert C. Cox, was killed as he landed. He had served overseas with the Royal Canadian Engineers 1940–43 before returning to Canada for a commission and was commander of the pioneer platoon in his battalion. His platoon sergeant has described the death of his officer: "He was killed in the landing on the Rhine crossing. The platoon glider was hit and crashed. He survived the crash but was almost immediately hit and killed by another glider. Known to his men as 'Babe' Cox, he was immensely popular and his loss was mourned."[36]

Though the airborne assault was considered conspicuously successful, there were 1,000 casualties among the 8,000 who took part in it.[37] An excellent account of a glider landing was written shortly after the event by CDN/390, Lieut. William J. Robinson, one of the CANLOAN officers in the 1st Battalion, the Royal Ulster Rifles (RUR):

We got up at about 0430 hr and had breakfast – five of us sat down and by lunch time that day two of them were gone. The takeoff was normal except that I had a severe attack of bladder trouble (nervous tension they call it). Before you knew it you were in the air and on the way. Out over the North Sea heading for Brussels where we were to link up with the Americans. What a sight they were ... it seemed that the whole sky was full of planes.

In we went over the Maas where we had left only a month before. Before you knew it the Rhine was in sight but the whole sky seemed to be filled with black clouds of smoke-flak! I sat down, strapped myself in, tried to adopt a carefree attitude, failed miserably, just sat there and tried not to think.

Bang! the first one hit us and what a hit – the gas tank in the jeep got it and the gas poured out all over the plywood floor. Bang! and the next one was really a doozer – the glider load had a jeep, trailer full of six pounder ammunition, two pilots, five of my men and myself. This shot hit the trailer ... We were now cast off and looking for the ground. The flak kept hitting us in the wings but no more hit the fuselage.

The pilot shouted "Hang on!" and boy did I ever hang on. We crashed down into a tree which banged off the end of the wing, spun us around and we ploughed head on into another tree which ended up between the two pilots in the nose. I was up, out the door and on the ground all in one movement. The others followed suit and by some miracle there wasn't a mark on any of us.

I twisted my map furiously around trying to orient myself. Finally I saw it – a railway car on a siding and I knew where I was. Meanwhile the corporal had been looking at the jeep and now informed me that it was useless to unload as there was no petrol left in it, so I gave the order, "Grab your packs and let's go."

Across the open fields we went in a straight line as well as I could judge it, heading for the bridge. I could see in the general direction a whole series of burning gliders with lots of noise from exploding ammunition, ack ack and the roar of planes away above us ... Just about that time I saw a glider coming in between us and the bridge at about 500 feet up. It was hit badly by flak and burst into flame from the front. Of course this was carried quickly along the whole length and at the little windows you could see the heads of the fellows inside silhouetted against the flames ... It landed on its back in pieces – nobody got out.

We finally reached an open stretch and about 250 yards ahead I saw some helmets appearing over the edge of a slit trench. Now came the luckiest and most stupid manoeuvre of my life. I told the boys to wait and I ran across the field towards the trench waving my red beret – still not knowing whether the round helmets were airborne or Jerry. When I finally got to them they were ours. They told me that part of their company was on the other side of the river so I got my men and waded through the river and met Major Dyball of the Ulsters on the other side. He was the only officer left standing in the company ... He said he would take the right side of the road to the bridge and that I was to take the left side ... Three of us reached the houses first. I sent a chap named Gardiner to look at what I thought was a root cellar. He opened the door and 17 German soldiers came out with their hands in the air.

I set out our Bren guns in a sort of defence with the chaps I had ... I had no sooner completed this than somebody shouted "tanks!" Sure enough up the road behind us came two Mk IV German tanks and an SP gun ... I shouted for a PIAT but of course nobody had one ... As they went up the road over the bridge one of them stopped, turned around and fired. The shot hit the barn which was connected to the house where we were and set it on fire.

A little later I saw our men, about a company in strength coming up the road from the main LZ [landing zone] and I knew that we were OK.

Every event of that day is so clear in my mind: how I felt thirsty, how hot it was as we worked with our full equipment on, with our faces covered with sweat and dirt. All the bodies lying about which nobody bothered about; the wounded, both our own and German; the planes dropping supplies; the Germans firing at us from the autobahn; greeting the different fellows and groups of fellows as they appeared; hearing about those who were killed; wondering about those whom nobody had seen.

The main thing was that the operation had been a success – quite large casualties – but the battalion had achieved all its objectives and was prepared to hold them. The Rhine had been crossed and the war was entering its last stages.[38]

By 28 March the bridgehead over the Rhine was 35 miles wide and 20 miles deep. Twenty divisions and 1,500 tanks were across, and it was time for the breakout. Field Marshal Montgomery ordered General Dempsey of the British Second Army and General Simpson of the US Ninth Army "to drive hard for the line of the River Elbe so as to gain quick possession of the plains of Northern Germany."[39]

The race to the Elbe involved virtually all the units in which the CANLOAN officers still in northwest Europe were serving. An exception was those serving in the 49th West Riding or Polar Bear Division, which had remained on "the island" as part of the Canadian I Corps during the Battle of the Rhineland. This division had a notable conclusion to the northwest European campaign when it captured Arnhem on April 13. A former company commander in 1/4 KOYLI, Colonel Barker-Harland, recalls the capable leadership of Lieut. Jack Young in the attack on Arnhem: "He was a splendid platoon commander. His men liked him and had confidence in him."[40] To Young he wrote recently, "For me you have always epitomized the best of the magnificent CANLOAN officers scheme."[41]

Jack Young and CDN/278, Capt. Richard Purdey had been in 6 DLI in the 50th Division in Normandy. This division was disbanded owing to heavy casualties, and the survivors went elsewhere as reinforcements. Young and Purdey joined 1/4 KOYLI in December. CDN/88, Maj. Robert Mainprize, who served with 1/4 KOYLI in Normandy, was wounded earlier in Holland.

Even the 6th Airborne Division was in the drive eastward, for much of the way having the novel experience of riding on tanks. Leaving Wesel on 23 March, the division reached Celle on 13 April and was with the spearhead of the British Army that crossed the Elbe on 29 April and headed towards the Baltic.[42] On the way it encountered spotty resistance, and in one action a CANLOAN officer, CDN/487, Lieut. John C. Pape, was killed. Former members of 7 Para. – Pape's company commander and members of his platoon – recall the circumstances of his death on 7 April at Wunsdorf airfield near Hanover, where his 4 Platoon was ambushed and both Pape and his platoon sergeant were killed by machine-gun fire along with approximately 30 other casualties. John Pape had served overseas with the Edmonton Regiment for three years before returning to Canada for a commission. He was one of the few CANLOAN officers who had served in Normandy with the 6th Airborne Division, had been wounded during the Battle of the Bulge on 4 January, and had rejoined his battalion in time for the Rhine airlift. Both he and his fellow CANLOAN officer in 7 Para., CDN/470, Lieut. William F. (Pat) Patterson, were considered competent and popular officers.

Once across the Rhine, the Allies met greatly reduced opposition. Altogether facing west there was the equivalent of only 26 divisions, which have been described as "the last scrapings of the manpower of the Reich collected for sacrifice – old men, sick men and boys. Nevertheless, there was much sharp fighting ahead, first on all fronts and then in pockets of small groups of SS troops or paratroops determined to hold out to the bitter end."[43]

A CANLOAN officer at this time described the nature of the warfare during the last month of the war:

> The German armies have lost all semblance of organized resistance after being chased across the Rhine, their defences smashed and armoured/infantry thrusts made deep into the heart of the Fatherland. Small groups have been left behind to delay these thrusts by sniping, blowing bridges, mines, road blocks and bazookas. They consist of men of a dozen units – sections with no knowledge of the whereabouts of the rest of their platoon, company or battalion, wherever a leader can persuade men to make a fanatical stand with him: parachutists, Volksturm, Pz Grenadiers, Commandos, youngsters of from 12 to 15 years in training centres, really guerrilla bands, living by looting their countrymen, killing when they have the advantage of surprise or numbers and surrendering or hiding when opposed with any strength.[44]

The goal of VIII Corps (6th Airborne, 11th Armoured, and 15th Scottish Divisions) was the Elbe from Celle; that of XII Corps (7th Armoured, 52nd, and 53rd Divisions) was Hamburg; and that of XXX Corps (Guards Armoured, 3rd, 43rd, and 51st) was Bremen. The British commanders were determined to end the war quickly and to avoid getting bogged down by ambushes in which a single soldier with a panzerfaust by a roadside could hold up an entire armoured division. The sense of urgency that was instilled into the troops in the breakout from the Rhine is conveyed in an account by Maj. Vince Lilley, 1/5 Queens, 7th Armoured Division:

> Our training had been designed to make us into a flexible, hard-hitting, mobile force, which it proved to be for the next two months. The composition of these mobile teams consisted of a company of infantry in Kangaroos, a squadron of Cromwell tanks, a troop of mounted artillery and a section of engineers, which included a scissors bridge ... The Desert Rats advanced on the centre line Wesel, Rhein, Bremen and Hamburg. My orders were: Here is your centre line. Patton is doing 40 miles a day and we expect you to do the same or else ... Our battle cry was "if you can't run over it go around it." This meant that the infantry div following us had a considerable amount of clearing up to do ... Several times when we hadn't made the mileage required I tried to make it up at night, much to the horror of the armoured boys who were used to forming a laager at night, protected by a ring of infantry.

Our attacks were launched quickly, giving verbal orders over the wireless net. One picture-book attack was a quick right flanking attack on the small village of Thedinghausen. Fortunately we had a thick smoke screen put down for the final infantry/tank assault and were not only surprised but fortunate to overrun six anti-tank guns before the remainder of the garrison surrendered.

The division bypassed Bremen and by the beginning of May had reached Hamburg where the 1/5 Queens was selected to be the first Allied troops to enter the city when it was surrendered on 3 May by the Mayor of Hamburg accompanied by the Army general commanding the area.[45]

During the advance of the 7th Armoured Division a CANLOAN officer, CDN/414, Lieut. Clarence Heald, a platoon commander in 2 Devon died of wounds on 31 March 1945. Heald had served in Normandy with 1 R. Hamps. in the 50th Division and had been wounded on 31 July. He joined 2 Devon at the end of November when that battalion was transferred to the 7th Armoured Division. A former officer in 2 Devon, Capt W.E. Wills, who at the time was a company sergeant-major, recalls that Heald was respected for his conduct under fire and that his platoon sergeant had said, "Mr Heald led from the front and was a man." Another fellow officer recalls, "He had, to our ears, a very pleasant accent ... and I can remember being in his company when someone said to him: 'Just talk and we will listen.'"[46]

In the advance towards the Elbe the 43rd Division was on the left flank. This meant that it re-entered and liberated part of Holland before continuing the general advance into Germany with its apprehensive, sullen, and hostile population. The most spectacular reception was at the liberation of the city of Hengelo, where, as the divisional history observes, "the enthusiastic welcome of their liberators passed all bounds,"[47] but similar welcomes occurred in every town and village, of which the following is an example:

I got my lads to dig in, though it was hardly necessary, and then, since we were likely to move at midnight, tried to get the lads to sleep in the loft of the barn except for sentries. But it was impossible. The Dutch family in the house were overjoyed at being liberated. There were two or three nuns in the house and when I returned from Coy HQ I found the Dutch – boys, girls, even old men and women as well as the nuns with British troops of all ranks hand in hand dancing in a ring and singing Dutch and English songs. I have rarely if ever seen such pure delight as was shown by these Dutch people.[48]

The most ambitious task of the 43rd Division – which it shared with the 3rd, 51st, 52nd, and 53rd Divisions – was the capture of Bremen, and it was here that the two final MCs of the war by CANLOAN officers were earned. The first, on 18 April, was a bar to the MC that had been awarded in Normandy to Lieut. Gordon Wright, 4 SLI, 43rd Division:

During the afternoon of 19 Apr Lieut Wright led a fighting patrol to find out whether the village of Uhlhorn south of Bremen was occupied by the enemy ... About 400 yards from the objective it was decided to take advantage of the cover of a road block to cross to the other side of the road ... The leading section had crossed over and the second one was halfway across when without warning simultaneous fire was opened from automatics to the front and rear and from a 20 mm gun on the right flank firing bursts. The patrol thus divided was almost impossible to control. Lieut Wright, without regard to his own safety, crossed and recrossed the road several times under fire and succeeded in reorganizing the platoon. He was able to effect the withdrawal in good order and without loss while he himself remained behind to the last with a Bren gun to cover them. Lieut Wright was wounded for the second time.[49]

A few days later another CANLOAN officer, Capt. Maurice Carter, 2 Seaforth, 51st Division, earned the MC when leading a patrol. The citation describes the ferocious enemy opposition that was typical of small local actions at that late stage of the war:

On 22 Apr the Bn was ordered to reconnoitre the village of Ganderkesee with a view to occupying it if it was not held. Capt Carter with a section of carriers was allotted this task. He approached the village and went forward with a patrol of 6 men on foot. When fired on by an MG post they dealt with it, killing one man and capturing another. Proceeding further the patrol assaulted another post, capturing 9 more enemy paratroopers. The patrol then came under heavy fire from both flanks and had to go to ground.

At this time the Bn was ordered to attack the village and a message was sent to Capt Carter to hold on where he was and to contain the enemy until a relieving force could come to him. This he did.

The enemy then became extremely offensive and 40 of them formed up and attacked Capt Carter's patrol of 6. The enemy rushed the post from two sides, screaming and firing as they came on. Two of his three Bren guns were knocked out and his post surrounded but the patrol stuck to its post, killed 7 of the attackers and eventually drove the enemy off. In this encounter Capt Carter and the NCO were wounded and one man killed. Of the 10 POW all except 3 escaped in the melee and rejoined the enemy. Undeterred Capt Carter personally gave chase after them in the face of determined and well directed fire, but his painful wound and the weight of opposition drove him back to his base where the patrol stuck to their remaining LMG, resisted further sorties by the enemy and inflicted further casualties.

When relieved by a company with tank support Capt Carter had his wounds dressed but although in considerable pain resumed command of his Carrier Platoon for the remainder of the action. The truly magnificent display by this officer and the resolution with which he carried out his task of containing a very active and fanatical enemy paratroop force led to the ultimate success of the Bn attack.[50]

In mid-April four CANLOAN officers in four different divisions were killed in four days. On 14 April Maj. Joseph Hemelryk of 1 HLI, 53rd Division, who had so recently earned the MC in the Rhineland, was killed in action. Two days later, on 16 April, Lieut. John Laurie, 1 R. Norfolk, 3rd Division, was killed in action, and CDN/ 304, Lieut. Eldon B. Mann, 6 RSF, 15th Scottish Division, died of wounds in hospital. Like Major Hemelryk, John Laurie had very recently been awarded the MC during the Battle of the Rhineland.

Eldon Mann was one of the remarkably great number of CANLOAN officers from

Prince Edward Island. After joining CANLOAN he was posted to 6 RSF, which he joined on 26 June, the first day of the Battle of the Scottish Corridor in Normandy. He was wounded four days later but was released from hospital in the United Kingdom in time to rejoin his battalion in August. Wounded for the second time on 27 March, after the crossing of the Rhine, he was sent to British and Canadian hospitals but died on 16 April. Earlier he had been awarded a Mention in Dispatches for gallantry.

The last fatal CANLOAN casualty of the war occurred on 17 April when CDN/80, Capt. John R. Harrison, 7 A. & S.H., 51st Division, was killed in action. He had served overseas 1940–43 with the Calgary Highlanders before returning to Canada for a commission. In CANLOAN he had gone to Normandy with 7 A. & S.H. and served continuously with them as commander of the carrier platoon until his death, so near the end of the war.

Another carrier platoon commander, Capt. Hank Henry of 4 KSLI in the 11th Armoured Division, continued to maintain the dashing image often associated with CANLOAN officers. A fellow officer in 4 KSLI reports:

In the final phase of the campaign in Germany during the advance on Osnabruck – a daring night attack in pouring rain on 2/3 Apr – Hank's own carrier was bazookered, much to his irritation. In the advance on Uelzen, 17 Apr, his platoon, with its three Vickers MGs and flame throwers were employed continuously in a variety of roles never contemplated in peacetime.[51]

Henry's exploits were recognized by a Commander-in-Chief's (C. in C.) Certificate to add to his Normandy MID.

The same award and a GOC certificate were earned by a CANLOAN officer in the 3rd Division, Lieut. Rex Fendick, 2 MX. As commander of a machine-gun platoon since shortly after D-Day, Fendick had consistently demonstrated leadership, competence, and daring. Fendick's companion, before, during and after CANLOAN, was Lieut. Francis "Conk" McConaghy, a platoon commander and company second in command in 2 MX. He created a minor furore in the last campaign near Lingen when he undertook an "unauthorized foray" to take German prisoners. After being missing for several hours he returned unscathed.

Among the honours awarded at this time was a second MID for Vince Lilley to add to his other MID for Normandy and MC for the Maas.

A notable CANLOAN event in the 51st Highland Division was the presentation by Field Marshal Montgomery of no fewer than five Military Crosses at the same ceremony to CANLOAN officers: Mo Carter, 2 Seaforth; Dick Coates, 1 BW; Robert (Bob) Gelston, 7 BW; Rod Mackay, 2 Seaforth; and Bill Mitchell, 1 BW.

As was observed earlier, many CANLOAN officers made determined if not desperate efforts to return to units in action, often to suffer additional wounds or death. Another of those was CDN/183, Lieut. Don J. Oland, 2 R. Warwick., 3rd Division. Though wounded in Normandy, he managed to return to his battalion and played an active part in the advance towards Bremen, capturing, for example, several prisoners in an attack at the Ems Canal on 10 April. Finally, near Bremen, he was wounded again and had to have a leg amputated.

A happier conclusion awaited Alex Cunningham, 4 KSLI, who had been wounded in his first attacks in both Normandy and the Rhineland. On being released from a hospital in Brussels, he hitched a ride back to 4 KSLI, arriving just in time for their assault on the bridge at the Dortmund-Ems Canal. After surviving this attack, Cunningham was promoted to captain in mid-April and given command of a company.

An interesting feature of the advance of the British Army deep into Germany was the capture or liberation of concentration and POW camps. An example is the liberation on 30 April of the notorious concentration camp of Sandbostel by 1 Gren. Gds., which then included three CANLOAN officers – Lieuts. Thomas Birchall, Frederick Burd, and Richard Chard. During the advance on the camp, which involved a river crossing, the walls of the camp were lined with inmates cheering on the Guards, who later released 30,000 prisoners. The following account was published years later in the *Canloan Review*:

> The war was nearly over. The Germans had gone and British troops of the Guards Armoured were in sight. The gates of the prison camp burst open and the inmates yelled and ran to meet their liberators. In the lead was Major John Foote, VC, the devoted Canadian padre who had remained with the wounded at Dieppe. He advanced to meet the efficient Gren Gds officer who was leading his platoon to them. His joy was mixed with amazement when he discovered that this officer was none other than Lieut Dick Chard, a boyhood friend from the same home town, Madoc, Ontario.[52]

More spectacular was the liberation of the Bergen Belsen concentration camp by the 11th Armoured Division. The following is one of many descriptions of the camp:

> No picture or words can ever adequately portray the horror of what I saw, of the 40,000 or 60,000 political prisoners of all nationalities. One could only hope for a quick death for the majority. The awful cloying stench of death was everywhere. There were piles of dead bodies, mere bags of bones from years of systematic starvation, but worst of all was the animal look and habits of so many of the prisoners still alive. All spark of human intellect seemed to have departed. The haunting memory of it will be with me till my dying day.[53]

A similar impact was made on the CANLOAN officers who observed the camp, including Leo Heaps, who was among the first to see it, and the CANLOAN officers in 4 Wilts., 43rd Division, whose battalion headquarters was in Belsen during the spring and summer of 1945.

By mid-April it was apparent to all that the war in Europe was nearing the end, and a new feeling of apprehension could be noted as the troops mentally promised themselves that they would try not to get killed at that stage of the war. One occasionally heard soldiers say, and officers read in the letters they censored, that they had no ambition to be the last soldier to be killed in the Second World War.

And soon it really was over. Probably every CANLOAN officer who was still in northwest Europe remembers what they were doing when the news of the armistice came – more often than not from signallers who picked up bootlegged messages over wireless sets. In many cases officers had been briefed for attacks the next day and some were actually on the way to a start line. Confirmation came on the evening of 4 May, when all units received the message: "All hostilities will cease at 0800 hours tomorrow morning 5 May."[54] On that day the surrender took place and the war in Europe officially ended.

The reaction to the end of the war in Europe by CANLOAN officers and their comrades in arms was not wild excitement. It ranged from Vince Lilley's succinct "went to sleep for 24 hours" to remarks overheard by Rex Fendick: "Well, I made it" and "Will I be sent to the Pacific now?" to more contemplative remarks such as the following:

> So that's it. 2" mortar flares, tracer, etc were fired into the air, a bit of shouting was heard, but on the whole everybody took the news very calmly. It was difficult to realize in a flash that the war was really over. No more barrages, attacks, digging in, moaning Minnies or Spandaus, no more night patrols or sniper bullets. Those who had survived had got themselves gradually adjusted to war and we couldn't change in a moment or realize just what peace meant. And when we did, any joy was more than balanced by the thought of all our "mates" who had given their lives to make peace and victory possible.[55]

12

The Irish Fusiliers
in Italy

THE FOUR CANLOAN infantry officers who served in the Italian campaign 1944–45 were unique in being the only exceptions to the policy that CANLOAN infantry officers were to be posted only to units in northwest Europe so that they would be available if needed by the Canadian Army. (As noted elsewhere there were also RCOC officers in Italy.) These four officers all came from the same Canadian regiment, the Irish Fusiliers (Vancouver Regiment), and all went to the same British regiment, which was affiliated with their Canadian regiment. The 1st Battalion, the Royal Irish Fusiliers (R. Ir. Fus.), was part of the Irish Brigade of the 78th (Battleaxe) Division, which had been in the British First, Fifth, and Eighth Armies in North Africa and Italy.

The four CANLOAN officers who were posted to 1 R. Ir. Fus. were serving in different Canadian units when they volunteered for CANLOAN, but all had served together in 1942 and 1943 in the 3rd Battalion, the Irish Fusiliers, when it was commanded by one of them, Lieut.-Col. Maurice Crehan.

Maurice Crehan had been born in Vancouver and had established a career in that city. When war was declared in 1939 he was 30 years old and married, a successful chartered accountant, and had had extensive experience as a militia officer. In September 1939, shortly after 1 Ir. Fus., a local regiment of the non-permanent active militia (NPAM), had been mobilized, he was enrolled as a major. When the 3rd Battalion was formed in June 1942 Crehan became its CO and took it to Vernon, British Columbia, where it was part of the 19th Infantry Brigade of the 6th Division.

Crehan retained command of the battalion until it was disbanded in August 1943. The impression made by Lieutenant-Colonel Crehan when the 19th Brigade was at Sarcee Camp near Calgary in the summer of 1943 is described by Reg Shelford, who was responsible for supply for the brigade and who later became a CANLOAN ordnance officer:

The CO [of the Irish Fusiliers] was Maurice Crehan, a real gung-ho man who was not satisfied that his unit was the best in the brigade; it was to be the best in the whole Army. When he received his rifles he blew up and sent a steaming telegram to Ottawa, stating that his unit was on active service and should not have been issued drill rifles. It became my job to explain to him that the painted red band around them did not make them drill rifles (that was a white band) but indicated that they were serviceable American rifles that used .30 ammunition and that the boxes of ammunition accompanying them also had the red band around them.[1]

Francis Augustus (Gus) Lefever had also grown up in Vancouver and was employed by a brokerage firm in the 1930s while working his way up in the Irish Fusiliers from signaller to pay sergeant before the battalion was mobilized on 26 August 1939. After service at Defence Headquarters and promotion to WO I he went, at the urging of Lieutenant-Colonel Crehan, to OTC at Gordon Head for a commission, obtained his second pip at Currie Barracks in Calgary, and returned to 3 Ir. Fus., initially as paymaster.

John A. (Jack) Chambers was born in Vancouver but lived in Winnipeg from 1925 to 1937 before returning to Vancouver, where he became a partner in a hardware company and in 1939 joined the 2nd (Militia) Battalion, the Irish Fusiliers, where he served as intelligence sergeant before qualifying for a commission. When 3 Ir. Fus. was formed in June 1942, Chambers transferred to it as a provisional second lieutenant. After officer training at Currie Barracks and an anti-tank course at Shilo, Manitoba, he was promoted to acting captain.

Alastair (Al) McLennan, another native of Vancouver, had attended the University of British Columbia and had been employed in the distilling industry before enlisting as a private at A-10 Training Centre in Vernon. Before approaching the Army, he had applied for the motor torpedo boat division of the RCN and the crash boat division of the RCAF. He joined 3 Ir. Fus. in August 1942 as a provisional second lieutenant and was acting OC of HQ Company when the battalion was broken up for reinforcements a year later.

When that happened, Lieutenant-Colonel Crehan was posted to NDHQ in Ottawa, where his boss was a loyal British Columbian, Maj.-Gen. Harry F.G. Letson, Adjutant-General and initiator of the CANLOAN scheme. Chambers, Lefever, and McLennan were posted to another battalion in the 19th Brigade at Vernon, the Prince Albert Volunteers (PA Vols.), which was stationed successively at Wainwright, Otter Point, Terrace, and Nanaimo. Chambers and Lefever attended a mountain warfare course near Terrace, British Columbia, in January 1944 and were kept on as instructors. McLennan went on the same course in February but was recalled to participate in the CANLOAN scheme.

There is no doubt that the three officers – Chambers, Lefever, and McLennan – would have volunteered for CANLOAN as a means of getting overseas if they had had an opportunity. It was not necessary, however, since their former CO, Maurice Crehan, who having learned about the scheme at the outset at his strategic location at NDHQ, jumped at the chance to get overseas himself, willingly reverted from colonel to captain in order to be accepted, and decided to share the good fortune with former officers of his old regiment. Before the notice about the CANLOAN scheme was received by the PA Vols., Chambers, Lefever, and McLennan received orders to report to A-34 SOTC, Camp Sussex.

The perpetrator of the plot to transfer officers from the Canadian Irish Fusiliers to their affiliated British regiment has been described by Jack Chambers:

> Maurice Crehan was a big man, about 6 ft 2 tall, broad and naturally heavy. But at the time he was appointed to command the 3rd Irish (VR) and we went to Sarcee Camp, Maurice was immense. He must have weighed 260 or 270 lbs. So he put himself on a diet – coffee, no cream or sugar; toast, no butter or jam; no bacon, no potatoes, no desserts – and Maurice loved chocolate and sweets of all kinds. Add to this, wherever we went for our early morning TEWT we went by truck but Maurice met us there, having run from the camp, and he ran back when we were finished. If there was a rugby game Maurice was in it; any marches, he was in them. I think we can all remember when, at Vernon, with his skin hanging like under-inflated balloons, Maurice hit the 200 lb target. It didn't stop there: he went on down to about 180 lbs and persevered until the sag was gone, his skin was tight and looked as though it belonged to him. When the unit was broken up in 1943 Maurice went to Ottawa while Gus, Al and I wound up with the PA Vols and it must have been Maurice who tipped us off to the CANLOAN operation. In any case the four of us wound up in Sussex (Maurice having reverted from Col to Capt for the purpose).[2]

The four ex-Irish Fusiliers officers travelled to the United Kingdom in two pairs. CDN/121, Capt. Maurice J. Crehan and CDN/178, Lieut. Alastair A.H. McLennan were in the third flight on the *Cavina*; CDN/532, Lieut. John A. Chambers and Lieut. Gus Lefever were in the fifth flight on the *Empress of Scotland*. In the allocation of officers to regiments Crehan and McLennan were informed that they could not join 1 R. Ir. Fus. because the battalion was in Italy – beyond the scope of the CANLOAN scheme. Instead they were posted to 5 R. Ir. Fus., which was redesignated the 2nd Battalion to replace the battalion that had been virtually eliminated in the battle for the island of Leros in November 1943. They discovered, however, that the new 2nd Battalion was to serve as a reinforcement unit for 21 Army Group in Normandy and would not go into action as a battalion. So Crehan obtained a posting back to London, where he entered into discussions with the most senior officers at the War Office and CMHQ. As Al McLennan put it, "After Crehan's machinations with the Adjutant General, Sir Ronald Adam, with, no doubt, great help from Maj Gen Letson, he rescued Lefever and Chambers from the Ulster Rifles and we joined up at the Marylebone Station Hotel."[3]

On arriving in the United Kingdom and being informed that 1 R. Ir. Fus. were off limits, Chambers and Lefever had chosen another Irish unit, a battalion of the Royal Ulster Rifles (RUR) and found, when they arrived at Bulford with five other CANLOAN officers, that it was part of the 6th Airborne Division. They were issued with red berets and airborne and glider patches and were about to begin a program of "para jumps and glider hops" when orders came for them to report to London en route to 1 R. Ir. Fus. in Italy. Chambers said, "I never inquired how this was achieved; I just assumed that Maurice knew all the strings to pull and buttons to push to get the four of us transferred to 1 Bn R Ir Fus."[4]

The CO of the Ulsters offered to fight the transfer, but the Canadians, partly welcoming the opportunity to join their affiliated regiment, partly resigned to the idea that Maurice would prevail in the end, declined the offer. The four sailed with a convoy assembled in the Firth of Forth and docked at Naples on 22 June. With three Inniskilling officers, they set off in a 15-cwt. to look for the 78th Division, rejecting offers to join the Coldstream Guards on the way. When they at last found the 78th Division, they learned that it was to move south out of the line, first to Tivoli – with visits to Rome – and then to Taranto, whence it would sail to Egypt for rest and training.

The 78th (Battleaxe) Division was created in June 1942 and sent as part of the First Army to take part with American troops in the Allied landing in North Africa. From the landing in Algiers in November to the capture of Tunis six months later, the division was engaged in fierce fighting and endured heavy losses. In March 1943 its 1st Guards Brigade was replaced by the 38th (Irish) Brigade, consisting of the 6th (later the 2nd) Battalion, the Royal Inniskilling Fusiliers (R. Innisks.)(the Skins), 1 R. Ir. Fus. (the Faughs), and the 2nd Battalion, the London Irish Rifles. This brigade arrived in the division in time for a series of attacks in April, after which the Army Commander said, "The 78th Division deserves the highest praise for as tough and prolonged bit of fighting as has ever been undertaken by the British soldier."[5]

In Sicily the 78th Division was in XXX Corps of the Eighth Army with the 1st Canadian Division and the 51st Highland Division. In Italy the division had advanced up the east coast as far as Termoli. In an attack by the Irish Brigade at San Salvo on 27–28 October 1943 the R. Ir. Fus. had lost their CO and their two leading company commanders (all killed) and all the leading platoon commanders, killed or wounded.[6] After the long winter, with the crossing of the Sangro, the move westward to Cassino, and the spring assaults on the Gustav and Hitler lines, the 78th Division was due for a rest and an opportunity to absorb reinforcements. The Irish Brigade, however, had managed the traditional enthusiastic celebrations of Barossa Day on 5 March and St. Patrick's Day on the 17th, and when relieved at the front put on an impressive performance of massed pipes and drums in Rome.

When the division sailed from Taranto, Crehan and Chambers were ill with malaria and after they arrived at the rest camp at Qassasin in Egypt spent two weeks in hospital. After being released and having had a brief opportunity to enjoy the comfort and pleasures of the leave centres and visits to Cairo and Alexandria, Crehan was hospitalized again with a burst eardrum but rejoined his unit in time to return with the division to Italy.

When the four Canadians joined 1 R. Ir. Fus. two of them had been assigned to B Company – Crehan, restored to the rank of major, as OC, and McLennan as a platoon commander. The other two went to A Company, Chambers, a captain, as second in command, and Lefever as a platoon commander. This disposition was changed in Egypt. Crehan and McLennan went to A Company and the CO, Lieutenant-Colonel Horsfall, asked Lefever to go to HQ Company as commander of the pioneer platoon and Chambers to Battalion HQ as intelligence officer (IO). These CANLOAN officers became immersed in their new duties at once. Lefever attended a school of engineering in Egypt and, after arriving in Italy, another engineering school at Capua to study mines and booby traps. Chambers attended lectures related to intelligence, such as photo interpretation and security, and constructed sand models of Italian battle zones.

The 78th Division arrived back in Italy on 15 September and moved up to the front in the Gothic Line in the northern Appenines. On 4 October it was transferred from V Corps in the British Eighth Army to the British XII Corps in the American Fifth Army. General Alexander said that in an effort to break through the steep mountains and gorges, he was sending the 78th Division: "It is my last remaining fully fresh division."[7]

The Irish Brigade relieved the US 351st Infantry Regiment in terrain described as "enormous precipices of slippery grey mud with slopes up to 300 feet high defended by strong enemy forces with elements of seven divisions."[8] After nearly two weeks of indecisive attacks on particular positions, the R. Ir. Fus. made a night attack towards Mount Spaduro, the predominant feature in the area, as described in the divisional history:

> The Irish Fusiliers attacked at nightfall towards Monte Spaduro. A Coy led in the darkness followed by B Coy. An hour later A Coy had a foothold on 387 ridge having taken the enemy by surprise. They soon overcame the opposition there and a number of Germans were killed or taken prisoner. B Coy then passed through and attacked towards point 396, the peak of Monte Spaduro. By dawn the battalion had attacked and captured the height. However, as the mist lifted the enemy machine guns opened up and at six o'clock a strong counter-attack came in against both companies. Casa Spinello, which the Irish Fusiliers had by-passed during the night, turned out to be strongly held by the enemy. The Irishmen fought stubbornly but they were out-numbered; when they ran out of ammunition they flung rocks at the advancing Germans, battered at them with rifle butts or grappled with their bare hands. Only a few got back from each company. The bare rocky hillsides were littered with dead from both sides; forty Fusiliers were taken prisoner, and Major Crehan, commanding A Coy, was found on the battlefield in the middle of a litter of German and Irish dead, all riddled with bullets. A smoke screen had to be put down at midday so that C Coy, which had been trying to go forward to help, could be withdrawn to safety.[9]

A similar account is contained in a letter to Al McLennan's mother from Lieut.-Col. J.H.C. Horsfall, CO of 1 R. Ir. Fus., who began by saying that Al was missing and that he was "desperately sorry to have to tell you that we couldn't look after him better for you. We all loved Al as did his platoon, although he had been with us only a short time." He continued:

> Al was lost in one of the most gallant actions ever fought by any part of our regiment. Al, with Maurice Crehan and A Company, had the task of capturing an important hill feature on the night of the 19th. Reports showed it to be weakly held. The attack went brilliantly and the objective was taken by midnight, a lot of Germans being taken and many more killed. The enemy were, however, in great strength, in fact they had a relief on that night so there were twice as many present as there would otherwise have been. Although A Company cleared the axis of the attack the enemy closed in on their flanks and behind, and at first light on the 20th launched a very heavy counter-attack. Maurice, Al and their boys put up a magnificent resistance but were overcome after fighting for two hours until their ammunition was exhausted. The German losses were very heavy. The Hill has since

been retaken. Maurice and many of his boys were found dead behind their weapons and also a very large number of Germans in and around their positions.[10]

It was very difficult for comrades to have to watch the counter-attack without being able to intervene. Jack Chambers and his sergeant were able, with binoculars, to identify Al McLennan because of a bandage on his neck. And McLennan, who was on the spot and now a prisoner, saw Maurice Crehan slumped in a slit trench. He did not know that Crehan had been killed (probably by a machine-gun burst in the throat) until after he was released from POW camp at the end of the war.

Maurice Crehan's widow received a letter from Maj.-Gen. P.J. Montague, CMHQ, London, in which he said that her husband's contacts with Sir Ronald Adam and himself "left a very deep impression and we considered him the finest type of officer." He enclosed a copy of a letter he had received from Lieut.-Gen. Sir Ronald Adam, AG, at the War Office:

I have just heard that Major Crehan has been killed whilst serving with the 1st Royal Irish Fusiliers in Italy. If you remember, we had some correspondence about him a few months back and I was very much impressed with him when I saw him here. I have also since had a letter from him.

It was a magnificent gesture on his part to give up his job and rank in Canada in order to fight with the British Army. I hope it may be possible to convey to his next of kin the British Army's appreciation of his action and of the great work he did under the CANLOAN scheme.[11]

By December 1944 the 15th Army Group, consisting of the Fifth (US) and the Eighth (Br.) Armies, had advanced 600 miles since their landing in Italy in September 1943 and had formed a front line along the Senio River in the plain of Lombardy. The winter campaign from January to April was a period of uncomfortable, bitter, static warfare that resembled campaigns on the Western Front in northwest Europe in the First World War.

The two remaining CANLOAN officers in 1 R. Ir. Fus. are remembered by Colonel P.C. Trousdell, who was a platoon commander at the time. He has reported that "Jack Chambers was very painstaking and dedicated as Bn Intelligence Officer." He was fully occupied by an active program of patrols and raids and was eventually promoted to major.

Colonel Trousdell recalls Gus Lefever as an energetic pioneer platoon commander:

Whatever task he was given he carried out with cheerful enthusiasm. Whether it was repairing the tracks leading to our positions in the mountains (the mud was appalling) or preparing some fiendish explosive device to hurl at the enemy when we were at close range with each other as on the River Senio flood banks in the Spring of 1945, Gus, with a large grin, would be in the centre of activity.[12]

Lefever's leadership was recognized by the award of a Mention in Dispatches.

Lefever and Chambers spent a pleasant leave in Rome, Naples, and Pisa in January, enjoyed the celebration of St. Patrick's Day, an important date in the calendar of the Irish Brigade, and contributed to hilarious pranks on 1 April. They were impressed with the speed of advances in the last stages of the campaign in Italy, which ended with the official cease-fire on 2 May 1945. Since 6 June 1944, when the Allies landed in Normandy, the soldiers in the Eighth Army in Italy had felt that they were not getting the recognition they deserved. This sentiment is expressed in the refrain to a popular Eighth Army song: "We are the D-Day Dodgers, in sunny Italy." The few CANLOAN officers had reason to feel especially neglected when the Canadian formations in Italy, chiefly the 1st and 5th Divisions, left to join the rest of the Canadian Army – the 2nd, 3rd, and 4th Divisions – in the Netherlands in the spring of 1945.

Jack Chambers has described the activities of 1 R. Ir. Fus. immediately after the cease-fire:

> We moved to Austria on 10 May and on the 11th we disarmed and transported to prepared camps 1200 SS troops and 130 civilians from an armoured train near San Andras ... On the 12th near Lavamond we accepted the surrender and gave safe passage to 4000 Cossacks and 3000 horses. They abandoned their mountain stronghold, leaving their weapons behind, only because we guaranteed safe passage from their positions in Yugoslavia.[13]

In view of the recent controversy concerning these troops the note on the subject in the history of the 78th Division is of particular interest: "The handing over to the Russians of 15,000 in the Cossacks and Caucasian divisions on 23 May was a distasteful task in view of their probable fate. At that time the 78th Division was feeding and looking after 120,000 surrendered personnel, military and civilian."[14]

On 6 July the 78th Division held its ceremonial victory parade. The whole division paraded before the army commander, and prominence was given to the pipes and drums of the Irish Brigade and the Argyll and Sutherland Highlanders.

On 15 October the CANLOAN officers received orders to report to a transit camp in Milan as the first stage in the journey to No. 1 Canadian Repatriation Depot in England. The round of farewell dinners and parties was so extensive that the Canadians felt that if they had not got away when they did they might not have survived. On the eve of their departure for Canada, Chambers and Lefever were separated at last. Chambers was designated as OC troops on an aircraft carrier on which 10 returning officers and 47 ORs had been fitted in. Lefever sailed home through the Panama Canal with 18 other passengers.

Meanwhile, Al McLennan's POW camp had been liberated by American troops just before VE-Day; he had been flown to the UK and after a brief convalescence sailed to Halifax on the *Neue Amsterdam*. After debarkation leave he attempted to join the Canadian Army Pacific Force with a view to transferring later to the 1st R. Ir. Fus., which was expected to be sent to the Far East. He was prevented from doing so by a reduction in his PULHEMS to L4 and, of course, the end of the war.

Sticking together and loyal to the Irish Fusiliers to the end, the three surviving CANLOAN Irish Fusiliers – Jack Chambers, Gus Lefever, and Al McLennan – all rejoined the Irish Fusiliers in Vancouver in 1946 and served in the battalion until 1958, when they retired, Chambers and Lefever as majors and McLennan as a lieutenant-colonel and commanding officer.

13

The CANLOAN POWs

OF THE 623 CANLOAN infantry officers, only 32 were captured, more than half of them in the final stages of the Battle of Arnhem. As noted earlier, these were almost all the surviving CANLOAN officers in the Airlanding Brigade of the 1st Airborne Division who had been wounded or overrun and were unable to escape across the Rhine. To their numbers – eight in 7 KOSB, six in 2 S. Staffords., and two in 1 Border – should be added Lieutenant Leo Heaps, MC, 1 Para., who was captured at Arnhem but quickly escaped, and Capt. Tom King of 4 Dorset, 43rd Division, who was captured while trying to help the 1st Airborne Division escape from Arnhem.

The remaining 14 CANLOAN POWs were from 13 different battalions in nine different divisions. They were captured, usually one at a time, over a period of ten months, from June 1944 to March 1945. Though their numbers were small, they had taken part in nearly all the most crucial battles in Western Europe in the last year of the war.

CDN/486, Lieut. George Marrs, 1 R. Hamps., was engaged in the bitter struggle waged by the 50th Division in the Hottot region in Normandy for more than a month after D-Day. He joined 1 R. Hamps. on 14 June and was a platoon commander when he was reported missing after an attack at Hottot on 19 June.

Lieut. Clifton Cassady and Lieut. J. Ed Davies were involved in the battle of the Scottish Corridor near the end of June. They had gone to Normandy with the 11th Armoured Division as platoon commanders in C Company of 3 Mons. As was reported earlier, this company was dropped off at Colleville on the night of 27 June before proceeding to the crossing of the Odon. In a heavy German attack at dawn the company was overrun in "Death Orchard," and in the ensuing fight it virtually ceased to exist. Many were killed and wounded; Lieutenants Cassady and Davies and 61 other ranks were reported missing presumed captured.

CDN/286, Lieut. Charles Ambery was captured during the bloody battles at Hill 112 in Normandy. He had joined 4 Dorset on 4 May and had gone to Normandy with the 43rd Division. After the attack on 10 July, in which the battalion suffered severe losses at Maltot, Ambery was reported missing.

CDN/462, Lieut. Maurice C. Joynt and CDN/404, Capt. Joseph O. "Blackie" Plouffe participated in the severe fighting of the 53rd Division near the Odon and Évrecy around the end of July when repeated attacks and fighting patrols were accompanied by heavy casualties. Captain Plouffe was a platoon commander in 1/5 Welch (the only CANLOAN officer in that battalion). Lieutenant Joynt, in 7 RWF, was one of two platoon commanders reported missing after a battle in which 100 other ranks were killed and 98 reported missing.

Another CANLOAN officer captured at this time was CDN/268, Lieut. Donald Gatenby, 1 E. Lan. R. He was active in the fighting in Normandy in which three CANLOAN officers in his battalion were killed in a period of two weeks in July.

The three CANLOAN officers from the 53rd Division were all captured during the week 16–23 July 1944.

CDN/288, Lieut. Floyd "Ding" Bell was one of three CANLOAN officers in 7 R. Norfolk of the 59th Division, which suffered such heavy losses in its three major battles in Normandy, particularly that of the Orne bridgehead. Bell was reported missing on 7 August, the first day of the bridgehead battle. The other two, Donald Smith and Andrew Bushell, were killed in action.

Lieut. John Surtees served the shortest period of confinement as a POW. Posted to 1/6 Queens in April 1944, he went to Normandy with the 7th Armoured Division. Wounded and taken prisoner on 5 August in the early stages of operation BLUECOAT, he was first reported missing. He was taken to Paris and operated on there and then transferred to a prison hospital near the French-German border. Here he was liberated by the US Army on 3 September, less than a month after he was captured. After being released from a hospital in England and convalescing in Northern Ireland, he rejoined the 7th Armoured Division in January 1945 and served with 1/5 Queens in the Rhineland and subsequent campaigns and in the Berlin garrison after VE-Day.

Lieut. Eric Fryer served in 1 S. Lan. R. in the 3rd Division and was captured at the Escaut Canal in September. The story of how his platoon was met by machine-gun fire while making an assault crossing of the canal has been related earlier.

Lieut. Alastair McLennan of 1 R. Ir. Fus. was wounded and captured in a counter-attack at Monte Spaduro in Italy on 20 October 1944, as was reported in chapter 12.

Capt. Philip Bordinat, 2 Oxf. Bucks., was one of the American citizens who volunteered for the Canadian Army to get into the war and then for CANLOAN to get overseas. In January 1945, he was sent on a two-man night reconnaissance patrol across the Maas River. At dawn he and the sergeant with him did not appear at the rendezvous with the pickup boat and the next day they were taken prisoner. After being liberated by American troops in southern Germany, Captain Bordinat was sent to the United States, returned to Canada, and then sent back to rejoin his unit in the UK in July 1945, ready to go to the Far East. In fact, he went to Palestine and stayed with the Oxf. Bucks. until 1946.

As was noted earlier, all the CANLOAN officers who were in the Battle of Arnhem, with the exception of Philip Turner and Alex Harvie of 2 S. Staffords., were either killed or captured. This included eight in 7 KOSB: CDN/136, Lieut. Donald A. Cameron; Lieut. Erskine Carter; CDN/482, Lieut. Lawrence Kane; Lieut. Martin Kaufman; CDN/177, Lieut. G. Smith Macdonald; Lieut. Peter Mason; CDN/465, Capt. James F. McCourt; and Lieut. James Taylor.

There were six in 2 S. Staffords.: CDN/434, Lieut. Albert E. Boustead; Lieut. James Erskine; CDN/455, Lieut. Arthur R. Godfrey; CDN/637, Lieut. John J. MacDonald; CDN/645, Lieut. Carlisle Norwood; and CDN/200, Lieut. Kenneth Taylor. The last two were from 1 Border: Lieut. Clifford Aasen and Lieut. George Comper.

Lieut. Leo Heaps was captured at Arnhem but since he escaped while being transported to a POW camp, he was only technically a prisoner of war.

One CANLOAN officer avoided capture at Arnhem. CDN/646, Lieut. Frank F. Palen had been posted to 2 S. Staffords. on 8 August 1944, a little more than a month before he landed at Arnhem with that battalion. He was severely wounded but was hidden by a Dutch family until he was fit to travel. He managed to get back to England where he joined 12 (Yorkshire) Parachute Battalion in the 6th Airborne Division less than two weeks before the airborne landing across the Rhine on 24 March 1945. In this operation Palen was wounded, and this time he was captured. Liberated three weeks later while still receiving medical treatment, he was returned to Canada 7 June 1945.

The last CANLOAN POW was CDN/376, Lieut. Leo Robillard, 1 RUR, in the 6th Airborne Division. He was captured on 2 April 1945 after the division's successful landing over the Rhine and during its subsequent drive towards the Baltic Sea.

A legitimate complaint of prisoners of war was the long time that it took to notify their families that they were POWs and hence alive, rather than missing. For CANLOAN officers it was necessary for their German captors to notify the Red Cross and for the Red Cross to notify the British War Office, which would notify CMHQ, which would finally notify the officer's next of kin. That often took an inordinately long time. When the six-month report on the CANLOAN scheme was prepared by CHMQ with statistics up to the end of October 1944 (by which time at least 25 CANLOAN officers were in POW camps), it reported only six CANLOAN prisoners of war but 30 missing. In fact, many who were listed as missing were POWs and others had been killed in action long before. For example, Ernest Cockburn and David Edwards, who had been killed in Normandy in June, were still listed as missing in December. Willard Caseley and Malcolm Rose, who had been killed on the same day in early August 1944, were still listed as missing in February 1945; and Richard Wilson, who had been killed in October, was listed as missing in April 1945. Most of the CANLOAN officers who were captured at Arnhem in September were reported as POWs in December. It is no wonder that Major MacLaren at CMHQ was anxious to interview Philip Turner, when he returned from Arnhem, about other missing CANLOAN officers.[1]

The journey from battlefield to POW camp was often long and tortuous. Such a journey, reported in a journal by Cliff Cassady, had the following stages:

27 Jun   Captured near Caen by 21 Pz Division.
28   Interrogated twice and arrived at first POW assembly point.

1	Jul	Arrived at Falaise.
3		Moved to Alençon.
7		Moved to Chartres.
15		Left Chartres via truck to Paris. Box cars from there.
16		Arrived at Rheims, from there to Chalons by bus.
27		Placed in solitary awaiting interrogation.
31		Interrogated.
1	Aug	Released from solitary. Half an English Red Cross parcel.
5		Left Chalons by box car.
9		Arrived at Triers. Canadian Red Cross parcel.
31		Br and Cdn Army officers left Triers by RR.
1	Sep	Arrived at Oflag 79, Brunswick. Cdn Red Cross parcel.[2]

The travelling conditions by rail were as follows:

> At the station in Paris we received a half loaf of bread each and a box of cheese between two. Then we were counted off and I believe it was 48 men to a box car and piled in. The SBO [Senior British Officer] begged for water but we did not receive any until he promised no one would attempt to escape. There was one pail put in our car. There was no ventilation and in the heat the stench became terrible from the dirty bodies and this cheese we had been issued with. We agreed that the men with dysentery only would use the latrine bucket.[3]

Similar experiences were reported by other CANLOAN officers en route to POW camps. Al McLennan was captured in Italy: "Sent back (walking) to interrogation centre and that night by truck to Mantova collection camp. There for a few days and by Forty and Eight to Stalag VII A near Munich."[4]

Jim Taylor was captured at Arnhem: "By truck to Apeldoorn. With 39 other officer POWs locked in a box car (designed for 8 horses or 40 persons). To Fallingbostel POW camp near Belsen. Train shot up by Mosquito night fighters. At Fallingbostel a week, then to Oflag 1XAZ at Rotenburg."[5]

Most of the CANLOAN POWs experienced the usual form of transportation for POWs: French box cars labelled *Huit chevaux ou quarante hommes.*

The treatment of prisoners of war was supposed to be governed by an international agreement, the Geneva Convention, to which all Allied countries and Germany had been signatories. There were several such conventions, beginning with one in 1864 that established the Red Cross. The Geneva Convention of 1929 dealt solely with the treatment of prisoners of war, and it was the terms of this agreement that were applicable to all signatories during the Second World War. It described in detail the treatment required for prisoners of war. They could not be coerced into giving information about their own forces – just their own name, rank, and number. They were to be provided with proper lodging with guarantees of hygiene and well-lit, insulated quarters. Provision was to be made for physical exercise. Minimum food requirements were specified. Limits were placed on disciplinary action, including penalties for escaping. Officers could not be forced to work. NCOs could work if they wished, and other ranks could be required to work if the work was not dangerous, related to the war, or more excessive than was required of civilians in the area.[6]

The Germans were certainly aware of all the provisions of the Geneva Convention, and probably there was a general intention to conform to them. There were, however, many exceptions, sometimes on the initiative of local commanders, but often because of circumstances, particularly in the last few months of the war, that prevented full compliance and that provided justification or excuses for violations. Cynics said that the Germans complied with the Convention only when it was convenient.[7] A balanced judgment of their performance is that "by and large prisoners of war in Germany were relatively well treated and life could be bearable as long as the POWs received more or less regular deliveries of mail from home and Red Cross food parcels."[8] These conditions did not apply in the latter stages of the war.

The German system for handling POWs was rather complicated. Each military service had its own camps. The Luftwaffe (German Air Force) handled air force POWs in camps called lufts. The Wehrmacht kept army POWs in camps called stalags. Officers were segregated in separate camps called oflags. Usually there was also segregation by nationality. Russian POWs were always in separate camps, there were sometimes separate camps for Americans, but often American officers were in the same camp with British and other officers. Even when officers of different nationalities were combined, there was a British compound that contained Commonwealth officers as well as Czechs, Poles, Free French, etc., the soldiers of occupied countries who were serving with British forces. An important person was the Senior British Officer (SBO), who might be a Canadian. He negotiated with the German captors on behalf of the POWs in the compound and had delegated to him by the Germans a great deal of authority, which a staff of fellow POW officers was required to help administer.

The Germans usually said to those whom they captured, "For you the war is over." This was only partially true, for life in a POW camp was a continuing fight by the prisoners to maintain their sanity and dignity. Even when creature comforts and living conditions were adequate, the mere fact of being a prisoner – the barbed-wire perimeter, the armed guards and dogs, the experience of confinement – imposed a psychological strain that never became more than endurable.

The Germans were suspicious of the CANLOAN officers because they could not find in their books of Allied divisional and regimental badges any British units that included the word "Canada." Even their fellow officers were sometimes suspicious of Canadians who claimed to be serving in British regiments. Jim Taylor, for example, was not given the necessary security clearance to listen to clandestine news broadcasts until his British company commander arrived to vouch for him.

One CANLOAN officer whose Canadian identity was an asset was Tom King. He was at Oflag VII B, where there were about 1,800 Allied officers, excluding the Americans. Of these about 90 were Canadians captured at Dieppe, about 50 of whom King knew: officers of the Royal Hamilton Light Infantry, the Essex Scottish, and the Royal Regiment of Canada. Among them were the COs of these battalions, Lieutenant-Colonels Labatt, Jesperson, and Catto. He recalls, "As the only Canadian outside of their group they generously gave me a credit of 1000 cigarettes, the buying currency for the camp exchange."[9]

The accommodation in most of the oflags was similar to that in Oflag 79 described by Clifton Cassady: "Prisoners live in two-storey barracks blocks which once housed men of the Luftwaffe. Roughly speaking each floor in a block houses a company of officers who live twelve to eighteen in a room [and sleep in double decker bunks]. Organization includes hospital, PRI [President Regimental Institutes] and Q stores."[10]

After the Allied victory in Normandy and particularly after the Battle of the Bulge (in the Ardennes), life in POW camps changed drastically. From January until the end of the war, deliveries of mail and of the precious Red Cross parcels fell victim to the disrupted and deteriorating transportation system. The basic German rations were often reduced or cut off completely for the POWs in order to feed German troops retreating before the Russians, and even civilians.

The German attitude towards escaping, the first preoccupation of officer POWs, changed, too. Until mid-1944 it was regarded as a cat-and-mouse game: the POWs planned escapes and dug tunnels, and the guards tried to find them and even returned without violence the few who managed to get out of the camp and were recaptured. After the successful Allied invasion in Normandy, the Germans feared that escaping officers would organize serious uprisings and considered them to be a threat that must be stopped. The execution of 50 officers from the "Great Escape" from Stalag Luft III was an indication of the new policy, and though it did not deter the continued planning and attempts to escape, in the last months of the war it was recognized that the chances of escaping and surviving were slight.

Next to plans for escape came the preoccupation with a wide range of organized activity. Clifton Cassady's journal describes something of the variety of activities:

> There is a "university" in the camp which offers most of the usual subjects. Perhaps 12% of the 2300 officers take advantage of it. There is a library, fiction and technical. The camp social structure is interlaced with societies ranging from the Law Society down to the short lived *Jorrocks Club* which was laughed out of existence. Entertainment includes a steady flow of light musical programmes and recordings, plays, readings and an occasional film. There are several wall newspapers, some of which are truly adult in outlook. Wall maps are well done and are a source of great attraction. Considering the artificial state of the self-contained community, friction is inevitable but little serious trouble arises.[11]

Participation in the various activities depended on individual inclinations and talents. Some, like Erskine Carter, took advantage of the educational facilities. As befitted a future Rhodes Scholar, he worked hard at studies in law and Latin. Jim Taylor was one of those who was active in sports. The Swedish Red Cross provided skates and hockey sticks, and a hockey league was formed in which Canadians were prominent. A loyal Calgarian, Taylor led the Stampeders. Less athletic POWs got their exercise by walking around the perimeter of the camp, known as "circuit bashing." Much effort went into a variety of theatricals, for which sets and costumes were made. Music was important, and musical instruments, including bagpipes, which were called "doodle sacks" by the Germans, were often obtained through the Red Cross. In spite of all the efforts to keep busy or entertained, the general impressions of a period in a POW camp have been summed up as "boredom, boredom, boredom," the results of which acquired various labels in "bag slang."

An exciting time for many POWs in September was the Arnhem airborne operation, which, it was hoped, would bring early liberation. Its failure was a great disappointment. Later Cliff Cassady ran a pool on the date and location of the first bridgehead across the Rhine.

Christmas 1944 was a notable event, partly because of the fabulous meal that was prepared by the POWs in most camps thanks to the prudent conserving of Red Cross parcels and the culinary talents of some of the POWs. All enjoyed the especially good British Christmas Red Cross parcel, although usually the Canadian Red Cross food parcel was preferred. Designed by Dr. Tisdall of the University of Toronto, it consisted of 2,070 calories, was intended to last one person a week, and was often assigned to two people. Though it was intended to supplement the German "goon" rations, POWs often existed primarily on the Red Cross parcels. Another reason why Christmas 1944 was notable was that it was virtually the last decent meal before the end of the war.

A special 1944 Christmas message from Queen Elizabeth was sent to all POWs, and a photograph of the King and Queen with their daughters was sent to each as a Christmas card. Indicative of the state of mail deliveries is the date when these messages arrived at Oflag 79 – 26 March 1945.

A distraction in many camps was the increasing number of Allied air raids in their areas. One CANLOAN officer counted 39 in October and 52 in November.

In most camps the cold caused much discomfort and even suffering during the winter of 1944–45 because of the shortage of fuel and blankets. One POW reported, "Most of the fellows are crawling into the sack early, going to bed with socks, gloves and Balaklavas with scarves twisted around our stomachs."[12]

Even more serious from January on was the shortage and irregular delivery of food. The food supply was as low as 500 calories per day, and the POWs were constantly hungry. One POW said, "When I get back I'll steal rather than be hungry again."[13] Another observed, "The food was the god damnest garbage you ever saw in your life."[14] On 25 February Cassady noted, "Red Cross parcel supply exhausted. German ration cut 20%."[15]

Worse was yet to come. As the Russians advanced from the east, and the Americans and British from the west, the POW camps were evacuated and the POWs taken on long marches all over Germany. Later they were called "death marches" because of the deaths from starvation, exhaustion, dysentery, and strafing by Allied aircraft. Tom King recalls, "As the Allies advanced we started to move south and east on foot. The day we marched out of camp 1800 strong we were strafed by Allied aircraft and had about 60 casualties. From then until we arrived at Lanshutt in Bavaria we could only march at night."[16]

Fortunately liberation was near. Most of the POWs were liberated by American troops, usually an armoured division. Virtually all CANLOAN POWs have engraved on their memories the moment of liberation, the speed with which, in most cases, they were flown in American or RAF planes to bases in Western Europe and on to England, and the fabulous food which was offered to them:

On 6 May US 14th Armoured entered camp. Moved by truck to Regensburg for one night. By C47 out to France, listening to VE Day in London on pilot's earphones. 28 to each plane. Landed at Airborne Division tented camp, fed chicken, mashed potatoes, white bread, ice cream and canned peaches, plus real coffee. Evening movie and each cot with clean linen. Most ill as stomachs rebelled.[17]

All the CANLOAN POWs were emaciated, having lost on an average 30 to 40 pounds. Some were down to 90 pounds and took some time to regain their proper weight. Others regained their weight very quickly. Cliff Cassady's weight zoomed from 125 to 180 pounds in a few days.

Other adjustments were necessary as well. For the first ten days in England, while he was staying with friends, Tom King had to sleep on the floor because the comfortable bed seemed to be suffocating him. Before long the visible effects of the POW experience disappeared, but the invisible and immeasurable effects lasted much longer.

Several conscientious CANLOAN ex-POWs reported at once to CMHQ, where Major MacLaren was considered to be not particularly sympathetic, being willing to have them posted at once to British regiments in the Far East while they were still underweight.

Some of the released CANLOAN POWs spent some time in hospital. Most had a short convalescence in England, but as soon as they were fit enough they were struck off strength of the CANLOAN scheme, posted to No 1. Repatriation Depot, and then returned to Canada.

14

The Ordnance Corps
CANLOAN

WINSTON CHURCHILL once wrote, "In the tale of war the reader's mind is filled with the fighting ... the fierce glory that plays on red triumphant bayonets dazzles the observer ... even the military student often forgets the far more intricate complications of supply."[1] Army ordnance services is a comprehensive term embracing all the activities concerned with the provision, receipt, storage, maintenance, and supply of warlike stores and clothing and general stores for the army, together with the personnel, both military and civilian, engaged in these duties. When the loan of 50 Royal Canadian Ordnance Corps officers was requested by the British War Office, no particular specialties were specified; thus all RCOC officers were eligible provided they met the conditions of rank, age, military qualifications, and physical fitness.

As was noted earlier, the enrolment of RCOC officers in the CANLOAN scheme differed in several respects from the recruitment of the infantry officer volunteers. In the first place, the initiative was taken entirely by the British when the War Office made a special request for 50 RCOC officers, whereas the initiative in the loan of infantry officers came from Canada. Second, the recruiting of the RCOC officers began two months later, about the time the enlistment of infantry officers ceased. Third, since there were no surplus RCOC officers in Canada, the loan of volunteers created the problem of finding replacements or spreading the workload. Finally, there was never any danger that the limited objective of 50 officers would not be attained. In fact, there was an embarrassment of riches. For example, there were no fewer than 94 volunteers from which the 20 officers in the second batch were selected.

Considerable attention has been given to the infantry officers who reverted in rank in order to be accepted by CANLOAN. This was even more prevalent in the case of the RCOC officers. Since there were so many volunteers to choose from, there was a tendency to favour those who had the highest seniority in the Ordnance Corps, which usually meant ranks higher than lieutenant. Approximately 25 percent of the volunteers from whom the second batch of 20 was selected were captains or majors, most of whom were obliged to revert in rank in order to be accepted.

The same conditions that had applied to the infantry officers, including the distribution by rank (one captain to eight lieutenants), applied as well to the RCOC volunteers. Of the 50 officers who were accepted, six were captains – four in the first batch of 30 and two in the second batch of 20 – and the rest were lieutenants. One who reverted from lieutenant-colonel to captain was CDN/561, Kenneth M. Dickson, who assumed the duties of senior officer of the group while at Sussex, en route to the United Kingdom, and at the RAOC training centre until the officers were assigned to units.

Though physical fitness was important in the selection of the RCOC volunteers and many were rejected for physical shortcomings, the medical examiners were not quite as adamant in insisting on "1s across the board" in PULHEMS as they had been for the infantry officers. In the first RCOC draft, for example, four of the 30 had a 2 in their PULHEMS. Two of them were E2, indicating good vision but slightly less than 20/20.

The stay at A-34 SOTC seems to have been considered a pleasant interlude – an opportunity to renew acquaintances and make new friends. CDN/560, Capt. Roger M. Smith observed, "We lived, trained and partied together. It was a good, happy time."[2]

The first group of 30 was there only five days, arriving on 5 June 1944 and leaving for embarkation from Halifax on the 10th. The RCOC officers were spared the rigours of battle drill that some of the less fit infantry officers recall with dismay.

The officers travelled from Sussex to the UK in the two groups. The first 30 went in the seventh CANLOAN flight on the *Cavina*, a two-week cruise that was remembered with the same pleasure and nostalgia as was the voyage of the third flight of infantry officers on the same ship. The remaining 20, crossing in a crowded troopship, the *Neue Amsterdam*, in only five days, 24–29 June, expressed less enthusiasm.

When the drafts of RCOC CANLOAN officers arrived in the UK, they went at once to the Royal Army Ordnance Corps Training Establishment at Leicester to become familiar with RAOC procedures. The first group docked on 25 June; the First War Ordnance Course for Canadian Officers began on the 28th and continued until 25 July. In the meantime various details were settled between the War Office and CMHQ. On 3 July the War Office confirmed that the correct badges for the Canadian officers would be the standard RAOC shoulder title on battle dress with a "Canada" badge underneath and the regular RAOC cap badge.[3]

The officers taking the course at Leicester were billeted in private homes. Most of them were treated well, and they welcomed the opportunity to become acquainted with the British people in such an intimate fashion.

The Commandant of the RAOC Training Establishment, Brig. K.F. Farquharson, was not inclined to rate the prior training or experience of the Canadian officers highly. It was soon apparent that the "familiarization" course was really a standard qualifying course for ordnance officers. On 29 June, the day after the first course began, the Commandant reported to the War Office, enclosing a copy of the syllabus for the four-week course, which covered "the necessary basic corps training and regimental training." He added,

It has been found, however, that of these 30 officers 2 are trained in ammunition duties, some 3 or 4 more have had experience in warlike stores and all the remainder have had no experience of ordnance stores except clothing and general stores. It is therefore suggested that they should carry out a further 2 or 3 weeks specialist training at the branches of the Training Establishment. They are all very keen to join field units, but the general standard of training is far from high.

He also suggested that those who were not qualified to drive lorries or ride motor cycles should obtain instruction at the Driver Training Battalion.[4]

In a progress report to the War Office a week later, the Commandant recommended that the CANLOAN officers have further regimental training before taking their places as officers in field force units. He proposed that at the end of the regular course on 25 July the 30 Canadian officers

> stay for a further week at the Battle Camp at Bradgate Park, which will enable them to be brought up to the regimental standard turned out on the War Ordnance Officers Course. After this I propose they should carry out a further three weeks training in the appropriate Branch of the Training Establishment. If you will inform me to what type of work these officers are to be posted I will arrange the specialist training accordingly.[5]

It is not surprising that at times the Canadian officers were instructed on subjects with which they were familiar. CDN/578, Capt. Reg H. Shelford recalls one such instance, a lecture on ammunition:

> During one of these lectures on a hot July afternoon in a quonset hut I fell asleep. The lecturer noticed, and after a certain point in the lecture asked a question. I had to ask him to repeat it and then gave him the text book answer. He came down to where I was sitting, offered me his pointer and asked if I would like to take the rest of the class. It appears I had given him a more detailed answer than he had given in his lecture. This is how the Brits found out they had two qualified IOOs [Inspecting Ordnance Officers] Jack Nelligan [CDN/582, Lieutenant] and myself.[6]

At the end of the course Shelford and Nelligan were excused from writing the specialization examination.

The RCOC CANLOAN officers undoubtedly profited from the expert instruction, and there seem to have been no serious complaints, but they were glad to be posted to ordnance depots in the UK at the end of the courses. The first group of 30 were granted leave from 17 to 23 August and joined their new units on 24 August. Some of them were joined later by officers from the second group of 20.

The same arrangements were made for the reception of the second group of RCOC officers, the last CANLOAN "flight." A memorandum from the War Office to the Commandant of the RAOC Training Establishment at Leicester on 21 July 1945 informed him that a Capt. P. Kitwood would meet the draft at Gouroch on 26 July and accompany the party to Leicester for the same type of basic, specialist, and driver training that their predecessors had been given.[7]

Similar reports were made on the lack of training and experience of the Canadian ordnance officers, but the six-month report on the CANLOAN scheme by CMHQ was much more favourable:

> In view of the early reports received from British authorities on the state of training of RCOC officers on arrival in the UK it is gratifying indeed to see the good results that were obtained by these officers on the 1st and 2nd Canadian War Ordnance Officers' Course.
>
> In fact the results of the courses were more than respectable. Examinations were given in three categories: regimental, organization and specialty. For the first course the average of the marks was 71%. The highest mark was 87% and officers referred to as outstanding were Captains Dickson, Campbell (CDN/563, Peter R) and Smith (Roger M) and Lieutenant Pepper (CDN/567, Philip R). For the second course the results were even better. The highest mark by Lieut Griffith (CDN/683, Walter M) was 90% and the average was slightly over 75%. The Commandant observed: "This was a good course. There were no outstanding personalities and everyone reached a good standard."[8]

The six-month report from CMHQ on the CANLOAN scheme continued:

> British authorities are more than satisfied with the Ordnance officers and though none of them has yet been posted to a theatre of operations, that is due largely to the RAOC reinforcement situation. Efforts are now being made to find vacancies for CANLOAN Ordnance officers in the theatres of operations.
>
> The Ordnance officers have settled down well to their new duties but are almost 100% anxious to get into action and this desire to serve more actively is undoubtedly to be commended. As will be seen from Appendix C, the majority of the Ordnance officers are employed in static Ordnance Depots.[9]

"Appendix C" was a list of the RAOC depots in which all 50 CANLOAN ordnance officers were serving. Fourteen were at Central Ordnance Depot (COD) Chilwell, seven were at COD Donnington, and from two to four were at each of the other 11 depots. Posting depended upon staff vacancies, and there does not seem to have been, as there was with the infantry officers, an opportunity to choose to serve with particular CANLOAN friends.

Lieut. Arnold Allen was one of the large number of CANLOAN officers posted to the COD at Chilwell, Notts., near Nottingham. This depot provided vehicles, armoured equipment, and related spare parts for all units and formations in the UK as well as all theatres of war.

Capt. Roger Smith; CDN/562, Capt. John W.I. Pollock; and CDN/574, Lieut. Tom T.A. Parker were posted to the COD at Old Dalby, which provided technical supplies to units and formations. While there, Roger Smith wrote a booklet for the depot on their storage and shipping procedures. The CANLOAN officers were billeted in comfortable homes near the depot but, like their colleagues in other depots, kept requesting to be posted to a war theatre. Their CO was sympathetic and willing to help. From Old Dalby Parker was posted to Bicester Central Ordnance Depot as officer in charge of the stores section, responsible for the preservation and packing of base workshop machinery destined for the tropics.

CDN/586, Lieut. Alex H. Ord and CDN/572, Lieut. Colin (Sandy) Gillis were posted to the Basing COD, where they were joined later by CDN/687, Capt. William J. (Jack) Carswell and CDN/678, Capt. W. Kenneth Bauer. The job of this depot was to provide stores directly to all units of 21 Army Group – as Ord said, "a non-glamorous but nonetheless vital service." Still, after more than seven months these officers were delighted to get postings to Italy.

Lieut. Reg Shelford and Lieut. Jack Nelligan were posted to the Advanced Supply Depot (ASD) at Working, Notts. On their arrival the Inspecting Ordnance Officer (OC), seeing their "Canada" flashes, remarked, "Oh, foreigners, eh! No wonder you got the dirty end of the stick." They worked hard fitting up units for transfer to 21st Army Group, and were glad when they, too, were posted to Germany.

For the RCOC CANLOAN officers it was satisfying to have upgraded or reviewed the knowledge of their field in the special courses provided for them. There was no doubt that they were making important contributions in their units, providing essential supplies to formations and units at the front. They were well treated by those with whom they served – officers, NCOs, and men – but they were not satisfied. They had volunteered for the CANLOAN scheme to get into field operations, and they missed no opportunity to seek postings to a theatre of war – anywhere. Long before provision was made for service outside northwest Europe by CANLOAN officers, many of the RCOC CANLOANs had volunteered for service in field units elsewhere. In early December 1944 it was reported that no fewer than 20 RCOC officers had volunteered for service in the Far East. It was a long wait, an average of about six months in depots in the UK, before postings abroad could be arranged, but eventually almost all were posted abroad – to northwest Europe, the Mediterranean, or the Far East. Five of them were sent to Egypt,[10] some to India, and at least two to Malaysia. Alex Ord expressed the sentiments of all the CANLOAN ordnance officers when at last he was posted to Italy: "It was a great joy to finally get a posting to the Continent!"[11]

The first four CANLOAN ordnance officers arrived in Italy on 27 December 1944: Capt. Arnold Allen, Capt. Ken Bauer, Capt. Roger Smith, and CDN/679, Capt. William D. (Bill) Timmerman. Six more arrived on 13 January 1945, and 11 more shortly afterward. Altogether more than 40 percent of the CANLOAN ordnance officers served in Italy.

Even when a posting to a theatre of war was obtained it was not always satisfactory, as is shown in the following account by Roger Smith:

> When our postings finally came they were all for base installations. We grumbled about this as we all wanted a more active unit, so the CO loaned us a jeep and we drove up to RAOC HQ and voiced our unhappiness. Much to our surprise instead of telling us to do as we were told, we were all given postings in the field. My own was as OC of OFP [Ordnance Field Park] for an Independent Armoured Brigade directly under Eighth Army command.[12]

In the distribution of postings it was rare for more than one RCOC CANLOAN officer to be assigned to the same unit. A good proportion of the postings were to active field units, such as OFPs for brigades, divisions, and corps. For example, Walter Griffith served the 78th Division, Peter Campbell the 10th Indian Division, and John Gray the 56th Division.

Occasionally RCOC CANLOAN officers managed to remain together. Tom Parker and CDN/581, Maj. Gordon Seymour, who were in the same draft to Italy, were posted together from the reinforcement depot at Brindisi to 500 Advanced Ordnance Depot (AOD), located at the port of Bari on the Adriatic side of Italy. It was here that some of the stores destined for Tito's troops in Yugoslavia were packed for parachute drops.

Most of the RCOC CANLOAN officers had arrived in Italy in time for the spring offensive from the Senio to the Po, which has been described by Arnold Allen:

> I remember this to be the busiest time in my life, before or since. Eventually we crossed the Po, then the Adige, through to Ferrare. The German defence was fighting with vigour but with continual bombardment by the Allied air forces, their supply lines cut and often outflanked on the east and west by both the Fifth Army and the Eighth Army divisions, many thousands of the enemy were cut off and long lines of POWs streamed past us to the rear areas. I can recall not sleeping for days at a time ... We were open for business continually, issuing stores and equipment, sometimes static, sometimes on the move. The constant activity and excitement left me at least in a high state of exhilaration.[13]

All of the RCOC CANLOAN officers performed their wartime duties well. The award of Member of the Order of the British Empire (MBE) to CDN/697, Lieut. Reginald S. Scholey was representative of their efforts; the citation suggests the nature of their contribution:

> This officer, in his capacity as officer commanding No 1 Ordnance Railhead Detachment, Royal Army Ordnance Corps, has dealt most efficiently with a volume of work which would have been normally beyond the capability of most officers of his rank and experience. His energy and determination in getting important ordnance stores to the fighting troops never flagged and it was his first consideration. Lieutenant Scholey succeeded in his task and always got the stores through despite all difficulties. Throughout he has shown a remarkable capacity for work and due to his energies the tonnage of stores handled by his unit exceeded all expectations and was far above the level for which his unit was designed. Despite pressure and volume of work this officer remained cheerful and displayed a very high devotion to duty throughout.[14]

With the cease-fire in northwest Europe and Italy, the RCOC CANLOAN officers undertook duties of occupation. Capt. Reg Shelford, for example, was involved in northwest Europe in the vital task of "disposal by demolition of unserviceable ammunition and battlefield clearance and disposal of all items with explosive content." He also contributed ideas for improving the packaging and delivery of ammunition in the Pacific.

In Italy several RCOC CANLOAN officers were in the interesting and potentially explosive area of Trieste, where Tito's partisans moved in just before the cease-fire and the Allied troops were obliged to accept the surrender of the Germans and prevent the Yugoslav partisans from establishing territorial claims without antagonizing them, pending a political settlement.

On 17 June 1945 Parker and Seymour were notified that their section, Returned Stores Sub-Depot (RSD) of 500 AOD, would be shipped on board a landing ship, tank

(LST) for movement to Venice. While loading was under way, they were notified that the Allied Military Government of Occupied Territories (AMGOT) wished to send a shipment of the new Austrian currency on their ship. The value was stated to be $400 million with a weight of 200 tons, all packed in more than 4,000 wooden cases. The treasure was duly loaded and handed safely to a Provost Corps guard in Venice.

Venice was a gathering point for some of the CANLOAN ordnance group. Parker remembers meeting CDN/556, Capt. Joseph G. Barber; CDN/568, Capt. Llewellyn F. Anderson; CDN/571, Capt. Alex Gray; CDN/579, Capt. Esmond L. Grant; and Capt. Roger Smith on visits there.

Several RCOC CANLOAN officers went to Austria with the Army of Occupation. 500 AOD, for example, went with the 46 Division to Graz, Austria, where they used a detachment of 186 German prisoners and about 90 Austrian civilians as labourers.

Most RCOC CANLOAN officers were kept busy in the Army of Occupation with a variety of assignments before they were repatriated. Repatriation from Germany seems to have been fairly straightforward: posting to the Repatriation Depot in England and to Canada as shipping space became available. From Italy repatriation was less orthodox, and at least two CANLOAN officers hitched rides to England in aircraft. In Naples Alex Ord met an RCAF crew who flew the "milk run" between London and Cairo. He hitched a ride that included a number of exotic stopping places – Benghazi, Cairo, Athens, Marseilles – on the way to London. Arnold Allen also hitched a ride to London in an RAF Lancaster with a Polish air crew. Gordon Seymour was one of those who volunteered to go to the Far East. A group of them was flown to England, expecting to have a leave in Canada before being transferred to the Far East, but they got no farther than England because of the Japanese surrender.

Roger Smith and Jack Carswell were serving together in a unit that was slated to go to Burma but was returned to the UK first for embarkation leave. To their surprise they were permitted to go to Canada for their leave, and when the Japanese surrendered and their unit was disbanded, they were posted to a technical supply depot near Hamburg. At the end of the CANLOAN scheme, in June 1946, they were returned to Canadian control and repatriated. Among the last RCOC CANLOAN officers to be repatriated were the two who had been serving in the RAOC in Malaysia, Capt. W.A. Finnie and Capt. John Gray. On 15 July 1946 a message from CMHQ notified 1 Canadian Repatriation Depot that these officers would be struck off strength of the CANLOAN scheme for return to Canada on 27 July 1946.[15]

The last to be repatriated was Reg Scholey, MBE, who did not arrive home from overseas until January 1947. When he returned from Austria he was posted by CMHQ to the Canadian Occupation Force in Germany, where he was first OC of a mobile laundry and bath unit; later, at Canadian Liaison HQ in Germany and Belgium, he arranged for the handing over of equipment to British disposal units as the Canadian forces prepared to leave. He was among the last to go.

About the middle of September 1945, when most of the RCOC CANLOAN officers were on the way home, each of them was sent a letter from the British Army Council thanking them for the valuable services they had rendered while they were serving in the British Army. (See Appendix G.) The thanks was well deserved. The spirit that these officers had shown in volunteering, their persistent efforts to get as near as possible to the front, their efficiency, and their enthusiasm were remarkable. They had the satisfaction of having succeeded in their objective of making a contribution to the waging and winning of the war, and in doing so they had had rich and rewarding experiences. It was clear that military rank was not of paramount importance to them, since so many had relinquished grades, but most of them were promoted during their service under the CANLOAN scheme. Originally the RCOC component of CANLOAN consisted of 6 captains and 44 lieutenants. At the end there were 13 majors, 28 captains, and 9 lieutenants, an 80 percent rate of promotion, which boded well for their post-war careers.

15

Occupation and Repatriation

While the war was being waged in Europe, CANLOAN officers seem not to have given much thought to what peace would be like. If they had, it would not have been unreasonable to expect some version of the routine and boring duties that those who had been involved in home-defence duties in Canada had escaped by joining CANLOAN. Nothing could have been further from the truth, for the immediate effect of peace in Europe was to open the door to a wide range of significant and amazing adventures.

The most urgent peacetime duty was the disarming of German troops. For soldiers who had become accustomed to associating even a handful of German troops with danger and violent death, it was a strange experience to face thousands of Germans, often bearing weapons, reaching to the horizon and advancing towards a road block where a few British troops, often less than a section, would disarm them and direct them to the nearest POW compound.

This happened throughout the sectors assigned to the divisions in the British Second Army, but particularly at the ports along the Elbe – Bremen, Hamburg, and Bremerhaven – which many German troops managed to cross in order to surrender to the British rather than the Russians, and on the Baltic coast, where the numbers of German troops were swelled by the thousands who had been evacuated by sea from East Prussia to avoid being captured by the advancing Russians. On 2 and 3 May alone the British Second Army captured nearly half a million German troops.[1]

Often important civilians were caught in the net. In the sector of the 11th Armoured Division, for example, the arrests included the notorious English renegade Lord Haw Haw. Elsewhere Heinrich Himmler was discovered disguised as an army sergeant – and bit his cyanide pill.

In addition to disarming German troops, the occupying armies searched for arms and ammunition. At Münster Lager quantities of mustard and phosgene gas were found and destroyed. In several places V2 fuel was found. In fact, the 5/7 Gordons occupied what had been a rocket fuel manufacturing plant where rockets were filled and then sent to launching sites. At least one CANLOAN officer was involved in the discovery of containers alleged to be filled with nerve gas.

Vince Lilley reported that the 1/5 Queens in the 7th Armoured Division – including his company with all CANLOAN officers – was posted at the Danish border to disarm hundreds of thousands of German troops as they returned to Germany. Several CANLOAN officers in 5 Kings had an interesting visit to Denmark, as related by Capt. Fred Burnaby, Acting OC of C Company:

> We were in Hamburg on VE-Day having taken part in the triumphal entry into the city after its surrender a few days before. Prisoners by the thousands were being marched through the rubble filled streets.
>
> On VE-Day plus 1 we were sent to Denmark ... There were 200 of us with three armoured cars, one DUCK and the usual motor transport. The sky was overcast, the country was dreary and the people we passed were shabby and depressed. There were hundreds of weary German soldiers straggling back voluntarily to prison camps singly and in groups.
>
> At the border the barricade was lifted, the clouds melted, the sun came out and we entered a country of green fields and well kept farms and neat houses. The streets and roads were filled with exuberant and happy Danes and sullen German troops struggling southward. Nobody paid any attention to the remnants of the defeated army.
>
> Just before we reached Horsens we stopped for lunch in a field. As we were eating, a Danish policeman on a motorcycle came up and asked us to follow him. The town was celebrating the liberation and the mayor wanted us to be their honoured guests ... The place was so crowded and our welcome so spontaneous we could hardly proceed. We were showered with flowers, besieged by autograph seekers and were only permitted to proceed after reviewing the local underground which lined each side of the street and presented arms as we proceeded slowly.
>
> The Kings party was asked to help the Danes get a certain German officer who had killed a Danish girl the day before.
>
> There were hundreds of German soldiers standing around each with a rifle. They were part of a group of several thousand stationed in the town ... The resulting negotiations in three languages finally persuaded the German commander to go back to camp and get the officer in question. I issued orders for our men to load their rifles and dispatched an armoured car to each end of the village to see that the officer did not escape by car. The German troops also loaded their rifles. A car with the officer in it appeared ready to make a getaway but when he saw the long line of our vehicles, which extended out of sight around a bend in the road, he decided to give himself up.
>
> We finally arrived at Aarhus about 2100 [hrs] all very weary and dirty. The town had prepared a banquet for the whole 200 of us and it had been ready since 1800 [hrs]. It was a welcome never to be forgotten. Besides I felt personally welcomed because everywhere there were signs and banners with the word "Fred" on them and my first name is Fred. Fred is the Danish word for Peace.[2]

Several CANLOAN officers took part in the disarming of German troops in Norway. Four CANLOAN officers in the reconstituted 7 KOSB were sent by air with a portion of the battalion to accept the surrender of German troops there: Maj. D.R.

Hartt; CDN/309, Capt. Ernest H. McMillan; CDN/116, Maj. Herrick M. Malloy; and CDN/643, Capt. Philip W.P. Newton. En route to Norway, Hartt's plane crashed. He was injured and several others were killed. The survivors walked to Sweden. Another CANLOAN officer who went to Norway was CDN/583, Lieut. Burton J. Hayman, 1 Border, also in the 1st Airborne Division.

At least one CANLOAN officer was concerned with the discharge of German soldiers who had been rounded up. Fred Chesham served from September to December 1945 with No. 50 Disbandment Control Unit, discharging German soldiers of all ranks. One of them introduced himself as Prinz zur Lippe, a kinsman of the Earl of Athlone, Governor General of Canada.

In addition to the German troops who were to be disarmed and detained, there were other groups to be looked after and provided with food, shelter, and medical services: the liberated American, British, and Canadian POWs, hundreds of thousands of inmates in scores of concentration camps, and the most difficult problem of all, the many thousands of forced labourers from a score of countries, the so-called DPs (displaced persons). Harry Hihn, 1 RUR, was one of the officers responsible for DP camps in the Ruhr. He reported:

Much trouble with Russian DPs. They were raiding farms, killing the cattle and murdering the farmers, and breaking into food larders. This all stopped when a raid by approximately 80 with sawed-off rifles attacked a farm home – actually a manor home with riding horses, four girls and two Yank deserters. I had Lieut Healy bring fire to bear on the retreating 80, enfilading Bren fire from the carrier into the bush, which they ran into. The next day we noticed several DPs wearing slings, etc. But the food stores and farms were not attacked again.[3]

Another CANLOAN officer, Burt Harper, 1 E. Lan. R., 53rd Division, had a confrontation involving DPs, also in the Ruhr. His platoon was guarding a camp for Russian workers. One day he was called to attend to a Russian, a former sea captain, an agitator who had been banned from the camp and was haranguing the inmates from outside the gate. When Harper signalled that he was to leave, he refused:

Turning to the guard I gave the order "Standing Load," and twelve rifles came up to the "On guard" position. Rifle bolts clicked forward placing rounds in breeches. Then I turned to the Russian, pointed down the street and to my watch, indicating that he was to disappear in that direction within one minute. I raised my arm like a race starter, my eyes on my watch. As the seconds ticked by the Russian just stood there smiling defiantly as before.

A deadly hush came over the spectators and actors. Even the birds seemed all at once to be silent. Another ten seconds ticked by. My mouth was suddenly dry and I cleared my throat nervously. This sound must have appeared to him to be preparatory to my next command because, heaven be praised, he suddenly turned and went pelting down the street, to the derisive shouts of some of the camp inmates, and to my indescribable relief.[4]

A similar problem with DPs existed elsewhere, including the area around Belsen near the Elbe, as described in letters at the time from a CANLOAN officer to his parents: "I am the Commandant here, a sort of local dictator or benevolent despot. When I came here with 30 men the Poles from nearby camps had been carrying on a reign of terror, killing cattle, stealing milk, eggs, bicycles, etc but we searched the camps for arms, enforced curfew, arrested and tried several and now things are quite orderly."[5] And later: "Germans cause no trouble at all but the Poles are a menace, looting and murdering and raping. Polish troops are supposed to keep order in the camps but one pulled a pistol on me when we were looking for a murderer in a camp and I nearly shot him."[6]

A different type of problem was encountered by Jack McBride, 7 BW, at an unusual DP camp in Holland. The notorious Vught concentration camp had been occupied earlier by the 7 BW and the Dutch inmates released. On 20 March McBride was ordered to pick a guard of 24 and report to Camp Vught. He has described his experiences:

> Arrived at the camp to learn that I was the wet nurse for 40,000 German DPs living as refugees in the camp. I was to ensure that nobody wandered off and then ultimately I was to escort them all back to Germany ... Here we were – a British Military Government Team commanded by a Canadian CO whose security was being protected by 24 Jocks under the command of a CANLOAN lieutenant.
>
> Able bodied men were put to work. Meanwhile I posted the guard and selected other able bodied Germans for mine-clearing duties out in the countryside. Then one day in marched six thousand SS prisoners. Nobody else seemed to know what to do with them. I now had a whole new batch of mine-lifters for the fields and who better than the SS?
>
> The Mil Gov people were busy with the domestic affairs of the civilians but they came to me with a problem. You see, to house this many people in a camp it was necessary to separate them into various barrack blocks: teen-age boys in one block, teen-age girls in another, mothers with small children together, fathers elsewhere – that sort of thing. Well, the marrieds were being deprived of their connubial bliss. They were willing to indulge themselves though sacrificing privacy. Thus I would provide an escort to march the husbands over to the wives' barracks every Thursday afternoon from 1400 to 1600 and stand guard outside to ensure they were not interfered with ... It is impossible to describe the sounds of ecstasy emanating from that hut. Keep in mind this had been a concentration camp and the bunks were three tiers deep.[7]

Other post-war events actually preceded the cease-fire in Europe. One was the entry into Hamburg by the 1/5 Queens, which has been mentioned earlier. It was an early test of the non-fraternization rule, as Vince Lilley recalled:

> I finally came to a street in my area that had not been too badly damaged and ordered my HQs to be located there and went off to position the infantry and tanks in strategic positions. On returning to my HQs I soon found out that they were occupying the largest whorehouse in Europe. Actually there were over 300 "ladies of the night" in one long street which had iron gates at both ends. What a headache it was to command the Reeperbahn for the next 36 hours, especially as there was a NO fraternization order. Although I closed the gates and posted sentries I soon found out that they could be bribed.[8]

Field Marshal Montgomery's non-fraternization order was dated 25 March 1945, just after the crossing of the Rhine, but it became significant only after the cease-fire in Germany. It forbade British troops to have any contact other than in the course of duty with any Germans, regardless of age or sex, and even applied to small children. The purpose was to ensure that both Germans and British troops were constantly aware of the enormity of the Nazi crimes, from which the German people would not be allowed to dissociate themselves. Monty is supposed to have said, "Last time we won the war and let the peace slip out of our hands. This time we must not ease off – we must win both the war and the peace."

James Lucas, in *The Last Days of the Reich*, writes, "In the hot summer of 1945 in the western zones the well-endowed German girls displayed themselves by lakes and in swimming pools to the only available men, the Allied soldiers."[9]

A CANLOAN officer who recalls an example of this display was stationed in a village near Celle through which ran a large stream or small river with a swift current. On most mornings, after tea in their mess, the officers in the company, wearing swimming trunks, were driven in the company jeep to the banks of the river, where they entered the water and were borne downstream by the current; at the bridge they were met by the driver and driven back to the starting point for more refreshing trips down the river. On the opposite bank there were always a number of young German women, some of them nude, having grown out of their child-sized bathing suits during the wartime shortages. They, too, entered the water and, though the girls were well aware of the non-frat rule and the officers were aware of having to set a good example to their men, some incidental contact may have been inevitable as they floated together down the stream, separating properly at the bridge.

The non-fraternization policy had an adverse effect on one aspect of the recreation program for the occupying troops – dancing. Though the number of female members of the British Armed Forces stationed in Germany increased rapidly after the cease-fire, the demand for dancing partners still far exceeded the supply. In these circumstances the reputation of Dick Coates was enhanced when he was able to provide partners by the hundred, as was related by a fellow officer in the Black Watch:

My company of 1 BW was detached in a small village near Hamburg and we wanted to organize a dance. No fraternizing was at that time allowed, so where were the girls? We heard that an all-girl Ack Ack Regt commanded by Mary Churchill was in Hamburg. That was all the information Dick needed. He borrowed four 3-tonners and departed to Hamburg. He returned that night with 100 girls – and Mary Churchill! What degree of Canadian charm accomplished such a feat is still unknown. But a happy time was had by all.[10]

The British troops grumbled about non-fraternization, chiefly because it seemed to be ignored by the nearby American troops. American jeeps and trucks passed regularly, their drivers accompanied by German girls. A strong deterrent to violation of the rule, however, was the punishment for fraternization, often an adjustment of points that would ensure that the culprit would be sent to the Far East instead of to the United Kingdom for discharge. By mid-June the "non-frat" order had been lifted.

Some of the early contacts made with Russian troops as the Russian and British Armies gradually established themselves along their boundaries, generally along the

Elbe and the sectors in Berlin, are described by Tom Anstey, 2 Oxf. Bucks., 6th Airborne Division:

> We went straight through to the Baltic, met the Russians near Rostock, sailed dinghies on a lake just north of Rostock for two weeks before VE-Day and drank some excellent German wine that we had to bottle before we could get it to the mess. Our General and our Brigadier insisted that all the Canadians go with them when partying so, as junior officers, we made out pretty well. Then the curtain fell on VE-Day. No more parties with the Russians.[11]

Victory in Europe was celebrated in the British Second Army in a series of formal and informal ceremonies. In some battalions the chaplain went to each decentralized rifle company immediately after the cease-fire to hold thanksgiving services. In other cases services were held at the battalion level. Most divisions had victory parades. The one for the 43rd Division was held in Bremerhaven on 12 May. General Horrocks had a victory parade for his XXX Corps in Bremen. Among the CANLOAN officers' most popular souvenirs is the printed program entitled *Second Army Thanksgiving Service on conclusion of the campaign in North West Europe, 6th June 1944 to 5th May 1945.* It contains hymns, selections from Scripture, and prayers. In colour on the cover are the badges of all the divisions and corps of the British Second Army.

The most prestigious ceremony was the victory parade held in Berlin in July in the presence of Prime Minister Winston Churchill and Field Marshal Montgomery. This was a memorable event for all those who took part, including the CANLOAN officers in the infantry brigade of the 7th Armoured Division – the 1/5 Queens, 2 Devon, and 9 DLI. This division was occupying barracks in Spandau, taken over from the Russians, which had been scrubbed by 100 German women before they were considered fit to occupy. With time, conditions in the garrison and relations with the Russians improved. Gordon Chatterton recalls visiting Russian messes at which huge quantities of caviar were served, and attending outstanding concerts by the Berlin Philharmonic and the Opera Orchestra.

There were other celebrations as well, including the presentation of awards by Field Marshal Montgomery. An unusual ceremony held at Königsplatz in Munich on 7 June has been described by John Anderson, a CANLOAN officer in the 5/7 Gordons, 51st Highland Division:

> The 5th and 7th Gordons had a bad time in Italy. The units were overrun and lost most of their equipment including their band instruments. Somewhere the U.S. 45th (Thunderbird) Division found a drum belonging to the Gordons. On 7 June at Konigsplatz in Munich a formal presentation involving at least four Generals was held. The drum was presented by a Capt O'Rorke to the GOC Seventh US Army, by him to Brig Sinclair, 51st Highland Division, and by him to the drummer.[12]

Incidentally, the regimental history of the Gordon Highlanders notes, "at the close of hostilities the 5/7 Gordons reckoned to have 18 pipes on parade. No other battalion can do better if as well."[13]

The army in which CANLOAN officers served had several designations, including British Western Expeditionary Force (BWEF) in the early stages in Normandy; British Liberation Army (BLA), often referred to as "Burma Looms Ahead" by those with few discharge points, from Normandy to the end; and finally British Army of the Rhineland (BAOR) from 25 August 1945 to the present. During the summer of 1945, the main preoccupation of this army was recreation.

There were the regular duties in each company and battalion, which provided for sports nearly every afternoon: soccer (football), cricket, (ground) hockey, and basketball, to which most CANLOAN officers added, or tried to add, baseball. The Canadians were impressed by the universal participation by the British. One of them observed at the time, "Every man plays every game whereas at home only the best players participate and the rest watch. Our CO was 4th in the 7-mile cross country run and he plays on all the teams."[14]

A serious handicap was the very limited quantity of sports equipment. The author was a battalion sports officer and spent considerable time and effort arguing with his two counterparts over the division of the trifling number of balls, bats, and nets available for an infantry brigade.

One CANLOAN officer, Dick Coates, MC, earned a great reputation for his achievements in this respect; a fellow officer in 1 BW recalls,

He really came into his own after the war ended when we were marking time in Germany and waiting to go home. We badly needed sports kit and Dick decided he would tackle the problem while staying on leave with his uncle, Viscount Bennet (former Prime Minister of Canada) at his home in Boxhill. So, while still in bed, he telephoned the War Office to inquire if there was anybody there who knew anything about sport kits. He eventually got through by sheer persistence to a rather irate Major-General (impressed no doubt by the address from which the call came) and a week later the Bn got a very fine collection of gear.[15]

In some battalions use was made of local facilities, as related by Alex Cunningham, 4 KSLI, 11th Armoured Division: "The battalion area in Flensburg was a former German army camp. The divisional engineers built a huge swimming pool. There was a riding stable with 10–15 horses. The OC, D Coy, was a former cavalry officer who insisted that all junior officers learn to ride and jump."[16]

Beyond the company were various competitions up to divisional, corps, or even Army level. Burt Harper did well in boxing, and John Anderson was one of those who participated in the Highland Games of the 51st Division on 1–2 August. The list of events included "drumming and bugling" competitions. A great spectator event in Hanover in July was a football game between the Liverpool professional team and an all-star Second Army side.

Every unit had messes and recreational facilities of various kinds. Officers' clubs were often quite luxurious. One in Hamburg had a favourite drink, a champagne cocktail garnished with a ripe strawberry. Another club in Celle specialized in "White Ladies" topped with shredded chocolate bars.

One CANLOAN officer, Fred Chesham, was in charge of leave hotels at Blankenberg from June to September 1945. Another, Gordon Booth, as Staff Captain, Welfare, in the 53rd Division, was responsible for welfare and entertainment. A newspaper reported on his operation of clubs and entertainment centres for officers and ORs in Düsseldorf:

> The most luxurious other-ranks club in Germany, known to the troops as "the Ritz of the Rhine" is run by a Canadian officer, Capt Gordon Booth, MC ... a former German restaurant which can cater to 5000 persons at a time with a beer parlour overlooking the river, the club offers a lounge, reading and writing rooms, room for skittles and ping pong and a room for checkers, dominoes and other quiet games, a beer cellar and a magnificent dining room in which the club's own orchestra plays.[17]

On 11 June a federal election was held in Canada, and Canadians overseas were entitled to vote in an advance poll. Although CANLOAN officers were complaining that the Canadian authorities seemed to have forgotten them, most were notified of the election, and a good proportion of them managed to get to Nijmegen to vote. One of the most successful expeditions was that by five CANLOAN officers in the 1/5 Queens, whose CO agreed to the trip without being overly concerned about the dates. On 5 June Lilley, Chatterton, Surtees, Craib, and Maclean departed in a 15-cwt. for Nijmegen, where they voted the next day. They returned by a circuitous route through some of their old haunts and didn't get back for nearly a week.

Several CANLOAN officers contributed to the economic development of Germany. CDN/650, Capt. Henry J. Richard was posted to Duisburg-Hamborn to administer the production and distribution of coal for the British North German Coal Control. This was vital with winter coming. Other CANLOAN officers were involved in wood-cutting activities. Norman Orr, 2 Essex, had a job with the military government to get the sawmills going in the province of Westphalia. With another Canadian officer in the Forestry Corps and four British officers, and despite the shortages of transport, fuel, and staff, they got the mills into production. With about five widely dispersed mills, each of them working from dawn to dark, Orr reported, "It was exciting, useful and taxed us to the limits of our ingenuity."

Another officer in 2 Essex, Capt. John A. Bannan, was called upon to produce the first daily newspaper in occupied Germany, with a circulation of from 150,000 to 350,000. Recruited by 21st Army Group because of his newspaper experience, he was transferred to an information control unit and assigned to the province of Schleswig-Holstein, where he was given command of the Hamburg Press Section. Finding one of the city's large dailies reasonably intact, he was able to produce a daily, starting with news of the German capitulation and continuing with other vital news and instructions. Later he was ordered to produce, in addition to the daily, a weekly newspaper with a circulation of a million for the whole region.[18]

During the summer of 1945, farewells were a frequent occurrence in the regiments in Germany in which CANLOAN officers served: officers were being posted to the military government or other positions or returned to the United Kingdom, for retirement if they had long service or for posting to the Far East if they had short service. Among those departing were the CANLOAN officers themselves. Sometimes, as was the case of those in the 1/5 Queens, each was given a warm letter from the CO and a gift such as cuff links bearing the divisional and regimental crests.

Sometimes, as was the case with those in 2 Glas. H., the departing officers made the occasion memorable, as related by Stewart Cameron:

> Having access to a huge supply of captured booze we decided to throw a party in true Pictou Highlander fashion ... A company commander who left the party early found himself on the floor under his upturned bed. The CO didn't appear, so in the morning, when we had missed our train to Hamburg, we appeared at Bn HQ and in spite of protests from the adjutant, barged in to the colonel and wouldn't leave until he had a swig from the bottle each of us had in our tunics. He wasn't overjoyed at such treatment but I'm sure he felt discretion the better part of valour and, thankful to see the end of us "Colonials," went through the motions as though he enjoyed it.[19]

CANLOAN officers attended farewell parties for other officers, too, and the following story by Hal Foster, 9 DLI, shows why so many of them have fond memories of their former commanders:

> We all knew that Col Mogg would be moved upward within the British Army. (He held many important posts including an important NATO appointment as Deputy Supreme Allied Commander, Europe.) Sure enough, not long after reaching Berlin Col Mogg was told to relinquish command and return immediately to the UK. He bade his farewell to the whole battalion, not without emotion. And the final drill was to be a farewell mess party after which he was to take a dawn flight to the UK. Someone suggested in the wee hours that since we had beaten Gerry about the only thing left to do would be to each grade our wrestling ability beginning with Col Mogg taking on the 2 i/c on down. This turned out to be a free for all. Shirts were off and with many glasses smashed after toasts we looked like we had just finished an action. John (Mogg) worked his way down to the 2 i/c of D Company, I believe, before it was time to leave for Templehof Airport. Off we went in a jeep with sufficient supplies to see him to his destination. I often wonder what people thought when he reached the UK.[20]

John Mogg is a Canadian who joined the British Regular Army as a young officer but always maintained his Canadian passport.

The six-month report on the CANLOAN scheme that was issued on 9 November 1944 contained references to two subjects that required new policies. The first was the question of permitting CANLOAN officers to accompany the British regiments in which they were serving if they were posted to the Far East after the end of the war in Europe. The second was the matter of repatriation and demobilization and whether distinct policies were required for CANLOAN officers in addition to the repatriation program for the Canadian Army Overseas.

The first subject involved a great deal of discussion in Ottawa and London during the first three months of 1945. Applications for permission to serve in the Far East were being received, and more could be expected. One of the first was from Lieut. William Edwards, 2 A. & S.H. Another, from CDN/503, Lieut. Austin Delaney, 12 Para., was supported by a special request from Major-General Down, Commander of the 6th Airborne Division. These and other applications had to be rejected because of the CANLOAN agreement of 23 March 1944, which limited the service of CANLOAN officers to northwest Europe and the Mediterranean. After discussions that included the two Adjutants-General, Sir Ronald Adam at the War Office, and General Walford at NDHQ, it was decided to change the agreement.[21] This, however, would take several months.

In the meantime it was decided in Ottawa that despite the apparent settlement of the "three months issue" earlier, requests by CANLOAN officers to return to Canadian control would be granted unless there were very good reasons to the contrary, such as special training for a particular operation. The Adjutant-General notified CMHQ: "While the British may not like it, criticism that has arisen here makes it necessary to insist on the ready acceptance of the principle that an officer can return to Canadian service in accordance with our interpretation."[22]

This proposal was discussed with the War Office, which pointed out that any large-scale withdrawals of CANLOAN officers would be most embarrassing in the first two weeks of February because of the impending operations (VERITABLE) and the shortage of infantry officers, but that otherwise the British would not try to hold any individual officers who were unhappy and applied for return.[23] Finally, in the middle of March 1945 the Minister of National Defence signed the new designation order that permitted CANLOAN officers to serve with their British units in any theatre of war.[24] By the end of hostilities about 50 applications to serve with the British Army in the Far East had been received from CANLOAN officers, some of them dating back to September and October 1944. In the meantime, the number had been reduced to 22 by casualties.[25]

A week later, a fairly extensive report on the CANLOAN scheme was presented to NDHQ in Ottawa by the Director of Personal Services, Colonel Carey, who had visited CMHQ and had, as he reported, "taken the opportunity of investigating thoroughly the question of CANLOAN officers":[26]

> [Major-General Hare, Director of Organization at the War Office] spoke in terms of the highest praise in regard to the work of CANLOAN officers. It appears that our officers were of the greatest assistance to the British and that Unit Commanders of British formations would be glad to get more of the same calibre. I found that all the staff officers to whom I spoke at the WO shared the same opinion.[27]

Colonel Carey had words of praise for Major MacLaren:

> He has a tactful, pleasant personality and is doing an exceptional job in keeping in touch with individual officers. He visits them in their Depots and in their Units in the Field. He knows their names and is familiar with their problems ... Recently MacLaren interviewed between 60 and 70 CANLOAN officers serving with British units in the field. All expressed a desire to remain with their units as they had adjusted themselves quite satisfactorily and in many cases had received promotions and decorations.[28]

Colonel Carey reported that problems of the past seemed to have been resolved. Mail had improved considerably. The situation at the South End Depot, where he had interviewed 25–30 CANLOAN officers awaiting postings after being wounded, was satisfactory. Sick or wounded CANLOAN officers were now treated in Canadian hospitals, and CANLOAN officers who were not employed operationally by the British were returned promptly to the Canadian Army. The matter of requests for return to the Canadian Army had ceased to be a problem. "The War Office follows the wishes of Major MacLaren in respect to the return of CANLOAN officers to the Canadian service."

Though the report covered CANLOAN problems of the past, it did not address the main problem of the near future, repatriation. In this matter Major MacLaren took the unusual step after VE-Day of consulting the CANLOAN officers themselves. In a memo of 18 May, intended for all CANLOAN officers, MacLaren wrote: "At present no concrete plan has been drawn up for the reallocation of CANLOAN officers. It is desirable, however, that this Headquarters obtain from you an expression of opinion regarding your future employment and your wishes in regard to reallocation. This correspondence, purely exploratory in character, is designed to obtain this." He pointed out that the main alternatives were to remain in the British Army or return to the Canadian Army. If they stayed in the British Army, there was no guarantee where they might serve, but they were not required to serve outside northwest Europe, the Mediterranean, or the United Kingdom against their wishes. They would be considered for repatriation and demobilization according to the point system as if they were serving in the Canadian Army overseas. If they returned to the Canadian Army, they could volunteer for service in the Canadian Far-East Force, be employed with the Canadian Army of Occupation in Europe, or be returned to the Canadian Army in the United Kingdom to await reallocation according to the number of points based on length of service that each had accumulated.[29]

It had been intended, apparently, to issue an annual report on the CANLOAN scheme on 31 May, but it was decided to wait until replies to the memo of 18 May had been received and analysed. Without giving the numbers who had opted for each alternative, Major MacLaren listed the six options and the proposed disposition of those in each:

a) Canadian Far East Force – to be returned en masse on 8 July or later to 1 Canadian Reception Depot, Aldershot, as if they were in the Canadian Army Overseas;

b) British Far East Force – British arrangements for leave, return to the UK and movement by units. Different arrangements from the CANLOAN scheme: allowances for service in India, for example.

c) remain with British unit until reallocated;

d) return to Canadian control for reallocation;

(For (c) and (d) officers were to remain in their British units until notified.)

e) Canadian Occupation Force; or

f) British Army of Occupation – arrangements with the British for release.

Points were awarded to all Canadian servicemen on the basis of the length of time they had served, two points being awarded for each month in Canada and three for each month overseas, regardless of rank but with a 20 percent bonus for married personnel. A soldier who had gone overseas with the 1st Canadian Division in 1939 would have about 180 points, whereas a CANLOAN officer who had graduated from university COTC in 1943 would have only about 60 points.

All CANLOAN officers who had 165 points or more were to be posted to 1 Canadian Reception Centre between 15 and 31 July to await a draft to Canada. Those with lower scores were to remain with their British units until their points category came up for repatriation, or be transferred to the Canadian Occupation Force. Of the 360 CANLOAN officers whose names and point scores were listed, approximately 70 had scores of 165 or more. Major MacLaren concluded, "If the above courses are followed the CANLOAN scheme will wind up in the next few months to the satisfaction, I believe, of all concerned."[30]

His expectations were justified. A report from CMHQ in London to NDHQ in Ottawa on 2 August listed the strength of CANLOAN officers on 31 July:[31]

Original number of volunteers	673
Returned to Canadian control	213
Medical repatriation	134
Liberated POW	27
Dismissed	2
Others (language, suitability, etc.)	50
Fatal casualties	128
Remainder	332
Volunteered for Canadian Army Pacific Force	42
Volunteered for British Far East Force	18
Volunteered for Canadian Occupation Force	15
Volunteered for British Army of Occupation	18
For reallocation with 140 or more points	83
Under 140 points	138
Replies awaited	18

Shortly after this, Major MacLaren reported to 21st Army Group that all the CANLOAN officers with 140 or more points had been returned to Canada and even those with fewer than 100 points could expect to return not later than March 1946.[32]

Less than a month after the report that showed 332 CANLOAN officers on strength, a report to NDHQ showed that the number had been reduced to 175. These officers fell into the following categories:

Volunteers for British Far East Force	17
Volunteers for British Army of Occupation	18
To be reallocated 15 October (110–139 points)	26
To be reallocated 15 November (90–109 points)	50
Under 90 points	61
Other	3

A few examples may suggest better than the mere reduction of numbers the activity in the summer of 1945 as CANLOAN officers made their choices and either awaited instructions or were transferred in various directions.

The 6th Airborne Division left Germany in June, returning to the United Kingdom to prepare for going to South East Asia. Lieutenant-General Browning, Commander of the 1st British Airborne Corps, called the Canadians to his office for an interview that is recalled by Tom Anstey:

> He asked if we wished to go with him. Six of us said "Yes." He immediately phoned CMHQ who said we could go. When he asked when we were to proceed on embarkation leave CMHQ laughed and told him we had had that. He then phoned British HQ and said he had six officers he wanted sent to Jungle Warfare School in Florida because the Division was going to SE Asia. We left the next day for New York where we were met at the gang plank on debarkation by a British officer with travel warrants to go anywhere in Canada. We were to report back in 30 days. We did, got to the middle of the Atlantic when the bomb dropped on Hiroshima. So we arrived in London for the VJ-Day celebrations.[33]

The six airborne volunteers were Tom Anstey, Philip Bordinat, and John Stone of 2 Oxf. Bucks., CDN/376, Capt. Leo J. Robillard of 1 RUR, and CDN/481, Capt. Claude W. Dansey of 8 Para., all of the 6th Airborne Division; and Leo Heaps, 1 Para., 1st Airborne Division. Tom Anstey took advantage of the leave in Canada to get married. Later Bordinat, Stone, Robillard, and Dansey, as well as CDN/109, Lieut. John M. Bennett, 1 RUR, served in Palestine with the 6th Airborne Division. Anstey continued his civilian career by spending six months at British agricultural research stations.

Harold (Moodie) Richards, 6 Green Howards, served for a time in Intelligence at the War Office (MI9) but was adjutant of his battalion when it was posted to Palestine. He was excused in time to return to university in Canada. John Davies, 3 Mons., went to India with 7 Worc. R. and, along with CDN/48, Lieut. William G. Whitney, 1 HLI, took glider training for the war with Japan. William B. Mottram had already served with the 7 S. Staffords. in the 59th Division and 5 Wilts. and 7 Som. LI in the 43rd Division when he went to India and joined 2 DLI. He went with this battalion to Singapore and had been promoted to second in command of the battalion before he came home. Two RCOC officers, CDN/580, Capt. William A. Finnie and CDN/680, Capt. John C M. Gray, served in Malaya.

There is a story behind almost every choice made by CANLOAN officers and the results of those choices during the summer of 1945. Sometimes they changed their minds. Wilf Smith, 4 Wilts., opted to remain with his unit in Germany but later volunteered for the Far East. CDN/253, Capt. George W.J. (Paddy) Gander, 9 Cameronians, returned to Canada and then went back to the Canadian Army of Occupation. Peter Pearce, 1 BW, transferred to the Cameron Highlanders of Ottawa in Germany and was discharged. He then served with the Allied Control Commission in Germany and retired to a business in Inverness, Scotland, which had become his home.

All those whose turn to be repatriated came up were posted to 1 Canadian Reception Centre in Aldershot, where they waited in one of several camps until their names appeared on the passenger list of a ship sailing for Canada. Since no serious attempt was made to organize training or other purposeful activity, those awaiting passage had little difficulty in obtaining permission for short leaves and none at all to go up to London for the day or even overnight. CANLOAN officers tended to congregate at Maple Leaf 4, the Junior Officers' Club in Kensington, which was staffed by Red Cross girls from the *Cavina* and which had always been an unofficial CANLOAN headquarters. The following incident concerns that club and CANLOAN repatriation, although the details are rather hazy after 47 years:

> One CANLOAN officer who was up to London for the day and having a quiet drink at the Club was approached by an RAF officer who was carrying a kilt and a Balmoral headdress. He asked if a Canadian officer in a Scottish regiment were about. He explained that he had been at a party the previous evening and had met the officer. He said he had always wanted to wear a kilt and both had retired to the men's room where the kilt and Balmoral were exchanged for the RAF cap, tunic and wings. Later they had become separated. The next day the RAF officer, whose leave was up that day, had gone to the club in Kensington which was said to be a haunt of Canadian army officers, seeking to recover his uniform. Unable to help, the CANLOAN officer returned to Aldershot where he discovered that his embarkation draft was ready to leave. Standing in line to return kit to stores he was relating the above story to a friend when another officer within earshot interrupted to ask if the RAF officer was still at the Club. He dashed off towards the railway station carrying an RAF cap and tunic.[34]

As early as July it was proposed at the War Office that on reverting to Canadian control each CANLOAN officer should receive a letter of thanks and best wishes from the British Army Council. The draft of the proposed letter expressed "thanks for the valuable services you have rendered" and added, "The Council hope that you will carry with you pleasant recollections of your service with the British Army and that you may find it possible to keep in touch with the regiment or corps with which you served." The draft was approved (see Appendix G) and there are lists of CANLOAN officers to whom the letters were supposed to be sent, although many did not receive them.

By February 1946, when only about 30 CANLOAN officers remained on loan to the British Army, steps were taken to wind it up. On 28 February Lieut.-Gen. J.C. Murchie at CMHQ wrote to the Under Secretary of State at the War Office: "It is now considered desirable that the Canadian officers should be returned to Canadian control by 30 June 46."

It was proposed that the remaining CANLOAN officers be given the option of remaining with their British units until 30 June or returning to the United Kingdom and being repatriated any time after 1 April. A questionnaire to this effect, signed by the newly promoted Lieutenant-Colonel MacLaren, was sent to them. Later the units in the 21st Army Group were urged to ensure that CANLOAN officers under their jurisdiction were sent to 1 Canadian Reception Centre before the deadline. A list of the 32 remaining officers revealed that 5 were in the Mediterranean theatre, 4 in India, 2 in Malaya and the remaining 21 in Germany. Of those, 7 were with their infantry battalions, several with Royal Army Ordnance Corps (RAOC) or Royal Army Service Corps (RASC) units, and the rest in various military government posts.

The end came before the 30 June deadline. On 20 June former CANLOAN Harold Foster wrote to CMHQ from Edmonton, asking for the names and number of those who were still overseas. The reply from Lieutenant-Colonel MacLaren on 4 July 1946 seemed to close the door on CANLOAN: "Please be advised that all former

CANLOAN officers have now been returned to Canadian control and dispatched to their respective District Depots in Canada."[35]

The CANLOAN scheme was short-lived. Its total length, from the approval of the scheme by Cabinet on 4 January 1944 to the effective end of the scheme at the end of June 1946, was less than two and a half years; the period of service in the British Army, from the arrival of the first "flight" to the departure of the last homeward-bound CANLOAN officers, was closer to two years, and the period in which the infantry officers were engaged in armed conflict, from D-Day to the cease-fire, was less than a year.

How well did the CANLOAN officers perform during their service in the British Army under the CANLOAN scheme? It is not fair to generalize, and there was, of course, no method of precise measurement, but two relevant indicators are promotions and awards.

Rank was related to position. The rank of a rifle platoon commander, for example, was lieutenant, that of the second in command of a company, captain, and a company commander was a major. One did not, however, automatically assume a higher rank by performing the duties of a position. If a lieutenant performed the duties of a company second in command continuously for six months as acting captain, he could be promoted to temporary captain. After another six months his captaincy could be confirmed. It was the same if he had been commanding a company all that time, since one could be promoted only one rank at a time, although one could be recommended for a second promotion before the first was approved. For example, Lieut. Allan Smith, 2 Glas. H., had two recommendations for promotion before either was approved: from lieutenant to acting captain on 3 July and from acting captain to acting major on 18 August 1944.[36] If an officer was wounded or transferred while in an acting rank, he automatically reverted to his former rank. It was not rare for a CANLOAN – or British – officer to command a company as a lieutenant or acting captain in a series of battles and then be replaced by a more senior acting captain from another company or by a reinforcement major or acting major from the UK, thus reverting to lieutenant platoon commander. In the Canadian Army promotion was faster, even with the same rules, because priority was given to those who were in position, and there was less emphasis on looking outside the battalion for officers with a higher seniority.

In spite of all these obstacles, the promotions of CANLOAN officers were numerous. The final figures were lieutenant to captain, 118; lieutenant to major, 10; captain to major, 27. There were 155 promotions in all.[37]

Thus 25 percent of the CANLOAN infantry officers received promotions during their service in the British Army. Most of the remaining 75 percent were lieutenant platoon commanders throughout their service. These figures, however, do not reveal the hundreds of occasions during which CANLOAN officers performed, for considerable periods, duties of higher positions for which they were not promoted. If there were complaints – and there were – it was against the system and not the way in which it was applied, because there was no feeling that CANLOAN officers were discriminated against because of their nationality. The Ordnance Corps CANLOAN officers fared much better in regard to promotion. Although they joined the scheme with the same ranks (one captain to eight lieutenants), most RAOC positions for officers were at the captain and major level. The final figures for CANLOAN ordnance officers were lieutenant to captain, 27; lieutenant to major, 8; captain to major, 5. The total number of promotions was 40.

This was a promotion rate during service in the British Army of 80 percent – quite remarkable.

The granting of awards was much less precise than the granting of promotions and depended upon several factors, including the knowledge of particular acts by a person who could recommend an award, the number of recommendations at the time by a battalion, brigade, or division, and the literary ability of the drafter of the recommendation. There were few complaints that the awards were not deserved, but it was generally believed that, for various reasons, at least as many deserving cases were not recognized. In Normandy, for instance, during a battalion advance, part of a company found itself in the middle of a minefield, and several men were killed or wounded by exploding mines. The acting company commander, the only officer present, withdrew the men from the minefield and, although he was a slight person, carried the wounded, one by one, to safety, becoming a victim himself on the last trip and losing a leg to an exploding mine. This story, told to the author much later by two privates who were there, was completely unknown to anybody who would have been likely to initiate a recommendation for an award for bravery.

When recommendations were made they had to compete with other recommendations for the limited number of awards considered available at a particular time. An MC, for example, had to be approved and signed successively by battalion, brigade, division, and army commanders and could be screened out at any level. Sometimes a lesser award was granted than the one for which an initial recommendation had been made. Many MIDs originated as recommendations for MCs. It has been noted earlier that Capt. Robert Marsh, recommended by the CO, 1/6 RWF, for a Victoria Cross, was awarded one of his two Mentions in Dispatches. So the awards that were finally approved (see Appendix I) were not reflective of the full extent of the meritorious acts performed. Again, CANLOAN officers were not discriminated against in the granting of awards, nor were they especially favoured, although their list of honours and awards, totalling 89, was impressive:

Military Cross with Bar	1
Military Cross	41
Mention in Dispatches (2)	2
Mention in Dispatches	22
Croix de Guerre (French)	5
Croix de Guerre (Belgian)	2
Silver Star (United States)	2
Distinguished Service Cross (United States)	1
Order of Leopold (Belgium)	2
Order of Orange, Knight (Netherlands)	1
Order of Bronze Lion (Netherlands)	1
Croix Militaire (Belgium)	1
Member of the Order of the British Empire	1
Commander-in-Chief's Certificate	4

In addition, one Distinguished Conduct Medal and six Military Medals had been awarded for performance at Dieppe to soldiers who later became CANLOAN officers. In the Korean War former CANLOAN officers were awarded two Mentions in Dispatches, one Order of Military Merit, and one Distinguished Flying Cross.

It has been suggested that awards for gallantry were more difficult to earn in Normandy than later in the campaign in northwest Europe because commanding officers, anxious to maintain high standards, were inclined to wait for standards of gallantry, beyond the call of duty, to be established. This may not be true, but it seems rather strange that in the three months of the campaign in Normandy (June–August 1944), when most of the CANLOAN infantry officers were engaged, only 8 MCs, 20 percent of the total, were awarded, compared to the 16 (40 percent) in the autumn campaign, September–December 1944, and the 16 (40 percent) that were awarded in the final stage of the campaign, January–May 1945.

Measures of performance other than honours and promotions were even less precise. There was a type of recognition and respect in the frequency with which a platoon commanded by a CANLOAN officer was designated as point platoon in an attack, in the number of patrols or other dangerous missions undertaken, in leadership qualities as exhibited in effective performance, and in personal regard by members of a platoon or company commanded.

There were undoubtedly a number of CANLOAN officers who were not outstanding or did not perform well on all occasions, but generally speaking it can be said that, as a group, the CANLOAN officers serving in the British Army had an excellent record of performance. An indication of the respect they earned is the reaction of two COs in the Airlanding Brigade of the 1st Airborne Division to the performance of CANLOAN officers at Arnhem. Lieut.-Col. R. Payton-Reid, CO, 7 KOSB, wrote in *Our Nine Days at Arnhem:*

> This particular platoon was commanded by Lieut J. Taylor, one of several Canadian officers who were seconded to the battalion under an arrangement known as CANLOAN. This officer, who was wounded later the same day gallantly leading a counter attack, was typical of these Canadians – fine upstanding, courageous young men with hearts of gold and the spirit of Crusaders. The Battalion was indeed fortunate in having them and I believe that, on their part, they carried back to their Western homes, some of the Borderers' traditions. Except for two of their number, Lieuts. A.E. Kipping and A.E.F. Wayte, whose bodies rest in the Dutch soil which they helped to liberate.

When Philip Turner escaped from Arnhem he was asked by Major MacLaren to provide CMHQ with information about his CANLOAN colleagues who had been killed or captured. Hearing about the visit to CMHQ, the CO of 2 S. Staffords. asked Turner to inform the authorities that his opinion of the CANLOAN officers who had served in his battalion was so high that he was anxious to obtain as many Canadian officers of similar quality as he could absorb. He was quoted as saying: "If you know of any Canadian officers who are available, for God's sake bring them back with you."[38]

Though the Battle of Arnhem was unusually long and intense, the expressions of appreciation by commanders in regard to the CANLOAN officers whom they commanded have been echoed by many other commanders. In considering their experience in the British Army, most CANLOAN officers were pleased to be considered, in the words of Brig. Milton Gregg's post-war greeting, "happy warriors and grand ambassadors for Canada."[39]

CANLOAN officers who can recall every detail of the trip to the United Kingdom in the spring of 1944 have little to say about the return voyage in 1945. There are several reasons for this. First, since most of them returned on large ocean liners like the *Queen Elizabeth II* with up to 15,000 passengers, there were no intimate cruises like those on the *Cavina* and the *Bayano*. Also, CANLOAN officers returned individually, not as part of a group, and encountered fellow CANLOAN officers only by accident if at all. Even in the smaller hospital ships the immobility of stretcher cases was a distinct deterrent to companionship. For example, at least three CANLOAN officers were on the hospital ship *Letitia,* which sailed on 3 January 1945, but neither Roger MacLellan, John Foote, nor Arnold Willick knew the others were there.

Generally speaking, few of those returning shared the CANLOAN companionship that had been so important an element in developing an esprit de corps on the voyages to the UK. But the speed with which the liners crossed the ocean was welcomed by all those who eagerly awaited their Canadian landfall.

Happy reunions with families and friends were held at railway stations all across Canada. The officers who were married (about one in three) were particularly happy to be reunited with their families. CDN/564, Capt. Arnold E. Allen rejoined his wife and the little son he had never seen. Gordon Chatterton was able to become acquainted with a son whom he had seen only briefly en route to Sussex. In some cases the returning officers were met by comrades who had arrived earlier.

The usual procedure on arriving home was to check in at the district depot, be given a month's debarkation leave, and then return to the depot for discharge or transfer to supplementary reserve. This happened in most cases, but there were a few exceptions. When John Druhan came to MD #6 Depot in Halifax for his discharge his documents could not be found. After waiting, "sitting in the mess," for a month he persuaded the authorities to give him a temporary discharge, which he had until 1960.

In several cases CANLOAN officers were given duties at the depot while awaiting discharge. This was true of CDN/625, Lieut. Gerald F. Hatchette, who was at MD #6 Depot for six months, and Bob Gelston, who was at MD #4 Depot for nine months. Martin Kaufman was promoted and remained at the depot in Regina for more than a year. Earlier, CDN/322, William G. (Pat) McLoughlin had been struck off strength of CANLOAN but became adjutant at the depot in Regina. Later he was accepted once more by the British Army, with which he served in Asia and Europe until 1953.

Several CANLOAN officers were given other assignments while awaiting discharge. Eric Hall gave lectures at Petawawa. Roger MacLellan undertook several assignments, at least one of them back at Camp Sussex. Harold (Moodie) Richards got permission to audit classes at the University of New Brunswick, where he was recruited again, this time as an administrative assistant, by Brigadier Gregg, who had become president of the university.

Also, at the MD 7 Headquarters in Fredericton, Doug Gage, who was being employed as personnel officer while his wounds were healing, was nearly overcome by CANLOAN reunions as returning officers checked in to get leave and then for discharge. A possible threat to his liver was a factor in his own early discharge.

Finally, there were those who stayed in the Army. With the drastic reduction of the Canadian Armed Forces after the war, it was not easy to be accepted for the permanent force, but a considerable number of CANLOAN officers were accepted and went on to successful military careers. They included CDN/491, Capt. Donald E. Holmes, Roy Reid, Vince Lilley, Rod MacKay, Phil Labelle, Jack Stobo, and many more.

The percentage of infantry CANLOAN officers who continued in the Army after the war was very small and was greatly exceeded by the RCOC CANLOAN officers who joined the regular force. The latter included Arnold Allen, Peter Campbell, John Carswell, John Pollock, Reg Scholey, Bill Timmerman, and many others.

Everybody was happy to be home, to be reunited with family, friends, and familiar haunts, to get away from the war. Even the large number of CANLOAN officers who had volunteered for the war in the Far East were glad that VE-Day made it unnecessary to go, and they had the satisfaction of knowing that they had done all they could to contribute to victory and peace right to the end. At home they relished the things they had missed in Britain and the British Army – good coffee, peanut butter, hamburgers, hot dogs, apple pies, and hot water.

There were, however, things they missed: the British pubs, tea breaks, their batmen, and the camaraderie of regiments, companies, officers' messes, and, especially, their platoons. It was hard to believe that it was only a year (for some less, for others more) since they had left Canada for the CANLOAN adventure and that all that had happened since had been compressed into such a short time. In many respects the Canadian officers who returned were not the same ones who had left Canada so light-heartedly such a short time before.

Many of them had not returned. One hundred and twenty-eight, a quarter of their numbers, were buried in Europe in one of the 30 Canadian and British war cemeteries in Normandy, the Netherlands, Belgium, and Italy. The comrades who mourned their loss realized that but for the grace of God they would be with them.

Many who returned had disabilities, from loss of limbs to loss of eyesight and hearing or invisible psychiatric damage. Even the majority who had escaped or recovered from their wounds had been deeply affected by their experiences. They had endured the horrors of war at the most brutal level as infantrymen. They had experienced hardship, fear, suffering, the loss of comrades, the strain of leadership, and the responsibility for the lives of men under their command.

On the other hand, the CANLOAN officers had been enriched by their experience: they had become more cosmopolitan from their experiences in many countries; they had acquired confidence by demonstrating courage, endurance, leadership, decisiveness, and initiative as well as adapting to the distinctive culture of the British Army.

Had they become more British while living for months at a time as the only Canadian in a platoon, often a company, and even a battalion? All would deny it, having been made constantly aware of the differences or peculiarities of Canadian vocabulary, accent, and attitudes. Yet the following anecdote shows that all were not completely immune to the British influence.

A CANLOAN officer en route to the Repatriation Depot at Aldershot shared a railway compartment with a Canadian sergeant from Italy. It was the first Canadian he had spoken to in months, and both enjoyed an exchange of war stories and the discovery of mutual acquaintances, perhaps joining in denunciation of Mackenzie King. As the train approached the sergeant's station and he rose to leave, the CANLOAN officer shook his hand, saying, "Well, cheerio, old chap." The sergeant drawled coolly, "So long, pal."

On the whole, though, there is no doubt that the CANLOAN officers retained their Canadian identity while enjoying pleasant associations with their British comrades as well as with the British civilians they met.

The CANLOAN officers who returned to Canada in late 1945 or early 1946 were well pleased with CANLOAN. It had brought them a permanent respect, admiration, and affection for the British people; an enduring pride in the British regiments in which they had served; and a deep personal regard for the fellow officers in their companies and battalions and particularly for the NCOs and men in their platoons, with whom they had shared experiences that had tried, and in most cases proved, their capacity to endure hardships and overcome obstacles. They were proud of having passed through the crucible of the experiences that the CANLOAN scheme had provided, and they felt enriched by these experiences. They were aware, too, that they had been in effect representatives of Canada and were quietly confident that the reputation of Canada and its fighting men had not suffered from their performance. They did not regret having participated in the scheme and felt that it had helped prepare them for challenges they would face in post-war Canada.

Epilogue

I

The Survivors

HOME AGAIN, the surviving CANLOAN officers turned their thoughts and efforts to re-establishing themselves in post-war Canada. There were 545 individual experiences. Some remained in the regular forces and many went back to their former jobs. The Department of Veterans Affairs (DVA) university training plan helped many to catch up where they had broken off and make a second start in business or the professions. A few had trouble settling down, many got off to a slow start, and some died young, but all in all, their post-war careers reflect the qualities and spirit that were evident in their CANLOAN experiences in 1944 and 1945.

Some of those who were handicapped by war injuries were obliged to spend months or years in hospital and endure several operations before they could pursue normal careers; but virtually all were able to overcome their physical handicaps and achieve success in their particular fields. One of them, Bill O'Connor, a paraplegic casualty, graduated with honours from Trinity College while a patient in Sunnybrook Hospital in Toronto. He had a brief but most successful career as a journalist and as a lecturer at the University of Buffalo. CANLOAN officers with amputated limbs, of whom Don Oland and Ross LeMesurier are examples, went on to attain national distinction in their fields. Many of the other CANLOAN officers who had been wounded were awarded pensions, varying from 5 percent to 100 percent on the DVA scale, but almost all of them were able to pursue normal careers.

More than one-third of the survivors chose to return to the jobs, companies, or professions they had left to enlist in the Army; some of them spent their entire careers in these occupations, usually rising through several managerial levels. Examples are Ross Ingram at Bell Canada, Arnold Willick at Ontario Hydro, Tom King at Dominion Glass, Hank Henry in banking, Jack McBride in advertising, and Reg Shelford and Dick Coates in journalism.

Several CANLOAN officers who initially went back to their old jobs later changed to quite different careers. Alex Cunningham returned to Loblaws but later became production coordinator at Northern Electric. Elmer Fitzpatrick started again at Trans-Canada Airlines but became a director-general of personnel in the federal government. John Druhan got his old position back as a CNR brakeman, was promoted to area superintendent, and then was for a time adviser on transportation to countries in Africa.

Nearly one-third of the CANLOAN survivors attended university after the war before embarking on or continuing professional careers, taking advantage of the welcome DVA credits for wartime service that often made it possible for them to attend university. Popular professional schools were those of law, medicine, and engineering. One post-war class at Osgoode Hall in 1949 included Roger Conant, Ross LeMesurier, Pat MacDonald, Bill Robinson, and Arthur Stone, all of whom were to have distinguished careers in law and business. Other CANLOAN lawyers, such as Robert Barr in Saskatchewan and Don Findlay and Don Diplock in Ontario, had qualified earlier and resumed their legal careers after the war. Jack Irwin returned to the ministry in the United Church of Canada, and Jack Ayers and Jack Brayley took orders in the Anglican and Roman Catholic Churches respectively. Jim Duncan, Gordon Chatterton, Alex Ord, and others went back to teaching. Stewart Cameron and Glen Harrison became doctors of medicine, and Joe Craib a doctor of dentistry. Sam Majury, Hugh Thompson, John Anderson, John Howe, and Russ Parke took degrees in professional engineering.

Several ex-CANLOAN officers, after obtaining degrees in various subjects, had careers in the federal government. They included Doug Gage, science, with the Defence Research Board; Harold "Moodie" Richards, accounting, in the Department of Finance; and Wilf Smith, history, as Dominion Archivist.

Three CANLOANs made important contributions to agriculture after attending university: Tom Anstey, Martin Kaufman, and Roger MacLellan, all agricultural research scientists. Anstey was director of the Department of Agriculture research stations in western Canada, director-general (western) in Ottawa, and author of *One Hundred Harvests*, the history of the research branch of the Department of Agriculture. Kaufman's scientific career was at the research station in Lacombe, Alberta, where he developed new varieties of wheat, barley, and oats. MacLellan was chief insect ecologist at the research station in Kentville, Nova Scotia, and author of the history of that station. Incidentally, Tom Anstey, Martin Kaufman, and Wilf Smith all obtained PhDs from the University of Minnesota at about the same time.

Others who attended university after the war had careers in higher education. They included Harry Crowe, Department of History, York University; Lew Miller, Department of Philosophy, University of Toronto; and Fred Burd, Head, Department of Psychology, Huron College, in London, Ontario.

Some ex-CANLOAN officers qualified in one profession but later achieved success in another. This was particularly true of law. For example, Erskine Carter, a Rhodes Scholar and graduate of Osgoode Hall, became a specialist in corporate and mining law and left a law partnership to set up the Patino Group in Canada, of which he was president and chief executive officer. Similarly, Ross LeMesurier graduated from Osgoode Hall, attended the Harvard School of Business Administration, became a specialist in corporate finance, and soon was a director at Wood Gundy Securities. A classmate at Osgoode Hall, William Robinson, also went into business and became a vice-president of Crown Trust.

A relatively small group of CANLOAN officers served in various capacities in the different levels of the public service in Canada. Some of them became heads of regional branches of the federal departments of Manpower and Immigration (Lou Boudreau), National Revenue (Art Miller and Don Thomson), Veterans Affairs (Bob Fee), and Trade and Commerce (Harry Hihn), and the Unemployment Insurance Commission (Al Graves). At the provincial level several were employees of the Ontario Department of Education (Gordon Chatterton), the Department of Highways (Cameron Brown), Ontario Hydro (Ev Baker and William Black), Quebec Hydro (Pierre Mercier), New Brunswick Electric (Gerald Hebb), and Nova Scotia Power (Warren Hingley). At the municipal level, several were engaged in hospital administration (Eric Brown and Graham Gilhooly), police (Alex "Sandy" Millar,

Rod Keary, and Jim Cairncross), taxation (George Comper), and education (Bob Rist). One of several who worked at more than one level of government was Hank Richard, who had positions in welfare services, emergency planning, and aging in New Brunswick and federal agencies.

The largest field of post-war endeavour of CANLOAN survivors, however, was the broad area of business.

Among those in insurance were John K. Brown and Bill Hudson (Great West Life), Ralph Brown (Crown Life), Jack Catley (Underwriters Adjustment Bureau), and Don Urquhart (Royal Insurance). Bankers included managers Eric Hall, Duncan MacDougall, Robert Robertson, and Gordon Lee.

George Beck (Bartlet Cayley and Co.), Gus Lefever (Brink, Hudson and Lefever), Al McLennan (Warren Investment Services), and Joe Barber (Diversified Investment Services) were all investment consultants. Bruce Fleming, Norm Orr, and Al Smith were in real estate, while Don Lang (CNR), Ken Taylor (Western Canada Greyhound Lines), and Gordon Robertson (president of the Bangor-Aroostock Railroad) worked in transportation.

The ex-CANLOAN officers who were in business engaged in the production or sale of a wide range of products too numerous to list but including aluminum, automobiles, food and beverages, furniture, lumber, paper, shoes, and steel.

A few ex-CANLOAN officers owned their own companies or businesses. Several of them were engaged in well-established family businesses – Don Oland, for example, as vice-president of Oland and Sons and Fred Hatfield as president of Hatfield Industries. Others established their own companies: Don Hartt's Hartt Lumber Co. and Bernard Kruger's Kruger Paper Co. are examples. One of the larger enterprises was Hansler Machine and Supply. After the war Len Hansler established his own firm in Peterborough, Ontario, which was so successful that he soon had branches in Brockville, Ottawa, and Watertown, New York. Tom Parker had several successive engineering firms. Archie Street (Street Chemicals), Alfred Sprange (Sprange Memorial and Tile), Donald Meagher (Meagher Bros and Co.), Russ Waters (Waters Florist Supply), and Wallie Ingraham (Ingraham's United) all did well. Among those who owned automobile sales companies, the most prominent was Maurice "Mo" Carter, president of Carter Motors and a succession of companies in different parts of Canada. Gordon Wright was the only one in the CANLOAN group who identified himself as a farmer, but another, John Davies, operated kennels, and Ted Watson raised turkeys.

It was to this group of businessmen that the editors of the first issue of the *Canloan Review*, organ of the Canloan Army Officers Association, sent an appeal to attend CANLOAN reunions, recognizing that most CANLOAN officers were in business, that it was more important to them than drinking with the boys, and that contacts at reunions could be good for business:

> Business is built on contacts and most of us are already in business. Those who haven't their own will some day help to run the firms they are with now. Most clubs such as Rotary and Kiwanis build their membership from business men seeking contacts. Haven't we a lot more to offer? Turn out to our meetings, make your contacts and in the bargain "chew the fat" with an old buddy over a pint or a slug.[1]

Several CANLOAN survivors remained in the Canadian Army's regular force. This was initially a small, select group, first because most of the returning officers were anxious to get on with other careers and second because there were few positions for officers in the much reduced post-war Army. Among those who were selected and who eventually attained ranks of lieutenant-colonel to major-general were Ken Brown, Bill Campbell, R.F. "Rex" Fendick, Jean Gauthier, Don Holmes, Phil Labelle, Vince Lilley, Rod MacKay, "Blackie" Plouffe, Roy Reid, and Bill Timmerman. Most were accepted as officers in the Interim Force until the Canadian Army Regular Force came into effect on 1 October 1946. In the next few years these officers served in a variety of training, staff, and regimental appointments at Army Headquarters in Ottawa, at the various area headquarters across Canada, at the Canadian School of Infantry, the Canadian Army Staff College, and other schools, and in infantry battalions and ordnance depots in the field. There were assignments to international peacekeeping missions, and to NATO and exchanges with British and other armed forces.

The proportion of ordnance CANLOAN officers who joined the regular force far exceeded that of the infantry officers. The fourteen ordnance officers who were at some time in the regular force constituted 28 percent of their numbers. The proportion of infantry officers was between 5 percent and 15 percent. Among the better known RAOC CANLOAN officers were Majors Arnold Allen, Peter Campbell, John Carswell, John Pollock, and Reg Scholey and Lieut.-Col. Bill Timmerman.

The adventurous instinct that had prompted Canadian Army officers to volunteer for CANLOAN in 1944 and for service in the Pacific in 1945 reasserted itself when the Korean War broke out and the Canadian Army Special Force was formed to participate in it. In December 1950 the *Canloan Review* contained a partial list of CANLOAN officers then in Korea with the 25th Canadian Infantry Brigade, "asking for another bash," as Major Jean Gauthier put it. Several rejoined the Army to fight in the Korean War; among them were Gordon Booth, Jim Carson, Burt Harper, Harry Hihn, Hugh Macdonald, Bill Mitchell, and Jim Taylor. Most of them remained in until they retired.[2] Most of those who had stayed in the Army in 1946 served in Korea as regular officers.

Although the number of ex-CANLOAN officers who took part in the Korean War was small, their performance was more than satisfactory. Major Vince Lilley and the other ex-CANLOAN officers in 2 Princess Patricia's Canadian Light Infantry share the United States Presidential Unit Citation that was awarded to the battalion, a rare honour. Maj. Don Holmes and Capt. Rex Fendick were awarded Mentions in Dispatches, and Capt J.O.F. "Blackie" Plouffe of the Royal 22nd Regiment was presented with the Distinguished Flying Cross of the United States for directing an air strike behind enemy lines as an observer in May 1950:

Captain Plouffe directed his pilot through intense enemy ground fire in a low reconnoitering pass to discover the location of six camouflaged enemy bunkers, four mortar positions and one artillery position behind a key hill. Disregarding his personal safety he directed the pilot in making these passes to mark individual targets with smoke rockets for orbiting fighter aircraft. One of the fighters was hit by ground fire during the ensuing attack and Captain Plouffe's pilot escorted it to the nearest emergency strip. Upon returning to the area he continued to direct the fighters onto the targets resulting in four bunkers, two mortar positions and one artillery position being destroyed. By his high personal courage, aggressiveness and devotion to duty Captain Plouffe brought great credit upon himself, the Commonwealth and the United States Air Force.[3]

After the Korean War, ex-CANLOAN officers in the regular force, in addition to performing staff and regimental duties in Canada, served with their regiments in BAOR in Germany, international observer teams in India and Pakistan, the International Commission for Control and Supervision (ICCS) in Vietnam, and United Nation Forces in Egypt, Palestine, and Cyprus. In the Congo in 1961 Maj. Arnold Allen, RCOC, was OC, Administrative Squadron, 57 Signal Unit, where he was called upon to direct a Christmas service for the troops, including playing the organ and delivering a sermon.[4] Several ex-RCA CANLOANs, including Smitty Drew, Cec Jeffries, Phil Newton, and others, returned to the RCA after the war and served in that corps until they retired.

Despite the small numbers of ex-CANLOAN officers in the regular force, they managed to make their presence felt, particularly in the few infantry battalions. In 1958, for example, 2 RCR was commanded by Don Holmes, two of the company commanders were Phil Labelle and Barry Maclean, and Hugh Macdonald was training adjutant. The total number in the regular Army ranged from about 20 in 1946 to a maximum of about 75 in 1956 and dropped off rapidly to about 15 in 1966.

The number in the part-time militia was much greater, and there were few militia regiments that did not have at least one former CANLOAN officer on its strength. A majority of them became company commanders, and a dozen or more became lieutenant-colonels commanding their regiments – a switch from the lowly subalterns of 1944–45. One, Alex McIntosh, became a militia area commander, with the rank of brigadier-general.

In Nova Scotia, ex-CANLOAN militia officers included Doug Gage, Jimmy Marshall, and Roger MacLellan, who became CO of the West Nova Scotia Regiment. Militia officers in New Brunswick included Erskine Carter, Fred Hatfield, Conc McConaghy, and Bill Schofield, as well as no fewer than three lieutenant-colonels – Doug Bursey, Don Hartt, and Bev Howard. Hartt and Bursey commanded in succession the unit they had left as captain and lieutenant respectively for CANLOAN in 1944. Bev Howard attained his rank and had a distinguished militia career in spite of having lost a leg while in CANLOAN. Commanding officers of militia units in Quebec included Doug Ward in the Eastern Townships. In Ontario, Hugh Campbell and Alex Cunningham in the Hastings and Prince Edward Regiment and Wilf Smith in the Governor General's Foot Guards were among the many militia officers who sometimes had reunions at summer camp. Commanding officers of militia regiments included John Hunter and Walter Spencer. Maj. Reg Shelford, then circulation manager of the *Winnipeg Free Press,* was chosen to go to London with the Canadian Coronation contingent in 1952. Among the active militia officers in the west were Jim Fetterly, who became CO, the British Columbia Dragoons, and, of course, on the west coast the Royal Irish Fusiliers had the CANLOAN trio from Italy of Lieut.-Col. Al McLennan and Majs. Gus Lefever and Jack Chambers. Even in the United States, ex-CANLOAN officers were active in the US reserve army. Tim O'Keefe, for example, became a lieutenant-colonel in the Connecticut State Guard.

The decade of 1945–55 was a critical period in the lives of former CANLOAN officers, as it was for the thousands of others who had served in the Armed Forces during the war. Not only were they getting re-established in their occupations but they were marrying and starting families. Each *Canloan Review* for the period contains lists of marriages and births as well as reports on new appointments, promotions, and moves.

Brig. Milton Gregg recognized the significance of this first post-war decade in his message on the occasion of the first CANLOAN national reunion in 1954, the 10th anniversary of the founding of the CANLOAN scheme: "With the exception of those who went with the contingents to Korea and Germany you have been reestablishing yourselves in civil life. In this tricky effort, conducted with the same buoyancy that characterized the old Canloan spirit, you have exhibited a resourcefulness and a scorn for difficulties worthy of your Canadian forbears."[5]

In a message as national president of the Canloan Association in 1968, Don Oland addressed the question "How are Canloans doing today?"

> The civilian Canloan is quite a success story. On the whole, pretty well all of the Canloans have done as well in civilian life as they did in the Army. Many are senior executives, partners, presidents of their own companies; three are members of the clergy, several have been mayors and many have been aldermen. One is a judge. Many are school teachers and there are Canloans in practically all the professions. So far, no Canloan has been Prime Minister of this country.[6]

In addition to their regular occupations, many CANLOAN officers found time for community service. Philip Turner of Peterborough and Pat Macdonald of Port Colborne were the first CANLOAN officers to be elected mayors. They were followed by other mayors, aldermen, and members of municipal councils and school boards. Conc McConaghy, for example, served for many years on the Council of Fredericton, New Brunswick, and, after he retired, of Oxford, Nova Scotia. At the national level John Hunter was a Liberal Member of Parliament; unsuccessful candidates included Maurice "Mo" Carter, Progressive Conservative, and Leo Heaps, New Democratic Party. In provincial politics, René Brunelle was an MPP and Minister of Lands and Forests in the Government of Ontario. Other CANLOAN officers held important non-political positions in provincial legislatures, Arthur Stone, for example, as senior legislative counsel for the Government of Ontario and Harold Long as sergeant-at-arms in the Legislature of Nova Scotia.

A number of ex-CANLOAN officers were engaged professionally in national, provincial, and community services. Phil Newton was provincial treasurer of St. John Ambulance, and Bev Howard and Bill Mitchell were regional directors of the Red Cross. Many more ex-CANLOAN officers acted as volunteers: Bill Robinson and others in United Appeal campaigns, Don Diplock in the Children's Aid, and George Beck as president of the Canadian National Institute for the Blind, for example. Many others were active in service clubs, churches, Boy Scouts, cadets, and other community organizations.

By the mid-1960s the cumulative tributes to the work of CANLOAN officers were impressive. To take law as an example, the recipients of appointments as Queen's Counsel (QC) included Robert Barr, Don Diplock, Don Findlay, Dennis Jordan, G. Smith "Pat" Macdonald, and Hugh Mackenzie. Two CANLOAN officers, Roger Conant in Ontario and Montague Trywhitt-Drake in British Columbia, were appointed judges. Similar recognition was accorded in other professions as well as in the public service. Wilfred Smith, for example, joined Brigadier Gregg as an Officer in the Order of Canada. CANLOAN officers were awarded Centennial and Jubilee medals. In the military field many earned Canadian Forces Decorations (CDs) and bars. Vince Lilley added to his MC and two MIDs the rare Order of Military Merit. In one year two CANLOAN officers were appointed honorary lieutenant-colonels of Canadian regiments: Lieut.-Col. Maurice "Mo" Carter, MC, of the Argyll and Sutherland Highlanders, and Lieut.-Col. Roger MacLellan, MC, of the West Nova Scotia Regiment. Two others were appointed colonels of regiments: Brig.-Gen. D.E. (Don) Holmes as colonel of the Canadian Airborne Regiment and Maj.-Gen. Roland "Roy" Reid, MC, as the colonel of the Royal 22nd Regiment. General Reid also received the rare and distinguished award of Companion of the Royal Victorian Order (CVO). As the editor of the *Canloan Review* observed in 1972: "One cannot help but be impressed by the scope and quality of Canloan leadership in the professions, in government and community service ... this is the continuing service of Canloan."[7]

Though the number of CANLOANs was small and "the man on the street" was unlikely to have heard of them, their influence was remarkably pervasive. In the armed forces the CANLOAN reputation commanded universal respect. CANLOAN officers seemed to be involved in most current events. In the Winnipeg flood of 1950, for example, Maj. Don Holmes (RCR) commanded the Flood Control Detachment, which included Capts. Charlie Brown and Robert "Buzz" Mainprize, both of the PPCLI.

During the CNR strike in the same year publicity was given to an air drop of food to an isolated iron ore mining town, Steep Rock, Ontario. The distribution was organized by a local clergyman, ex-CANLOAN Rev. Jack Ayers. The strike was settled through the efforts of CANLOAN's godfather, Milton Gregg, then federal Minister of Labour.

The response to the Korean War has been noted. During the Hungarian revolt of 1956, ex-CANLOAN Leo Heaps organized efforts to assist the refugees.

Former CANLOAN officers were involved in several aspects of the Centennial celebrations and Expo '67. Brigadier-General (later Major-General) Reid was Canadian Equerry for Her Majesty the Queen during her Canadian visit. Lieut.-Col. Jean Gauthier was a co-ordinator of visits for the many heads of state who came to Canada during the Centennial year. Lieut.-Col. Rex Fendick, just returned to HQ Mobile Command from an appointment as deputy secretary general in the ICCS in Vietnam, co-ordinated VIP attendance at the Military Tattoo during Expo on behalf of the Minister of National Defence and the commander, Mobile Command. The Montreal CANLOANs were busy hosts, and Don Oland entertained on board his schooner *Bluenose II* at Expo '67. For the Olympics in 1976 Major-General Reid, too senior then to be an equerry, was in charge of security, with a staff if 103,000 to protect the 11,000 athletes.

A considerable number of CANLOAN officers were engaged in civilian aspects of international relations. Jack Young, for example, took on special assignments for multinational corporations and on eight occasions spent Christmases in eight different countries. Arnold Willick directed hydro installations in Iran, Kuwait, India, and other countries in the region. John Druhan's assistance to countries in Africa regarding transportation has been mentioned. Jim Marshall, also from Nova Scotia, spent several years in Africa with UNICEF. Dr. Don Good undertook a medical mission to Pakistan. Bill Burnett, who had been president of the 1967 International Trade Fair in Vancouver, became director of the Voluntary Agencies Division of the External Aid Office in Ottawa, and Moody Richards was seconded to the Government of Malaysia by Canada to advise on the setting up of a fiscal system there.

Among the 545 CANLOAN officers who survived the Second World War, it is doubtful if any one of them could be considered typical. Yet there are characteristics that are associated with the group and that perhaps can be illustrated by the careers of a number of CANLOAN officers. The following is one selection but others would serve the same purpose.

Roland "Roy" Reid was the last ex-CANLOAN officer to retire from the Canadian Armed Forces in 1977; he attained the highest rank, that of major-general. His career can be considered the fruition of the potential of the junior officers of 1944. As a CANLOAN officer he commanded a rifle company in 2 Devon in the 50th and 7th Armoured Divisions from Normandy to Berlin, was wounded twice, and earned an MC. After the war he commanded a company in the 2nd Battalion, Royal 22nd Regiment, in Korea, served in peacekeeping missions, commanded the Collège Militaire de St. Jean, and was entrusted with delicate and responsible tasks as equerry during Royal visits and the security of the Olympic games. Reid is honorary colonel of the Royal 22nd Regiment. He is the complete soldier.

Don Holmes, who retired from the Canadian Army as a brigadier-general in 1975 after 37 years' service, was an example of the boldness with a trace of recklessness that has been considered characteristic of CANLOAN officers. Rising from private to lieutenant, he joined CANLOAN and served with 12 Para., 6 AB Division, where he was promoted to captain and wounded. After the war he was company commander and commanding officer of an RCR battalion, commanded the Royal Canadian School of Infantry and Combat Arms School, was Military Attaché in Poland, and finally commanded the Canadian contingent of the United Nations force in the Middle East. After his retirement, the *Canloan Review* reported the following incident:

> In 1959, while at Petawawa with his RCRs, Don used the field telephone to call at midnight Prince Philip (the Colonel-in-Chief RCR) at Buckingham Palace, the PM (Diefenbaker), General Eisenhower and the Commandant of the US Marine Corps in a quixotic attempt to volunteer the RCRs for a Cuban campaign. The RCRs were not committed and Don was buried at AFHQ, Ottawa, for a short time.[8]

Jack Brayley was famous as a battle drill instructor and lecturer at Brockville and Sussex (as "Jack the Ripper"), and fearless as a company commander in the Gordons in the 51st Highland Division. After the war he was ordained a Roman

Catholic priest (his ordination was attended by Brigadier Gregg and Gen. A.G.L. McNaughton), and he dedicated himself to the service of the unfortunate and de prived. He founded Project Christopher, which offered teenagers an opportunity to share in the life of needy communities and to develop leadership, self-reliance, and Christian brotherhood. He himself has shared the life of those in physical and spiritual need, particularly on Indian reserves, an example of initiative, leadership, and compassion.

Jim Carson also is an example of courage and compassion. With CANLOAN he served in 10 HLI in the 15th Scottish Division. After being discharged, he began a career in social work but rejoined the Army to serve in Korea and later in the personnel branch at Army Headquarters. He returned to social work, where his ministry has included family counselling, re-establishing the mentally ill, prison work, and work with the Ontario ombudsman. On New Year's Eve 1976 when he was returning home on a Toronto subway train, he jumped to the defence of two Sikhs who were being bullied by a group of young rowdies. He received a broken nose and bruised shins for his trouble, but, as the *Canloan Review* reported, "his courageous stand against ugly racism made Jim an instant hero. The Sikh Society presented him with a splendid Sikh ceremonial sword and his courage has been responsible for a revulsion [against hooliganism] by the community."[9]

Leo Heaps has been referred to as a free spirit who was most effective in the relative flexibility of the CANLOAN scheme. His remarkable experiences at Arnhem and in assisting the "escapers" to freedom afterwards have been related in his books. His initiative, leadership, and compassion for those seeking to escape from danger and distress have been demonstrated often since the Second World War. He assisted Hungarian refugees, helped the "boat people" from Vietnam, and has helped those in need anywhere, interrupting his career as art dealer and author to do so.

Martin Kaufman was one of the CANLOAN officers who fought in the Battle of Arnhem and then spent time in a POW camp. After the war he became a research scientist in agriculture. He is representative of those who have been able to combine a busy and successful career with a wide range of activities in the service of his community. His professional work has been acknowledged by life memberships in several associations, by awards, and by membership in the Alberta Agricultural Hall of Fame. He had also been president of his local home and school association, the Lions Club, and the Royal Canadian Legion, and for 15 years commanded the local Royal Canadian Army Cadets.

Maurice Carter represents the combination of energy and versatility that many CANLOAN colleagues would like to emulate. After distinguished service with 2 Seaforth in the 51st Highland Division he became a businessman, owning a succession of automobile franchises in Winnipeg, Edmonton, and Hamilton. He has also had careers as a radio and television sports announcer. He drove his own cars in Canadian and American road-racing championships until he was 60. In all his activities, his high standard of excellence has been recognized. In 1974 the Automobile Dealers of Ontario elected him "Quality Dealer." Recently he was appointed Honorary Lieutenant-Colonel of the Argyll and Sutherland Highlanders of Canada.

The contributions of George Beck should be described in the context of the Canloan Association, of which he has been the heart and soul, deserving well the title "Mr. CANLOAN." Although severely wounded in Normandy he has demonstrated to a remarkable degree a combination of qualities: professional success, significant contribution on a national scale to the handicapped through the CNIB, and an appreciation of the British spirit of kinship in the UK in Canada. He has ignored his physical disabilities in his life of service and dedication to his family, his business, his comrades, and his country.

II

The Canloan Army Officers Association

The crest of the Canloan Association is based on the English pub sign that hangs outside the Red Lion Inn in Colchester, England, and CANLOAN officers like to believe that their association was founded at the informal gathering, described earlier, of a number of CANLOAN officers at the Red Lion on the evening of 8 September 1944. Certainly in the course of a pleasant evening devoted to eating corn on the cob, drinking beer, and singing around a piano, it was proposed that an association of CANLOAN officers be formed, with Brigadier Gregg as honorary president and with a secretary whose medical category would keep him out of battle. But nothing was done about it then. The meeting in Colchester established that the idea of an association was popular among CANLOAN officers, and the presence of artist James Buchanan and his ready pen produced the basis of a crest. These became valuable elements in the CANLOAN story, but these preliminaries would never have borne fruit had it not been for a strong spirit of kinship and postwar initiatives in Canada.

The senior officers in Ottawa and London who made such a fuss about the lion and beaver crest did not contemplate an association of CANLOAN officers. Nor did Major MacLaren when he organized the reception for more than 100 CANLOAN officers at the Royal Empire Society in London on 4 November 1944. Even the officers who attended the gathering at the Red Lion do not seem to have considered taking steps to implement the proposal they had so readily endorsed.

The origins of the Canloan Association have been described briefly by Brigadier Gregg and in more detail by George Beck in the *Canloan Review:* "The seed for CANLOAN was sown at Sussex, NB and flowered shortly thereafter in countless small and informal reunions at holding units, Colchester, Southend, and London. Almost immediately following repatriation CANLOAN coalesced in spontaneous informal (with a capital I) reunions in the larger centres."[10]

In Toronto in the summer of 1946 the first large reunion at the Royal York Hotel was organized by Jim Carson, Stumpy Ford, Bus Pelton, and others. CANLOAN officers who had been meeting in London, Ontario, joined those in Toronto to sponsor this reunion. It was referred to later as "the first riotous and infamous CANLOAN reunion." There were more than 100 CANLOANs present, as well as Wilson Woodside, the unfortunate speaker. The boisterous young celebrants let it be known that they were not in the mood for political commentary. In Ontario, beginning in

1946, an annual reunion was held on the first Saturday after Thanksgiving, and though there was not a formal constitution, a group known as the South Ontario Canloan Association was formed with CDN/1, Don Findlay as president 1947–49. These were difficult years when re-establishment was the chief occupation of CANLOAN officers, and attendance at reunions sometimes dwindled to a corporal's guard. Don Findlay's guidance probably ensured the survival of the association, and the founding of a newsletter, the *Canloan Review*, under his direction, provided the basis for a national association and an essential tie for the widespread members.

The first editors of the *Canloan Review* were Jack Bannan and Jack Bedford. George Beck and Art Connor assisted Don Findlay with the printing and mailing. The first issue of the newsletter, intended as a quarterly, appeared in February 1949 as a four-page leaflet. It contained a message from Brigadier Gregg, news about the activities of CANLOAN officers, and appeals for attendance at reunions, for news items, and for addresses of CANLOAN officers. The second issue, in May 1949, reported a meeting of Toronto CANLOAN with Brig. Gregg, suggested one dollar for an annual subscription to the *Review*'s four issues, and began with the subtitle *A Quarterly paper from South Ontario Canloan to inform Canloan everywhere about all Canloan everywhere*. It noted that copies had been sent to the presidents of Canloan Associations in Montreal, Winnipeg, Halifax, and Vancouver for distribution to their members, expressing the belief "that the Review can serve to maintain the Canloan spirit especially now when it seems to be at a low ebb."[11]

The associations in the four cities mentioned all held periodic meetings. In Nova Scotia Don Oland rounded up a number of CANLOAN officers for a dinner at the Nova Scotian Hotel in the fall of 1946, and in 1947 a larger Maritime reunion was held at Moncton. By 1950, news items from all four cities were appearing in the *Canloan Review*, which by 1951 was also receiving letters from CANLOAN officers in Korea.

On 13 October 1951 the South Ontario Canloan Association, the only regional association to have reunions every year from 1946 on, adopted a constitution. Earlier, in 1950, George Beck had replaced Jack Bedford as co-editor of the *Review*. He was compiling a roster of CANLOAN officers and already had 330 out of 545 names. Support for a national association was being expressed in letters from all over Canada. The *Review* encouraged the formation of local CANLOAN groups and the holding of regular provincial reunions as a stage towards a national reunion and a national association. Editorial urging continued: "There are only 540 of us left and we are spread across the country in all walks of life. Most of us are well established. Individually we are regimental 'orphans.' Collectively we are a unique brotherhood, jealous of our record and concerned for each other's well-being. Let's get together and stay together."[12]

Continued interest in a national association was evident, and in March 1953 it was announced in the *Canloan Review* that the first national reunion would be held in Toronto in 1954 on the anniversary of D-Day. Lieut.-Gen. Sir Archibald Nye, British High Commissioner to Canada, and Brig., the Hon. Milton Gregg, Minister of Labour, had agreed to be patrons of the reunion. The Brig. promised to present on that occasion his log book containing photographs of all the CANLOAN volunteers as they were recorded at A-34 SOTC in Sussex in 1944. Meanwhile Field Marshal

Montgomery, when in Toronto to open the Canadian National Exhibition in August 1953, had paid a tribute to the CANLOAN officers, which was recorded on tape.

The first national CANLOAN reunion, held at the King Edward Hotel in Toronto 4–6 June 1954, established a national association and a pattern of events for CANLOAN reunions that has been followed ever since. One such precedent was the publication of a special issue of the *Canloan Review* for each national reunion. The first of these, in 1954, contained the messages from Montgomery, Nye, and Gregg, and an eloquent account of the reunion by George Beck. The reunion itself began with a "pub night" at which CANLOAN officers squeezed into their wartime battle dress blouses, drank beer, swapped yarns, and sang wartime songs in a recreated British pub, a product of the efforts of an artistic CANLOAN officer, Lorne Ballance, and his talented wife, Pat.

A constitution (see Appendix H) was adopted at the general business meeting. The highlight of the reunion, the formal dinner, was held that evening. On another occasion George described this meal:

> Our Reunion Dinner, when the National CANLOAN family sit down to their family feast but once in every three years, is the manifestation and celebration of the quintessential spirit of CANLOAN. The traditional Regimental Mess Dinner in its formality and dignity is thus the apex of all our reunions. From the Grace, the Loyal Toast, through Fallen Comrades, the Association, the Divisional Roll Call, the British Regiments and the always splendid reply by a British brother officer, those decisive days so far away become very present.[13]

At the first national reunion dinner, the Consul General of France presented bottles of Calvados from Normandy, Brig. Gregg presented his Sussex log book to the new association, and General Nye, described as "the epitome of the distinguished British soldier," was a popular guest speaker with his praise for the infantry soldier.

A memorial service was held on the Sunday morning for the CANLOAN fallen comrades; it included the reading of their names, the laying of wreaths, and the Last Post. The reunion concluded with a reception for the next of kin and a picnic at Russ Waters's farm, which was to become an annual event for many years for Ontario CANLOAN and their children, the CANLOAN Mark IIs.

The organization of the first national reunion, attended by 127 CANLOAN officers and more than 30 wives, entailed 20 months of intensive planning and work under the direction of George Beck, assisted by Don Findlay, Art Connor, and many other local CANLOAN.

The constitution that was adopted in June 1954 established the name of the organization as the Canloan Army Officers Association, whose objects were to: (1) provide liaison among all CANLOAN everywhere, (2) advance the interests of CANLOAN, and (3) aid the national interests of Canada.

As a federation the membership consisted of all constituent CANLOAN associations, of which eight were named, one for each province except Newfoundland and Prince Edward Island, which were combined with Nova Scotia and New Brunswick respectively. The association was to be governed by a National Council consisting of representatives selected annually by the constituent associations. The Council would annually appoint from its members a president, a secretary-treasurer, and a delegate for national affairs. National reunions were to be convened every five years. Each constituent association would pay a supporting fee of $10 annually to the national association. The first executive comprised Don Findlay as president of council, Art Connor as secretary-treasurer, and Bev Howard as delegate for national affairs.

It was in the constitutions of the constituent CANLOAN associations that individual members were defined as

> all commissioned officers of HM Canadian Army who volunteered for active service with the Imperial Army in the year 1944 and who have an official serial number prefixed by the letters CDN being known as CANLOAN officers, who are resident in the geographical area of this association and whose membership is approved by the Executive Committee and such persons who are elected to Honorary Membership by the Executive Committee or at the Annual Meeting.

The first annual meeting of the National Council was held in Toronto on 20 November 1955. The first national president, Don Findlay, had resigned because of the pressure of his legal practice, and George Beck was elected to succeed him. It was decided that a charter should be issued to each provincial association, that any CANLOAN guilty of conduct unbecoming to a CANLOAN officer could be expelled from membership, that welfare was a matter of rehabilitation within the jurisdiction of the provincial associations, that the *Canloan Review*, hitherto published by the Ontario Association, be taken over by the National Council as "the National Quarterly of the Canloan Army Officers Association." Subjects discussed at this first meeting included a national memorial tablet to fallen comrades, an official history, a CANLOAN roster, and CANLOAN emblems.[14]

Great activity all across Canada followed the national reunion of 1954. In 1955 provincial associations were formed in all provinces except Saskatchewan and Alberta, and even in Alberta a meeting of CANLOAN officers in Calgary was held. Reports were received from British Columbia, Manitoba, Quebec, and the Maritimes about reunions. In addition, Don Oland was planning the first of a series of hunting and fishing trips in Nova Scotia. Annual Ontario reunions, held regularly since 1946, were to be in Toronto in alternate years, following a successful reunion in Peterborough.

The second National Council meeting was held in Montreal on 4 May 1957. In honour of the occasion the Quebec association organized a dinner that was attended by 42 CANLOAN officers and by the Brig., who made a special trip from Ottawa. At the business meeting an invitation from the Quebec association to hold the second national reunion in Montreal in 1959 was accepted. A new roster was to be issued at that time. A blazer crest was being designed with the help of James Buchanan. The name of the Canloan Army Officers Association had been registered with the appropriate authorities in the federal government and in Ontario. The first major project, a national CANLOAN memorial, was in the early planning stage.

In the next two years the momentum of regional associations continued. Reports of reunions in Ontario, Quebec, Nova Scotia, New Brunswick, and Manitoba were published in the *Review*. The annual "fishing convention" was held in Nova Scotia, and the annual dinner in Montreal. In 1958 CANLOAN officer Lew Miller, then director of talks and public affairs for the CBC, arranged for a talk by George Beck, "The CANLOAN Story," to be broadcast on Sunday evening 9 November.

The second national reunion, which was held in Montreal 4–6 June 1959, was just as successful and well attended as the first reunion five years before. The guest speaker was Gen. Sir Neil Ritchie, known and respected as the former commander of XII Corps in northwest Europe. Also present was the British High Commissioner to Canada, Sir Saville Garner.

During the Montreal reunion there was a flurry of excitement in the media over an attack on Field Marshal Montgomery by Franklin Roosevelt Jr., son of FDR. Responding to recent criticism by Monty of the fighting qualities of American troops, Roosevelt accused him of using Canadian officers as cannon fodder in Normandy, claiming that the casualties of the officers who were loaned far exceeded those of the British Army. When asked to comment publicly on these charges, the CANLOAN officers in Montreal quickly came to the defence of Montgomery, pointing out that they had jumped at the chance to volunteer, and that their casualties were not unusual for junior infantry officers in battle.[15]

The most ambitious project of the Canloan Association was the construction of a national memorial to CANLOAN fallen comrades. After a great deal of negotiations and planning over a seven-year period, it was agreed by all the parties concerned that a memorial would be designed and constructed in the National Capital on a site on the east bank of the Rideau River near Ottawa City Hall, a site also close to the residences of the British High Commissioner and the French Ambassador. A CANLOAN goal was set to raise the $5,000 required for labour and materials. Within six months this amount had been paid or pledged by CANLOAN officers, and another $1,000 was contributed by British regiments (in response to a letter from Brigadier Gregg to the colonels of the regiments), and by next of kin and friends.[16]

The memorial was unveiled on 3 June 1961. A special memorial issue of the *Canloan Review* described the success of this first CANLOAN national project and what has been called CANLOAN's greatest parade. The memorial was unveiled by Governor-General Vanier in the presence of 125 CANLOAN officers, 80 wives, next of kin of the fallen CANLOAN, and representatives of the British and Canadian governments and armed forces. The memorial is a three-sided granite column with a bronze cap and plaques bearing the names of 128 CANLOAN dead, with their CDN numbers and regiments. The many tributes to Don Diplock, who had laboured for so long with the negotiations and arrangements, were well deserved.

George Beck insisted, "It is imperative that we find new projects to keep our Association keen,"[17] and thoughts turned towards a pilgrimage to Britain and the battlefields of northwest Europe, but in the meantime other national reunions were held in Halifax in 1963 and Winnipeg in 1965.

Recalling the "East Coast Canadian port" from which the CANLOAN officers had sailed so long ago, the Association held its 1963 reunion in Halifax, where the festivities included a harbour cruise and lobsters for lunch. The Brig. and others were photographed wearing authentic sou'westers and pretending to row a fisherman's dory. Several new precedents were set. Ladies were present at all events. The Union Jack that had been used at the unveiling of the national memorial in Ottawa was used at the memorial service at the Halifax cenotaph as the CANLOAN colour. Berets were worn for the first time and became part of the CANLOAN uniform – and the "Last Toast" was introduced. A Canadian distillery presented the Association with a bottle of Canadian whiskey of 1944 vintage, and it was agreed that the last two surviving CANLOAN officers would share a toast at the last reunion. Mounted in a lined case with a specially printed label and fitted with two crystal glasses, this whiskey is exhibited at all reunions, accompanied by a book in which those who wish to enter the contest can inscribe their names, and from which names are deleted, with a cross, as the numbers diminish.

At the fourth national reunion in Winnipeg in 1965 George Beck resigned as president and delivered an address which captured elements of the CANLOAN spirit. He noted that Brigadier Gregg "in one short month transformed 673 mutinous and eccentric reinforcement officers into Canada's best bundle for Britain," and that

> the leadership training received 25 years ago is still at work ... This must be the essence of continuing CANLOAN. Let no one imagine that CANLOAN is merely a sentimental group of "old sweats." Rather it is the reaffirmation of that dauntless spirit of voluntary service to one's community and the world which is so well demonstrated by the continuing record of the peacetime service of CANLOAN ... For 22 years we have kept this spirit going. Today we resolve that it will continue as it was lighted as a beacon for national and international peace and goodwill.[18]

Succeeding Beck as national president, Don Oland proved to be an active and inspirational leader, visiting CANLOAN groups from coast to coast. A new roster was prepared in 1967. But from 1964 on, most of the organization's attention was given to the plans for an overseas pilgrimage; Lorne Ballance was chairman of the Reunion Committee.

The fifth national reunion, the overseas trip, was an exciting, unforgettable experience for the 51 CANLOAN officers and their wives and families who participated. During the 22-day tour the members of the CANLOAN party were invited guests at the Trooping of the Colour; the Royal Military College, Sandhurst; Windsor Castle; Westminster Abbey; the Lord Mayor's lunch at the Guildhall, at which a memorable speech provided the Association with its motto, *Transiens in Britanniam*; and a reception by the Queen Mother and other members of the Royal Family at St. James's Palace. On the Continent the group visited the battlefields and cemeteries of Normandy, Holland, and Germany and were given enthusiastic receptions. For example, they were formally received as guests of the City of Paris at the Hôtel de Ville and by the Canadian Ambassador at Brussels. In Edinburgh, just before their departure, they were guests of Scottish Command at its HQ, where they were bade farewell by a Retreat Ceremony by the massed bands of Scottish regiments.

While national reunions were organized in Calgary in 1971, followed by a trip to the Pacific coast, and in Ottawa in 1974, another CANLOAN project was being considered. It was proposed that the association donate a memorial chair to the CANLOAN Officers' Mess of the Infantry School at Camp Borden, to join those that had been donated by Canadian infantry regiments. This proposal was dropped when the Combat Arms School was transferred to Camp Gagetown. An illuminated scroll containing a brief history of CANLOAN, headed by the new motto, *Transiens in Britanniam,* and surrounded by coloured corps and divisional badges of the Second British Army (including the 78th Division in Italy), was prepared by Rex Fendick and Lorne Ballance. The first of 100 numbered copies was presented to the Canadian War Museum and the second copy to the Infantry School at Camp Gagetown. An additional copy was accepted by the Imperial War Museum in London. Several CANLOAN officers presented copies to their British regiments and to appropriate museums.

The seventh national reunion in Ottawa was, in part, a response to the overseas trip in 1968 when so many CANLOAN officers had been reunited with their regiments and had been recipients of warm hospitality. A special effort was made to have British guests at the reunion on the 30th anniversary of the origin of the CANLOAN scheme. A highlight was the presence of Gen. Sir John Mogg as the guest of honour. He noted in his speech at the reunion dinner that in the room was the first CANLOAN officer he had seen 30 years before when he was CO of a DLI battalion. Elmer Fitzpatrick was delighted to be with his former CO, as was Hal Foster, who had last seen him at his battalion's farewell party in Berlin in 1945.

In the last decade or so there has been no diminution in interest in the Canloan Association. Quite the contrary. Reunions have never been so well attended nor enthusiasm so high. One reason, of course, is that most CANLOAN officers have reached retirement age and have more free time to attend reunions. To a considerable extent, though, the enthusiasm is a product of long association, of the friendships of officers and their wives that have developed over the years.

Like most organizations, the Canloan Association has been maintained by a handful of its members. Reunion chairmen and members of their committees have risen to the challenge in organizing periodic national or provincial reunions. The national presidents have all made distinct contributions to the development of the Association. But the real success of the Canloan Association has depended on the *Canloan Review* and its editors; the *Canloan Roster*; the decision to include wives in all activities; the steady reliability of Art Connor as the only secretary-treasurer for the last 35 years; and the infectious enthusiasm and dedication of George Beck, who has earned well the title "Mr. CANLOAN."

By the 1980s the Canloan Association was beginning to look ahead to its dissolution. At the meeting of the National Council in 1980 a committee was appointed "to review the constitution with a view to the eventual devolution of the association."[19] Such arrangements were about due, as was emphasized by the casualty lists of CANLOAN comrades. A 1982 issue of the *Canloan Review* contained a list of 24 CANLOAN officers who had died since the last issue. Another list in March 1986 contained 20 names.

At least two projects remained. At the 11th national reunion in Ottawa in 1986, the publication of a history of CANLOAN was approved by the National Council, to be written by Wilf Smith, a professional historian who had retired as Dominion Archivist, with the assistance of a history committee. And on the anniversary of D-Day in 1987 a memorial to commemorate the connection between CANLOAN and the late Brig. Milton Gregg was unveiled at the Infantry Combat Arms Centre at Camp Gagetown.

CANLOAN officers have no illusions about their future. They know that they and their association will cease to exist in a very few years. In that time they must make provision for the perpetual care of their monuments to their fallen comrades and their revered leader, for custody of their records and artifacts, and for the publication of their history. This is all they can do to ensure that any of those in future generations who may be interested can have access to information about an unusual incident, which can serve as a study in leadership illustrating human courage and adaptability and the brotherhood of shared ideals and experiences.

Canloan Army Officers Association

Officers of National Council

Honorary President
Brig., the Hon. Milton F. Gregg, VC, CBE, MC, ED, Frederiction, NB

Honorary Members
Lieut.-Col. H.M. Jones, MBE, ED
Lieut.-Col. D.L.M. Gibbs, DSO, Tavistock, Devon, England

Past Presidents

Maj. Donald M. Findlay, ED, QC	1945–55
Lieut. George H. Beck	1955–65
Lieut. Don J. Oland	1965–71
Lieut. Lorne W. Ballance	1971–77
Lieut. J. Norman Orr, MC	1977–83
Capt. James R. Fetterly, MC	1983–86

President
Major Douglas G. Gage, CD, Ottawa, Ont.

Vice-Presidents
Capt. Maurice C. Carter, MC, Campbellville, Ont.
Lieut. William J. Hudson, Winnipeg, Man.
Capt. Martin L. Kaufman, CD, Lacombe, Alta.
Lieut. C. Russel Parke, Ottawa, Ont.
Maj.-Gen. Roland A. Reid, CVOMC, CD, ADC, Montreal, Que.
Capt. Leonard B. Robertson, MC, Chatham, NB
Capt. Edward A. Watson, Whonnack, BC

Secretary-Treasurer
Lieut. Arthur Connor, Scarborough, Ont.

Delegates to National Council

Capt. John W. Druhan	Atlantic
Lieut. John E. Moxley	Quebec
Capt. Norman A. Barnes	Ontario
Capt. Ronald C.S. Maclean	Ontario
Lieut. Thomas A. Parker	Ontario
Maj. Delmar H. Struck, MC, CD	Ontario
Maj. Eric Brown	British Columbia

The Association

CANLOAN is organized in provincial associations and in 1954 a national constitution and council were established. Provincial reunions are held regularly and the following reunions have been held on weekends of 6 June:

Toronto	1954
Montreal	1959
Ottawa, CANLOAN Memorial Dedication	1961
Halifax	1963
Winnipeg	1965
Overseas	1968
Calgary	1971
Ottawa	1974
Montreal	1977
Toronto	1980
Vancouver	1983
Ottawa	1986
25th Anniversay of CANLOAN Memorial Dedication	1989
Quebec City	1992

Reunion Chairmen

1954 – Lieut. George H. Beck
1959 – Lieut. Alfred H. Pierce
1961 – Lieut. D. Donald Diplock, QC
1963 – Lieut. Don J. Oland
1965 – Lieut. Jack R. Brown
1968 – Lieut. Lorne W. Ballance
1971 – Lieut. William F. Patterson
1974 – Col. Reginald F. Fendick, CD
1977 – Lieut. Norman Orr, MC
1980 – Lieut. Thomas A. Parker
1983 – Lieut. Francis A. Lefever
1986 – Lieut. Douglas G. Gage, CD
1989 – Lieut.-Col. Maurice C. Carter, MC
1992 – Maj.-Gen. Roland A. Reid, CVO, MC, CD, ADC

III

The British Connection

It is evident that most of the men who volunteered for CANLOAN did so because they wanted to get overseas and into action, not particularly because they wanted to serve in the British Army. That was, for most, a means to the end. But when the war was over in Europe, the CANLOAN officers left the British Army with deep regret. Their attachment had been illustrated by the efforts of many who were wounded and evacuated to get back to their regimental "home." During their relatively short time in the British Army they had acquired a fierce pride and devotion to the regiments in which they served, respect and affection for their British fellow officers, and a relationship akin to a close-knit family with the members of the platoons they commanded. As they parted amid expressions of continuing fellowship, addresses were exchanged with sincere assurances that they would always keep in touch. Reinforcing the intention to maintain a permanent relationship with friends in the UK were the considerable numbers of CANLOAN officers who had married or were about to marry young British women.

Once back in Canada and engaged in the absorbing activities of re-establishing themselves, however, they rarely achieved their intention to keep in touch with regimental mates. Some of them kept in touch with one member of a former regiment, a platoon sergeant, a company commander, even a commanding officer. Fred Burnaby, for example, kept in touch with a former company commander in 5 Kings, Don Oland and Jack Young with their former commanding officers in 2 Royal Warwick. and 1/4 KOYLI respectively, and Martin Kaufman with a former private in his platoon.

Some CANLOAN officers, of whom Hank Henry, Vince Lilley, and Jack Chambers are examples, maintained a correspondence with former comrades for several years. Others kept in touch because of the initiative of former British fellow officers. Rex Fendick's former CO, Lieut.-Col. (later Maj.-Gen.) G.L.P. "Pat" Weston, kept in touch and visited once in Ottawa before his death, and a former company commander, Col. Tony Hewett, retired in Australia, has recently re-established contact with the 2 MX CANLOAN. Outstanding in this respect was Brig. A.E.C. "Speedy" Bredin, who wrote regularly to all the CANLOAN officers who had served under him in two battalions of the Dorsetshire Regiment – Ken Brown, Hal Foster, Bill Hudson, and others. Only a few CANLOAN officers, such as Hank Henry and Vince Lilley, corresponded regularly with several members of their former battalions.

One CANLOAN, Gordon Chatterton, took the initiative in 1950 to organize a 1/5 Queens Canloan Association with a newsletter that was sent to the eight CANLOAN officers who had served in the battalion and an equal number of British comrades who contributed news. His only continuous contact since then, however, has been with Bill Crook, a former 1/5 Queens British fellow officer.

Perhaps letters were not the best medium for those whose shared experiences were so limited and brief, and in any case most people are poor correspondents. Certainly when opportunities for visits in Canada or the United Kingdom occurred, the spontaneous pleasure was often a moving experience. Such visits were limited initially to CANLOAN officers whose business or occasional vacations took them abroad. Among them were Don Oland and Hank Henry, who visited friends, as well as Al McLennan and Vince Lilley, who attended several regimental reunions. When Lilley and Rex Fendick were at Bisley several times with Canadian rifle teams, they took the opportunity to visit old comrades.

Fred Chesham and Ross LeMesurier were among those who, during periodic visits to the UK, became reacquainted with regimental friends. Tom King donated his Canadian battle dress with the Dorset, 43rd Division, and Canada badges on it to the Dorset regimental museum.

Sometimes CANLOAN officers were in the UK for a considerable time and had extended opportunities to look up old friends. Rod MacKay, for example, was an exchange instructor at the British School of Infantry for several years. Civilian ex-CANLOAN officers, too, sometimes lived in the UK for fairly long periods – Leo Heaps, for example, whose overlapping careers of art dealer and author were based in London for several years, and Jack Young, whose business headquarters was in London for shorter periods.

The two CANLOAN officers who stayed in the UK after the war – Peter Pearce in Scotland and John Stone in Devon – were, to all intents and purposes, British.

As time went on, especially after retirement, the frequency of visits by CANLOAN officers to the UK and by their British comrades to Canada increased, but never ceased to evoke the magic and pleasure of shared vital experiences. This was most vivid in reunions after many years: Jim Duncan was a guest at a mini-reunion of officers with whom he had served, at a dinner at the Savoy Hotel in 1968; Wilf Smith was surprised by a similar reunion at a luncheon at Wiltshire Regimental Headquarters in Salisbury in 1986; Stewart Cameron was overwhelmed by the hospitality of the Glasgow Highlanders in 1968 and 1982. The reception of British officers visiting their CANLOAN comrades in Canada was equally extensive and fully appreciated, as is attested by many reports published in the *Canloan Review* over the years.

A new element in the British connection was introduced with the founding of the Canloan Army Officers Association in 1954, for it could express formally the feelings or wishes of CANLOAN officers towards Britain and the British. For example, a telegram on behalf of the new association was sent in 1954 to Sir Winston Churchill on his 80th birthday: "All honour, health and happiness to our illustrious warrior from surviving CANLOANs."[20] Subsequent messages were sent to HM the Queen on her Silver Jubilee in 1977 and on the occasion of the Falklands War: "Canada and CANLOANs rejoice with Great Britain and her Armed Forces in their great victory and the reaffirmation of their determination to stand fast."[21]

A continuing relationship with representatives of the British government was established with the construction and unveiling of the CANLOAN National Memorial in Ottawa in 1961. When the memorial was being planned and it was evident that money needed to be raised, the British High Commissioner, Sir Saville Garner, suggested that the British regiments in which CANLOAN officers had served should be invited to contribute. The British Defence Liaison Staff (BDLS) in Ottawa, under the direction of Brig. Hugh Tyler, assisted in contacting those British regiments. Letters signed by Brigadier Gregg were sent to the colonels of the regiments, and virtually all of them, more than 40, responded by contributions to the memorial fund and warm tributes to the service of the CANLOAN officers. Brigadier Tyler then arranged for Sir Saville to attend the dedication of the memorial and a subsequent reception at Earnscliffe, the High Commissioner's residence.

Since the dedication of the memorial in 1961, CANLOAN officers from Ottawa and farther afield have gathered at the memorial on 6 June and on Remembrance Day each year to pay tribute to their fallen comrades. On all occasions the BDLS has been present and joined the CANLOANs in placing wreaths at the memorial. A number of Brigadier Tyler's successors have been guests at CANLOAN national reunions.

After the war the British Army underwent a major reorganization, as a result of which a great many of the old and famous British infantry regiments disappeared though amalgamation into new composite units. Thus many of the regiments in which CANLOAN officers served now exist only in the form of regimental associations, maintained by veterans of the former regiments. Nevertheless, the ties remain strong, and recognition of the connection with CANLOAN is gratifyingly sincere and wholehearted.

The composition of the Ottawa contingent of CANLOAN was rather unstable, since for years it included many CANLOAN officers still in the Army who were stationed at Headquarters for only brief stints. Faced with the challenge of arranging for the construction and unveiling of a national memorial, the Ottawa CANLOAN were mobilized under the direction and leadership of Don Diplock, and 18 of them participated in the memorial arrangements. From 1961 on, the memorial has become a continuing charge for Ottawa CANLOAN, who are responsible for the wreath-laying ceremonies twice a year. Even so, at times the attendance was small. In 1964 Don Diplock reported that on 11 November the five CANLOAN officers were nearly outnumbered by the four Brits on parade. This has changed, as more CANLOAN officers from Montreal, Toronto, and elsewhere have begun to come to Ottawa regularly for the ceremonies, particularly on Remembrance Day.

Almost immediately the British High Commissioner began the practice of inviting the CANLOAN officers and their wives to lunch at Earnscliffe after the wreath laying. Then, when it became known that some out-of-town CANLOAN were arriving on 10 November, the senior officer at BDLS began the practice of inviting all the assembled CANLOAN to dinner or a reception. Very soon a bond of friendship with the staff officers at BDLS and their wives was firmly established. It was extended to a wider circle of CANLOAN outside Ottawa as the senior staff officers were regularly invited and accepted invitations to virtually all CANLOAN reunions. In 1965 Col. J.M.A. Tillett, then Deputy Senior Army Liaison Officer, wrote an article for his regimental newsletter, the *Royal Green Jackets Chronicle*, in which he described the fourth national CANLOAN reunion which he had just attended and the special relationship with CANLOAN of the British representatives in Canada.

During Expo '67, the General Manager of British Trust House hotels presented the Canloan Association on board Don Oland's *Bluenose II* with a replica of the Red Lion sign of the inn in Colchester, which had become a part of the CANLOAN legend. This is in the form of a red and black cast metal sign and stand which is a table piece at CANLOAN dinners. The presentation generated a number of stories about CANLOAN in the British press.

The CANLOAN pilgrimage overseas in 1968 had the effect of rekindling the feelings of kinship with British comrades on a far greater scale than had been possible in occasional private visits and infrequent correspondence. CANLOAN officers and their wives were delighted with the warmth of the welcome which they received and were impressed with the British mastery of the ceremonial and respect for tradition. Particularly notable was the presentation to members of the Royal Family by the colonels of their regiments. In Edinburgh it was discovered that the names of CANLOAN officers who had been killed in action while serving with Scottish regiments had inadvertently been omitted from the regimental books of remembrance in Edinburgh Castle. This omission was quickly remedied.

The 1968 trip generated a series of contacts between the families of CANLOAN officers and those of former comrades that have continued to the present. From 1968 on, the *Canloan Review* reports frequent contacts of CANLOAN officers with their regiments, including visits to friends, attendance at regimental reunions, the presentation of CANLOAN scrolls to British regiments, participation in such events as the unveiling of a 3rd Division memorial at Caen in Normandy, and the 300th anniversary of the Royal Highland Fusiliers, which was attended by a strong contingent of CANLOAN HLI officers.

In 1977 the 3rd Infantry Division, the only formation remaining in the peacetime British Army of those in which CANLOAN officers served in 1944–45, was reorganized in the British Army of the Rhineland into an armoured division, thus ending its continuous tradition as an infantry division since 1809. To mark the change, the GOC authorized the publication of a divisional history. On hearing of this, former CANLOAN officers who had served in the 3rd Division were quickly in touch with the author. Consequently the history included a section on CANLOAN in the division quite out of proportion with the 170 years' events covered. Subsequently, when the 3rd Division in Germany organized memorial services in Normandy and at their home station at Soest to mark the 40th anniversary of the division's assault landing on Sword Beach on D-Day, they made a particular effort to invite former CANLOAN officers. Those who attended were given a very special reception, both by the staff of the current division and by old comrades attending from the UK.

The eighth national reunion in Ottawa in 1974, on the 30th anniversary of the CANLOAN scheme, was, in a way, a response to the British hospitality in 1968 with emphasis on the continuing relationship of CANLOAN officers with their British regiments. Officers were urged to invite their former commanding officers and others to attend. Post-reunion tours from coast to coast were arranged, and all were delighted that the British Army was represented by Gen. Sir John Mogg, Deputy Supreme Commander of SHAPE and a former CO of several CANLOAN officers.

A number of isolated circumstances prevented the attendance of as many British guests as had been expected. Even Brig. "Speedy" Bredin couldn't make it. But it was a success, and for those who did attend and were surrounded by former members of their regiments or divisions amid expressions of comradeship and brotherhood, it was obvious that CANLOAN affection for their British comrades was as strong as ever. Col. Nick Nice was a focal point of the Queens CANLOAN, indeed of all those who served with the 7th Armoured Division "Desert Rats"; Maj. Jerry Jarvis represented the South Staffordshire Regiment and 59 Division; Jack Young brought his former CO of 1/4 KOYLI, Col. Godfrey Harland-Barker; and all the 2 Glas. H. were glad to renew acquaintance with Majors Archic Mason and Gordon Lightbody. As Colonel Barker-Harland remarked, "It was interesting and touching to find that so many CANLOAN officers still retain their affection for the British Regiments and, indeed, for the Divisions in which they served so gallantly thirty years ago. The CANLOAN story is interesting and the record is a proud one."[22]

If one looks for an explanation for this strong regimental bond, it is difficult to improve on the remarks of Sir John Mogg at the CANLOAN banquet in 1974: "The events of 1944–1945 burned themselves into the memory of all of us who were involved and I know that we forged unbreakable friendships in the heat of battle. All too many of them to be tragically broken but some thankfully still fresh and rewarding after having survived more than a quarter of a century."[23]

Brigadier Gregg was always surprised at the strong esprit de corps, sense of identity, and kinship of CANLOAN, since it seemed to have such an insubstantial base in brief casual meetings of young men with diverse origins. Surprise can be expressed as well that these same officers could retain for nearly half a century strong bonds of friendship with people in a country across the Atlantic with whom they had such brief association. In both cases the key is the sharing of vital and significant experiences that cannot be forgotten and that provide a special bond. A regiment can symbolize, too, the shared ideals of those who served in it, the memory of comrades who did not survive, the traditions of which it is the custodian.

The number of individuals who are involved in the British connection of CANLOAN officers is small, will disappear completely in a few years, and has had no great influence on British-Canadian relationships as a whole. There are, however, elements in the CANLOAN story that illustrate interesting facets of human behaviour: the motivation of persons who volunteer for certain danger, leadership of junior officers in battle, adaptation to alien customs and groups, the relationship between wartime experiences and civilian careers, and, not least, the nature of group loyalties.

Just as it is impossible for any soldier who has been in action to explain "what it was like" to someone who was not, so too, no CANLOAN can ever describe what binds him to his regiment, his division, or his comrades of that time. But the intense regimental and divisional loyalties remain. They were forged in fire, and they have not weakened. They are, in the words to CANLOAN by the Lord Mayor of London in 1968, paraphrasing Edmund Burke, "strong as iron but light as air."

Appendix A

Brochure for Potential CANLOAN Volunteers

Opportunity for Early Overseas Service with the British Army

Questions, Answers and General Information Concerning
Loan of Canadian Officers to the British Army

The Canadian Army having a surplus of Reinforcement Officers and the British Army being in need of Lieutenants and Captains (Infantry), arrangements have now been completed whereby Officers of the Canadian Army may volunteer for service on loan to the British Army.

This plan provides an opportunity for Canadian officers to see Overseas service in the very near future and to acquire valuable experience with the British Army without sacrificing any of the rights and privileges enjoyed as officers of the Canadian Army. Officers on loan will continue to draw Canadian rates of pay and allowances, and the Canadian Government will continue to be responsible for pay, pension claims, etc. All rehabilitation entitlements will be granted on exactly the same basis as to officers who serve Overseas with the Canadian forces. Officers may be recalled to Canadian service as and when needed, with due regard to operational requirements.

Volunteers may also be accepted from R.C.A. and R.C.A.S.C. provided they are willing to take a refresher course to obtain the necessary infantry qualifications, and transfer to the Canadian Infantry Corps. Officers on loan may continue to wear their Canadian badges and regimental insignia on service dress and "Canada" together with such British insignia as necessary, on battle dress. Wherever possible, officers of Canadian regiments will be posted to the British regiment of which the Canadian regiment is an affiliate.

The purpose of this booklet is to endeavour to answer questions which have been raised by Canadian officers considering this transfer. If you are of Overseas age and Pulhems profile, and eager to see action in the near future, secure from your Commanding Officer the details regarding service with the British Army.

PROBABLE QUESTIONS IN CONNECTION WITH VOLUNTARY SERVICE WITH THE BRITISH ARMY

1. Q. What procedure is necessary to volunteer for service with the British Army?
   A. Application to Commanding Officer.

2. Q. How would my pay and allowances, and eligibility for pension be affected by voluntary service with the British Army?
   A. Not affected – still retained on strength of Canadian Army and services only loaned.

3. Q. Would my Dependents' Allowance be affected?
   A. No.

4. Q. Which Government (British or Canadian) would be responsible for my pay and allowances?
   A. Canadian.

5. Q. Would service with the British Army affect my Canadian post-war rehabilitation?
   A. No.

6. Q. Would I be expected to pay British rates of Income Tax, or would I be exempt – similarly to Canadian serving Overseas?
   A. Exempt.

7. Q. Under what jurisdiction would I be for discipline, etc?
   A. While on loan the officer would be under the jurisdiction of his Commanding Officer as in the case of Canadian Service, but provision is being made for the control of the more severe disciplinary actions by the Overseas Canadian authorities.

8. Q. Can I withdraw from serving with the British Army for one reason or another – compassionate grounds, inability to get along with British officers, unhappiness, etc?
   A. After a minimum period of three months service with the British an officer may, through his Commanding Officer at that time, make application for return to Canadian Overseas authorities. This provision has been made, however, to meet exceptional circumstances and will not be utilized to facilitate the return of officers to Canadian service for other than essential reasons, prior to recall by Canadian Army.

9. Q. Can the British Army have me returned to the Canadian Army and, if so, how would this procedure affect my military career?
   A. The War Office may, where the services of a Canadian Officer have been found in any way unsuitable, return him to Canadian service but in no case shall this action be taken until the officer has served a minimum of three months with the British and until C.M.H.Q. has concurred in this procedure. The effect of such a return to Canadian Service on the military career of an officer would necessarily depend on the circumstances in each individual case.

10. Q. Would I have any channel of communication other than through regimental channels in connection with complaints, etc?
    A. Normal channel through Officer Commanding, but Liaison Officers will be at C.M.H.Q. to watch interests of officers on loan.

11. Q. By volunteering for British service, is an officer likely to miss an opportunity to proceed Overseas in the immediate future as a Canadian Reinforcement Officer?
    A. No – He should proceed Overseas much earlier.

12. Q. Upon the cessation of hostilities, how soon would a volunteer be returned to the Canadian Army?

    A. As soon as the necessary administration arrangements can be completed.

13. Q. Does service with the British Army affect my eligibility for confirmation of rank or promotion?

    A. No.

14. Q. What are the prospects of promotion while on loan?

    A. Officers will be employed in British formations and will be eligible for promotion on those establishments on British recommendation, approved by Canadian Overseas authority. An officer consequently by leaving the reinforcement pool for service in unit becomes eligible for promotion earlier than would now be possible.

15. Q. In what theatre of operations would I serve?

    A. European or Mediterranean.

16. Q. Would other Canadian officers be with me in larger or smaller formations?

    A. Yes.

17. Q. Was the idea of loaning Canadian officers to the British Army instigated by Canada or Great Britain?

    A. Canada.

18. Q. Why was the question of a loan of officers developed with the British?

    A. The Canadian Army can now afford to loan officers to the British to *secure necessary active service experience* and also the British are in need of the services of a great number of officers to complete their formations. (Amended by deletion of italicized words.)

19. Q. Would I keep my identity as a Canadian, through the wearing of "Canada" badges?

    A. Yes.

20. Q. Officer qualification in what branches of the service are required at the present time?

    A. Only officers qualified in Infantry will be loaned at the present time, but volunteers from R.C.A.S.C. and R.C.A. (Coast Defence and Anti-aircraft Artillery) will be accepted. These officers will be given special qualification courses in Infantry prior to dispatch but will be given assurance of inclusion in quota of loan to British when qualification completed.

21. Q. What training standard is necessary?

    A. As for qualified Canadian Reinforcement Officers, Infantry.

22.   Q.   What medical standard is necessary?
      A.   As for qualified Canadian Reinforcement Officers, Infantry.

23.   Q.   What age groups are required?
      A.   As for qualified Canadian Reinforcement Officers, Infantry.

24.   Q.   What ranks are required?
      A.   Captains and Lieutenants on basis of one Captain to eight Lieutenants.

25.   Q.   Is any specialized training planned?
      A.   One month at Special Officers' Training Centre before dispatch Overseas.

26.   Q.   Would a fully trained Canadian Infantry Officer have any difficulty with different standards of training in the British Army?
      A.   Standards are not essentially different.

27.   Q.   Can the British Army reject volunteers upon arrival in the United Kingdom?
      A.   No.

28.   Q.   Is there a sufficiently large officer surplus in Canada to spare whatever numbers may be required for service with the British Army?
      A.   Reinforcement officers for Canadian Army are now available in such numbers as to preclude their early service Overseas and consequently their services can be made available to the British but only in numbers as can be spared.

29.   Q.   Are French-Canadian Officers eligible?
      A.   Yes, if thoroughly bilingual.

30.   Q.   Would compassionate leave be granted under such circumstances as would warrant such leave in the Canadian Army?
      A.   Yes.

31.   Q.   Would a volunteer lose seniority in the Canadian Army?
      A.   No.

32.   Q.   Would a volunteer be given an opportunity to remain in the permanent British Army after the war?
      A.   British authorities are encouraging applications for service in post-war Army.

33.   Q.   Can an officer with unit affiliation in Canadian Army be posted for service in a battalion of the same regiment in the British Army?
      A.   The British Army will, wherever possible, post an officer to the British unit to which his unit in the Canadian Army is affiliated.

34.   Q.   Was a similar plan operated in the last war, and were results satisfactory to all concerned?

A. No, but over 21,000 Officers and Other Ranks transferred to British Units from Canadian in World War I. Hundreds of officers and thousands of other ranks are serving in conjunction with British in this war.

35. Q. Is it not possible that a Canadian officer might be posted to a Welsh or Highland unit, and experience difficulty in adapting himself to unfamiliar accents, etc?
     A. No difficulty is anticipated. English is the common language of the soldier.

36. Q. What are the advantages of volunteering for service with the British Army?
     A. The advantages are numerous, but principally are:

     (a) Opportunity for early Overseas service.
     (b) Having the benefit of active service experience before returning to command experienced Canadian troops *in event of recall to Canadian Service*. (Amended by addition of italicized words.)
     (c) Opportunity for earlier promotion.
     (d) Avoiding prolonged delay in Canada due to large backlog of reinforcements presently in training here.
     (e) Material advantages such as tax exemption.

Appendix B

Acknowledgment Signed by CANLOAN Volunteers

APPENDIX "A" TO H.Q.C.8932–1 F.D.12 (Pers 2) of 23rd February 1944

Acknowlegment

I,   , an officer of the Canadian Army serving on active service, do hereby acknowledge that I have of my own volition expressed my willingness to be placed by the appropriate Canadian Service Authorities, as an Officer of His Majesty's Military Forces raised in Canada, at the disposal of the Army Council of the United Kingdom for attachment, pursuant to the Visiting Forces British Commonwealth Act, 1933, to the Military Forces of His Majesty raised in the United Kingdom, hereinafter referred to as "the United Kingdom Forces," for service with the said last mentioned Forces under the following conditions: –

(i) That, subject to what is hereinafter contained, I shall serve with the United Kingdom Forces until such time as I may be recalled therefrom by the appropriate Canadian Military Authority, but in any event such service shall not extend beyond the termination of the state of war now existing;

(ii) That if, in any exceptional case, I consider that I have just and reasonable cause for so doing, I may request that I be returned to the Canadian Military Forces for service therein, provided, however, that in no event will I make such request within a period of three months from the date of commencement of my service with the United Kingdom Forces, and provided further that the granting of any such request will be at the discretion of the appropriate Canadian Military Authority if, in the opinion of that Authority, said request is in the circumstances just and reasonable;

(iii) That during my attachment to the United Kingdom Forces I shall be subject at all times to the Military and other laws applicable to such Forces and the members thereof except to such extent as the same may be adapted or modified by Order of his Majesty in Council;

(iv) That while attached as aforesaid to the United Kingdom Forces I shall continue to be paid the Canadian rates of Pay and Allowances as are applicable to or in respect of the rank or appointment I may from time to time hold; and shall be eligible for pension, rehabilitation grant and other non-effective benefits in like manner and to the same extent as if my service while so attached to the United Kingdom Forces had been served with the Canadian Military Forces in like rank or appointment therein.

The foregoing shall not be deemed to be or construed as an admission or acknowledgment on the part of His Majesty in the right of Canada, or of the Canadian Service Authorities, that my consent or willingness, as an Officer of the Canadian Army serving on active service, to be placed at the disposal of the Army Council of the United Kingdom for attachment to the United Kingdom Forces is a legal prerequisite to my being so placed at such disposal as aforesaid and being so attached in consequence thereof. This document is to be construed solely as an acknowledgment on my part that I voluntarily express my willingness to be placed at such disposal for attachment as aforesaid and that I understand fully the general terms and conditions under which I shall serve with the United Kingdom Forces whilst so attached thereto.

DATED at   this   day of   19   .

_____   _____

Witness   Signature of Officer

Appendix C

Flights of CANLOAN Officers

Flight Number	Depart			Arrive			Ship	Number of CANLOANS	CDN Numbers
	Date		Port	Date		Port			
1	29	Mar	Halifax	6	Apr	Liverpool	*Andes*	52	1–52
2	3	Apr	Halifax	10	Apr	Liverpool	*Louis Pasteur*	57	53–109
3	7	Apr	Halifax	24	Apr	Edinburgh	*Cavina*	93	110–202
4	14	Apr	Halifax	1	May	Liverpool	*Bayano*	48	330–368
5	3	May	Halifax	11	May	Liverpool	*Empress of Scotland*	250	202–557
6	19	May	Sydney	2	Jun	Greenoch	*Beaverhill*	34	494–59
7	10	Jun	Halifax	25	Jun	Greenoch	*Cavina*	30	560–589
8	16	Jun	Halifax	23	Jun	Greenoch	*Empress of Scotland*	88	590–677
9	24	Jul	Halifax	29	Jul	Greenoch	*Neue Amsterdam*	21	678–697

Appendix D

Leaflet from General Sir Ronald Adam, War Office

To   _____

_____

With the compliments of
General Sir Ronald Adam, Bt., K.C.B., D.S.O., O.B.E.,
Adjutant-General to the Forces.

The War Office,
April, 1944.

---

1. The object of this leaflet is to welcome you on your arrival in England and to explain to you the reason for your posting to the British Army and conditions of your service while so posted.

2. The Army Council wish to extend to you their most cordial welcome and assure you that the Army, and in particular the unit to which you are now being posted, will receive you in the same spirit.

3. The reason for this most generous loan by the Canadian Government of the services of a large number of Canadian officers is the considerable officer shortage in British Infantry which the Canadian Government are helping to make good by the loan of your services.

   The officer commitments of the British Army do not end with the British Army itself. They are world wide and include the provision of officers for the Indian Army; for the large Force which has been raised in West Africa; for the East African Forces and for numbers of other smaller Non-European Forces, such as the Sudan Defence Force, the Transjordan Frontier Force, etc.

   It is these large outside commitments which have led to the shortage, together with the demands on the potential officer material made by the other fighting Services.

4. On being posted, as you will be immediately, to a British Army unit, you will become, to all intents and purposes, as much a part of that unit as are those officers of the British Service now serving with it. You will be posted to units for service in European or Mediterranean Theatres of War and not in Theatres of War in India and the Far East.

   Wherever possible Canadian officers belonging to Canadian Regiments affiliated to British Regiments are being posted to their affiliated Regiments.

5.   Your conditions of service whilst you serve with the British Army will be very much the same as those of the other officers of your unit and, broadly speaking, you will be treated as if you were a British Army officer. There are, however, certain matters which are handled differently in the two Armies, and as you will continue to be a Canadian Army officer, certain modifications in administrative procedure are necessary. These are stated briefly in the following paragraphs.

6.   Pay and Allowances. – You will receive all your emoluments (pay, dependents' allowances, allowances in lieu of accommodation and rations, and travelling allowances and expenses) from Canadian Army Paymasters at Canadian Army rates. When serving outside the United Kingdom, however, you will receive travelling allowances and expenses from British Army Paymasters at British Army rates.

Food and accommodation when provided in kind, which will probably be the general rule, will be in accordance with British Army scales.

7.   Promotion. – Any promotion which you receive will be in accordance with the Canadian Army system of acting and temporary rank. The appropriate British Army authority will be empowered to promote you to and revert you from acting rank and in this respect the normal British Army rules will be applied. Acting rank will normally be relinquished when you cease to perform the duties of that rank, though under British rules you are entitled to retain such rank for limited periods when sick, on a course, on temporary duty and so on. Conversion of acting to temporary rank will, however, be effected by Canadian Military headquarters on the recommendation of the British Army authority. Acting rank must be held for *six* months before it can be converted to temporary rank. Broken periods may be reckoned cumulatively.

Once you are granted temporary rank by Canadian Military Headquarters it will be regarded as equivalent to war substantive rank in the British Army.

8.   Dress. – Your dress whilst serving with the British Army will be battledress with the badges of the unit to which you are posted, and the shoulder strip "CANADA." When in service dress you may wear your own Canadian Army uniform and Canadian badges if you wish.

9.   Documentation. – You have been asked to complete two copies of Army Form B199A (Officers' record of service). One copy is required at the War Office so that your location and other particulars may be available if needed there. The duplicate will be sent by your unit to 2nd Echelon where it will be maintained for the same purpose.

It is not the purpose of this leaflet to set out the full details of administration and documentation which have been adopted in your case. That is being done in an Army Council Instruction which is being printed and issued to all concerned. A copy is available in your unit.

But you will no doubt wish to know at once that arrangements have been made for all information affecting you to be reported to Canadian Military Headquarters with all possible speed. Canadian Military Headquarters will in turn transmit this information to Canada wherever and whenever this is necessary, and should you become a casualty it is the aim to ensure that your next of kin are informed as certainly and as quickly as they would be if you were serving overseas with the Canadian Army.

It is for this reason that (among other things) you have been given a personal number with a prefix "CDN" so that you can be picked out quickly from reports on British Army officers. *It is therefore in your interests to see that this number and prefix are used in all documents relating to you.*

10. Medical procedure. – Medical procedure will be as for British Army officers, and if you are admitted to hospital you should make quite certain that the authorities know that you are a Canadian Army officer serving with the British Army. Reports about your state of health will be forwarded to the Office-in-charge Records, Canadian Military Headquarters, who will transmit them to Canada. Hospitals in this country have been told to regard him as your next of kin for this purpose.

The British Army system of Medical Categories will be used. This you will learn about in your unit.

Should you become permanently medically unfit for service with the British Army, arrangements would be made with Canadian Military Headquarters for your return.

11. Return to Canada. – Should you have strong compassionate reasons for wanting to return to Canada you should apply to your Commanding Officer. Your application will be sent, via the War Office, to Canadian Military Headquarters where it will be considered and a decision given. You will understand that operational considerations must influence that decision and that the general policy to be followed will be that adopted for the Canadian Army overseas as a whole.

(SO 4548) Wt. 59600–9994 2M 4/44 H & S, Ltd. Gp. 393

Appendix E

British Regulations Concerning CANLOAN Officers

ARMY COUNCIL INSTRUCTION No. 504 of 1944 Circulated down to Companies, Batteries and Equivalent Units

The War Office *15th April, 1944*

---

504.   Canadian Officers Specially Lent to the British Army – Conditions of Service and Procedure for Administration, Documentation, and Accounting.

1. Arrangements have been made for a number of officers of the Canadian Army to be posted to units of the British Army for service during the present emergency. The total number of officers involved will be large and it is expected that the first party (approximately 250) will be available for posting to British units at the beginning of April, 1944. The code word for the scheme is "CANLOAN."

2. The officers will be volunteers, and will be of the rank of captain or lieutenant. They will be available for posting to units for service in European or Mediterranean theatres of war only and will not be available for service in theatres of war in India or the Far East.

3. They will retain their identity as Canadian Army officers but from the date on which they are posted to units of the British Army they will be treated as if they were British Army officers.

Except as stated in this A.C.I. and Appendix A, the normal British Army administrative procedure, including channels of communication, will be followed in dealing with them.

A.C.I.222 of 1943, which refers only to officers of the Canadian Army *temporarily attached* to units of the British Army, does not apply to CANLOAN officers.

4. Officers will be provided, under arrangements being made by the War Office, with a leaflet containing brief details of the conditions of service, and an outline of the procedure for their administration, while they are serving with the British Army.

5. *Postings and Transfers* – Officers will be posted initially to units of their own arm of the Service by the War Office. Subsequent postings within the same arm or to staff employment may be made by commands to whom authority to post has been delegated by the War Office. Transfers between arms or employment in another arm will not be effected by

commands, whether with or without the officer's consent. All such applications will be forwarded to the War Office.

6. *Dress* – Officers will, normally, wear battledress with the badges of the British Army unit to which they are posted, and the shoulder strip "CANADA". Officers appointed to staff or extra regimental employment will, when in battledress, wear the badges of the unit which they were wearing on appointment. When wearing service dress they may, if they wish, wear Canadian pattern uniform with the badges and insignia of their parent Canadian regiment or corps.

7. *Pay and allowances*

(a)   Subject to the exception in sub-para. (b) below, the rules governing the pay and allowances for CANLOAN officers will be those in force in the Canadian Army.

(b)   While serving in the British Army they will be paid all emoluments (pay, dependents' allowances, allowances in lieu of accommodation and rations, and travelling allowances and expenses) by the Canadian authorities at Canadian rates, except that when serving outside the United Kingdom they will be paid travelling allowances and expenses by British paymasters at British rates.

The Canadian Government will continue to be responsible for pension claims, etc.

(c)   These officers will be eligible for Canadian rehabilitation entitlement and, for this purpose, service with the British Army will count as service with the Canadian Forces.

(d)   The British and Canadian Governments will reciprocally not recover from each other any expenses incurred under sub-paras. (b) and (c) above.

8. *Promotion* – CANLOAN officers will be promoted in accordance with the Canadian Army system of acting and temporary rank. Canadian temporary rank is equivalent to, and held under the same conditions as, British Army war substantive rank.

Officers will be eligible for the grant of acting rank within the War Establishments exactly as British officers. Acting rank will be paid, and when held for six months (182 days) will be convertible to temporary rank, retrospectively for this period, subject to confirmation by the Canadian military authorities. Broken periods of acting rank while serving with the British Army will count towards the grant of temporary rank. Apart from these modifications the normal British Army rules for acting rank will apply.

The grant or relinquishment of acting rank, and the conversion of acting to temporary rank will be notified to command headquarters in the same manner as for British officers. Such casualties will be published in a special Appendix (headed "CANLOAN officers") to command or routine orders, four copies of which will be despatched by the command concerned direct to the O.i/c Records, Canadian Military Headquarters, with a copy to the War Office. These casualties will not appear in War Office Orders, but Canadian Military

Headquarters will confirm all promotions to temporary rank to the command and to War Office. All appointments, promotions, relinquishments, etc., will in due course, be re-published in Canadian Supplements to Overseas Routine Orders.

9. *Hospital treatment* – The procedure will be the same as for officers of the British Army but recoveries for treatment in hospital will not be made except in cases of alcoholism, including drug addiction; such recoveries will be decided, and effected, by the Canadian authorities.

10. *Discipline* – Officers will be attached under the provisions of the Visiting Forces (British Commonwealth) Act, 1933, Section 4 (2) (i). Consequently, they become subject to United Kingdom military law and will be treated for disciplinary purposes as if they were officers of the British Army of equivalent rank.

Instructions will be issued later for dealing with the case in which a CANLOAN officer is convicted by court-martial and sentenced to death, or to be cashiered or dismissed.

A.C.I.810 of 1942 will not apply to CANLOAN officers.

11. *Powers of command and punishment* – Officers will have the like powers of command and punishment over members of the United Kingdom forces to which they are attached as if they were members of the United Kingdom forces of equivalent rank.

12. *Confidential reports*

(a)   Confidential reports will be completed by the British authorities on A.F.B 194 series.

(b)   Adverse reports which recommend the return of an officer to the Canadian Service will be at the direction of the appropriate British commander not below the rank of major-general, and will be sent from force or command headquarters direct to Canadian Military Headquarters, which authority will take action on them in consultation with the War Office. A copy of A.F.B 194 will be sent by the force or command headquarters direct to the War Office (M.S.4). Such a report will not be initiated on an officer until after three months from the date of his first posting to a British unit.

(c)   Other reports on A.F.B 194 series, including recommendations for advancement on the staff or for command, will be completed in duplicate and will be forwarded through the usual channels to the War Office (M.S.4), who will pass the duplicate copy to Canadian Military Headquarters for information and retention.

13. *Return to Canadian Army* – The Canadian Army authorities will not consider applications from CANLOAN officers to return to the Canadian Service, except as provided in para. 15.

14. *Return to Canada on compassionate grounds* – Should an officer have strong compassionate reasons for wanting to return to Canada he should apply to his C.O. setting

forth all available information, with copies of any supporting documents. The application will be sent direct from the unit to the War Office who will transmit it to Canadian Military Headquarters for decision.

15. *Representation of grievances* – When a CANLOAN officer considers he has a grievance and on application to his C.O. does not receive the redress to which he may consider himself entitled he may make representations in writing setting out all relevant facts. These representations will be disposed of, as found necessary, by successive commanders in the chain of command. If the officer is still dissatisfied, the case will be referred to the War Office for disposal. If redress has not been provided by any higher British authority the representations, which may contain a request for return to Canadian Service, will be passed by the War Office as expeditiously as possible to Canadian Military Headquarters. Any such officer may, in his representations, include a request for an interview with an officer representing Canadian Military Headquarters, in which case appropriate arrangements will be made.

16. *Honours, Awards, and Service Medals*

(a)   While serving with the British Army CANLOAN officers will be treated for the purpose of Honours and awards, as though they belonged to the British Army. The War Office will advise Canadian Military Headquarters of any awards made, sending copies of the citations.

(b)   While serving with the British Army CANLOAN officers may qualify for British service or campaign medals under the same conditions as for British officers. Claims for such awards will follow normal British procedure.

(c)   Applications for purely Canadian service medals will be forwarded by units direct to the O.i/c Records, Canadian Military Headquarters.

17. *Channels of communication* – Except as specially provided in this A.C.I. all questions regarding the posting, administration and documentation of CANLOAN officers will be submitted by units through the usual channels for decision.

Matters of a routine nature (*e.g.*, observations on Part II Orders [Officers]) relating to individual casualties may be dealt with direct between the O.i/c Records, Canadian Military Headquarters and British units. In such cases, copies of the correspondence will be despatched to the War Office.

Questions regarding an individual's pay and allowances may be settled direct with the Chief Paymaster, Canadian Army Overseas, Bromyard Avenue, Acton W.3.

100/Miscellaneous/1482 (A.G.1 (Officers)).

CANLOAN Officers – Detailed Instructions for Administration, Documentation and Accounting

Note: The full addresses of the Canadian authorities referred to in the A.C.I. and this appendix are:–

(a) Canadian Military Headquarters:–

> 2, Cockspur Street, London, S.W.1.
> Telephone No.: Abbey 9090
> Telegraphic address: Canrecords, Lesquare.

(b) O. i/c Records, Canadian Military Headquarters:–

> Government Buildings, Bromyard Avenue, Acton, W.3.
> Telephone No.: Shepherds Bush 3120
> Telegraphic address: Canrecords, London.

(c) Chief Paymaster, Canadian Army Overseas:–

> Government Buildings, Bromyard Avenue, Acton, W.3.
> Telephone No.: Shepherds Bush 3120
> Telegraphic address: Canrecords, Lesquare.

prefaced "for C.P.M."

1.   *Documentation*

(a)   Each officer, on being posted to a British unit, will be allotted a personal number by the War Office. This number will have, as an additional means of identification, the prefix "CDN", *e.g.* CDN/96. The numbers will be quoted in all communications, and upon all documents, in connexion with individual officers. It is important that the prefix always be used.

(b)   *Record of Service* – A.F.B 199A (reprint 2/43) will be completed in duplicate by each officer before being posted to a British unit. The *original* will be held at, and maintained by, the War Office. The *duplicate* will be handed by the officer to his unit on first joining; this copy will be retained by the O.C. unit unless the unit is administered by a G.H.Q., 2nd Echelon in which case the form will be transmitted by the unit to that G.H.Q. after extraction of the particulars required.

Any other records peculiar to the Canadian Army held by the officer will be retained by the unit and will be disposed of with other documents held on reposting to another unit.

(c)   A.B.439 *(Officer's Record of Service),* will be issued by the unit to which an officer is posted.

(d) *Document of Identity* – Each officer will be in possession of Form MFM 182 which will be retained by him. A.F.B 2606 series will not be issued.

(e) *Identity Discs* – Identity discs already in his possession will be stamped with the prefix and personal number allotted (*see* sub-para. (a) above) under unit arrangements.

2.   A.F.B 158 *(Series)*.

(a) CANLOAN officers will be shown on A.F.B 158A and A.F.B 158 (War) exactly as British officers, and the return will have the normal distribution.

(b) G.H.Q., 2nd Echelons administering CANLOAN officers will, in addition to A.F.B 158, submit on the last day of each month to the O.i/c Records, Canadian Military Headquarters a roll (in quadruplicate), showing the following particulars of all CANLOAN officers in units:–

   (i)   Personal number.
   (ii) Rank, name and initials.
   (iii) Corps in Canadian Army, and British Army unit.

3.   *Part II Orders (Officers)*

(a) Casualties, both Sections A and B (*see* A.C.I. 789 of 1943) affecting CANLOAN officers will be published as for British officers. Full personal particulars will be given where each CANLOAN officer's name appears
   Sections A and B casualties occurring to an officer while he is temporarily attached to another unit will be reported to the O.C. unit to which he is posted, for publication in that unit's Part II Orders (Officers).

(b) When units holding CANLOAN officers on their posted strength are not administered by G.H.Q., 2nd Echelons four copies of all Part II Orders (Officers) will be sent to the O.i/c Records, Canadian Military Headquarters.

(c) Units administered by G.H.Q., 2nd Echelon will report all casualties on A.Fs.W 3010 and W 3011 Series as in the case of British officers.
   For the purpose of publishing Part II Orders (Officers) G.H.Q., 2nd Echelon will regard CANLOAN officers as being of a separate category; and, where required, will publish a separate series for them for each arm (*e.g.*, Canadian Infantry Corps, R.C.A.S.C.) of the Canadian Army.
   The distribution of each series for CANLOAN officers will include the O.i/c Records, Canadian Military Headquarters (four copies).

4.   *Accounting* – Normal strength returns compiled by units and by G.H.Q., 2nd Echelons for statistical purposes will show CANLOAN officers separately from British officers.

5.   *Battle and Sickness Casualties in a theatre of operations*

(a)   Reports of such casualties may be sent simultaneously, or in close succession, from two sources, *viz,* 2nd Echelon, or a hospital in the United Kingdom to which the wounded or sick officer has been evacuated.

(b)   Reports by 2nd Echelon will be sent direct to the O.i/c Records, Canadian Military Headquarters by the quickest means and a copy will be sent at the same time to the War Office.

(c)   Reports of admissions to hospitals in the United Kingdom will be made in the normal manner of A.F.W 3017, E.M.S. Form 105 or (in Scotland) H.O.4 to the War Office. The War Office will transmit the contents of this report by the quickest means to the O.i/c Records, Canadian Military Headquarters.

(d)   Seriously ill and dangerously ill cases will be dealt with as under:–

(i)   Those received by 2nd Echelon will be reported direct to the O.i/c Records, Canadian Military Headquarters.

(ii)   Those admitted to hospitals in the United Kingdom. The telegram usually sent to the next-of-kin will be despatched by the hospital to the O.i/c Records, Canadian Military Headquarters, who will be regarded as the next-of-kin for this purpose irrespective of where the next-of-kin at the time resides.

(e)   Extracts from reports on A.F.W 3034 and W 3034A will be made by 2nd Echelon and despatched direct to the O.i/c Records, Canadian Military Headquarters by quickest means.

(f)   Should the O.i/c Records, Canadian Military Headquarters require further information he will ask 2nd Echelon or the hospital concerned direct for the particulars required, which must be furnished.

6.   *Sickness and deaths outside a theatre of operations*

(a)   *Sickness* – Reports of admissions to, transfers between, and discharges from hospitals in the United Kingdom of officers serving with units not controlled by a 2nd Echelon will be made in the normal manner as laid down in A.C.I. 498 of 1943 (as amended by A.C.Is. 1084 and 1720 of 1943). The procedure in para. 5(c), (d)(ii) and (f) above will be followed.

(b)   *Deaths* – The normal advance notification by the O.C. unit in the case of death other than in hospital, or by the O.C., hospital, if the death takes place in hospital, will be made by telegram only to the O.i/c Records, Canadian Military Headquarters, who for this purpose, will be regarded as the next-of-kin.

7.   *Reports to next-of-kin* – No communications to the next-of-kin of CANLOAN offic-
       ers will be made except by the Canadian authorities. Any such communication
       originating in British Army units will, therefore, be sent to the O.i/c Records,
       Canadian Military Headquarters for disposal.

8.   *Discipline*

   (a) *Offence reports* – At least two copies of all offence reports on A.F.B 122 will be
        forwarded to the War Office.

   (b) *Courts of Inquiry* – When CANLOAN officers are involved, two copies of proceed-
        ings of courts of inquiry on A.F.A 2 will be transmitted to the War Office.

   (c) The War Office will forward one copy of each of the documents referred to in sub-
        paras. (a) and (b) above to the O.i/c Records, Canadian Military Headquarters.

9.   *Action in the event of death*

   (a) *Presumption of death* – Authority to presume death will be vested in the O.i/c
        Records, Canadian Military Headquarters, the British Army authorities (War Of-
        fice or G.H.Q., 2nd Echelon) furnishing all available evidence.

   (b) *Burial Reports* – A.Fs.W 3314 and W 3314A will be forwarded to the O.i/c

        Records, Canadian Military Headquarters.

Appendix F

British Regiments and Corps
in Which CANLOAN Officers Served

Formal Name	Abbreviation
The Argyle & Sutherland Highlanders (Princess Louise's)	A. & S.H.
The Bedfordshire & Hertfordshire Regt.	Bedfs. Herts.
The Black Watch (Royal Highland Regt.)	BW
The Border Regt.	Border
The Buckinghamshire Regt. (TA)	Bucks.
The Cameronians (Scottish Rifles)	Cameronians
The Corps of Royal Engineers	RE
The Devonshire Regt.	Devon
The Dorsetshire Regt.	Dorset
The Duke of Cornwall's Light Infantry	DCLI
The Duke of Wellington's Regt. (West Riding)	DWR
The Durham Light Infantry	DLI
The East Lancashire Regt.	E. Lan. R.
The East Yorkshire Regt. (The Duke of Yorks Own)	E. Yorks.
The Essex Regt.	Essex
The Glasgow Highlanders (TA)	Glas. H.
The Gloucestershire Regt.	Glosters.
The Gordon Highlanders	Gordons
The Green Howards (Alexandra, Princess of Wales's Own Yorkshire Regt.)	Green Howards
The Grenadier Guards	Gren. Gds.
The Herefordshire Light Infantry (TA)	Hereford LI
The Highland Light Infantry (City of Glasgow Regt.)	HLI
The King's Own Scottish Borderers	KOSB
The King's Own Yorkshire Light Infantry	KOYLI
The King's Shropshire Light Infantry	KSLI
The King's Regt.	Kings
The King's Royal Rifle Corps	KRRC
The Lancashire Fusiliers	LF
The Liverpool Scottish (The Queen's Own Cameron Highlanders TA)	Livpl. Scot.
The Loyal Regt. (North Lancashire)	Loyals
The Manchester Regt.	Manch.
The Middlesex Regt. (The Duke of Cambridge's Own)	MX
The Monmouthshire Regt. (TA)	Mons.
The North Staffordshire Regt.	N. Staffs.

The Oxfordshire & Buckinghamshire Light Infantry	Oxf. Bucks.
The Parachute Regt.	Para.
The Princess Louise Kensington Regt.	PLKR
(The Middlesex Regt. Duke of Cambridge's Own TA)	
The Queen's Own Cameron Highlanders	Camerons
The Queen's Royal Regt. (West Surrey)	Queens
The Royal Army Ordnance Corps	RAOC
The Royal Hampshire Regt.	R. Hamps.
The Royal Irish Fusiliers (Princess Victoria's)	R. Ir. F.
The Royal Leicestershire Regt.	R. Leicesters.
The Royal Lincolnshire Regt.	R. Lincolns.
The Royal Norfolk Regt.	R. Norfolk
The Royal Scots Fusiliers	RSF
The Royal Scots (The Royal Regt.)	RS
The Royal Ulster Rifles	RUR
The Royal Warwickshire Regt.	R. Warwick.
The Royal Welch Fusiliers	RWF
The Seaforth Highlanders	Seaforth
(Ross-shire Buffs, The Duke of Albany's)	
The Sherwood Foresters	Foresters
(Nottinghamshire and Derbyshire Regt.)	
The Somerset Light Infantry (Prince Alberts)	Som. LI.
The South Lancashire Regt.	S. Lan. R.
(The Prince of Wales's Volunteers)	
The South Staffordshire Regt.	S. Staffords.
The South Wales Borderers	SWB
The Suffolk Regt.	Suffolk R.
The Tyneside Scottish (TA)	Tyne. Scot.
The Welch Regt.	Welch
The Wiltshire Regt. (The Duke of Edinburghs)	Wilts.
The Worcestershire Regt.	Worc. R.
The York & Lancaster Regt.	Y. & L.
The Hallamshire Regt. (Y. & L.)	Hallams.

Note: After the Second World War many regiments, including some of these, disappeared as a result of reorganization within the British Army.

Appendix G

Letter of Thanks from British Army Council

December 1945.

Sir,

On the termination of your service with the British Army during a period of grave emergency, I am commanded by the Army Council to convey to you their thanks for the valuable services you have rendered, and to express to you their good wishes for the future.

The Council hope that you will carry with you pleasant recollections of your service with the British Army, and that you may find it possible to keep in touch with the regiment or corps with which you served.

I am, Sir,

Your obedient Servant

E. W. Lambert
(Signed)

(Rank and Name of CANLOAN officer)

(CDN number, Unit with which he served)

Appendix H

Canloan Army Officers Association Constitution

I. Name – The name of the Association shall be – Canloan Army Officers Association

II. Objects – The objects of the Association shall be –

(a) To provide liaison among all Canloan everywhere.
(b) To advance the intersts of Canloan.
(c) To aid the national interests of Canada.

III. Membership –

(a) The membership shall consist of all constituent Canloan Associations which in turn shall consist of Canloan resident for the time being in the areas of those associations and those not resident in any of such areas who associate with the area association of their choice and who were commissioned officers of H.M. Canadian Army who volunteered for active service with the Imperial Army in the year 1944 and who have an official serial number prefixed by the letters CDN, being known as Canloan officers and whose membership is approved by the executive committee of his constituent association and such persons as who are elected to Honorary Membership by National Council. At the adoption the recognized constituent associations are as follows:

Atlantic Canloan Army Officers Association.
Quebec Canloan Army Officers Association.
Ontario Canloan Army Officers Association.
Manitoba and Saskatchewan Canloan Army Officers Association.
Alberta Canloan Army Officers Association.
British Columbia Canloan Army Officers Association.

(b) National Council, on the recommendation of the constituent associations concerned, be empowered to withdraw membership privileges of any Canloan whose conduct is unbecoming to a Canloan officer, and that National Council, on its own authority, may withhold membership privileges from any Canloan whose conduct is unbecoming to a Canloan officer and who is not a member of any constituent association.

IV. Government –

(a) The affairs of the association shall be governed by National Council of Canloan which shall consist of the following representatives selected annually by constituent associatons, in Atlantic – two, in Quebec – three, in Ontario – four, in Manitoba and Saskatchewan – two, in Alberta – two, in British Columbia – two, the national reunion chairman and deputy chairman and the past presidents of National Council. In addition to the permitted number of delegates to National Council, up to two alternates should be elected so that one may substitute for delegate upon certification of the constituent association and will have full voting power.

(b)   The National Council shall annually appoint one of its members to be President of Council and one or more of them to be Vice-President(s) of Council. It shall also appoint a Delegate for National Affairs, a Secretary and a Treasurer or a Secretary-Treasurer who, if not appointed from among its members, shall thereby become members of National Council.

(c)   Person appointed under this Section shall hold such appointments until their successors are appointed.

(d)   Whenever a vacancy exists for reunion chairman or deputy chairman or the other representatives stipulated, which is unlikely to be filled in the normal course, the Council shall have power to fill the same by a pro tem selection.

(e)   Mail vote – Council may act upon a mail vote taken by mail upon a two-thirds majority of those eligible to vote. Should less than the required two-thirds vote by mail affirmatively, the motion may be again put to a Council meeting.

V.   National Reunions –

National reunions of Canloan shall be convened at intervals of not more than five years and at such times and places as Council shall determine. A national reunion shall be presided over by a reunion chairman and deputy chairman respectively who shall be appointed by a general session of the Canloan present at the next previous national reunion.

VI.   Constituent Associations –

(a)   New constituent associations may be chartered by Council on application of Canloan in any recognized distinctive geographical area and will be named "... . Canloan Army Officers Association" inserting the name of the area.

(b)   Voting representatives to the National Council constituent associatons may not exceed the following in number:

Atlantic	– two
Quebec	– two
Ontario	– four
Manitoba and Saskatchewan	– two
Alberta	– two
British Columbia	– three

(c) Any representations to governments and their officials, to the national press, to other Canloan Associations or to any national organizations that are desired by constituent associations shall be referred to Council or a reunion.

(d) Constituent associations established by Section iii above or hereafter recognized, unless and until they have adopted a constitutional organization of their own choosing, which they are free to do, shall be organized under the local form of constitution set out in Appendix "A" hereto.

(e) Constituent associations shall be autonomous in welfare and all other matters save in this constitution provided.

VII. Fiscal –

(a) The fiscal year of the national association shall end on December 31st of each year.

(b) The constituent associations shall each pay such general supporting fees and such supporting fees of Canloan Review as National Council shall from time to time establish by resolution circulated to them and shall pay such further special assessments as agreed by the majority of the constituent associations by correspondence.

VIII. Patrons –

Council shall from time to time between national reunions make such arrangements for the patronage of distinguished persons as Council shall see fit.

IX. Constitutional Amendments –

This constitution may be amended by a two-thirds vote of Canloan voting at a general session of a national reunion or upon the recommendation of Council confirmed by the resolution of two-thirds of the constituent associations adopted at local general meetings.

Adopted 5 Jun 54
Amended 8 Jun 63
Amended 5 Jun 71
Amended 10 Jun 89

Appendix I

CANLOAN Roster

CDN	Surname	Name(s)	Rank	Honour Roll[1]	Decorations[2]	British Regiments in Which Served
285	AASEN	Clifford M .	Lieut.			1 Border
430	ABRAM	Lloyd	Lieut.			10 HLI
122	AGNEW	William H.	Lieut.			5 Cameronians
599	AITKEN	John A.	Lieut.	k/a 27-8-44		2 Gordons
509	ALLARD	Lionel J.	Lieut.			1 Glas. H.
431	ALLCROFT	Morgan G.	Lieut.			2 Oxf. Bucks.
564	ALLEN	Arnold E .	Capt.			RAOC (56)
286	AMBERY	Charles C .	Lieut.			4 Dorset
123	ANAKA	Harry J .	A./Capt.	k/a 4-10-44		7 R. Hamps.
124	ANDERSON	Albert G .	Capt.			5 S. Staffords.
600	ANDERSON	John	Lieut.			5/7 Gordons
568	ANDERSON	Llewellyn F.	Capt.			RAOC 2 Arm. Bde. Wksp.
601	ANDREW	Francis F .	Capt.			1 KOSB
60	ANDREWS	Ellis G.	Capt.	k/a 8-8-44	MC	4 Dorset
9	ANGRIGNON	Joseph R .F.	Capt.		C.Mil.(Bl.)	1 E. Lan. R.
478	ANSTEY	Thomas H.	Lieut.			2 Oxf. Bucks. 6 AL Bde. HQ
61	ARNETT	Francis L.J.	Lieut.	d /w 25-3-45	MID	5 Cameronians
10	ARTHURS	Ralph B.	Lieut.	k/a 11-7-44		5 DCLI
110	ATKINSON	Francis S.	Capt.			3 Mons.
589	AUBIN	Norman D.	Capt.			RAOC
432	AYERS, Rev.	Wm. Jack	Capt.		MID	1 Suffolk R. 2/6 S. Staffords. 7 E. Yorks.
685	BACAL	Louis	Capt.			RAOC
62	BAKER	Charles T.	Lieut.	k/a 25-6-44		11 DLI
330	BAKER	Everett O. (Ed)	Lieut.			5 Wilts.
287	BAKER	Maxwell L.	Capt.		MC, MID	1/5 Queens 6 Bedfs. Herts. 6 DWR
2	BALDWIN	George W.	Capt.			9 Cameronians
433	BALDWIN	Ivor B.	Lieut.	k/a 24-6-44		1 Dorset
252	BALLANCE	Lorne W.	Lieut.			2 E. Yorks.
232	BANIUK	William T.	Capt.			2 Essex
236	BANNAN	John A.	Capt.			2 Essex
566	BARBER	Joseph Gerald	Capt.			RAOC HQ 86 Area
207	BARNES	Norman A.	Capt.			7 S. Staffords. 2 R. Lincolns.
203	BARONS	Harry H.D.	Lieut.			12 Devon, 1 Para.
260	BARR	Robert M.	Capt.			5 BW
125	BARTHOLOMEW	Bart A.	Lieut.			7 A. & S.H.

[1] Date killed in action (k/a) or died of wounds (d/w).
[2] Orders, decorations, and awards received during Second World War.

602	BATE	Holland K.	Lieut.			2 S. Staffords.
678	BAUER	W. Kenneth	Capt.			RAOC
						665 Tank Wksp.
126	BEATON	Gordon E.	Lieut.	k/a 25-9-44		2 Gordons
378	BECK	George H.	Lieut.			7 S. Staffords.
127	BEDFORD	John T.	Lieut.			10 DLI, 11 DLI
						9 Kings
63	BELANGER	Henry E.	Lieut.	k/a 28-6-44		10 DLI
288	BELL	Floyd (Ding)	Lieut.			7 R. Norfolk
128	BELL	Harry D.	Lieut.			1 KOSB
320	BELLAVANCE	Georges A.J.	Capt.		MC	1/5 Welch
64	BENNETT	Cecil A.	Lieut.			7 DWR
109	BENNETT	John M.	Lieut.			1 RUR, 1 Worc. R.
65	BENNETT	William A.	Lieut.	k/a 18-7-44		4 Dorset
66	BERRY	Gregory L.	Lieut.			1/4 KOYLI
603	BIRCHALL	Thomas H.	Lieut.			1 Gren. Gds.
261	BIZZELL	Lloyd G.	Lieut.			1 RUR, 1 Para.
111	BLACK	William H.	Maj.			7 RWF
129	BLACKHAM	John P.	Lieut.	k/a 29-6-44		8 RS
379	BLACKMORE	Bert A.H.	Lieut.			1 KOSB, 4 KOSB
11	BLANCHARD	René	Lieut.			1/7 Queens
380	BOOTH	Gordon J.	Lieut.		MC	4 Welch
370	BORDINAT	Philip	Capt.			2 Oxf. Bucks.
505	BOUCHER	Joseph L.P.	Lieut.		MC	RE 204 Fd. Co.
407	BOUDREAU	Louis J.	Lieut.			2 Glas. H.
538	BOULTER	Donald R.	Lieut.			1 Border
539	BOURBONNAIS	Rene S.	Lieut.			2 SWB
112	BOURGET	Joseph A.R.	Capt.	k/a 8-7-44		2/6 S. Staffords.
434	BOUSTEAD	Albert E.	Lieut.			2 S. Staffords.
540	BOVILLE	Percy G.	Lieut.			1 Border
130	BOWMAN	John E.	Lieut.	k/a 22-6-44		6 RSF
331	BOX	Vernon E.	Lieut.	k/a 22-2-45		6 rSF
408	BRADSHAW	Glendon D.	Lieut.			2 Glosters.
67	BRADY	Frank J.L.	Lieut.			2 A. & S.H.,
						2 Army HQ, 10 BW
400	BRAIS	Joseph C.Y.	Lieut.	k/a 30-9-44		1/5 Welch
494	BRAYLEY	John A.	Maj.		MC	5/7 Gordons
435	BRETZ	Howard C.	Maj.			3 Mons.
325	BRIDEN	William H.	Capt.			6 Green Howards
131	BROWN	Colin M.	Capt.			2 A. & S.H.
590	BROWN	D. Kenneth	Capt.			5 Dorset
289	BROWN	Eric	Maj.			1/6 Queens
						3 Mons.
604	BROWN	F. Cameron	Lieut.			2 Seaforth
						5 Seaforth
132	BROWN	Gordon M.	Lieut.	d/w 30-7-44		2/5 L.F.
68	BROWN	Hector J.B.	Lieut.		Silver Star (US)	1/6 DWR, 2 SWB
436	BROWN	John K.	Lieut.			4 Welch
541	BROWN	Norman A.	Lieut.	d/w 14-8-44		2 E. Yorks.
479	BROWN	Ralph M.	Capt.			1 Suffolk R.
113	BROWN	Trevor P.	Capt.			2/6 S. Staffords.
605	BROWNLEE-LAMONT	Wilfred W.N.	Lieut.	k/a 16-9-44		2 Gordons
437	BRUNELLE	René J.N.	Lieut.			1 R. Hamps.
						2 Mons.
422	BRYGIDER	Adam	Capt.		DCM	1 Worc. R.
237	BUCHANAN	James M.	Lieut.			2 Gordons, 7 KOSB
238	BUCHANAN	James W.	Capt.			2 Gordons
438	BUCHANAN	John S.	Lieut.		MM	1 Suffolk R.
133	BUCKLE	William F.	Capt.			4 KSLI,
						11 S. Staffords.
						30 Loyals
606	BURD	Frederick W.	Lieut.			1 Gren. Gds.

381	BURDEN	Arthur R.	Capt.			2 Gordons
332	BURNABY	Frederick H.	Capt.			5 Wilts.
						2 Glosters.
						5 Kings
607	BURNETT	William J.	Lieut.			1 Gren. Gds.
439	BURSEY	Douglas F.	Capt.			6 KOSB, 1 PLKR
134	BUSHELL	Andrew F.	Lieut.	k/a 8-8-44		7 R. Norfolk
135	CAIN	Kenneth	Lieut.			5 E. Lan. R.
333	CAIRNCROSS	James R.	Lieut.			2 Essex
70	CAMBRIDGE	Richard B.	Lieut.			5 Dorset
136	CAMERON	Donald A.	Lieut.			7 KOSB
542	CAMERON	Earl W.	Lieut.			7 Seaforth
159	CAMERON	Stewart H.	Lieut.			2 Glas. H.
608	CAMPBELL	Clarence V.	Lieut.			7 KOSB
69	CAMPBELL	Hubert J.	Lieut.			5 BW
510	CAMPBELL	James R.	Capt.			2 Glas. H.
563	CAMPBELL	Peter R .	Maj.			RAOC
440	CARRUTHERS	Philip Wm.	Capt.			4 KOSB
610	CARSON	Jim J.F.	Capt.			10 HLI
16	CARSTAIRS	Kenneth W.	Lieut.	d/w 23-8-44		1 BW
687	CARSWELL	William J.	Capt.			RAOC
71	CARTER	Fred F.J.	Lieut.			1 Tyne. Scot.
						11 A. & S.H.
609	CARTER	Erskine E.R.E.	Lieut.			7 KOSB
543	CARTER	Maurice C.	Lieut.		MC	1 Worc. R.
						2 Seaforth
611	CASELEY	Willard S.	Lieut.	k/a 6-8-44		1 KOSB
334	CASSADY	C. Clifton	Lieut.			3 Mons.
544	CATLEY	Jack E.	Capt.			1/7 Queens
						1/5 Welch
137	CATLIN	Harold B.	Lieut.			4 R. Lincolns.
441	CAWSEY	Aubrey C.	Capt.	d/w 7-8-44		5 S. Staffords.
532	CHAMBERS	John A.	Maj.			1 RUR, 1 R. Ir. F.
72	CHAPMAN	Robert D.	Lieut.			6 KOSB
612	CHARD	Richard N.	Lieut.			1 Gren. Gds.
613	CHARMAN	Lionel W.	Lieut.			7 KOSB
442	CHATTERTON	Wm. Gordon	Capt.		ED	6 Bedfs. Herts.
						1/5 Queens
209	CHERRETT	Robert B.	Capt.			4 Som. LI
154	CHESHAM	Frederick A.N.	Capt.			7 R. Hamps.
443	CLARK	David G.	Lieut.			7 Cameronians
585	CLARK	Hubert D.	Capt.			RAOC
12	CLOUTIER	Earl C.	Lieut.			1/7 Queens
233	COATES	Kenneth	Lieut.	k/a 16-9-44		6 KOSB
14	COATES	Richard B.	Capt.		MC	1 BW
409	COCHRANE	James	Lieut.	k/a 24-3-45	MC	2 Oxf. Bucks.
410	COCKBURN	Ernest E.	Capt.	k/a 12-6-44		2 SWB
335	COFSKY	J. Paul	Lieut.			2 Devon
423	COHEN	Lawrence	Lieut.	k/a 8-7-44		2 R. Warwick.
138	COLBERT	William A.	Lieut.			1 Border, 7 Som. LI
545	COLL	William J.	Lieut.	k/a 17-7-44		1 Dorset
519	COLLIE	Robert T.	Lieut.			7/9 RS, 8 RS
444	COLLINGWOOD	Al J.A.	Lieut.			1/6 S. Staffords.
290	COMOLLI	Benoit D.J.	Lieut.	k/a 11-7-44		5 DCLI
139	COMPER	George W.	Lieut.			1 Border
73	COMPTON	Neil	Lieut.			6 KOSB
546	CONANT	Roger G.	Capt.			2 SWB
15	CONNOR	Andrew	Capt.			5 BW
551	CONNOR	Arthur	Lieut.			1 R. Hamps.
						1/6 Queens
547	COOPER	Charles W.	Lieut.	d/w 12-7-44		10 DLI

480	COPE	Alfred R.	Lieut.	k/a 18-9-44		1 S. Lan. R.
13	CORISTINE	C. Fraser	Lieut.			1 BW, 4 BW, 7 BW
614	CORSTON	George	Capt.			2 Seaforth
74	COWAN	Duncan R.H.	Lieut.	k/a 16-9-44		7 RWF
615	COWAN	William M.	Lieut.	k/a 16-11-44		5 BW
204	COX	Hubert C.	Lieut.	k/a 24-3-45		12 Devon
140	CRABB	Allen P.	Lieut.	d/w 5-6-44		1 Border
17	CRAIB	Joseph S.	Lieut.			1/6 Queens
						1/5 Queens
114	CRASKE	William D.	Capt.			1 R. Leicesters.
121	CREHAN	Maurice J.	Maj.	k/a 20-10-44	ED	1 R. Ir. F.
141	CRIGHTON	Arthur D.	Lieut.	k/a 10-7-44		6 RWF
445	CROWE	Harry S.	Capt.		MC	4 Welch
371	CUDDY	Deloss C.	Lieut.			4Welch, 5 Wilts.
689	CULVER	A. Gerry	Maj.			RAOC, 16 Veh. Co.
446	CUMMINGS	Gordon P.	Lieut.			4 Wilts.
						1/7 Queens
210	CUNNING	Thomas H.	Lieut.			9 Cameronians
142	CUNNINGHAM	Alexander W.	Capt.			4 KSLI
383	CYPIHOT	Joseph G.	Lieut.			2 KSLI
481	DANSEY	Claude W.	Capt.		OoL. (N.),	8 Para.
					Cr. de G. (Bl)	
262	DARROCH	Walter H.	Lieut.			2/7 S. Staffords.
						1 S. Lan. R.
144	DAVIES	James E.	Lieut.			3 Mons.
548	DAVIES	John E.O.	Capt.			3 Mons., 1 Worc. R.
						4 Worc. R.
143	DAVIES	Walter F.	Lieut.			11 RSF
292	DAVIS	Milton G .	Lieut.			RAOC
447	DAVISON	George H.	Maj.			1/4 KOYLI
263	DAY	Irwin M.	Maj.			34 RHU
395	DAY	James P.	Lieut.	d/w 1-8-44		1 E. Lan. R.
293	DE LUCA	Orlando	Capt.			1 Hereford LI
549	DE SERRES	Anthony C.F.	Lieut.		Cr. de G. (Fr)	7 Seaforth
503	DELANEY	Austin E.	Lieut.			12 Para.
411	DELONG	Howard R.	Lieut.			6 RSF, 11 RSF
240	DEMPSTER	Jim J.J.	Capt.			5 Wilts., 10 DLI
369	DENMAN	Sydney D.	Maj.			5 BW
211	DEZIEL	Robert J.	Lieut.			4 Som. LI
561	DICKSON	Ken M .	Maj.			RAOC
508	DILLON	Thomas S.	Lieut.			CRASC 45 Tpt. Col.
688	DINSLEY	Thomas H.	Lieut.			RAOC
241	DIPLOCK	D. Donald	Lieut.			1/5 Welch
212	DOUGHERTY	MacIsaiah	Lieut.			1 R. Hamps.
496	DOWNEY	Patrick J.	Lieut.			11 RSF
616	DREW	Sydney S.	Capt.			10 HLI
255	DRUHAN	John W.	Capt.			7 Seaforth
336	DUCLOS	Pierre	Lieut.	k/a 28-6-44		4 KSLI
448	DUFF	Robert A.	Lieut.			2 Devon
449	DUHAULT	Maurice C .	Capt.			1 RUR, 1 Para.
692	DUNCAN	Charles J.	Capt.			RAOC
450	DUNCAN	Donald A.	Lieut.	k/a 9-7-44		4 Welch
514	DUNCAN	James C.	Maj.		MC, MID	7 Cameronians
617	DUNLOP	Harold A.	Lieut.			2 S. Staffords.
518	DYNES	Frederick J.	Lieut.	k/a 7-8-44		1 BW
550	EAMON	William L.	Lieut.		MID	2 A. & S.H.
583	EDDIE	James W.E.	Capt.			RAOC
264	EDWARDS	David E.	Lieut.	k/a 27-6-44		1 S. Lan. R.
337	EDWARDS	William T.	Capt.			2 A. & S.H.
618	ELLEKER	Bruce A.	Capt.			5 Cameronians
						2/7 R. Warwick.

294	ELLIS	Fred G.	Lieut.		2 Mons.
557	ELLS	Frederick A.	Lieut.	k/a 24-7-44	1 E. Lan. R.
452	ERSKINE	James S.	Lieut.		2 S. Staffords.
145	EVANS	Frederick	Lieut.	Cr. de G. (Fr.)	2 Mons.
18	EWART	Charles B.	Lieut.	MC	7 Seaforth
669	FAZACKERLEY	Lawrence	Lieut.		1 Gren. Gds.
396	FEE	Robert C.	Lieut.		4 Dorset
453	FENDICK	Reginald F.	Lieut.	CCC	2 MX, 6 KSOB
					1/7 MX
75	FERRIN	Clarence W.	Lieut.		10 DLI
265	FESTON	John	Lieut.		1 Dorset
267	FETTERLY	James R.	Lieut.	MC	7 R. Hamps.
					2 E. Yorks.
1	FINDLAY	Donald M.	Maj.	ED	1/6 Queens
580	FINNIE	William A.	Capt.		RAOC
338	FISET	Henri P.	Lieut.		1 Worc. R.
55	FISHER	Charles L.	Maj.		4 RWF
619	FISHER	Gordon R.D.	Lieut.		5/7 Gordons, 4 RWF
620	FITZGERALD	James M.	Lieut.		2 Seaforth
146	FITZPATRICK	Elmer J.	Lieut.		11 DLI
591	FLEMING	Bruce E.B.	Capt.		1 R. Hamps.
266	FLORENCE	Merle D.F.	Lieut.		6 N. Staffs.
					1 R. Hamps.
295	FLYNN	Magnus S.G.	Lieut.		5 Dorset
696	FOLLETT	F. Bert	Capt.		RAOC
621	FOOTE	John K.A.	Lieut.		4 Dorset
296	FORBES	John D.	Lieut.		4 KSLI, 6 RWF
297	FORD	William F.	Lieut.		1 R. Leicesters.
19	FORGUES	Lucien	Lieut.		5 KSLI
684	FORSTER	Rex H.	Maj.		RAOC, 1-Hereford
397	FOSTER	Hal H.D.	Capt.		1 Dorset, 9 DLI
623	FOX	Archie F.	Capt.		5 Cameronians
622	FOX	Richard C.	Lieut.		2 R. Warwick.
					2 KSLI, 5 Seaforth
504	FRANSHAM	John H.	Lieut.		2 Glas. H.
76	FRASER	Donald M.	Lieut.		6 DWR, 2 SWB
384	FREEMAN	Earl M.	Lieut.		10 DLI
454	FRYER	Eric	Lieut.		1 S. Lan. R.
339	GAGE	Douglas G.	Lieut.		4 Welch
					6 N. Staffs.
405	GAGNÉ	Bernard B.G.	Capt.		2 Gordons,
					HQ 21 Army Gp.
340	GAGNON	Joseph G.	Capt.		6 RWF
584	GALBRAITH	James K.	Capt.		RAOC
253	GANDER	George W.J.	Capt.	ED	9 Cameronians
268	GATENBY	Donald	Lieut.		1 E. Lan. R.
298	GAUTHIER	Joseph H.J.	Maj.	MID	5 DCLI,
					HQ 214 Inf. Bde.
77	GAUTHIER	Joseph W.A.	Lieut.		9 DLI
115	GELSTON	Robert J.	Maj.	MC	10 DLI, 7 BW
					1 Tyne. Scot.
372	GIBSON	Harold G.	Lieut.		12 Devon
587	GIBSON	Robert F.	Capt.		RAOC
299	GILHOOLY	H. Graham	Lieut.		4 KSLI, 1 Dorset
572	GILLIS	Colin L.	Lieut.		RAOC
78	GILMOUR	James H.	Lieut.	d/w 18-6-44	1 Gordons
499	GLASS	Edward D.	Lieut.	k/a 15-8-44	1 Gordons
412	GODDARD	Ronald M.	Lieut.	k/a 10-7-44	4 Dorset
533	GODDU	François	Capt.		1 R. Hamps.
					4 Wilts.
455	GODFREY	Arthur R.	Lieut.		2 S. Staffords.

242	GOOD	Donald M.	Lieut.			1/5 Welch
269	GOOD	Vernon V.J.	Lieut.			2 Devon
385	GOURDEAU	Joseph A.H.	Lieut.			RASC
456	GRAHAM	Donald L.	Lieut.			10 HLI, 13 RWF
534	GRANDA	Adolphe M.	Capt.			2 Glas. H.
579	GRANT	Esmond L.	Capt.			RAOC
341	GRAVES	Albert E.	Lieut.			1/7 R. Warwick.
571	GRAY	Alex	Capt.			RAOC
						26 Armd. Bde.
680	GRAY	John C.M.	Maj.			RAOC
254	GREENE	Lloyd G.	Capt.			2 Glas. H., 7 KOSB
147	GREENHALGH	James	Lieut.			1 Gordons
148	GREGORY	George K.	Lieut.			5 E. Lan. R.
683	GRIFFITH	Walter M.	Capt.			RAOC, 38 Ir. Bde.
213	GUIDOTTI	Melville A.	Lieut.			2 E. Yorks.
342	HADDOW	Robert W.	Lieut.			2 A. & S.H.
3	HALL	Eric W.	Maj			1/5 Queens
23	HALL	Leon E.	Lieut.			5 S. Staffords.
386	HAMBLY	Sam G.	Capt.			4 KSLI
398	HAMILTON	James B.	Capt.			1 HLI, 2 Gordons
149	HANSLER	Leendert	Lieut.			3 Mons.
327	HARCOURT	Earl H.	Lieut.	k/a 16-7-44		8 RS
25	HARDING	Albert R.	Lieut.	k/a 29-6-44		10 HLI
300	HARDY	Marcel W.	Lieut.			5 DCLI
670	HARKNESS	Robert H.	Lieut.			5 Cameronians
624	HARLEY	Bruce F.	Capt.		MC	1/7 Queens
552	HARPER	Burton E.	Lieut.		Cr. de G. (Fr.)	1 E. Lan. R.
					CCC	
79	HARRIS	Alfred J.	Lieut.	k/a 6-11-44		2 SWB
457	HARRISON	Glen S.	Lieut.			7 Cameronians
80	HARRISON	John R.	Capt.	k/a 17-4-45		7 A. & S.H.
24	HARTMAN	William G.	Lieut.	k/a 8-8-44		1 Oxf. Bucks.
459	HARTT	Donald R.	Maj.			6 KOSB, 1 Manch.
150	HARVIE	W. Alex	Lieut.		MID	2 S. Staffords.
151	HASTINGS	Donald K.	Lieut.	k/a 11-7-44		1 R. Hamps.
625	HATCHETTE	Gerald F.	Lieut.			1 Border
413	HATFIELD	Frederick H.	Lieut.			2 SWB
460	HAYES	Harold A.	Lieut.			7 KOSB, 1 Gordons
553	HAYMAN	Burton J.	Lieut.			1 Border
414	HEALD	Clarence F.	Lieut.	d/w 31-3-45		2 Devon
415	HEAPS	Leo J.	Lieut.		MC	1 Para.
626	HEATH	Fred	Lieut.			1 Border
507	HEBB	Gerald D.	Lieut.		MC	2 E. Yorks.
4	HEMELRYK	Joseph	Maj.	k/a 14-4-45	MC, MID	1 HLI
627	HEMMINGSEN	Robert M.	Capt.			7 Seaforth
152	HENRY	Harold F.	Capt.		MID, CCC	4 KSLI
153	HIHN	Harold J.	Capt.			1 HLI, 2 RUR
154	HILBORN	David G.	Lieut.	k/a 29-6-44		10 HLI
155	HILL	William A.	Lieut.			2 Essex
156	HINGLEY	Warren V.	Lieut.			2 Gordons, 6 KOSB
535	HINGSTON	Basil W.H.	Capt.	k/a 19-9-44		2 S. Staffords.
157	HISCOCKS	William J.	Capt.			5 Dorset
343	HISLOP	James A.	Lieut.			3 Mons.
						5 S. Staffords.
81	HITCHCOCK	John H.	Lieut.		MC	2 Gordons,
						7 Gordons
8	HOBBS	Leonard J.	Capt.			8 RS
628	HODGINS	James F.	Capt.			Allied Forces HQ
20	HOGARTH	Bruce A.	Capt.			1/6 Queens
158	HOLLIER	Hubert	Lieut.			7 S. Staffords.
491	HOLMES	Donald E.	Capt.			12 Para.

160	HOPKINSON	George G.	Lieut.	k/a 10-10-44		1 Hereford LI
695	HOPPS	Herbert L.	Lieut.			RAOC
558	HOWARD	Beverley R.	Maj.		ED	6 Cameronians
22	HOWARD	Eric B.	Lieut.			5 BW
214	HOWARD	George M.	Lieut.			1/7 R. Warwick.
461	HOWE	John A.	Lieut.			6 Bedfs. Herts.
						1/7 Queens, 4 KSLI
161	HOWLETT	Robert G.	Lieut.			6 DWR
162	HOWLETT	Robert R.	Capt.			4 R. Lincolns.
565	HUBBELL	MacPherson	Capt.			RAOC
416	HUDSON	Bernard	Capt.			2 Glosters.
629	HUDSON	William J.	Lieut.			5 Dorset
501	HUGGAN	Lloyd M .	Capt.			1 KOSB
401	HUGHES	Harry F.	Lieut.	d/w 28-6-44		1 S. Lan. R.
163	HUNT	William G.	Lieut.	d/w 7-11-44		1 Worc. R.
421	HUNTER	John W.G.	Maj.		MC	7 Green Howards
21	HUNTER	Robert L.	Lieut.			7 BW
215	HURLEY	Richard F.	Lieut.			4 RWF
344	HURST	G. Vernon	Lieut.			2 Glas. H.
451	ILSLEY	Albert	Lieut.			1 Border
630	INGRAHAM	Hugh W.	Lieut.			1/6 Queens
						3 Mons.
301	INGRAM	Ross G.	Lieut.			4 Dorset
387	INMAN	Robert E.	Lieut.			2 E. Yorks.
						7 E. Yorks.
164	IRWIN	John T.	Lieut.			2 Essex
520	JACKSON	Robert J.	Capt.			5 HLI, 10 HLI
165	JAMES	William A.	Lieut.	k/a 1-7-44	MC	11 DLI
631	JEFFRIES	Cecil B.	Capt.			4 Dorset
424	JEFFRIES	Peter	Lieut.	k/a 16-7-44		6 S. Staffords.
166	JOHNSON	Henry	Lieut.			4 Wilts.
506	JONES	Hubert M.	Lieut.	k/a 8-7-44		7 Som. LI
576	JORDAN	W. Dennis	Maj.			RAOC
462	JOYNT	Maurice C.	Lieut.			7 RWF
482	KANE	Lawrence	Lieut.			7 KOSB
345	KARLS	Justin T.	Lieut.	k/a 16-7-44		5 E. Lan. R.
167	KAUFMAN	Martin L.	Lieut.			7 KOSB
26	KEARY	Roderick C.	Capt.		MID	7 Seaforth
388	KEAST	Robert J.	Lieut.	k/a 24-9-44		2 R. Warwick.
483	KELLY	Bernard J.	A./Capt. k/a 18-7-44			2 KSLI
168	KEMSLEY	Sydney A.	Capt.			1 R Norfolk
						9 R. Warwick.
216	KESLICK	William C.	Lieut.			7 Green Howards
						7 KOSB
302	KING	Thomas B.	Capt.			6 Bedfs. Herts.
						4 Dorset
169	KIPPING	Albert E.	Lieut.	k/a 18-9-44		7 KOSB
217	KIRBY	Alfred T.	Lieut.			7 Cameronians
402	KNIGHT	Alfred T.	Lieut.		MM	1/4 KOYLI
270	KOTCHAPAW	William J.	Lieut.	k/a 10-9-44		1 Hereford LI
271	KRAMER	Gerald L.	Capt.			5 E. Lan. R., 6 DLI
						2/7 R. Warwick.
573	KRUGER	Bernard J.	Lieut.			RAOC
205	KUHL	Allen W.	Lieut.	k/a 17-7-44		4 RWF
218	LABELLE	Philip A.	Lieut.			6 RSF, 2 Gordons
403	LABONTE	Paul E.	Capt.			1 Oxf. Bucks.
						6 RSF
						2 Gordons
244	LAFOND	Raymond	Capt.			1/5 Welch
28	LALONDE	William J.	Lieut.	k/a 3-8-44		1/7 Queens
406	LAMARRE	Maurice J.	Capt.			1 Oxf. Bucks.
						8 DLI, 11 RSF

592	LAMB	Murray B.	Capt.		7 Som. LI
82	LAMBERT	Dominique	Lieut.		7 DWR
598	LANG	Donald A.D.	Capt.	MID	5 Kings
83	LANGSTAFF	Harvey W.	Lieut.		1/6 S. Staffords.
					1/6 Queens, 4 KSLI
245	LAPERRIER	Laurent	Lieut.		2 E. Yorks.
170	LARRET	Edward F.	Lieut.	MID	7 Som. LI
171	LAURIE	John A.	Lieut.	k/a 16-4-45	MC	1 R. Norfolk
85	LAUZIÈRE	Joseph A.	Capt.		6 RWF
172	LAVALLÉE	Joseph A.J.	Capt.		11 Y. & L.
632	LAWRENCE	Arthur E.	Capt.		1/7 Queens
					1 Suffolk R.
84	LAXER	Benjamin	Lieut.		1/6 S. Staffords.
					Army Ed Corps
321	LEE	Donald K.	Lieut.	k/a 28-9-44	8 RS
484	LEE	Gordon J.	Lieut.		9 Para.
463	LEFEVER	Gus F.A.	Capt.	MID	1 R. Ir. F., 1 RUR
173	LELIÈVRE	Joseph L.	Lieut.		2 LF
633	LeMESURIER	J. Ross	Lieut.	MC	5 Cameronians
417	LEVINE	John O.	Lieut.	k/a 2-7-44	2 Glosters.
86	LILLEY	C. Vincent	Maj.	MC, MID (2)	1/6 S. Staffords.
					1/5 Queens
					1/6 Queens
256	LONG	Harold C.	Capt.		2 Glas. H.
27	LUDFORD	Raymond	Lieut.		5 Wilts.
425	LUFFMAN	George H.	Lieut.	k/a 1-8-44	8 DLI
87	LYNN	Brian F.	Lieut.	k/a 8-7-44	6 N. Staffs.
33	MacDONALD	Alistair K.	Lieut.	d/w 25-3-45	1 Gordons
177	MACDONALD	G. Smith	Capt.		7 KOSB
32	MACDONALD	Hugh G.	Lieut.		1/5 Queens
					1/6 Queens
418	MacDONALD	Hugh W.	Lieut.		2 A. & S.H.
671	MACDONALD	Ian M.	Lieut.	MC	6 KOSB
637	MacDONALD	John J.	Lieut.	MM	2 S. Staffords.
466	MacDONALD	Vernon L.	Capt.	MC	2 A. & S.H.
273	MacDOUGALL	Duncan	Lieut.		9 DLI
346	MacEWAN	Chester	Lieut.		9 Cameronians
638	MACINTOSH	Joseph D.	Capt.		7 KOSB
56	MacKAY	Roderick F.	Maj.	MC	2 Seaforth
347	MacKENZIE	Allan M.	Capt.		4 Welch
246	MacKENZIE	Hector	Lieut.		1/7 Queens
348	MacKENZIE	Hugh S.	Lieut.		8 RS
6	MACLEAN	Ronald C.S.	Capt.		1/5 Queens
554	MacLELLAN	C. Roger	Lieut.	MC	2 Glas. H.
374	MACMILLAN	Donald A.	Lieut.		11 Devon
91	MacQUARRIE	Donald K.	Capt.		11 RSF
174	MAIN	Harold W.	Lieut.	k/a 19-8-44	6 RWF
88	MAINPRIZE	Robert B.	Maj.		1/4 KOYLI
634	MAJURY	Samuel S.	Lieut.		7 Seaforth
116	MALLOY	Herrick H.	Maj.		7 KOSB
304	MANN	Eldon B.	Lieut.	d/w 16-4-45	MID	6 RSF
53	MANNING	Charles A.	Capt.		2 Seaforth
89	MANNING	Edward P.	Lieut.		1 Tyne. Scot.
486	MARRS	George G.	Lieut.		1 R. Hamps.
485	MARSH	Robert G.	Capt.	k/a 24-20-44	MID (2)	6 RWF
90	MARSH	John W.M.	Lieut.	MM, ED	5/7 Gordons, 1 BW
175	MARSHALL	James A.	Capt.		8 RS, 1 Gordons
5	MARTINEAU	Raymond D.	Capt.		1 BW
176	MASON	Peter B.	Lieut.		7 KOSB
305	MASSEY	Richard	Capt.		5 Wilts.
349	MATTHEW	John B.	Lieut.	k/a 27-3-45	2 Glas. H.

672	MATTHEWS	Harold S.	Lieut.			5 Dorset
307	McALLISTER	Howard C.	Lieut.	k/a 29-6-44		8 RS
92	McAULEY	Lionel H.	Lieut.			6 RWF, 5 E. Yorks.
29	McBRIDE	John	Lieut.			7 BW
467	McCABE	Roy A.	Capt.			10 HLI
464	McCONAGHY	Francis A.	Lieut.			2 MX, 6 KOSB
673	McCORMICK	Hubert F.	Capt.			5/7 Gordons
465	McCOURT	James F.	Capt.			7 KOSB
221	McDERMOTT	George A.	Lieut.	k/a 26-6-44	MM	9 Cameronians
234	McDONALD	Alex G.F.	Capt.			HQ 176 Bde.
						1 Bucks.
118	McGREGOR	James A.	Capt.	k/a 6-6-44		2 E. Yorks.
93	McGUIRE	Wesley B.	Lieut.			11 RSF
57	McHARG	J. Sydney	Maj.		ED	1/5 Welch,
						HQ 3 Br. Inf. Div.
						2/5 LF
593	McINERNEY	George H.F.	Capt.			5 Seaforth
94	McINTOSH	Alexander R.	Maj.		MID	5/7 Gordons
468	McINTOSH	John A.	Lieut.		MC	10 RSF
555	McIVER	W. Aubrey	Lieut.		MID, CCC	2 Mons.
639	McKENNA	James L.	Lieut.	k/a 22-9-44		11 Para.
640	McKIBBIN	Hugh D.	Lieut.	k/a 12-1-45		5/7 Gordons
308	McKINNON	Gerald F.	Capt.			1/7 R. Warwick.
34	McLAUGHLIN	Patrick C.	Lieut.			1 KOSB
350	McLEAN	Baron	Lieut.			10 HLI
178	McLENNAN	Alastair A.H.	Lieut.			2 R. Ir. F.
						1 R. Ir. F.
373	McLEOD	Hugh D.	Capt.	d/w 26-7-44		1 HLI
322	McLOUGHLIN	William G.	Capt.			1 R. Hamps.
						1/5 Queens
309	McMILLAN	Ernest H.	Capt.			7 KOSB
223	McMILLAN	Ian F.	Capt.			10 HLI
469	McRAE	George D.	Lieut.			7 Cameronians
7	MEAGHER	Donald B.	Maj.		ED	6 KOSB, 1 Foresters
500	MEEK	Kenneth R.	Capt.			2 A. & S.H.
						2 BA HQ
594	MERCHANT	Evatt F.A.	Capt.	k/a 18-11-44		5 Cameronians
247	MERCIER	Pierre	Lieut.		MID	7 Som. LI
248	MICHAUD	Adrien H.	Capt.			1/7 R. Warwick.
219	MICKLE	William J.	Lieut.			2 SWB, 4 RWF
274	MIDWINTER	John C.	Lieut.			1 Suffolk R.
117	MILLAR	Alexander M.	Maj.			2 Glas. H.
						2 Seaforth
257	MILLER	Arthur F.	Lieut.			9 Cameronians
635	MILLER	D. Lewis C.	Lieut.			5 BW
588	MILLER	William J.	Lieut.			RAOC
569	MILLIKEN	Robert R.A.	Capt.			RAOC 15 + 16,
						Veh. Coy.
677	MITCHELL	D. William	Capt.		MC	1 BW
306	MORLEY	Henry J.	Maj.			6 DWR
30	MORRIS	Desmond H.	Capt.			2 A. & S.H., 7 KOSB
513	MORRIS	H.W.O. (Bill)	Capt.			6 Cameronians
419	MORRISON	Carson E.	Lieut.			8 DLI, 10 DLI
275	MOTTRAM	William B.	Maj.			7 S. Staffords.,
						5 Wilts., 2 DLI
						7 Som. LI
636	MOXLEY	John E.	Lieut.			5 Seaforth
31	MULCAIR	Jack K.	Capt.			1 Oxf. Bucks.
577	MULLIN	Alex H.	Capt.			RAOC
351	MURRAY	Michael G.	Lieut.			1/7 R. Warwick.
641	NATION	R. John	Lieut.			7 Seaforth

642	NEILSON	William A.	Lieut.		5 Cameronians
179	NEILY	Melbourne H.	Lieut.		2 E. Yorks.
310	NELLES	Larry D.	Lieut.	k/a 11-7-44	7 Seaforth
582	NELLIGAN	Jack E.	Lieut.	•	RAOC
180	NEWSTEAD	Robert R.L.	Capt.		7 S. Staffords.
					2 Mons.
643	NEWTON	Philip W.P.	Capt.		7 KOSB
95	NICHOLSON	Havelock H.R.	Capt.		1 Tyne. Scot., 5 BW
644	NICHOLAS	William E.	A./Capt. k/a 10-12-44		2 Glosters.
426	NIZNICK	Harry	Lieut.	k/a 9-9-44	8 DLI
181	NOBERT	J.L. Fern	Capt.		Hallams (Y. & L.)
					7 KOSB
182	NOISEUX	Joseph A.C.A.	Lieut.	k/a 14-6-44	Hallams (Y. & L.)
645	NORWOOD	Carlisle	Lieut.		2 S. Staffords.
352	O'CONNOR	William R.	Lieut.		5 E. Lan. R.
224	O'HALLORAN	Roy L .	Lieut.		9 DLI
96	O'KEEFE	Arthur B.	Capt.		7 BW
183	OLAND	Don J.	Lieut.		2 R. Warwick.
586	ORD	Alex H.	Capt.		RAOC
249	ORR	Norman J.N.	Lieut.	MC	2 Essex
184	OUELLET	Roland J.B.	Lieut.		4 R. Lincolns.
					1 Bucks.
353	OUELETTE	Georges	Lieut.		4 KSLI
354	OUELETTE	Yvon	Capt.		7 DWR
58	OUIMET	Joseph J.G.	Capt.		2 Gordons
497	OWEN	Jack H.	Capt.		10 HLI
681	PACE	Donald J.	Maj.		RAOC
37	PAFF	Lorne H.	Lieut.	k/a 26-6-44	9 Cameronians
646	PALEN	Frank F.	Lieut.		2 Green Howards
					2 S. Staffords.
					12 Para.
487	PAPE	John C.	Lieut.	k/a 7-4-45	7 Para.
250	PARENT	Guy S.N.	Lieut.		3 Mons.
258	PARKE	C. Russell	Lieut.		2 Glas. H.
574	PARKER	Tom T.A.	Lieut.		RAOC, 8 Army
					500 AOD
38	PATCH	Colin M.	Lieut.	MID	4 KSLI
311	PATRICK	John G.	Lieut.		1 Dorset, 5 Wilts.
470	PATTERSON	William F. (Pat)	Lieut.		7 Para.
35	PATTISON	L.V.P. (Pat)	Lieut.		1 KOSB
					1 Livpl. Scot.
647	PAWLING	John D.	Lieut.		1 Border
185	PEARCE	Joses D.	Lieut.		5 Cameronians
36	PEARCE	Peter P.C.	Lieut.		1/6 Queens, 1 BW
495	PEARCE	Wilfred A.	A./Capt. k/a 25-9-44		Hallams (Y. & L.)
488	PEARCY	William A.	Capt.		6 RWF
					35 Movt. Cont. Gp.
471	PEARSON	Fred V.	Lieut.		2 Mons.
648	PEAT	Norman N.B.J.	Lieut.		2 Seaforth
375	PELTON	R.R. (Bus)	Maj.		7 E. Yorks., 6 KOSB
					2/6 S. Staffords.
186	PENNINGTON	John W.	Capt.	MID	5 Cameronians
567	PEPPER	Philip R.	Capt.		RAOC
					21st Army Grp.
595	PEVERLEY	Harold M.	Capt.		5/7 Gordons
355	PHELPS	Thomas A.	Lieut.	k/a 18-7-44	1 E. Lan. R.
596	PHILLIPS	George W.E.	Capt.		5 Kings
356	PIERCE	Alfred H.	Lieut.		2 A. & S.H., 6 KOSB
277	PILCHAR	Walter A.	Capt.		4/5 RSF,
					1 S. Lanc. R.
323	PLANT	James V.	Capt.		1 R. Hamps.

404	PLOUFFE	Joseph O.	Capt.		1 Welch
357	POCOCK	John L.	Lieut.		6 Green Howards
					2/6 S. Staffords.
187	POIRIER	Yvon	Lieut.		2/5 LF, 2 Essex
562	POLLOCK	John W.I.	Maj.		RAOC
188	PORTELANCE	Ferdinand	Lieut.		5 LF, 1 Dorset
427	PRIMEAU	Arthur J.	Maj.	MID	2 Devon
284	PURCHASE	John R .	Lieut.	k/a 17-7-44	4 RWF
278	PURDEY	Richard	Capt.		11 DLI, 6 DLI
					1/4 KOYLI
649	QUINN	James C.	Lieut.		8 RS
189	RADWAY	Norris E.B.	Lieut.		2 S. Staffords.
59	REID	Roland A.	Capt.	MC	2 Devon
190	REID	Stirling A.	Lieut.	k/a 13-7-44	2 E. Yorks.
259	RICE	Lorne A.	Lieut.		2 Glas. H.
650	RICHARD	Henry J.	Capt.		5 BW
651	RICHARDS	Harold F.	Lieut.		6 Green Howards
191	RICHARDSON	Leonard J.	Lieut.	k/a 9-7-44	2 R. Lincolns.
523	RICHARDSON	Ogden B.	Capt.		5 KOSB
					1 Corps Staff
389	RIST	Robert G.	Lieut.		1/7 Queens
97	ROBERTSON	Charles S.	Capt.		2 A. & S.H.
192	ROBERTSON	Leonard B.	Capt.	MC	2 E. Yorks.
193	ROBERTSON	Robert	Lieut.		1 KOSB, 7 KOSB
329	ROBERTSON	Robert K.	Lieut.	k/a 10-8-44	7 S. Staffords.
358	ROBERTSON	W. Gordon	Capt.		6 RSF
493	ROBICHAUD	Gerry J.G.	Maj.		5 Wilts.
376	ROBILLARD	Leo J.	Capt.		1 RUR
225	ROBINSON	William B.	Lieut.	d/w 10-8-44	11 RSF
390	ROBINSON	William J.	Lieut.		1 RUR
676	RODDAN	Samuel M.	Lieut.		6 KOSB
98	RODDAN	Stuart	Lieut.		2 Seaforth
429	RODGER	Anderson	Lieut.	k/a 24-3-45	1 Gordons
472	RODGER	William S.	Lieut.		2 Devon
99	RODGERS	Clarence J.	Capt.		7 DWR
652	ROPER	Harry C.	Lieut.	k/a 1-10-44	5 Wilts.
502	ROSE	Malcolm R.	Lieut.	k/a 6-8-44	1 KOSB
653	ROSENTHAL	Hyman	Lieut.	k/a 9-2-45	1 BW
39	ROSENTHAL	Moe	Lieut.		3 Mons., 9 RWF
675	ROWLES	William H.	Lieut.		6 KOSB
498	RUMBLE	Stanley G.	Lieut.		10 HLI
279	RUSH	Mathew C.P.	Lieut.	k/a 9-7-44	5 DCLI
359	RUSSELL	Ralph A.	Lieut.		9 Cameronians
360	RUTHERFORD	James H.	Lieut.		4 Wilts.
100	SABOURIN	Wilfrid M.	Lieut.		7 RWF
597	SCHOFIELD	William A.	Capt.		2 Seaforth
697	SCHOLEY	Reginald S.	Capt.	MBE	RAOC
313	SCHWARK	Harold L.	Lieut.	d/a 28-8-44	6 RSF
208	SCOT-BROWN	Charles L.	Capt.		1 Gordons
314	SCOTT	Frederick	Lieut.	k/a 11-7-44	7 Seaforth
315	SCULLY	Joseph B.	Capt.		10 HLI
536	SELVAGE	Donald J.	Capt.	MC	4 Wilts., 2 Essex
581	SEYMOUR	Gordon R.	Maj.		RAOC, 8th Army
					500 AOD
428	SHARMAN	John C.	Lieut.		1/6 S. Staffords.
					13 Para.
44	SHEELY	Henry G.	Lieut.	k/a 8-7-44	1/7 R. Warwick.
578	SHELFORD	Reginald H.	Capt.		RAOC, BAOR,
					9 L. of C.
194	SHORT	Charles G.	Maj.	MC	3 Mons.
195	SHUTTLEWORTH	Ostend W.	Lieut.		4 Som. LI

575	SILVER	Harris M.	Capt.		RAOC
690	SLOANE	Philip	Maj.		RAOC
693	SMITH	Adriane C.	Lieut.		RAOC
42	SMITH	Allan F.	Maj.	Cr. de G. (Fr)	2 Glas. H.
391	SMITH	Donald J.	Lieut. k/a 8-7-44		7 R. Norfolk
196	SMITH	Lawson M.	Capt. k/a 30-10-44		7 Seaforth
682	SMITH	Martin F.	Capt.		RAOC
560	SMITH	Roger M.	Maj.		RAOC
197	SMITH	Thomas A.M.	Lieut. k/a 8-7-44		2/6 S. Staffords.
198	SMITH	Wilfred I.	Lieut.		4 Wilts.
101	SNEATH	Lloyd G.	Capt.	MID, Cr. de G. (Fr.)	Hallams (Y. & L.)
226	SPENCE	Harvey B.	Lieut.	OoBL (N)	5 Dorset, 2 Devon
41	SPENCER	Walter S.	Lieut.		3 Mons., 1/6 Queens
654	SPRAGGE	Harold G.	Capt.		6 KOSB
199	SPRAGUE	Richard P.H.	Lieut.		11 DLI
570	SPRANGE	Alfred L.	Capt.		RAOC
102	STAINTON	William J.	Lieut.	MC	4 R. Lincolns.
280	STAMP	George G.M.S.	Capt.		7 Green Howards 7 N. Staffs.
511	STANSFIELD	Samuel S.	Lieut.		6 Cameronians
377	STEADMAN	Dean O.	Capt.		1 RUR
281	STEINHOFF	Guy S.	Lieut.		7 Green Howards
655	STEPHENSON	John C.	Capt.		7 BW
473	STEVENSON	Howard M.	Lieut. k/a 16-7-44		5 S. Staffords.
227	STEWART	Fernie B.	Lieut. k/a 28-9-44		9 Cameronians
392	STEWART	Francis E.	Lieut.		8 DLI
361	STEWART	Jackson	Lieut. k/a 15-9-44		8 RS
656	STEWART	Richard N.	Lieut. k/a 25-2-45		5 BW
40	STILLING	Lester A.	Lieut.	MID	1/6 & 1/7 Queens, 1/5 & 1/6 S. Staffords.
228	STOBO	Jack R.	Capt.	MC	8 RS
362	STONE	Arthur N.	Lieut.		6 N. Staffs. 1 Gordons
474	STONE	John K.	Lieut.		2 Oxf. Bucks.
316	STREET	Archibald J.	Capt.	MID	6 RSF
515	STRUCK	Delmar (Del) H.	Capt.	MC	5 HLI, 10 HLI
282	SUFFRON	Douglas G.	Lieut.		9 DLI, 10 DLI
694	SUMNER	Charles J.	Maj.		RAOC
43	SURTEES	John R.	Lieut.		1/5 Queens 1/6 Queens
283	SUTTIE	James M.	A./Capt. k/a 22-10-44	MC	4 RWF
674	SWEENEY	George E.	Capt.		6 KSOB
393	TAYLOR	Gordon B.	Maj.	OoL (N) Cr. de G.(2)(Bl)	5 BW
475	TAYLOR	Harry A.	Capt.	MC	7 R. Hamps.
489	TAYLOR	James W.	Lieut.		7 KOSB
200	TAYLOR	Kenneth M.	Lieut.		2 S. Staffords.
103	TESSIER	Trevor R.	Lieut.	OoO (N)	5/7 Gordons 1 Bucks
328	THARP	Walter	Lieut.		7 Som. LI
517	THIRGOOD	Ernest	Capt.	MM	6 Cameronians
657	THIRNBECK	Woodie O.	Lieut.		3 Mons.
229	THOMPSON	Donald C.	Lieut.		4 Som. LI
658	THOMPSON	Hugh E.	Lieut.		11 RSF
201	THOMPSON	Warren	Capt.		9 Cameronians
363	THOMSON	Raymond W.	Lieut. k/a 9-7-44		6 N. Staffs.
659	THORESEN	Raymond F.	Lieut. k/a 14-1-45		7 Seaforth
364	THORNBER	Leslie	Lieut.		7 DWR 6 Green Howards

679	TIMMERMAN	William D.	Maj		RAOC
					HQ 5 (US) Army
119	TOWNSEND	J. Stuart	Capt.		7 Som. LI
660	TRAPLIN	Arthur M.	Maj		1/5 Queens
251	TRUDEAU	Maurice A.	Lieut.	k/a 12-8-44	1/5 Welch
537	TUNIS	Charles W.	Maj		2 A. & S.H.
476	TURNER	Philip H.	Capt.	DSC (US)	2 S. Staffords.
317	TYRWHITT-DRAKE	Montague L.	Lieut.		5 Wilts., HQ 8 Bde.
					2 E. Yorks.
531	URQUHART	Donald J .	Capt.		4 KOSB
324	VANCE	William E.	Capt.		7 RWF, HQ 2 Army
					21 Army Gp.
106	VERONNEAU	Joseph C.M.	Lieut.		6 RSF, 1/5 Welch
45	VEZINA	Robert	Lieut.		1 R. Norfolk
202	WALKER	Ritchie J.R.	Lieut.	MC	1 KOSB
394	WARD	Allan	Lieut.	k/a 26-6-44	5 E. Yorks.
235	WARD	Douglas Wm.	Lieut.		1 R. Leicesters.
365	WATERS	J. Russ	Capt.		1 Hereford LI
					HQ 8 Corps
230	WATERSON	Harry	Lieut.		9 DLI
366	WATSON	Edward A.	Capt.		1 HLI
49	WATSON	Raymond	Lieut.		1 BW
					1/7 R. Warwick.
477	WAYTE	Albert E.F.	Lieut.	d/w 20-9-44	7 KOSB
490	WEBB	Neil H.	Capt.		8 Para.
318	WELLBELOVE	John A.	Lieut.	k/a 25-9-44	1 Border
691	WELLS	Robert W.C.	Capt.		RAOC, (HQ 21 Army)
662	WENMAN	Arthur F.	Lieut.		5 Seaforth
661	WEST	Philip G.	Lieut.	d/w 24-9-44	6 RWF
512	WESTON	George W.	Lieut.		2 Glas. H.
367	WHITE	Charles A	Lieut.		1 E. Lan. R.
368	WHITE	Francis C.	Capt.		5 S. Staffords.
559	WHITE	Thomas E.	Lieut.		6 KOSB
46	WHITEHOUSE	Fred W.	Lieut.		1/5 Queens
48	WHITNEY	William G.	Lieut.		1 HLI
104	WHITTINGTON	Cyril D.	Lieut.	ED	10 HLI, 6 RWF
686	WILLIAMS	George G.O.W.	Lieut.		RAOC, 157 Veh. Pk.
47	WILLICK	Arnold J.	Capt.		5 Wilts.
663	WILSON	Donald G.	Lieut.		1 BW, 7 Som. LI
420	WILSON	Edward A.	Lieut.	k/a 1-7-44	11 RSF
51	WILSON	Kenneth J.	Lieut.		1 R. Norfolk
664	WILSON	Richard N.	Lieut.	k/a 2-10-44	1/7 Queens
206	WINSHIP	Robert	Lieut.		1 Tyne. Scot.
120	WITH	Ronald A.	Capt.		4 Dorset
105	WOOD	Dudley H.	Lieut.	d/w 26-6-44	6 RSF
665	WOODBURY	Leon G.	Lieut.		3 Mons.
50	WRIGHT	Gordon V.	Lieut.	MC & Bar	4 Som. LI
556	WYKES	Nevill G.	Lieut.		7 A. & S.H.
231	YEOMANS	C.H. (Ted)	Lieut.		8 MX
52	YOUNG	Allister M.	Capt.	Silver Star (US)	1 KOSB
667	YOUNG	Everett E.	Lieut.	k/a 22-2-45	7 Seaforth
666	YOUNG	Jack A.	Lieut.		6 DLI, 1/4 KOYLI
668	YOUNG	Leland A.	Lieut.	k/a 4-12-44	7 Seaforth
107	YOUNG	Peter B.	Lieut.	k/a 16-7-44	8 RS
108	YOUNG	Richard O.	Lieut.	d/w 29-6-44	8 RS
319	YOUNG	Robert L.	Capt.		1 S. Lan. R.

Glossary

AA	anti-aircraft
AC	Army Council
ACI	Army Council instruction
ADC	aide-de-camp
AFHQ	Armed Forces Headquarters
AG	adjutant-general
AMGOT	Allied Military Government of Occupied Territories
AOD	advanced ordnance depot
ASD	advanced supply depot
ATk	anti-tank
AVRE	assault vehicle, Royal Engineers
bde.	brigade
BDLS	British Defence Liaison Staff
BLA	British Liberation Army
bn.	battalion
BAOR	British Army of the Rhineland
BOC	British Army of Occupation
Br.	British
Bren	light machine gun, standard for Commonwealth infantry platoons. See also LMG.
Brig.	brigadier
Bt.	baronet
bty.	battery (artillery)
Buffalo	amphibious tracked personnel and cargo carrier
BWEF	British Western European Force
Capt.	captain
carrier	light, fully tracked open-topped vehicle often called a Bren carrier
CASF	Canadian Active Service Force
CB	Companion of the Order of the Bath
CBC	Canadian Broadcasting Corporation
CBE	Companion of the Order of the British Empire
CCS	casualty clearing station
CDN	prefix for CANLOAN numbers – Canadian
CDO	commando
CGS	chief of the general staff (Canadian)
CI(B)TC	Canadian infantry (basic) training centre
CIDA	Canadian International Development Agency
CIS	Canadian infantry school
C. in C.	commander-in-chief
CITC	Canadian infantry training centre
CMHQ	Canadian Military Headquarters (London)
CNIB	Canadian National Institute for the Blind
CO	commanding officer (battalion)
COCTU	Canadian officer cadet training unit
COD	central ordnance depot

Col.	colonel
comm.	communication
COTC	Canadian Officers' Training Corps
coy.	company
Crab	Sherman tank with mine-clearing Flail (see Flail)
CRC	Canadian Reception Centre – a camp where military personnel were collected before returning to Canada
Crocodile	Churchill tank equipped with a flame thrower
CSM	company sergeant-major
CVSM	Canadian Volunteer Service Medal
CWAC	Canadian Women's Army Corps
cwt.	hundredweight
DAAG(L)	deputy assistant adjutant-general (liaison)
DAAG(O)	deputy assistant adjutant-general (operations)
DAG	deputy adjutant-general
DAG(A)	deputy adjutant-general (administration)
DAG(O)	deputy adjutant-general (operations)
DCM	Distinguished Conduct Medal
DD tank	duplex drive (amphibious) tank
DOC	district officer commanding
DP	displaced person
DSO	Distinguished Service Order
DUKW	2.5-ton amphibious truck
DVA	Department of Veterans Affairs
ED	Efficiency Decoration (Canadian)
88-mm dual purpose	German 88-mm anti-aircraft and anti-tank gun
ENSA	Entertainments National Service Association, which provided entertainment for the troops
FDS	field dressing station (medical unit)
Flail	Sherman tank with a front roller and chains to activate mines in its path. Code name Crab.
fmn.	formation: above battalion such as brigade, division, or corps
Gen.	general
GOC	general officer commanding
GOR	gun operations room
GRO	general routine order
HAA	heavy anti-aircraft artillery
HE	high explosive
HQ	headquarters
HQC	headquarters command
hr.	hour or hours
Hun	German (slang)
i/c	in command, e.g., 2 i/c: second in command
IO	intelligence officer
IOO	inspecting ordnance officer
ITC	infantry training centre
jerry	German soldier (slang)
Kangaroo	tank (usually Sherman) with turret and internal gear removed used for transporting troops quickly and safely
KBE	Knight Commander, Order of the British Empire

KCB	Knight Commander of the Order of the Bath
Kraut	German soldier
LAA	light anti-aircraft (artillery)
LC(A)	landing craft, assault
LC(I)	landing craft, infantry
LC(T)	landing craft, tank
L./Cpl.	lance corporal
Lieut.	lieutenant
Lieut.-Gen.	lieutenant-general
LMG	light machine gun (see also Bren)
LOB	left out of battle
LSI	landing ship, infantry
LST	landing ship, tank
LZ	landing zone
Maj.	major
Maj.-Gen.	major-general
MC	Military Cross
MD	military district
MG	machine gun
MID	Mention in dispatches
MLBU	mobile laundry and bath unit
MM	Military Medal
MMG	medium machine gun
MO	medical officer
NAAFI	Navy, Army, Air Force Institute, which provided canteens, usually staffed by women volunteers, for the troops
NCO	non-commissioned officer
NDHQ	National Defence Headquarters
NPAM	Non-Permanent Active Militia
NRMA	National Resources Mobilization Act. Soldiers conscripted under this Canadian Act were called "zombies" in military slang.
OBE	officer of the Order of the British Empire
OC	officer commanding, company
OCTU	officer cadet training unit
OFP	ordnance field park: a depot where military equipment is stored and issued
O. Gp.	orders group
OP	observation post
ORs	other ranks (other than commissioned officers)
OSAC	officer selection and appraisal centre
OTC	Officers' Training Centre
PBI	poor bloody infantry
PIAT	projector infantry anti-tank: a weapon fired from the shoulder like a rifle for knocking out tanks
pl.	platoon
P./Lieut.	provisional lieutenant
PMC	president, mess committee
POW	prisoner of war
PRI	president, regimental institute
PT	physical training

Q.	quartermaster; often used to describe any military supply organization.
RAF	Royal Air Force
RAOC	Royal Army Ordnance Corps
RAP	regimental (medical) aid post
RCASC	Royal Canadian Army Service Corps
RCOC	Royal Canadian Ordnance Corps
recce	reconnaissance
regt.	regiment
rft.	reinforcement
RHQ	regimental headquarters
RHU	reinforcement holding unit
RN	Royal Navy
RSD	returned stores depot
RSM	regimental sergeant-major
RTU	return to unit
rv.	rendezvous
Schumine	small German anti-personnel mine of wood and plastic; almost undetectable with electric mine detectors
SITREP	situation report
SBO	senior British officer (of POW Camp)
SOS	struck off strength; also *Silhouettes of Sussex* (a unit newspaper of A34, SOTC); the defensive fire targets on which artillery, MGMs, and mortars remained laid when not otherwise engaged
SOTC	Special Officer Training Centre (Sussex, New Brunswick)
SP	self-propelled (gun) e.g., a 25-pr or 105-mm field gun on a converted tank chassis
spandau	German infantry machine gun (soldiers' slang)
stonk	heavy shelling
TCV	troop-carrying vehicle
TEWT	tactical exercise without troops
trg.	training
2 i/c	second in command
UNICEF	United Nations International Children's Emergency Fund, now called the United Nations Children's Fund
VC	Victoria Cross
Vickers	medium (.303-in) machine gun standard Br/Cdn
VIP	very important person
Wasp	universal carrier equipped with flame thrower
WE	war establishment: the authorized personnel of a unit. For example, the WE of a rifle company consisted of a major, a captain, and three platoons, each consisting of a lieutenant and 30 NCOs and men

Notes

Chapter 1: The CANLOAN Scheme

1 *Toronto Telegram*, 22 May 1959. Quoted in *Canloan Review* 12 (Mar. 1960).
2 See, for example, *Canloan Review* 10 (Mar. 1968): 18.
3 *Canloan Review* 29 (Mar. 1977): 14.
4 National Archives of Canada RG 24, 24/Reports/1/3, Report 145, 27 Sept. 1945, 1.
5 King's College, London, Liddell Hart Centre for Military Archives, Gen. Sir Ronald Adam Papers, Memoirs, chap. 2.
6 Ibid., chap. 1
7 Ibid.
8 Dec, 1943 9 Col. C.P. Stacey, *Six Years of War* (Ottawa, 1955), 127–29.
9 Ibid., 129.
10 Ibid., 130–32.
11 Ibid., 139.
12 RG 24, vol. 10015, 9/Loan/5, Defensor to Canmilitry, 22 Sept. 1943.
13 Ibid., Fleury to Montague, 30 Sept. 1943.
14 Ibid., Montague to DAG/MS, 4 Oct. 1943.
15 Interview with Maj.-Gen. H.W.E. Letson. General Letson who, as an infantry officer in the First World War had enjoyed contacts with the British Rifle Brigade, which was affiliated with his Vancouver regiment, was particularly keen about the idea of Canadian volunteers being posted to British regiments that were affiliated with their Canadian regiments.
16 RG 24, HQC 8932–1, vol. 2, Report of visit of AG and DAG(A) to War Office, 1 Nov. 1943.
17 Ibid., Roome to Carey (D. Pers.), 25 Nov. 1943.
18 Ibid., Memo re proposed loan of junior officers to British.
19 RG 24, vol. 10015, 9/Loan/6, Defensor to Canmilitry (AG 90), 4 Dec. 1943.
20 Adam, Memoirs, chap. 2(see n. 5 above).
21 RG 2, 7c, reel 4876, Letson to Minister, 28 Dec. 1943, Minutes and Documents of the Cabinet War Committee, vol. 15, 5 Jan. 1944.
22 Ibid., Letson to Minister, 4 Jan. 1944.
23 Ibid.
24 RG 24, vol. 10015, 9/Loan/6, Minutes of conference at the War Office, 4 Feb. 1944.
25 Ibid., War Office to CMHQ, 21 Feb. 1944.
26 Ibid., Montague to Secretary of State, War Office, 10 Mar. 1944.
27 Hon. J.L. Ralston, Debates, House of Commons, 16 Feb. 1944.

Chapter 2: The Volunteers

1 RG 24, 8932–1, vol. 2, Carey (D. Pers.) to AG, 10 Feb. 1944.
2 Ibid., Deputy CGS to CGS, 11 Feb. 1944.
3 Ibid., vol. 3, AG to GOCs, 11 Feb. 1944.
4 Carey (D Pers) to AG, vol. 3, AG to GOCs, 11 Feb. 1944.
5 CDN/339, Douglas G. Gage, CANLOAN History Questionnaire [hereinafter Questionnaire].
6 CDN/29, Jack McBride, "A Slit-trench View of the Normandy Bridgehead," unpublished memoirs, 1–4.
7 RG 24, 8931–4, vol. 4, Lieut. J.B. Matthews to CO, PEI Highlanders, 18 Feb. 1944.

8 CDN/159, Stewart H. Cameron and CDN/255, John W. Druham, Questionnaire.

9 Maj.-Gen. George Pearkes, GOC Pacific Command, strongly opposed the CANLOAN scheme, which he believed would bleed his battalions to an extent which would make them close to inoperative. Reginald H. Roy, *For Most Conspicious Bravery* (Vancouver, 1977), 211.

10 CDN/47, Arnold J. Willick, Questionnaire.

11 CDN/515, Delmar H. Struck, Questionnaire.

12 CDN/198, Wilfred I. Smith to parents, 2 Jan. 1944.

13 Leo Heaps, *The Grey Goose of Arnhem* (London, 1976), 30.

14 CDN/478, Thomas H. Anstey, Questionnaire.

15 CDN/380, Gordon J. Booth, Questionnaire.

16 CDN/606, Frederick W. Burd, Questionnaire.

17 CDN/651, Harold F. Richards, Questionnaire.

18 RG 24, 8932–1, vol. 3, AG to GOCs, 23 Feb. 1944.

19 Ibid., vol. 11, Brig. C.B. Topp to Secretary, Department of National Defence, 25 Feb. 1944.

20 Ibid., 1 Mar. 1944.

21 Ibid., 3 Mar. 1944.

22 Ibid., vol. 3, Capt. W.Z. Estey to DAG(O), 28 Feb. 1944.

23 Ibid., vol. 3, AG to GOCs, 9 Mar. 1944.

24 Ibid., vol. 4, O i/c Promotion to DAG(O), 13 Mar. 1944.

25 Ibid., vol. 4, Director Army Recruiting to District Recruiting Officers, 14 Mar. 1944.

26 Ibid., vol. 4, District Recruiting Officer MD 3 to Director, Army Recruiting, 27 Mar. 1944.

27 PULHEMS was a medical classification of physique, upper limbs, lower limbs, hearing, eyesight, mentality, and stability. Ratings in each were from a high of 1 to a low of 5. Officers were accepted into CANLOAN if they had a 1 in each category.

28 Ibid., vol. 4, AGs to DOCs, 10 Apr. 1944.

29 RG 24, 24/Reports/1/3, Interview with Maj. A.B. MacLaren, 31 Aug. 1945.

30 RG 24, 8031–1, vol. 4, Master General of Ordnance to DAG(O), 30 Mar. 1944.

31 CDN/586, Alex H. Ord, Questionnaire.

Chapter 3: From Sussex to the Second Army

1 RG 24, 8932-1, vol. 3, Minutes of conference concerning facilities for SOTC, 18 Feb. 1944.

2 Ibid., Chief of General Staff to Master General of Ordnance, 19 Feb. 1944.

3 The *SOS (Silhouettes of Sussex)*, Camp Sussex, May 1944, 3.

4 RG 24, vol. 10015, 9/Loan/6, NDHQ Training Instruction No. 1, 8 Mar. 1944.

5 RG 24, 8931–1, vol. 8, Gregg, Commandant A-34 SOTC: "Training Directive #1 to Instructors," Feb. 1944.

6 From the beginning, at Camp Sussex, the various outgoing drafts were called "flights."

7 CDN/453, Reginald F. Fendick, unpublished memoirs, 3.

8 *Canloan Review* 29 (Mar. 1977): 4.

9 Officer cadets at OTCs wore a white flash on each epaulette and on their field cap.

10 Gage, Questionnaire.

11 CDN/142, Alex Cunningham, Questionnaire.

12 CDN/560, Roger Smith, Questionnaire.

13 Anstey, Questionnaire.

14 RG 24, 8932-1, vol. 5, Gregg, Commandant A 34, SOTC to Roome, NDHQ, 2 Apr. 1944.

15 Ibid., Gregg to Roome, 29 Apr. 1944.
16 RG 24, vol. 10015, 9/Loan/6, Defensor to Canmilitry, 21 Mar. 1944.
17 Ibid., Army Council Instruction No 504 of 1944, 5 Apr 44.
18 McBride, Memoirs, 13.
19 Willick, Questionnaire.
20 *Canloan Review* 14–15 (Dec. 1962–Mar. 1963): 7.
21 Ibid., 8–9.
22 *Canloan Review* 1 (Sept. 1949): 2.
23 *Canloan Review* 24–25 (Dec. 1962–Mar. 1963): 9–10

Chapter 4: Getting Acquainted

1 CDN/146, Elmer Fitzpatrick, Questionnaire.
2 RG 24, vol. 10015, MacLaren (DAAG(L)) to AAG(M5), 18 Apr. 1944.
3 Fendick, Memoirs, 8.
4 CDN/499, Edward D. Glass to CO 48th Highlanders of Canada, 9 Aug. 1944.
5 Anstey, Questionnaire.
6 Nigel Hamilton, *Monty, Master of the Battlefield, 1942–1944* (London, 1983), 561.
7 RG 24, vol. 10015, 9/Loan/8, War Office to 21 Army Group, 18 July 1944.
8 Burd, Questionnaire.
9 CDN/258, Russell C. Parke, Questionnaire
10 McBride, Memoirs, 22.
11 RG 24, vol. 10015, 9/Loan/6, Log of DAAG(L) MacLaren, 19 Apr. 1944.
12 Lieut.-Col. J.E. Taylor to author, 26 Mar. 1987.
13 Col. K.L. Whitehead to author, 21 Sept. 1987.
14 Col. G.M. Thornycroft to author, 5 June 1987.
15 *Canloan Review* 6 (Mar. 1954): 6.
16 CDN/192, Leonard B. Robertson, unpublished memoirs, 3.
17 Willick, Questionnaire.
18 Parke, Questionnaire.
19 Brig. A.E.C. Bredin to author, 9 June 1987.
20 Whitehead to author, 21 Sept. 1987.
21 CDN/417, John O. Levine to author, 25 June 1944.
22 W.I. Smith to parents, 30 May 1944.
23 McBride, Memoirs, 22.
24 Ibid., 24.
25 Percy Mason to author, Dec. 1987.
26 John Sendall to author, 10 Mar. 1987.
27 *Canloan Review* 6 (Mar. 1954): 6.
28 Adam, Memoirs, chap. 2.
29 CDN/362, Arthur N. Stone, unpublished memoirs, 3.
30 W.I. Smith to parents, 28 Apr. 1944.
31 CDN/86, C. Vincent Lilley, Questionnaire.
32 Levine to author, 25 June 1944.

Chapter 5: Normandy: The Bridgehead

1 Cornelius Ryan, *The Longest Day* (New York, 1959), 54.
2 Ibid., 239. The Second British Army, under General Montgomery's 21 Army Group, commanded all the British and Canadian assault troops. Under General Dempsey, each assault beach, Gold, Juno, and Sword, was the responsibility of a corps: Sword Beach

was the objective of 3 British Infantry Division (1 Corps), led by 2 E. Yorks. of 8 Brigade (with 4 Commando and 2 Special Service Brigades); Juno Beach was given by 1 Corps to 3 Canadian Infantry Division and Gold Beach to 50 Infantry Division, led by 69 Brigade and followed by 231 Brigade and 46 Commandos.

3 Robertson, Memoirs, 7–9.
4 Ryan, *Day*, 251.
5 Department of National Defence, Directorate of History, Citations, Honours and Awards [hereinafter DND, Citations].
6 McBride, memoirs, 109.
7 CDN/36, Peter Pearce, Questionnaire.
8 Col. C.P. Stacey, *The Victory Campaign* (Ottawa, 1960), 129.
9 Maj.-Gen. H. Essame, *The 43rd Wessex Division at War, 1944–1945* (London, 1952), 23.
10 Alexander McKee, *Caen: Anvil of Victory* (London, 1964), 136.
11 Max Hastings, *Overlord: D-Day and the Battle for Normandy* (London, 1984), 138.
12 DND, Citations.
13 Ibid.
14 Ibid.
15 Maj. I.R. English to author, 2 Mar. 1987.
16 Quoted in Robertson, Memoirs, 14.
17 P.R. Nightingale, *A History of the East Yorkshire Regiment in the War of 1939–45* (London, 1952), 188.
18 Carlo d'Este, *Decision in Normandy* (London, 1983), 244.
19 Eversley Belfield and H. Essame, *The Battle for Normandy* (London, 1965), 265.
20 McKee, *Caen*, 232.
21 Essame, *43rd Division*, 33.
22 George Molesworth, *History of the Somerset Light Infantry, 1919–1945* (London, 1951), 151.
23 Essame, *43rd Division*, 43.
24 Jack Foster to author, 18 Aug. 1987.
25 Druhan, Questionnaire.
26 DND, Citations.
27 Public Record Office, London [hereinafter PRO], WO 171/1390, War diary, 6th Bn Royal Welch Fusiliers, 30 July 1944.
28 DND, Citations.
29 Ibid.
30 Lieut.-Col. C.C.S. Genese to author, 30 July 1987.
31 Major John Baker to author, 24 Jan. 1987.
32 Bredin to author, 9 June 1987.
33 D'Este, *Normandy*, 282–83, and Hastings, *Overlord*, 177–79.
34 *Canloan Review* 7 (Dec. 1955): 8.

Chapter 6: Normandy: Infantry Officers in Battle

1 Fitzpatrick, Questionnaire.
2 Essame, *43rd Division*, 26.
3 Ibid., 33.
4 Nightingale, *East Yorkshire Regiment*, 202.
5 Lilley, Questionnaire.
6 McBride, Memoirs.
7 Elmer Fitzpatrick to War Office, 31 July 1945.

8 Robertson, Memoirs, 11.

9 Lieut.-Col. E. Jones to author, 27 June 1987.

10 PRO, WO 171/1390, War diary, 6th Bn, RWF, 29/30 July 1944.

11 Majors A.D. Parsons, D.I.M. Robbins, and D.C. Gjilson, *The Maroon Square* (4th Bn, The Wiltshire Regiment, 1939–46) (London [1946]), 33–35.

12 McKee, *Caen*, 158–59.

13 Ibid., 159, note.

14 PRO, WO 171/1326, War diary, 4th Bn, The King's Shropshire Light Infantry, 28 June 1944.

15 Essame, *43rd Division*, 82, 88.

16 Lieut.-Col. H.S. LeMesurier to author, 7 June 1987.

17 CDN/153, Harold J. Hihn, Questionnaire.

18 CDN/397, Hal H.D. Foster, Questionnaire.

19 McBride, Memoirs, 185.

20 CDN/3, Eric Hall, Questionnaire.

21 CDN/442, W. Gordon Chatterton, Questionnaire.

22 CDN/249, Norman Orr, Questionnaire.

23 Belfield and Essame, *The Battle for Normandy* (London, 1965), 183.

24 D'Este, 508.

25 Ibid., 509.

26 DND, Personnel files, extracts.

27 McBride, Memoirs, 150.

28 Quoted in John Keegan, *The Face of Battle* (London, 1976), 217.

29 Keegan, *Face of Battle*, 218.

30 *Canloan Review* 10 (June 1958).

31 Gen. Sir John Hackett, *The Profession of Arms* (London, 1983), 220.

32 D'Este, *Normandy*, 283.

33 McKee, *Caen*, 298

Chapter 7: Normandy: The Breakout

1 D'Este, *Normandy,* 370.

2 Belfield and Essame, *Normandy*, 147.

3 McKee, *Caen*, 254.

4 Belfield and Essame, *Normandy*, 151.

5 Capt. U.D. Urquhart to author, 24 Feb. 1988.

6 PRO, WO 171/1326, War diary of 4 KSLI, 19 July 1944.

7 Maj. M.J.D. Sayer to author, 25 Mar. 1987.

8 Hamilton, *Battlefield*, 768.

9 Belfield and Essame, *Normandy*, 205.

10 Winston S. Churchill, *The Second World War*, vol. 6 (Boston, 1953), 30.

11 Chester Wilmot, *The Struggle for Europe* (London, 1952), 406.

12 DND, Citations.

13 Ibid.

14 Ibid.

15 Ibid.

16 Essame, *43rd Division,* 72.

17 McKee, Caen, 322.

18 Ibid., 324.

19 DND, Citations.

20 Ibid., 327.
21 George Beck, *Canloan Review*, Mar. 1954, 12.
22 John E. Sendall to author, 10 Mar. 1987.
23 DND, Citations.
24 Ibid.
25 Stacey, *Campaign*, 257.
26 Belfield and Essame, *Normandy*, 238.
27 Hastings, *Overlord*, 339.
28 McBride, Memoirs, 189–90.
29 DND, Citations.
30 Stacey, *Victory*, 270–71.

Chapter 8: Hospitals and Reinforcement Holding Units

1   John Ellis, *The Sharp End: The Fighting Man in World War II* (New York, 1980), 174.
2   Ibid., 167.
3   W.I. Smith, Memoirs, 44.
4   All CANLOAN officers were envied by their British colleagues because of the recognized superiority of the Canadian battle dress over the British battle dress. They had a more attractive olive green colour, were made of material of a finer and less abrasive texture, and had pocket flaps to hide the buttons. CANLOAN officers strove to keep their Canadian battle dress even when it was torn and blood soaked.
5   PRO, War Diary, 4 Bn KSLI, 1944, WO171/1326. This policy changed later when field General Hospitals were established in Normandy. Then only those who could not be made fit for battle in a reasonable time were evacuated.
6   Stone, Memoirs.
7   RG 24, vol. 10015, 9/Loan/6/2.
8   CDN/337, William Edwards, Questionnaire.
9   CDN/51, Kenneth Wilson, Questionnaire.
10 Stewart Cameron, Questionnaire.
11 RG 24, vol. 12577, file 206/4 MacLaren to AMD2, 13 Oct. 1944.
12 Ibid., Dir. Med. Services to MacLaren, 31 July 1944.
13 Ibid., 16 Aug. 1944.
14 RG 24, vol. 10015, 9/Loan/6/2, War Office to 21 Army Gp, 31 May. 1944.
15 W.J. Smith to parents, 10 Sept. 1944.
16 RG 24, vol. 10015, 9/Loan/6/2/ 31 Oct. 1944.
17 *Canloan Review* 29 (Mar. 1977): 14.
18 CDN/241, Donald Diplock, Questionnaire.
19 W.I. Smith to parents, 10 Sept. 1944.
20 RG 24, HQC 8932–1, vol. 2.
21 Ibid., vol. 10015, 9/Loan/6, T.M. Fletcher to War Office, 10 July, 1944.
22 RG 24, vol. 10015, 9/Loan/6, Montague to DND, 15 Aug. 1944.
23 Ibid., 9/Loan/6/2, Maclaren to AAG(MS), 23 Aug. 1944.
24 Ibid., Letson to CMHQ, 24 Aug. 1944.
25 RG 24, HQC 8931-1, vol. 2, Ivor to DND, 16 Sept. 1944.
26 RG 24, vol. 10015, 9/Loan/6/2, Canmilitry to Defensor, 17 Feb. 1945.

27 Ibid., MacLaren to AAG(MS), 28 Sept. 1944.

28 RG 24, vol. 10015, 9/Loan/8, MacLaren to Knox, 27 Sept. 1944.

29 Ibid., 9/Loan/8/2, MacLaren to AAG(MS), 9 Oct. 1944.

30 Ibid., S S21 Dec. 1944.

31 RG 24, vol. 10015, 9/Loan/6/2, Montague to DND, 31 Oct. 1944.

32 Ibid., App. C.

33 RG 24, vol. 12757 24/Reports/1/3, Comments by Capt. J.H.J. Gauthier on Report 145, 26 Mar. 1947.

34 RG 24, vol. 10015, 9/Loan/6/2, Canmilitry to Defensor, 6 Nov. 1944.

35 Ibid., 9/Loan/8/2, Maclaren to Fleury (no date).

36 Ibid., 9/Loan/6/2, Maclaren to ADAG(MS), 3 Feb. 1945.

37 *Canloan Review* 6 (Mar. 1954).

38 RG 24, vol. 10015, 9/Loan/6/2, MacLaren to ADAG(MS), 3 Feb. 1945.

39 Ibid.

40 Ibid.

41 RG 24, vol. 10015, 9/Loan/6/2, Report of Col. F.H. van Nostrand, 27 Sept. 1944.

42 Ibid., 9/Loan/8/2, Maclaren to ADAG(MS), 13 Mar. 1945.

43 Smith, Memoirs, 66.

44 Ellis, *Sharp End*, 317

Chapter 9: The Canals and Arnhem

1 McBride, Memoirs, 216–17.

2 Stone, Memoirs, 47.

3 CDN/289, Erik Brown, Questionnaire.

4 Robertson, Memoirs.

5 Nightingale, *East Yorkshire Regiment,* 220.

6 Wilmot, *Struggle*, 469.

7 Ibid., 434.

8 Cornelius Ryan, *A Bridge Too Far* (New York, 1974), 49.

9 Lilley, Questionnaire.

10 DND, Citations.

11 Wilmot, *Struggle*, 486.

12 DND, Citations.

13 P.K. Kemp, *The Red Dragon: The Story of the Royal Welch Fusiliers, 1919–1945* (Aldershot, 1960), 204.

14 *A Short History of the 6th Battalion, the Royal Welch Fusiliers* (London, 1946), 32.

15 Ibid., 36.

16 CDN/552, Burton Harper, Memoirs.

17 Maj. Ian English, letter to author, 2 Mar. 1987.

18 Maj. K.H. Crawford, letter to author, 8 July 1987.

19 Wilmot, *Struggle*, 483.

20 Ryan, *Bridge*, 125

21 Sir Brian Horrocks, *Corps Commander* (London, 1977), 98.

22 Ryan, *Bridge*, 128–29.

23 Ibid.,166.

24 Ibid., 163.

25 Ibid., 132.

26 *By Air to Battle: The Official Account of the British Airborne Divisions* (London, 1945), 10.

27 CDN/489, James Taylor, Questionnaire.

28 Leo Heaps, *Grey Goose*, 30–31.

29 Ryan, *Bridge*, 188.

30 Ibid., 345–46.

31 Ibid., 404.

32 Nigel Nicholson, *The Grenadier Guards in the War of 1939–1945*, vol. 1 (Aldershot, 1949), 137.

33 Citation for United States Distinguished Service Cross, in possession of CDN/476, Philip Turner.

34 Erskine Carter, "Nine Days at Arnhem" (unpublished memoirs), 36–37.

35 CDN/489, James Taylor, Questionnaire.

36 Carter, "Arnhem," 40.

37 Ibid., 39–40.

38 Ibid., 46.

39 A. Wilson to author, 8 May 1987.

40 CDN/302, Thomas King, Questionnaire.

41 Brig. A.E.C. Bredin to author, 9 Apr. 1987, quoting Major M. Whittle.

42 Carter, "Arnhem," 64.

43 DND, Citations.

44 Wilmot, *Struggle*, 522.

45 Field Marshall the Viscount of Alamein, *Memoirs* (London, 1958), 296.

46 *By Air to Battle*, 134.

Chapter 10: Stalemate

1 Wilmot, *Struggle*, 539.

2 Ibid., 532.

3 Stacey, *Victory Campaign*, 655.

4 Wilmot, *Struggle*, 570.

5 DND, Citations.

6 Lieut.-Col. E. Jones to author, 3 June 1987.

7 DND, Citations.

8 Ibid.

9 Essame, *43rd Division*, 141–47.

10 Ibid., 148.

11 Lilley, Questionnaire.

12 Leo Heaps, *Escape from Arnhem* (Toronto, 1945) and *Grey Goose*.

13 *A Short History of the 6th (Cameronion and Anglesey) Battalion, The Royal Welch Fusiliers in North West Europe, June 1944 to May 1945* (n.p., 1946), 36.

14 *A Short History*, 51–53, and Kemp, *Royal Welch Fusiliers*, 218.

15 CDN/180, Robert Newstead, Questionnaire.

16 W. Denis Whitaker and Shelagh Whitaker, *Tug of War: The Canadian Victory that Opened Antwerp* (Toronto, 1984), 256.

17 Ernest Thirgood, unpublished memoirs, 14.

18 Whitaker, *Tug of War*, 372.

19 CDN/600, John Anderson, Questionnaire.

20 Hall, Questionnaire.

21 Fendick, Memoirs, 72.

22 Horrocks, *Corps Commander*, 135.

23 Willick, Questionnaire.

24 Richards, Memoirs, 17.

25 Fendick, Memoirs, 85.
26 Fitzpatrick, Questionnaire.
27 DND, Citations.
28 Ibid.
29 Ibid.
30 Ibid.
31 CDN/630, Hugh Ingraham, Questionnaire.
32 Anderson, with Questionnaire.
33 Memoirs, 18.
34 Essame, *43rd Division*, 159.
35 DND, Citations.
36 Johan Van Doorn to author, 4 June 1987.
37 DND, Citations.
38 Ibid.
39 Ibid.
40 Ibid.
41 Ibid.
42 Nightingale, *East Yorkshire Regiment*, 227.
43 Essame, *43rd Division*, 176.
44 Sir Brian Horrocks, *A Full Life* (London, 1960), 235.
45 Fitzpatrick, Questionnaire.
46 DND, Citations.
47 Ibid.
48 Ibid.
49 Published in *Canloan Review*.
50 Alan E. Scott to author, 2 June 1987.

Chapter 11: To the Rhine and Beyond

1 Wilmot, *Struggle*, 672.
2 Author's copy.
3 Horrocks, *Corps Commander*, 187.
4 Bernard Fergusson, *The Black Watch and the King's Enemies* (London, 1950), 292.
5 W. Denis Whitaker and Shelagh Whitaker, *Rhineland, the Battle to End the War* (Toronto, 1989), 85.
6 *Historical Records of the Queen's Own Highlanders, 1932–1948* (Edinburgh, 1952), 139.
7 Whitaker, *Rhineland*, 103.
8 Fergusson, *Black Watch*, 301.
9 Horrocks, *Corps Commander*, 185.
10 Ibid., 187.
11 Essame, *43rd Division*, 207, 213.
12 Parsons, Robbins, and Gilson, *Maroon Square*, 150.
13 Smith, Memoirs, 90.
14 Stacey, *Victory Campaign*, 482.
15 Horrocks, *Corps Commander*, 187.
16 DND, Citations.
17 Ibid.
18 Ibid.
19 Ibid., 194.
20 Stacey, *Victory Campaign*, 524.

21 W.I. Smith to parents, 19 Feb. 1945.

22 Montgomery, *Memoirs*, 329.

23 Horrocks, *Corps Commander*, 207.

24 Stone, Memoirs, 57.

25 Anderson, Questionnaire.

26 Horrocks, *Corps Commander*, 210.

27 CDN/543, Maurice Carter, Questionnaire.

28 Clippings enclosed in a letter from M. Campbell to Hon. A.G.L. McNaughton, 17 May 1945, RG 24, 8932-1.

29 Fergusson, *Black Watch*, 308.

30 Stone, Memoirs, 64.

31 Stacey, *Victory Campaign*, 538.

32 PRO, WO 171/5158, War Diary of 1 BW, 24 Mar. 1945.

33 DND, Citations.

34 Ibid.

35 Ibid.

36 Eddie Harrel to author, 16 Aug. 1987.

37 *By Air to Battle*, 144.

38 William Robinson, unpublished account.

39 Wilmot, *Struggle*, 684.

40 Col. G. Barker-Harland to author, 2 Mar. 1987.

41 Ibid.

42 Stacey, *Victory Campaign*, 604.

43 Christopher Chant et al., *World War II* (London, 1977), 179.

44 W.I. Smith, Memoirs, 148–49.

45 Lilley, Questionnaire.

46 Capt. W.E. Wills to author, 2 Aug. 1987.

47 Essame, *43rd Division,* 247.

48 W.I. Smith, Memoirs, 133.

49 DND, Citations.

50 Ibid.

51 Major U. Thorburne, letter to author, 18 Mar. 1987.

52 *Canloan Review* 6 (Mar 1954): 13–14.

53 Maj.-Gen. G.L. Verney, *The Desert Rats: the 7th Armoured Division, 1938–1945* (London, 1956), 276.

54 Horrocks, *Corps Commander,* 219.

55 W.I. Smith, Memoirs, 178.

Chapter 12: The Irish Fusiliers in Italy

1 CDN/578, Reg H. Shelford, Questionnaire.

2 CDN/533, J.A. Chambers, Memoirs, 5.

3 CDN/178, Alastair McLennan, Questionnaire.

4 CDN/532, John A. Chambers, Questionnaire.

5 Cyril Ray, *Algiers to Austria: A History of 78 Division in the Second World War* (London, 1952), 47.

6 Ibid., 95.

7 Ibid., 161.

8 Ibid., 162

9 Ibidi, 170

10 Lieut.-Col. J.H.C. Horsfall to Mrs. McLennan, 25 Oct. 1944.

11 Attached to official personal file of Maj. Maurice Crehan.
12 Col. P.J.C. Trousdell, letter to author, 25 Apr. 1987.
13 Chambers, Memoirs, 33.
14 Ray, *Algiers to Austria*, 229.

Chapter 13: The CANLOAN POWs

1 MacLaren memo to file, 2 Dec. 1944, RG 24, vol. 10015, 9/Loan/8/2.
2 C. Cassady, Journal.
3 C. Cassady, Claim for maltreatment, with journal.
4 McLennan, Questionnaire.
5 Taylor, Questionnaire.
6 Daniel G. Dancocks, *In Enemy Hands: Canadian Prisoners of War* (Edmonton, 1983), xii.
7 Ibid.
8 Ibid.
9 King, Questionnaire.
10 President, Regimental Institute. The term was used to describe soldiers' comforts, generally bought through regimental funds – similar goods to a NAAFI issue. In POW camps the purpose was somewhat different, but the term was familiar to British troops.
11 Cassady, Journal.
12 James Macleod, unpublished memoirs.
13 Ibid.
14 Dancocks, *Canadian POWs*, 79.
15 Cassady, Journal.
16 King, Questionnaire.
17 A. McLennan, Memoirs.

Chapter 14: The Ordnance Corps CANLOAN

1 William F. Rannie, ed., *To the Thunderer His Arms: The Royal Canadian Ordnance Corps* (Lincoln, Ont., 1984), 3, dedication.
2 R. Smith, Questionnaire.
3 RG 24, vol. 10015, file 9/Loan/8, 217, War Office to CMHQ, 3 July 1944.
4 Ibid., 9/Loan/6, 290, Commandant RAOC Trg. Estab., 29 July 1944.
5 Ibid., 291.
6 Shelford, Questionnaire.
7 RG 24, vol. 10015, 9/Loan/8, 236, War Office to Commandant, 21 July 1944.
8 Ibid., 100–10, CMHQ to DND, 31 Oct. 1944.
9 Ibid.
10 Rannie, *Thunderer*, 211.
11 Ord, Questionnaire.
12 R. Smith, Questionnaire.
13 CDN/564, Arnold Allen, Questionnaire.
14 DND, Citations.
15 RG 24, vol. 10015, file 9/Loan/6/4, CMHQ to 1 Cdn. Repat. Depot, 15 July 1946.

Chapter 15: Occupation and Repatriation

1 Field Marshal Viscount Montgomery, *Memoirs* (London, 1958), 333.
2 *Canloan Review* 6 (Mar. 1954): 12–13.

3 CDN/153, Harold Hihn, Questionnaire.
4 Harper, Questionnaire.
5 W.I. Smith to parents, 17 June 1945.
6 Ibid., 29 July 1945.
7 McBride, Memoirs.
8 Lilley, Memoirs.
9 James Lucas, *The Last Days of the Reich* (Toronto, 1986), 229.
10 Major J.N. Davis-Colley to author, 4 Aug. 1987.
11 Anstey, Questionnaire.
12 Anderson, Questionnaire.
13 Wilfred Miles, *The Life of a Regiment: The Gordon Highlanders*, vol. 5, *1919–1945* (Aberdeen, 1961), 366.
14 W.I. Smith, to parents, 17 June 1945.
15 Davis-Colley, 4 Aug. 1987.
16 Cunningham, Questionnaire.
17 CDN/380, Gordon Booth, Questionnaire.
18 *Canloan Review*, 11(Mar.–June 1959): 24–27.
19 Cameron, Questionnaire.
20 Foster, Questionnaire.
21 Adjt-Gen to Minister, 2 Jan. 1945, RG 24, vol. 10015, 8931-1, vol. 8.
22 Ibid., Adjt-Gen to Col. Fleury (ADAG), 5 Jan. 1945.
23 Ibid., Canmilitry to Adjt-Gen, 30 Jan. 1945.
24 RG 24, vol. 10015, 8931–1, vol. 9.
25 Ibid.
26 Ibid., Col. Carey (D. Pers.) to DAGO, 22 Mar. 1945.
27 Ibid.
28 Ibid.
29 RG 24, vol. 10015, 9/Loan/6/2.
30 Ibid.
31 Ibid., 9/Loan/6/3.
32 RG 24, vol. 10015, 9/Loan/6/3.
33 Anstey, Questionnaire.
34 W.I. Smith, Memoirs.
35 RG 24, vol. 10015, 9/Loan/8/3, 234–35.
36 Ibid., vol. 10010, 9/Loan/6/2, 113.
37 DND, Historical Section, nominal roll of CANLOAN, file 195.91065.
38 Ibid., Memo to file, 2 Dec. 1944, 9/Loan/8/2, 78.
39 *Canloan Review* 1 (Feb. 1949): 1.

Epilogue

1 *Canloan Review* 1 (Feb. 1949): 2.
2 *Canloan Review* 2 (Dec. 1950): 1.
3 *Quebec Chronicle-Telegraph*, 30 Aug. 1956.
4 *Perspective* (Dept. of Health and Welfare), Dec. 1971, 10–12.
5 *Canloan Review* 6 (June–Dec. 1954): 1.
6 *Canloan Review* 19 (June 1967): 18.
7 *Canloan Review* 24 (Sept. 1972): 16.
8 *Canloan Review* 29 (Mar. 1977): 26.
9 Ibid., 28.

10 *Canloan Review*, 17 (June–Dec. 1965): 22.
11 *Canloan Review* 1 (May 1949): 2.
12 *Canloan Review* 2 (Dec. 1950): 2.
13 *Canloan Review* 27–28 (1975–76): 9.
14 *Canloan Review* 7 (Dec. 1955): 2–3.
15 *Canloan Review* 11 (Dec. 1959): 26.
16 *Canloan Review* 12 (Dec. 1960): 2.
17 *Canloan Review* 13 (June–Dec. 1961): 2.
18 *Canloan Review* 17 (June–Dec. 1965): 23.
19 *Canloan Review* 33 (Mar.–Dec. 1982): 9.
20 *Canloan Review* 7 (Mar. 1954): 24.
21 *Canloan Review* 33 (Mar.–Dec. 1982): 32.
22 Ibid., 37.
23 Ibid., 12.

Index

SUBJECT INDEX

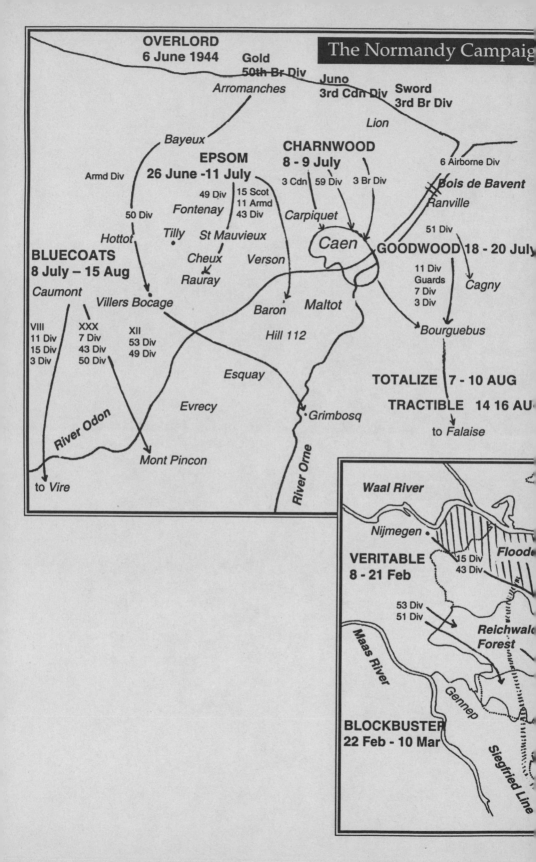

OVERLORD
6 June 1944

Gold
50th Br Div

Juno
3rd Cdn Div

Sword
3rd Br Div

The Normandy Campaig

Arromanches

Bayeux

Lion

6 Airborne Div

EPSOM
26 June -11 July

CHARNWOOD
8 - 9 July

Armd Div

3 Cdn | 59 Div | 3 Br Div

Bois de Bavent

Ranville

49 Div | 15 Scot
11 Armd
43 Div

Fontenay

50 Div

Carpiquet

51 Div

Hottot

Tilly

St Mauvieux

Caen

GOODWOOD 18 - 20 July

BLUECOATS
8 July – 15 Aug

Cheux

Verson

11 Div
Guards
7 Div
3 Div

Cagny

Rauray

Caumont

Villers Bocage

Baron

Maltot

Bourguebus

VIII
11 Div
15 Div
3 Div

XXX
7 Div
43 Div
50 Div

XII
53 Div
49 Div

Hill 112

Esquay

TOTALIZE 7 - 10 AUG

Evrecy

Grimbosq

TRACTIBLE   14 16 AU

to *Falaise*

River Odon

Mont Pincon

to *Vire*

River Orne

Waal River

Nijmegen

VERITABLE
8 - 21 Feb

15 Div
43 Div

Flood

53 Div
51 Div

Reichwald
Forest

Maas River

Gennep

BLOCKBUSTER
22 Feb - 10 Mar

Siegfried Line